# THE WTO AT THE CROSSROADS

## About the Editor

Professor Paramita Dasgupta is currently Dean of Training & Conferences and Director, Centre for Economics and Finance at the Administrative Staff College of India, Hyderabad. She has been a faculty member at the Administrative Staff College of India, Hyderabad for the past 17 years. She holds a PhD in Economics from the Jawaharlal Nehru University, New Delhi. She was a EFMD Visiting Fellow at the Rotterdam School of Management, Erasmus University, The Netherlands working on issues relating to Indo-EU Trade. She has been working on the area of WTO and international trade for the past decade and has been continuously involved in designing and conducting training programmes for civil servants, corporate executives and scientists in this area. Also, she has been a Consultant to UNDP and has led and participated in major research and consultancy assignments of Government of India, State Governments and international organizations including the Delegation of the European Commission and the UNCTAD, on areas relating to international trade.

# The WTO at the Crossroads

*Edited by*

**PARAMITA DASGUPTA**

**CONCEPT PUBLISHING COMPANY, NEW DELHI-110059**

**Cataloging in Publication Data—DK**
*Courtesy:* D.K. Agencies (P) Ltd. <docinfo@dkagencies.com>

**The WTO at the crossroads** / edited by Paramita Dasgupta.
p. cm.
Contributed articles.
Dealing with key issues that have assumed importance in India's international trade scenario in recent years.
Includes bibliographical references.
Includes index.
ISBN 13: 9788180694431
ISBN 10: 8180694437

1. World Trade Organization. 2. Foreign trade regulation—India. 3. Foreign trade regulation—Developing countries. I. Dasgupta, Paramita. II. Title: World Trade Organization at the crossroads.

DDC 382.920 954 22



ISBN-13: 978-81-8069-443-1
ISBN-10: 81-8069-443-7

First Published 2009



*Published and Printed by*
Ashok Kumar Mittal
**Concept Publishing Company**
A/15-16, Commercial Block, Mohan Garden
New Delhi-110059 (INDIA)

*Phones* : 25351460, 25351794
*Fax* : 091-11-25357103
*Email* : publishing@conceptpub.com

*Dedicated to*

**My Parents**

# Preface

Over the past thirteen years of its existence, the WTO has emerged as one of the most controversial international organizations. This is mostly because negotiations in the WTO have cut across a wide range of areas of critical importance to the economies of the member countries. In fact under the umbrella of the WTO areas such as intellectual property rights and services have found a place in international trade negotiations for the first time.

The scope of multilateral negotiations in the WTO is vast-spanning issues relating to agriculture, industrial tariffs, intellectual property rights and services among others which have significant and complex ramifications for domestic policy and the economies of member countries. While member countries recognize the importance of the negotiations, they have often been unable to reach an agreement on these areas. It is not difficult to understand the reason for such lack of agreement among member countries. Thus, for instance, while agriculture is a livelihood issue for developing countries like India concerning the interest of millions of farmers, it is a heavily subsidized sector in the developed countries thereby creating controversial issues relating to market access and international competitiveness. Similarly areas like intellectual property rights and the implementation of the TRIPS agreement have given rise to a range of controversial cross cutting issues across the economies of all developing member countries, including India. However, notwithstanding the differences at the current juncture it is important that the negotiations are carried forward through agreement in the above areas.

The on-going Doha Round of negotiations has thrown up major challenges. While the Hong Kong Ministerial had ended with broad agreement in important areas including agriculture, NAMA and services and shown a way forward, negotiations had to be suspended a year later due to what appeared to be major differences primarily in the area of agriculture. Subsequently, there has been a revival of the stalled Doha Round with member countries attempting to arrive at an agreement in key areas. Negotiations in the WTO are currently at the crossroads. The future of the multilateral negotiations depends upon the ability of the member countries to reach an agreement in critical areas.

This book brings together a set of papers dealing with key issues that have assumed importance in India's international trade scenario in recent years. India has been involved in negotiations in the WTO in some of these areas. Apart from dealing with issues in the negotiating agenda, the papers discuss implications of these issues for current economic policy. The issues discussed in the papers are topical and the book will thus be of interest to a wide cross-section of readers drawn from academic and policy-making circles.

**Paramita Dasgupta**

# Acknowledgements

I would like to express my gratitude to the Delegation of the European Commission, New Delhi for awarding a project entitled " Enhancing Benefits from the Doha Development Agenda for India" to the Administrative Staff College of India, Hyderabad. A number of papers in this volume are revised versions of papers presented at workshops organized under this project. Earlier versions of the following papers, listed below have been prepared with the financial assistance of the European Community. The views expressed therein are those of the author and can in no way be taken to reflect the official opinion of the European Community. The papers are:

- Multilateral Framework on Investment under WTO: A Developing Country Perspective: *Dipayan Datta Chaudhuri*
- Competition Policy, Mergers and Acquisitions and the Relevance of a Multilateral Framework for India: *Paramita Dasgupta*
- Trade Facilitation Issue and India: *Nirmal Sengupta*
- Trade Facilitation and Transaction Costs as an Agenda for Global Trade Negotiations: *Jayanta Roy*
- Efficacy of a Multilateral Agreement on Transparency in Government Procurement: A Developing Country's Perspective: *Thilotham R Kolanu*
- Traditional Knowledge and Intellectual Property Rights: *Nirmal Sengupta*
- WTO Non-Agriculture Market Access: Implications for Indian Industrial Tariffs: *Rajesh Mehta and Pooja Agarwal*
- Social and Economic Aspects of Agricultural Biotechnology: *Suman Sahai*

- ❖ TRIPS Patent System and Doha Declaration—Implementation by India: *B.K.Keayla*

There are many persons who have contributed directly and indirectly over the past few years in the process of publishing this book and whom I must mention. I owe a debt of gratitude to Shri M. Narasimham, Chairman, Court of Governors Administrative Staff College of India and Dr. S.K. Rao, Director General, Administrative Staff College of India for their constant encouragement and guidance in my endeavour to understand the complexities of the WTO and write on it , Ambassador S. Narayanan who is a pillar of support and who on many occasions has patiently clarified many complex aspects of the WTO to me, Dr. E.A.S. Sarma, Former Principal, Administrative Staff College of India for being extremely supportive, Professor Biswajit Dhar, Professor and Head, Centre for WTO Studies, IIFT, Dr. Jayanta Roy, Principal Advisor, Confederation of Indian Industry and Dr. Veena Jha, India Programme Coordinator, UNCTAD, for their help.

I thank Mr. Samik Shome, Senior Research Fellow, ASCI who has painstakingly helped with the editing and references of the book. I would also like to thank Mrs. P. Mahalaxmi and Mrs. K. Usha Rani for their meticulous help in editing and proof reading of the manuscript. A note of thanks to my husband, Amitabha Dasgupta without whose steady support, patience and constant encouragement this book could not have been written. Any errors which remain however are solely mine.

**PARAMITA DASGUPTA**
*Hyderabad*

# Contents

# List of Tables & Boxes

## BOXES

# List of Figures

# Introduction

Multilateral trade negotiations in the WTO have assumed a great deal of importance in the current global scenario mainly because they have cut across a wide range of issues, political, social and economic and have complex ramifications for all cross sections of civil society.

Currently major efforts are on to continue the stalled Doha Round of Negotiations. The negotiations in the WTO had been suspended earlier. This had happened primarily because member countries could not agree on the modalities of negotiations in important areas. The Doha Round of Negotiations had received its first major setback at the Cancun Ministerial Conference in 2003 due to a considerable divide between the developing countries and the developed countries, the latter being primarily the US and EC, mainly on the area of agriculture. There was a revival of negotiations, however, with a Framework Agreement in July/August 2004 (WTO, 2004) when the member countries agreed to what came to be known as the 'July Package'. There was considerable advance in negotiations in agriculture in the July Package. Among other major areas, which received attention in the July Package, were negotiations on non-agricultural market access (NAMA), where negotiations continued without a specific agreement, and the Singapore Issues. As far as the Singapore Issues are concerned, three of the four issues were dropped from the negotiating agenda. Among the four issues on Investment, Competition Policy, Transparency in Government Procurement and Trade Facilitation, only Trade Facilitation remained and negotiations were to continue on it. The Hong Kong Ministerial that followed in 2005, ended with agreement in three areas, namely, agriculture, NAMA and services. Ongoing negotiations are mostly concentrated in these three areas. As Bhaumik (2006) aptly writes, "The story of the WTO today is essentially a story of growing North-South Conflict" and "The biggest challenge before the WTO today is meaningful management of the North-South Conflict". With member countries being unable to agree on modalities of negotiations and consequent suspension of negotiations, the WTO is at the crossroads today. At one end is the road to regional agreements and bilateralism and at the other end is the multilateral agenda and commitments to it.

While international trade is growing rapidly over the past few years, some areas have attracted attention for reasons both economic and political. The first of these is trade in agriculture. Agriculture has also undoubtedly been the most contentious area in multilateral trade negotiations. This is mostly because of imbalances in international trade in agriculture caused by the huge domestic and export subsidies that were paid out by the governments of some developed countries. Market access has also been affected by peak tariffs in existence on selected agricultural products in countries like US, EU and Japan. This has affected other countries including developing as well as developed countries, which are agricultural exporters, primarily in terms of preventing access into the concerned developed country markets.

Agriculture was brought into the multilateral negotiations for the first time in the Uruguay Round. The Agreement on Agriculture proposed to discipline the subsidies that were being given by developed countries to their farmers and also to provide market access through reduction in tariffs on agricultural products. The objective of the Agreement on Agriculture (AOA) was to establish a fair and market oriented agricultural trading system by providing for substantial reduction in agricultural support and other types of protection so as to remove distortions on markets for agricultural products. Accordingly as signatories to the AOA, developed as well as developing countries were committed to reduction of their Aggregate Measure of Support, mostly the Amber Box subsidies, over periods of six and ten years. Commitments included reduction in export subsidies and reduction of tariffs to ensure market access.

The major problem which began to brew around the late 90s and the beginning of the new millennium was regarding implementation of the Uruguay Round commitments on these three areas. It was noticed that total domestic subsidies given by some developed countries, primarily the US and EC were still huge and in the case of the US, had been actually increasing. Similarly on market access, there were tariff peaks, higher than those in developing countries, in existence in US, EC and Japan—all this in spite of the Agreement on Agriculture and its declaration on free and fair trade.

The Doha Ministerial Declaration in 2001 (WTO, 2001) reiterated the objective of the Agreement on Agriculture to establish a fair and market oriented trading system by taking steps to ensure that restrictions and distortions in world agricultural markets are prevented. The Declaration commits itself to "reductions of, with a view to phasing out, all forms of export subsidies; and substantial reductions in trade distorting domestic support." The commitments made also included providing S&D treatment to developing countries and taking note of their development needs, including food security and rural development.

The Doha Ministerial was followed up by negotiations and with views and counterviews being expressed by the developed countries like US-EC on the one hand, the Cairns Group of countries and developing countries like India, Brazil and the African group of countries on the other. The process led up to the Cancun Ministerial in September 2003, which failed. At Cancun there was a major divide between the US-EC on the one hand and nearly all the developing countries on the other and the Cancun Ministerial collapsed.

The Framework Agreement, or the 'July Package' signed in August 2004 (WTO, 2004) carried the negotiations forward by agreeing on a package of modalities, among other areas on agriculture. The Framework Agreement marked a substantial progress in agricultural negotiations among other things in defining total trade distorting domestic support as a sum total of final bound level of AMS, de minimis support and Blue Box measures, capping of Blue Box measures, deeper cuts in higher tariffs in market access, designation of special products for developing countries on the criteria of rural development, food security and livelihood security etc. There were however several areas where modalities still required to be sorted out, e.g. setting of a date for elimination of export subsidies, agreement on the tiers for reduction of domestic support, bands for tariff reduction etc. The July Package was hailed as a positive step in the direction of continuing negotiations. The Hong Kong Agreement (WTO, 2005)marked substantial progress on the July Package in terms of negotiations on agriculture. The following were specifically the areas on which there was agreement at Hong Kong: On market access, a tariff reduction from bound tariffs using a tiered approach with four bands of tariffs has been agreed. There will be deeper cuts on higher tariffs. On domestic support it was agreed to cut substantially the overall trade distorting support based on negotiations, based on three bands and on export subsidies it was agreed to completely phase out export subsidies by 2013. Developing countries are to be allowed to self designate an appropriate number of products as special products on the grounds of food security, livelihood security and rural development and there would be more flexible treatment for these products. Developing countries can also take recourse to special safeguard mechanism. The measures to allow developing countries to designate special products and also to take recourse to special safeguard mechanism were much acclaimed since they would provide developing countries with the much sought after flexibility in a scenario where quantitative restrictions are no longer allowed. Also, the provision of a special safeguard mechanism is expected to provide protection in a situation of import surges.

In spite of the movement forward at Hong Kong, recently the WTO talks were suspended in July 2006 mostly due to lack of agreement on reduction of domestic subsidies by developed countries.

For India, agriculture is an issue connected to rural livelihoods. At the same time Indian agriculture is confronted with cheap subsidized imports from the developed countries. India does not have the requisite resources to increase its domestic support to a level compatible with countries like the US and EU. As far as the WTO negotiations are concerned, India therefore needs to resist further demands for tariff reduction in its agriculture sector in the absence of firm commitments on reduction of subsidies from the developed countries. India also needs to focus on the sanitary and phyto-sanitary measures which are posing non-tariff barriers to its exports to developed countries and the special and differential treatment provisions and needs to select products that can be designated as 'special products' on the grounds of rural livelihoods and food security.

A second critical area at the current juncture is the NAMA negotiations which basically concentrate on industrial tariffs. Industrial tariffs constitute a major policy tool for industrialization for developing and least developed countries and are used by these groups of countries to protect selected industries from external competition. The structure of industrial tariffs varies across developed and developing countries. In developed countries, while average tariffs are low, there are peak tariffs in existence for specific products and also tariff escalation. These are issues of concern to developing countries since they prevent market access of their exports into these markets. Apart from peak tariffs and tariff escalation, developing countries are also concerned about non-tariff barriers in the form of Sanitary and Phyto-sanitary measures (SPS) and Technical Barriers to Trade (TBTs) being applied by the developed countries as well as the use of anti-dumping and safeguard measures. In spite of these problems however, developing countries were opposed to bringing industrial tariffs on to the Doha agenda. This is because developing countries feared that bringing industrial tariffs on to the negotiating agenda would lead them to be pressurized to bring in more stringent tariff reductions on sectors where they were not prepared to make such commitments. Major concern was expressed by the least developed countries, (LDCs) including the ACP countries. Apart from the fact that tariffs were perceived by these countries as a tool for industrialization for protecting certain industry sectors from external competition—customs revenues constituted a substantial share of total revenues in many of these countries which would be adversely affected with lowering of tariffs (Khor and Chien, 2004).

Thus there was no agreement between the developed countries on the one hand and developing and least developed countries on the other on bringing industrial tariffs on to the agenda of negotiations. However in spite of this lack of agreement, negotiations on NAMA was brought on to the Doha agenda.

The basic mandate in the Doha Declaration concentrated upon reduction or elimination of tariff peaks, high tariffs and tariff escalation, as well as non-tariff barriers in particular on products of export interest to developing countries, and also noted that negotiations were to take fully into account the special needs and interests of the developing countries and the LDCs, including through less than full reciprocity in reduction commitments.

The Chairman of the Negotiating Group on Market Access (NGMA) set up after the Doha Work Programme was adopted, prepared a draft proposal on NAMA in May 2003, followed by a revised text in August 2003. While the Chairman's draft proposals were broadly acceptable there were concerns expressed by the developing countries and least developed countries (LDCs), primarily the African countries. While the larger developing countries were more concerned with tariff peaks and tariff escalation, LDCs were more concerned with their issues of domestic industrialization and drop in customs revenues concomitant with a drop in their tariffs. (Khor and Chien, 2004).

It is well known that while at Cancun a draft containing proposals on a framework on modalities on NAMA was circulated, there was no agreement at Cancun on any of the elements of the draft and there was no mention of a tariff reduction formula.

The Framework Agreement of August 2004 (WTO, 2004) was mostly based on the Cancun draft. The need for additional negotiations was however mentioned in the Framework Agreement. Between the Framework Agreement and the Hong Kong Ministerial, there was no major progress on NAMA negotiations. Developing countries like India and Brazil expressed their doubts about the Swiss Formula and its suitability from the point of view of developing countries. However despite this situation, at Hong Kong, the Swiss Formula was accepted without much clarification about the type of formula and the specifics regarding the coefficients to be adopted.

The negotiations on NAMA are therefore at the crossroads. There is no agreement yet on the specifics regarding the coefficient to be adopted, whether there should be two or more coefficients or different coefficients for different countries. Member countries are in the process of submitting proposals. Issues such as special and differential treatment to be provided to developing countries, treatment of unbound tariffs, sectoral tariff elimination and non-tariff barriers need to be tabled and sorted out to the best interests of developing and least developed countries.

The issue of industrial tariffs and their reduction is a major policy issue in India's liberalization efforts and economic growth process. A holistic approach to the NAMA negotiations encompassing negotiations around the appropriate coefficients to be adopted in the formula, the sectoral tariff elimination issue, special and differential treatment and non-tariff barriers need to looked at in a way as to ensure maximum market access for Indian products into developed country markets, while at the same time preserving the use of tariffs as a competitive tool for domestic industry. This is the challenge of NAMA negotiations.

The issue of service sector liberalization is very important for India. Service sector is the most rapidly growing sector in the Indian economy. Currently, the services sector accounts for around 54.1 per cent of India's GDP. Services exports increased by almost 106 per cent between 2003/04 and 2005/06 in India. India is one of the top five exporters of services among developing countries.

Negotiations in the WTO on the GATS Agreement are therefore important provided they result in opening up of markets for India's exports particularly in sectors of interest to India like IT and IT enabled services where India has a competitive strength. As discussed by Jha in her paper in this volume, for India, these negotiations are important because on the one hand, it may lead to commitments from developed countries like US and EC to open up their markets and modify their regulations, and on the other, it is expected to lead to continuity, sustained commitments and clarity in domestic policy which help to enhance exports.

Services continue to be a complex area in international trade especially since they are subject to regulations of different kinds in each country. These regulations vary from country to country and are based on national policy objectives and direction. Thus there are regulations on foreign direct investments, on movement of people across borders, on entry of investment into particular sectors, on the nature of foreign investments etc.

Prior to the Hong Kong Ministerial, many developed countries had filed revised offers, including among others, the US and the EC. However the offers did not include many new openings for trade for developing countries like India. India has also made revised offers covering 11 sectors and 94 sub-sectors which represents substantial improvement over its earlier offer.

At Hong Kong, agreement on the area of GATS included a number of new clauses including proposals for strengthening commitments under Mode 1 and Mode 4 and changing the structure of negotiations to include negotiations on a plurilateral basis. This is a major change since earlier negotiations in the GATS had been based on bilateral requests and offers and/or unilateral, autonomous commitments by members.

India's major focus on the GATS is to persuade developed countries to make commitments in Mode 1 and Mode 4. This is because on the one hand, Mode 1 will ensure predictability in terms of entry in the areas of IT and IT enabled services, where India has a tremendous competitive advantage and on the other hand commitments under Mode 4 will facilitate entry of professionals in key areas. At present there are a large number of entry barriers for professionals in developed countries in a variety of forms ranging from visa requirements, qualifications, licenses to practice, labour market tests, etc. Simultaneously India will also require to be clear about its own commitments in specific sectors, and ensure transparency in its own regulations.

The issue of bringing intellectual property rights (IPRs) on to the multilateral trade agenda has been contentious since the early eighties and as expected, the TRIPS Agreement has been one of the most controversial areas of the WTO. Developing countries always felt that IPRs should not be brought on to the platform of multilateral trade negotiations and had initially opposed the inclusion of the TRIPS Agreement on the WTO agenda since they felt that signing of this Agreement would affect their development concerns adversely in a multitude of ways. However despite this opposition, the TRIPS Agreement was signed and intellectual property rules were introduced in the multilateral trading system for the first time.

The Agreement establishes minimum levels of protection that each member country has to give to the seven categories of IPRs specified in the Agreement. India has amended its Patent Law through three successive amendments and is now fully compliant with the TRIPS patent regime.

Implementation of the TRIPS Agreement has raised a host of complex issues among developing countries. These issues span areas as diverse as industry, health, research and development, genetic engineering, plant breeder's rights, farmers' rights, folklore and culture. In fact the TRIPS Agreement has emerged as the most complex area among all the WTO Agreements in terms of its coverage and ramifications.

A major concern was and continues to be regarding public health. Developing countries were concerned that signing of the TRIPS Agreement would prevent them from taking measures to protect public health. In fact in response to these concerns, a Declaration on the TRIPS Agreement and Public Health was adopted in the Doha Ministerial Conference. The Declaration confirmed that each member would have the freedom to grant compulsory licences and to determine the grounds upon which such compulsory licences are granted. Each member is also given the freedom to determine what constitutes a national emergency. Public health crisis in the form of HIV/AIDS, tuberculosis, malaria and other epidemics can constitute a national emergency.

Several issues arose in the context of this Declaration—primarily that least developed countries (LDCs), which do not have adequate manufacturing capacity cannot make use of the compulsory license provision to manufacture their own drugs if faced with a public health crisis.

Among other controversies that the TRIPS Agreement has generated in India is that regarding the adverse impact of the Agreement on price of pharmaceutical products and its consequent adverse impact on public health. India is now compliant with the product patent regime mandated by the TRIPS Agreement. The issue of patents and specifically, patentability, has raised a range of concerns. Concern ranges from impact of the new patent regime and increased drug prices on public health, to genetic engineering and plant breeders rights. Article 27.3 of the TRIPS Agreement on patentability has raised a great deal of debate. Micro-organisms and microbiological processes are now patentable. Hence genetically modified (GM) crops are being patented by multinational corporations with adverse implications of different sorts for the agricultural sector in developing countries. There are serious consequences for the biotechnology industry as well. The other issue is that of patenting of traditional knowledge and folklore. Developing countries like India are gravely concerned with protection of its traditional knowledge. Appropriate policy regulations are required at the domestic level and those that are in existence need to be further fine tuned to suit the present requirements.

Views on the impact of the TRIPS Agreement and the new patent regime vary. Keayla for instance in his paper in this volume holds the view that the TRIPS Agreement provides flexibilities which should be utilized in India's patent law. This, according to him, has not been done adequately, especially in the context of the TRIPS Agreement and public health. Rao on the other hand in his paper in this volume argues that the impact of the TRIPS Agreement on public health and the pharmaceutical industry will be negative since the TRIPS Agreement and compliance with the patent regime will lead to an increase in drug prices and increased technological dependence of the developing countries on the developed countries.

Thus while there is compliance with the TRIPS Agreement in India in the area of patents, implementation of the Agreement continues to lead to complexities cutting across different segments of civil society and different sectors of the economy.

The four Singapore issues have been a major bone of contention between the developed and developing countries in the WTO negotiations. In the first Ministerial Conference at Singapore, the developed counties primarily comprising E.C. and U.S. tried to place the issues comprising trade and investment, trade and competition policy, trade facilitation and transparency in Government procurement on the negotiating agenda.

This was staunchly resisted by developing countries and instead Working Groups were constituted in each of the four areas to undertake study in these areas. However, submissions made by member countries to the Working Groups on core principles relating to these four issues like transparency, non-discrimination, pre-investment commitments, procedural fairness etc., showed that there was no consensus on these issues regarding placing them on a multilateral framework since different countries have different policy priorities. Despite this, the four issues were placed on the Agenda in the Doha Ministerial and it was stated in the Doha Ministerial Declaration (WTO, 2001) that "negotiations will take place after the fifth session of the Ministerial Conference on the basis of a decision to be taken by explicit consensus at that session on modalities of negotiations."

The above phrase led to some ambiguities in interpretation. On the basis of a clarification issued by the Chairman of the Doha Ministerial Conference, the developing countries understood that negotiations would start in the Fifth Ministerial subject to explicit consensus on modalities. Developed countries, on the other hand claimed that negotiations were mandated and only the modalities were subject to consensus. The fifth ministerial meeting at Cancun collapsed. The current status as far as the negotiating agenda is concerned, as noted in the Framework Agreement of August 2004, (WTO, 2004) is that three of the four Singapore issues are no longer a part of the Doha work programme. Only trade facilitation remains on the negotiating agenda and negotiations are continuing as per the modalities set out in Annexure D of the Framework Agreement (WTO, 2004).

Does India require to have a multilateral framework in these areas?

Quite apart from the WTO Agenda the issue of foreign direct investment (FDI), competition policy, transparency in Government procurement and trade facilitation are important domestic policy concerns for India. Let us take the case of FDI. The issue is, does liberalisation of FDI inflow lead to greater FDI? As pointed out by Datta Chaudhuri in his paper in this volume, studies undertaken in these areas with reference to India and other developing countries do not indicate a positive correlation between these two factors. Rather FDI appears to depend more upon factors like size of the market, availability of infrastructure, income distribution etc. (Correa and Kumar, 2003). In this situation, appropriate and timely domestic policy regulation of FDI appears to be a critical need for entry of FDI into the desired areas in a developing country like India. Thus, placing these issues on a multilateral framework with its concomitant requirements do not appear to be necessary to achieve the desired objective of higher levels of FDI.

For competition policy, given the wave of mergers and acquisitions, joint ventures and corporate restructuring that is going on in India, a policy for regulating such combinations and preventing monopolies from emerging is necessary and domestic competition policy is required to be tuned to this purpose. However, as regards adopting a multilateral framework, while the additional costs of compliance including setting up infrastructure etc., are clear, additional benefits ensuing are not very clear. This is because of the following reasons: on the one hand multilateral rules, it is perceived, will take away the freedom of developing countries to regulate their own combinations according to their economic requirements, while on the other hand without assured cooperation from the developed countries in particular, regarding information on their rules and assured technical support, it may not be possible for developing countries to undertake prosecution of international cartels and combinations. Thus a multilateral framework may not be of benefit to the developing countries.

Similarly, the linkage between transparency in government procurement and trade related objectives are not clear. Thus, as noted by Kolanu in this volume, while achieving transparency in Government procurement is an important domestic governance issue, bringing it on to the multilateral platform does not involve any substantial gains in the perception of the developing countries.

Trade facilitation presents a slightly different picture. There is little disagreement on the fact that a holistic approach towards trade facilitation including customs procedures, trade related information together with physical infrastructure like ports, service, transport, storage facility is certainly beneficial for India since, as noted by Roy in his paper in this volume, it will lead to enhanced competitive advantage for India's exports through reduced prices and enhanced quality. Adoption of a multilateral framework as mandated in the WTO, however, raises certain issues. As discussed by Sengupta in his paper in this volume, the modalities as spelt out in the Framework Agreement, 2004 and reiterated in the Hong Kong Declaration have positive implications for India if they are adhered to. However, it would involve costs to the developing countries in the form of infrastructural investment and other costs of compliance. So, while there are many positive aspects to adopting a multilateral framework on trade facilitation for India, whether the outcome will be positive will depend upon whether the modalities as spelt out in the Framework Agreement are adhered to. There is need to concentrate on these negotiations. Negotiations are thus at the crossroads. They may either lead to a framework that is beneficial for developing countries or to one that does not pay importance to the developing countries' requirements for trade facilitation.

This volume brings together a collection of papers on key issues in India's international trade scenario as discussed above. India has been involved in negotiations in these areas in the WTO. While WTO negotiations in these areas have had significant impact on different aspects of India's economy and on the structure of domestic policy regulations, they have also been very controversial with regard to their implications for India. Currently the WTO negotiations are at the crossroads. The member countries are unable to come to an agreement in critical areas. The future of the multilateral negotiations will depend upon the ability of the member countries to agree on critical issues. Hence whether multilateral negotiations will survive or will be replaced completely by the spate of regional and bilateral agreements already well under way will depend upon the approach adopted by the member countries to the negotiations. The papers in the volume contain an analysis of these critical issues in international trade in India, in the context of the impact of WTO Agreements on these issues and suggest policies for the future that will be beneficial for India.

**Paramita Dasgupta**

## REFERENCES

Bhaumik, T.K. (2006). *The WTO A Discordant Orchestra*. New Delhi: Sage Publications, p. 20.

Correa M.E. and Kumar, N. (2003). *Protecting Foreign Investment—Implications of a WTO Regime and Policy Options*. London: Zed Books.

Khor, M. and Chien, Y.G. (2004). 'The WTO Negotiations on Non-Agricultural Market Access: A Development Perspective', *Third World Network*, November, available at twnet@po.jaring.my

WTO, (2001) Ministerial Declaration. Ministerial Conference, Fourth Session, Doha, 9-14 November 2001.

WTO, (2004) 'Doha Work Programme—Decision adopted by the General Council on 1st August 2004'. WT/L/579, August 2.

WTO, (2005) Doha Work Programme. Ministerial Declaration. Adopted on 18 December 2005. Ministerial Conference, Sixth Session, Hong Kong, 13-18 December 2005 WT/MIN(05)/DEC.

# *Chapter* 1

# WTO Non-Agriculture Market Access: Implications for Indian Industrial Tariffs

RAJESH MEHTA* and POOJA AGARWAL**

The World Trade Organisation's (WTO) Sixth Ministerial Conference in Hong Kong saw 149 WTO member nations of the world assembled together for the first time to pave the way for multilateral trade negotiations. This time all the 149 trade ministers were set to conclude the unfinished agenda of the Doha development round launched on the eve of Fourth Ministerial Conference of WTO held at Doha in November 2001. But the apathetic attitude of select developed countries towards the needs and concerns of developing countries that got reflected in the disagreement over the issue of agriculture subsidies and market access led to another deadlock in the negotiations.

The Doha Ministerial Declaration it may be recalled had mandated for undertaking negotiations on market access for non-agriculture goods so as to enable the free flow of goods across borders by a reduction of tariff barriers. In this regard the Negotiating Group on Market Access (NGMA) had been created within WTO. The draft Hong Kong Ministerial Text, circulated by the Chairman of General Council of WTO, recommits to complete the work programme of Doha Declaration in the near future. Besides other areas, this draft has proposed a framework of modalities for negotiations on non-agricultural products. As India is a member of the WTO with products of export interest for developing and developed countries it has to

* Senior Fellow, RIS, India Habitat Centre, New Delhi.

** Research Assistant, RIS, India Habitat Centre, New Delhi.

take care of its development strategy and trade policies. In this paper therefore an attempt has been made to assess the implications of the Development Round of WTO negotiations on Indian industrial tariffs. Section I provides the background for these negotiations with a review of Doha mandate on market access of non-agriculture products. In Section II we discuss the various elements of NGMA-Chairman draft (NGMA-CD) proposal and examine the formula proposed in this draft and the Hong Kong Ministerial Declaration with its likely impact on Indian industrial tariffs. In addition we have identified the items that are receptive to sectoral elimination as also items that have to be left unbound. Section III contains the outcome of the 'NGMA—possible options' draft on Indian bindings. The NGMA Chairman released this draft just a month before the Cancun meet to advance the process of Non-Agriculture Market Access (NAMA) negotiations. At the same time, EC-US-CANADA also came up with a joint proposal on NAMA negotiations. This also presents the results of the tariff cutting exercise conducted as per the pure Swiss formula proposed by the EC-US-Canada. Briefly this section also outlines the major difference in the consequences of the non-linear formulae proposed by Hong Kong Declaration on Indian industrial bindings. Section IV puts forth the important observations noticed in lieu of the Hong Kong Ministerial Text with respect to NAMA modalities and presents concluding observations.

## I. Doha Declaration

The Fourth Ministerial Conference of the WTO was held in Doha, Qatar in November 2001. The Ministerial Declaration contained the mandate on a number of issues. As part of this mandate (paragraph16) it was decided that the negotiations on market access for non-agriculture goods should be conducted. Paragraph 16 says that,

> "We agree to negotiations which shall aim, by modalities to be agreed, to reduce or as appropriate eliminate tariffs, including the reduction or elimination of tariff peaks, high tariffs, and tariff escalation, as well as non-tariff barriers, in particular on products of export interest to developing countries. Product coverage shall be comprehensive and without *a priori* exclusions. The negotiations shall take fully into account the special needs and interests of developing

> and least-developed country participants, including through less than full reciprocity in reduction commitments. To this end, the modalities to be agreed will include appropriate studies and capacity-building measures to assist least-developed countries to participate effectively in the negotiations" cf, WTO, *Ministerial Declaration*, WT/MIN (01)/DEC/W/1, Nov. 14, 2001, Doha, 9-14, November 2001.

This Doha mandate raised important issues that concerned India and other developing countries.

The Declaration highlighted the need for reduction and elimination of tariffs, tariff peaks, high tariffs, tariff escalation and non-tariff barriers. In this context, India has to be very careful about an elimination of tariffs. It is sometimes said that elimination of tariffs by developed countries may provide a higher market access to India and developing countries, because most of the developed countries are members of mega-trading blocs (with preferential and free tariffs). Elimination of tariffs, it may be pointed out will not provide a preferential market to member countries of Regional Trading Associations (RTAs) for intra-regional trade. Hence non-member countries like India could obtain access to markets of member countries of mega-trading blocs.

The Declaration also talked about reduction in and elimination of high and peak tariffs. The definition of high and peak tariffs has not been made very clear in the modalities before negotiations start. Peak tariff in the literature is defined at a specified level, i.e., 10 per cent, 12 per cent or 15 per cent (WTO, 2001a). The level of the peak tariffs cannot be assumed as being the same for all member countries—developed countries, developing countries and LDCs. In fact, there is a case that it must be linked to average tariff (Mehta, 2001).

The Ministerial Declaration also mentioned the reduction or elimination of tariff escalation as well as of non-tariff barriers. In this context, it should be remembered that the Uruguay Round negotiations led to an increase in the tariff escalation of developed countries; particularly for the products in which India and other developing countries had export interest (Mehta, 2003).

The Declaration does not mention the modalities of the negotiations. It merely states that the modalities have to be decided upon, and goes on to add that such decisions should take into consideration the appropriate studies and capacity-building measures to assist LDCs.

The Doha Declaration does not mention anything about the base rate (the tariff rate for starting negotiations) of the negotiations.

The Doha Declaration also states that a member country could not *a priori* exclude an item/product from the negotiations. In other words, India and other developing countries cannot keep any item in the unbound list on a unilateral basis.

There is no mention of "credit for autonomous liberalization".

The Declaration does not make any reference to an increase in transparency and predictability through a significant expansion of the scope of tariff bindings and through simplifying members' tariffs. A large number of developed countries are defining tariffs in the form of specific and compound duties, which have been found to be relatively very high. It is very difficult to put them in the negotiations without knowing the *ad valorem* equivalence and the other implications of such duties.

The Declaration talks about the reduction or elimination of non-tariff barriers, in particular for products of export interest to developing countries. However, it does not talk about the different types of non-tariff barriers be it hardcore or soft. Different issues relating to NTBs, namely identification, examination, linkage with other areas of the Doha Declaration, modalities, etc. remained untouched.

In the negotiation process it is expected that there will be mounting pressure on India and other developing countries to reduce/eliminate their tariffs. A number of studies do however suggest [(UNCTAD, 1999-2000, 2003), (Mehta, 2001, 2003), (Bacchetta and Bora, 2003)] that developing countries should emphasize the following aspects:

- *Elimination of Tariffs:* Developing countries should completely reject the issue of elimination of tariffs as one of the core objects of the Doha Declaration. Elimination of tariffs will lead to very high reductions by developing countries as compared to those made by developed countries and a further reduction (or even complete elimination) in the industrial tariffs of developed countries would not lead to a substantial increase in market access for countries like India. It will not be consistent with the development dimension of the present Round. It will also not be consistent with the principle of 'less than full reciprocity'. Elimination of low/nuisance tariff should not be considered as equivalent to high or deeper reduction by developed countries.

- *Reduction of Tariffs:* Developing countries should not concentrate on a reduction in the average tariff but their concerns should be centred on other aspects such as peak tariffs, tariff escalation, 'credit for autonomous liberalisation', non-*ad valorem* duties, etc.
- *Non-ad valorem Duties:* A large number of developed countries are used to the practice of imposing specific and complex duties rather than *ad valorem* duties. The total number of commodities with custom duties imposed in the form of specific/compound duties is very large in the case of developed countries, for instance, in the EU (for 1780 tariff lines and 1455 tariff lines in the US). In most cases, non-*ad valorem* duties[1] consist of one single specific tariff. However, many are mixed and complex, consisting of several specific and *ad valorem* tariffs associated with a condition of relationships between them. There are many variants of specific duties in the schedules of different countries. Some of these variants are very complex [(UNCTAD, 1998a), (Mehta and Mohanty, 2001)]. It has been noticed that the developed countries have imposed specific duties on a large number of commodities when compared to the number of commodities with such duties in the developing countries. Although most of the countries believe that the specific duties should be replaced by *ad valorem* rates, no decision was made in the Uruguay Round (UR). In fact, a significant number of UR bound rates had been committed in the form of specific duties. It has been noticed that these specific duties conceal the fact that the countries are indirectly imposing high tariffs (Mehta and Mohanty, 2001) without explicitly mentioning them in different forums [(UNCTAD, 1998a), (Mehta and Mohanty, 2001)]. The specific duties are not suitable for analytical and comparative purposes, and require more common *ad valorem* tariffs. Hence these specific duties should be converted to *ad valorem* equivalence (Mehta and

Mohanty, 2001) (AVEs). A study by UNCTAD (1999-2000) has computed the *ad valorem* equivalence of specific duties for 18,000 commodities of different countries. It shows that the *ad valorem* equivalence of a large number of products, whose customs duties are defined in the form of specific tariffs in national custom tariff schedules, is very high. The custom tariff database of the US for August 1999 (Mehta, 2001) also proves the above-mentioned observation. In this database, the US defines specific duties for around 600 industrial commodities (national lines) and provides the corresponding *ad valorem* equivalent rates of most of the specific duties. It shows that the average tariff rate of commodities with non-*ad valorem* duties is almost three times higher than the average tariff rate of the commodities whose custom duties are defined in the form of *ad valorem* rates. In this context, it is worth highlighting that the *ad valorem* equivalence of bound rates is still not available in the literature.

- *Tariff Peaks*: Even if the tariffs are reduced by developed countries, tariff peaks seem to be a major hurdle for the market access in certain sectors where the developing countries have a good export potential.

In most of the literature [(UN, 1998), (UNCTAD, 1999-2000)] a cut-off point has generally been carried out for the identification of commodities with peak tariffs. The level of the cut-off point is generally taken as 12 per cent (and sometimes 10 per cent or 15 per cent). All those commodities, with a tariff rate more than a 12 per cent *ad valorem* rate, are called commodities with peak tariffs. In the existing literature, the selection of a cut-off point is arbitrary and has no relationship with the average tariff. Further, it does not make any distinction between different groups of countries.

Besides, a number of attempts have been made to identify the commodities with peak tariffs. Notably the study by UNCTAD (UNCTAD, 1999-2000) concludes that, "both frequency and levels of tariff peak rates remain a matter of concern. Over 10 per cent of the tariff universe of the Quad countries, corresponding to an aggregate 4,000 tariff line, will continue to exceed 12 per cent *ad valorem*. All four countries maintain a high variance in tariff rates. One-fifth of the peak tariffs of the US, one-quarter of those in EU and Japan, and about one-tenth of those of Canada exceed 30 per cent. In the four *selected developing countries, tariff peaks are more frequent but reach less extreme rates* than in the major developed countries" (emphasis added).

Mehta and Mohanty (2001) also prove this point using detailed data of five developed countries.

- *Tariff Escalation*: The tariff structures of many countries have traditionally displayed significant escalation favouring domestic processors for a large number of commodities. It was expected that tariff commitments in the UR would provide for a gradual reduction of escalation by applying relatively higher cuts to finished goods. However, rapidly rising tariffs have been noticed from low rates for raw material to higher rates for intermediate goods and sometime peak tariffs for finished products. A number of studies [(UNCTAD, 1999-2000), (Mehta, 2001)] have confirmed that tariff escalation has continued after the UR for a large number of sectors, particularly, for fish and fish products, textile and textile products, leather and rubber products, footwear and to some extent wood and wood products. Basically, the results confirm that tariff escalation is still a major constraint for export industries in India and for developing countries.
- *Non-Tariff Barriers*: The developed countries have an impressive array of new measures of protection and government interventions. These have been imposed through different instruments, including non-tariff barriers (NTBs). The agreements of the UR have changed the intensity of different types of NTBs. Some measures of NTBs have lost their importance. However, a significant increase has been noticed in some other measures of NTBs.

The non-tariff barriers continue to affect the growth of world trade and the UR could not tackle these issues successfully. On the one hand, the importing countries generally term these as NTBs, the imposing countries insist that 'these instruments are policy objectives'. Developing countries should emphasise a coherent approach for dealing with such issues and participate actively in setting up new (and clear) rules and provisions (Mehta, 2005).

In short, the priorities of developing countries should be focussed on Peak Tariffs, Tariff Escalation and NTBs to market access, and to see that such trade measures are consistent with the development dimension and with "less than full reciprocity".

## II. NAMA Proposals: From Doha to Hong Kong

The Negotiating Group on Market Access (NGMA) was created in the WTO to initiate negotiations on market access for non-agriculture products.

### II.1 NGMA Proposals for Tariff Reduction (WTO, 2003c)

As part of negotiations a number of meetings of NGMA were held and member countries had submitted many proposals[2] particularly relating to the modalities for reducing tariff. The different modalities can be categorised into the following five broad categories, namely:

1. Request and offer,
2. Formulae,
3. Sector by sector,
4. Zero for zero, and
5. Mixed.

A list of formulae submitted by some members to NGMA is given in WTO (2003) (WTO, 2003a). Based on different submissions, the Chairman of NGMA prepared a document, 'Draft Elements of Modalities for Negotiations on Non-Agricultural Products', WTO, TN/MA/W/35, 16 May 2003. This draft was later revised on 19 August 2003, TN/MA/W/35/Rev.1. The major components for establishing modalities in market access for non-agricultural products as stated in the NGMA Chairman's documents are:

#### *II.1.1 Modified Swiss Formula Proposed by NGMA-Chairman*

The core modality of negotiations is based on a non-linear formula. This formula can substantially reduce high and peak tariffs even if the average tariff of a country is low. The application of the formula would be based on the following elements:

- *Base rate*: A tariff reduction or elimination on all non-agricultural products[3] from the present level of *bound rates* after full implementation of current concessions.[4] However, for *unbound items,* the basis for commencing the tariff reductions shall be two times the MFN applied rate;[5]
- The *base year* for MFN applied tariff rates shall be 2001;
- *Non-ad valorem duties* shall be converted to *ad valorem* equivalents;
- *HS nomenclature*: Negotiations to commence on the basis of Harmonized System (HS) 1996, and negotiations to be finalized in HS 2002 nomenclature;[6] and
- For import data, the years 1999-2001, hereinafter "*reference period*", shall be used in order to mitigate yearly fluctuations.

All non-agricultural tariffs shall be reduced on a line-by-line basis using the following formula[7] applied to the base rates outlined in above paragraph:

$$t_1 = \frac{B \times t_a \times t_0}{B \times t_a + t_0} \quad \ldots(1)$$

where

$t_1$ is the final rate, to be bound in *ad valorem* terms,
$t_0$ is the base rate,
$t_a$ is the average of the base rates, and
$B$ is a coefficient with a unique value to be determined by the participants (member countries of the WTO).

### *II.1.2 Sector-by-Sector/Zero-by-Zero Approach*

The sectoral elimination approach can be used to eliminate and bind all tariffs of the products which are of export interest to developing and least developed countries. The NGMA-CD has proposed this approach for seven sectors namely: Electronics and Electrical goods; Fish and Fish products; Footwear; Leather goods; Motor Vehicles parts and components; Stones, Gems and Precious Metals; and Textiles and Clothing.

### *II.1.3 Supplementary Modalities*

In addition to the above two approaches, the NGMA-CD proposes that member countries should adopt other procedures for *additional tariff reduction and elimination*. The countries that have a less than 35 per cent binding coverage are *expected to bind all* non-agricultural lines and bind tariffs at a level that does not exceed the overall average of bound tariffs for all developing countries after full implementation of the current concessions.

The original (WTO, 2003b) version of the NGMA-CD proposal says that "for developing countries ...reference period" up to 5 per cent of tariff lines may remain unbound provided they do not exceed 5 per cent of the total value of a member's imports. Later in the revised NGMA proposal (WTO, 2003c) this condition was made more strict that is up to 5 per cent of tariff lines may remain unbound provided no more than 1 per cent (1 per cent of the total value of a member's imports) could be taken in one HS chapter.

### *II.1.4 NGMA Proposals: Some Observations*

Keeping in mind the priorities of developing countries, the following paragraphs make some relevant observations on the modalities mentioned in the different drafts of the NGMA-CD proposal:

The core modality is based on the formula.

The NGMA-CD proposal is hushed on the tariff escalation of non-agricultural products, since the formula captures it. In case this formula is used, the rate of the tariff escalation may also decline in comparison to the Uruguay Round.[8] However, the 'supplementary modalities' may lead to an increase in tariff escalation and may not meet the priorities of developing countries.

The NGMA-CD proposal is clear that all items for which duties are defined in the specific or complex form should be included in the negotiations. It says "... Non-*ad valorem* duties shall be converted to *ad valorem* equivalents (AVEs) according to the procedures..." The proposal also mentions the formula for working out an *ad-valorem* equivalence of specific duties using simple methods. However, it is well known how some of these specific duties are defined and it is very difficult to calculate an *ad-valorem* equivalence of these duties [(UNCTAD, 1998b), (Mehta and Mohanty, 2001)]. The proposal suggests that in such cases "Non-*ad valorem* tariffs for which AVEs cannot be calculated by the Secretariat because of the technical nature of the duties concerned shall be assumed to have an AVE equivalent to the tariff average ($t_a$) as used in the formula". India and developing countries should keep a close watch on this, because it has been noticed that the *ad valorem* equivalence of specific duties, indeed is relatively very high as compared to those commodities whose duties are defined in the form of *ad-valorem* rates.

The NGMA-CD proposal however, is not very clear on how to deal with non-tariff barriers. It talks about: (i) identification and examination of various types of NTBs, (ii) categorisation, (iii) collection of information, and (iv) inter linkage with other bodies of the WTO. It says that the modalities could include request/offer, horizontal or vertical approaches. Developing countries should ask for a clear interpretation of such steps towards NTBs. A similar unresolved state exists in the post Hong Kong era.

## II.2 Impact of NGMA-CD Formulae on Indian Industrial Tariffs: Some Simulation Results

### *II.2.1 Methodology*

The formula, as represented by equation (1) contains following variables/parameters:

1. $t_0$—the base rate (bound or unbound) of all tariff lines of India,
2. $t_a$—the average of the base rates,
3. *B*—a coefficient with a unique value to be determined by the participants.

The tariff cutting exercise starts from the Uruguay Round bound rates that are the base rates. These rates are collected for non-agricultural commodities defined in HS-1996 at the 6-digit level. With all these rates the simple average i.e. $t_a$ was found out. Then we arbitrarily (WTO, 2003c) chose the values of *B* that were 0.25,0.5,1.0,1.5, and 2.0. After fitting these values in the formula for different scenarios of *B* consequential were the post-Doha Development Round rates. The results are presented in Table 1.1.

### *II.2.2 Proposed Bound Rates*

The range of proposed bound rates after the Doha Development Round based on the NGMA-CD proposal under alternate scenarios

**Table 1.1:** India: Proposed Bound Rate (%) in Post-DDA based on NGMA-CD proposal, under alternate scenario of B (excluding commodities of seven sectors)

| | *Base rate** | *B = 0.25* | *B = 0.5* | *B = 1* | *B = 1.5* | *B = 2* | *No. of Tariff Lines (at 6-digit HS)* |
|---|---|---|---|---|---|---|---|
| | 0.00 | 0.00 | 0.00 | 0.00 | 0.00 | 0.00 | 67 |
| | 3.00 | 2.36 | 2.64 | 2.81 | 2.87 | 2.90 | 7 |
| | 5.00 | 3.45 | 4.08 | 4.49 | 4.65 | 4.73 | 10 |
| | 10.00 | 5.27 | 6.90 | 8.17 | 8.70 | 8.99 | 28 |
| | 12.50 | 5.89 | 8.00 | 9.76 | 10.53 | 10.96 | 1 |
| | 13.30 | 6.06 | 8.32 | 10.24 | 11.09 | 11.57 | 2 |
| | 20.00 | 7.15 | 10.53 | 13.80 | 15.39 | 16.33 | 15 |
| | 25.00 | 7.70 | 11.77 | 16.01 | 18.19 | 19.52 | 395 |
| | 26.70 | 7.85 | 12.14 | 16.69 | 19.07 | 20.54 | 1 |
| | 30.00 | 8.12 | 12.78 | 17.92 | 20.70 | 22.44 | 9 |
| | 32.50 | 8.29 | 13.21 | 18.78 | 21.86 | 23.81 | 3 |
| | 34.00 | 8.38 | 13.45 | 19.27 | 22.53 | 24.60 | 1 |
| | 35.00 | 8.44 | 13.60 | 19.59 | 22.96 | 25.12 | 8 |
| | 36.00 | 8.50 | 13.75 | 19.90 | 23.39 | 25.63 | 1 |
| | 37.70 | 8.59 | 13.99 | 20.41 | 24.09 | 26.48 | 1 |
| | 38.90 | 8.65 | 14.15 | 20.76 | 24.58 | 27.07 | 1 |
| | 40.00 | 8.70 | 14.30 | 21.07 | 25.01 | 27.60 | 1698 |
| | 46.70 | 8.98 | 15.07 | 22.79 | 27.48 | 30.63 | 1 |
| | 50.00 | 9.10 | 15.40 | 23.54 | 28.59 | 32.01 | 72 |
| | 55.00 | 9.25 | 15.84 | 24.60 | 30.15 | 33.99 | 1 |
| | 70.00 | 9.60 | 16.88 | 27.21 | 34.17 | 39.18 | 720 |
| | 150.00 | 10.36 | 19.38 | 34.32 | 46.19 | 55.86 | 1 |
| | 300.00 | 10.73 | 20.71 | 38.75 | 54.60 | 68.64 | 1 |
| Average (%) | 43.97 | 8.53 | 14.14 | 21.19 | 25.49 | 28.41 | 3044 |

* Final Bound Rate or two times MFN Applied Tariff Rate (for unbound items) in 2001.

*Note*: The analysis is carried out for 3044 commodities on the basis of 6-digit HS Level. The range of proposed bound rates is found out after excluding seven sectors under 'Sectoral Elimination' Approach. Although the average value (44.5%) is used while calculating the proposed rates, it was based on all commodities.

of B for non-agricultural products, excluding seven sectors[9] (identified for sectoral tariff elimination) defined at the 6-digit HS level are given in Table 1.1 and in Fig. 1.1.

India's average tariff rate for the base year (2001) comes to 44.5 per cent for all non-agricultural products. The range of base tariffs is 0 to 70 per cent except for two items. Most of the items in the base year have a rate of 25 per cent, 40 per cent and 70 per cent. In case $B = 1$, the proposed average bound rate in the post-DDA comes to 21.2 per cent (excluding seven sectors). This will lead to an average reduction of 51.8 per cent.

In case $B = 1.0$, the bound rate of a large number of items will be 21.1 per cent (1698 items), 27.2 per cent (720 items), and 16.0 per cent (395 items). The frequency distribution of Indian non-agricultural bound rates, defined by commodities at the 6-digit HS-1996, is illustrated in Fig. 1.2. The range of India's proposed tariffs would be 0 to 27.2 per cent. Two items with mega-tariffs of 150 per cent (types of alcohol) and 300 per cent (passenger goods), in the base year, will be 34.3 per cent and 38.7 per cent, respectively.

The increase in $B\,(> 1)$ does not lead to any significant difference in reduction of tariffs; while a decline in $B$ below 1 (i.e. $B < 1$) reduces the post-DDA bound tariffs significantly.

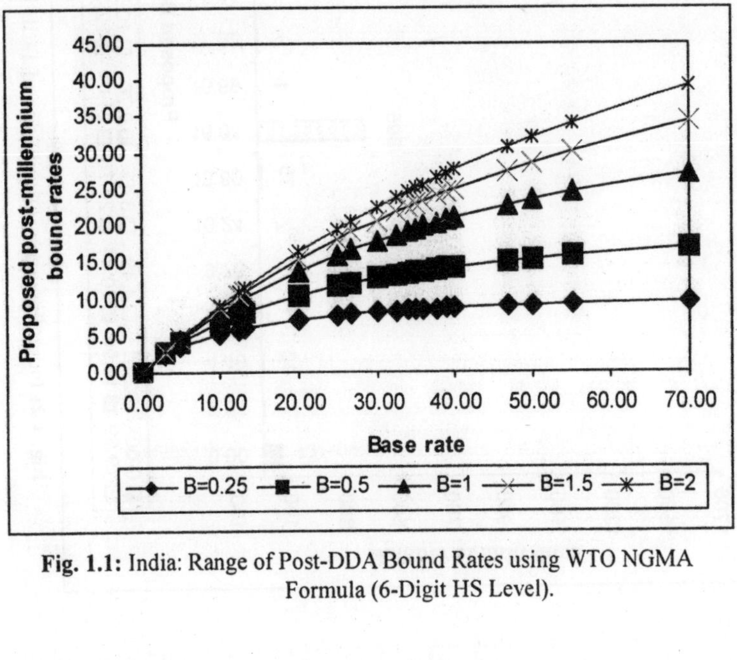


**Fig. 1.1:** India: Range of Post-DDA Bound Rates using WTO NGMA Formula (6-Digit HS Level).

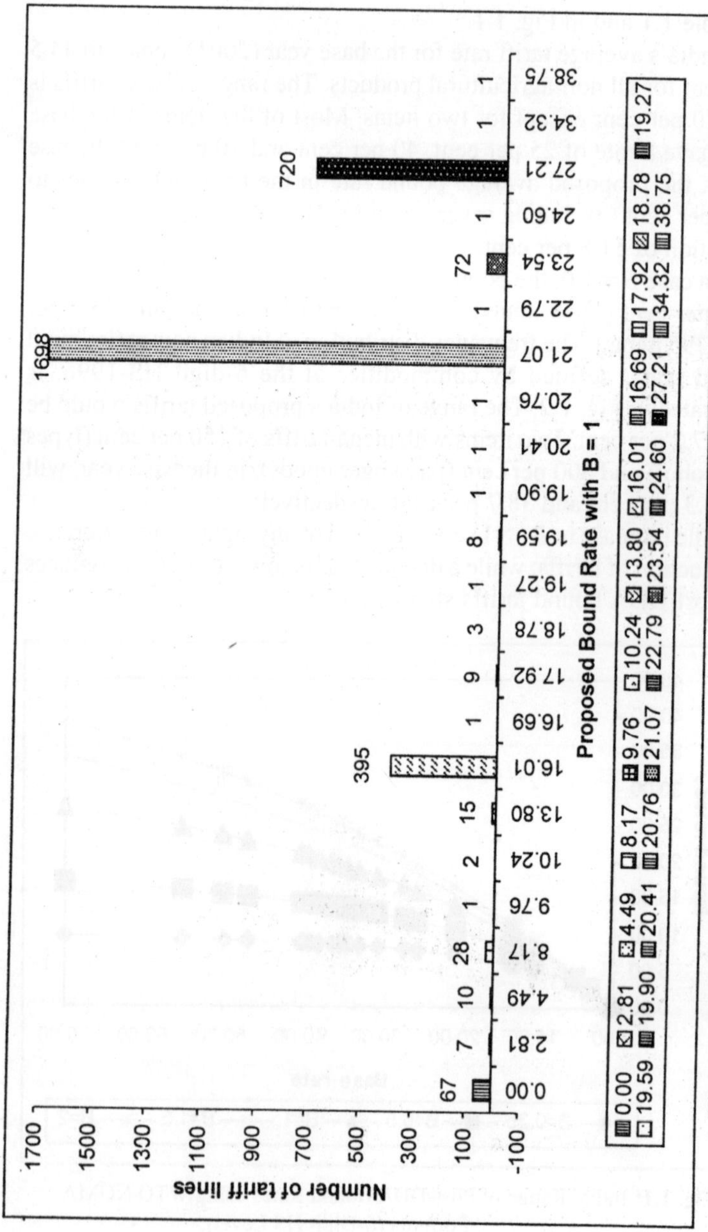


**Fig. 1.2:** India: Frequency Distribution of Tariff Lines of Post-Millennium Bound Rates (6-Digit HS Level)

### *II.2.3 Sectoral Tariff Elimination*

The NGMA-CD proposal talks about sectoral tariff elimination in seven sectors. We have defined seven sectors as per Table 1.2.

**Table 1.2:** A Definition of Seven Sectors

| *Special Sectors* | *HS Chapters* |
|---|---|
| Fish and fish products | 3,15,16 |
| Leather goods | 42 |
| Textiles and clothing | 50-63 |
| Footwear | 64 |
| Stones, gems and precious metals | 71 |
| Electronics and electrical goods | 85 |
| Motor vehicles parts and components | 87 |

The sensitive items falling in these seven sectors are identified after conducting an analysis of all non-agriculture products that amounted to 9467 items (defined by the HS 8-digit Indian Trade Classification) by categorizing them into five groups:

(i) *Group I: Bound Item-Significant Cut: Identification of items where bound rates are very high and India could bring them down. These commodities are selected on the basis of various criteria for example:*

(a) Those commodities that have a low price elasticity, i.e. lower than the average value (1.29).

(b) Also taken into consideration are those commodities for which the difference between tariff rates and bound rates are less than or equal to 5 per cent points during the year 2000-01.

(c) The recommendations of the apex industrial bodies, specific industries, Government departments, etc. regarding the reduction of bound levels for certain commodities.

(d) Commodities with a very high share (value) of exports during the year 2000-01 and with a positive growth rate of exports during the last five years.

(e) Commodities with a very high share (value) of exports during the year 2000-01 and with a negative growth rate of exports for the last five years but with a zero share value of imports during the year 2000-01.

(f) Commodities with a very high share (value) of exports during the year 2000-01 and with a negative growth rate of exports for the last five years but with a very low share value of imports for the same year and with a negative growth rate of imports for the last two years.
(g) Then, the rest of the commodities with a zero share (value) of imports during the year 2000-01 (and 2001-02) irrespective of their export share.
(h) Commodities with a low import share (value) during the year 2000-01 (and 2001-02), a negative rate of growth of imports for the last two years and a positive rate of growth of exports for the last five years irrespective of their export share.
(i) Commodities with a very low import share during the year 2000-01 (and 2001-02) and with a growth rate of imports less than 10 per cent.
(j) Commodities whose imports are not increasing.
(k) Commodities with a low import share.
In the case of textile items, the following two additional criteria have been used.
(l) This contains items of the textile industry, i.e. items under Section XI of the ITC HS classification for which the committed level of the final bound rate is to be achieved by 1 March 2005. This identifies the items with bound rates that are high and could be brought down. Items of the textile industry are identified separately, because the WTO committed level has to be achieved by 1 March 2005, and that level can be significantly lower than the present level of the MFN Tariff Rate. Further, there will not be a significant time difference between for example: (i) the implementation period of the present level of the committed rate, i.e. 1 March 2005, and (ii) the initiation of the process of implementation of the DDA.
(m) As mentioned earlier, items of the Indian textile industry have been renegotiated after the UR, and the binding rates have been generally defined in the form of mixed duties, i.e. "*ad valorem* percentage, or Rs. A per unit whichever is higher". Given the nature of these duties, i.e. mixed duties, we have not applied a large number of the criteria mentioned above, in identification of 'sensitive items'.

(ii) *Group II: Bound Items—No Significant List of tariff lines where the existing bound levels are considered adequate and effort can be made to see that these rates remain at a high level.* The various criteria used for identification of commodities in this list are as follows:

(a) This may be on the basis of recommendations of the apex industrial bodies regarding increase in tariff rates.

(b) Commodities reserved exclusively for the small-scale industries. In this case we have not taken into consideration those commodities, which were "free" during 1998 to 2001.

(c) Commodities, for which imports have increased in recent times, i.e. 2001-02 as per reports from various sources, economic dailies, G.O.I, particularly those for which the QRs were removed in April 2001.

(d) Commodities on which anti-dumping duties are imposed but are not categorised above.

(e) Commodities on which safeguard duties are imposed.

(f) Recommendations of the Ministry of Chemicals and Fertilizers, Department of Fertilizers, Government of India. The criteria stated here were not applied to commodities of the textile industry, for which import duty is defined in the form of "mixed duty".

(iii) *Group III: Bound Items—Sufficient Rate: Tariff lines where the existing levels of binding rates are considered just sufficient to provide the adequate protection.*

This list consists of all the bound lines, which are not included in the above two mentioned lists (Group I and Group II), excluding items of textile industry and information technology.

(iv) *Group IV: Unbound Item—High Binding Rate: Tariff lines, which due to domestic sensitivities, cannot be bound or need to be bound at high levels.*

All the criteria used for the identification of bound items are used here also for unbound items. Along with those criteria, all the unbound lines for which QRs were removed in April 2001, with very high import values for the period April-August 2001 and with very high growth rates of imports calculated for the periods April-August 2000 and April-

**Table 1.3:** Number of Items (at 8-Digit HS-96) in which India can Eliminate Tariffs

| Sectors | Total No. of Lines | Group I | Group II | Group III | Group IV | Group V | Sensitive Items, where Elimination can be Problem |
|---|---|---|---|---|---|---|---|
| | | Bound Items—Significant Cut | Bound Items—Inadequate Rate | Bound Items—Sufficient Rate | Unbound Items—High Binding Rate | Unbound Items—Significant Cut | |
| (1) | (2) | (3) | (4) | (5) | (6) | (7) | (8) = (4)+(5)+(6) |
| Fish and fish products | 134 | 6 | | | | 128 | — |
| Leather goods | 54 | | | | | 54 | — |
| Textiles and clothing | 2220 | 1024 | 4 | 302 | 18 | 872 | 324 |
| Footwear | 62 | | | | 1 | 61 | 1 |
| Stones, gems and precious metals | 88 | 50 | | | 1 | 37 | 1 |
| Electronics and electrical goods | 555 | 329 | 4 | 38 (125)* | 3 | 56 | 45 |
| Motor vehicles parts and components | 138 | 65 | | | 47 | 26 | 47 |
| **Total** | **3251** | **1474** | **8** | **465** | **70** | **1234** | **418** |

* We have excluded 125 commodities which fall under ITA agreement and whose binding is already fixed at zero

*Source*: RIS Study, Indian Industrial Tariffs: Towards WTO Development Round Negotiations, 2003.

August 2001 are shifted here. It also includes some fertilizers of the canalised route.

(v) *Group V: Unbound Item—Significant Cut*: *Tariff lines of low trade interest, which may be bound at low levels.*

This list includes the unbound items, which are not included before. The items falling under Group II, III and IV are considered sensitive.

Our results show that the tariff rates of all the items under 'fish and fish products', 'leather products', can be significantly cut. There are some items in the textile sector (324 out of 2220) where the tariff cut cannot be made significant, or eliminated. Out of 3251 items from the seven sectors of India (at 8-digit), 2833 can be easily reduced or eliminated (*see* Table 1.3).

### *II.2.4 Special and Differential Treatment for Developing Countries*

As a special and differential treatment, developing countries will be granted longer implementation periods for tariff reductions. Besides this developing countries can probably keep up to 5 per cent of tariff lines unbound.

**Table 1.4:** Indian Non-Agricultural Sensitive Items: Number of Tariff Lines and Value of Imports

| *Group* | *Category of Sensitive Items* | *Number of Sensitive Lines** | *% Share (of sensitive item) in all Non-Agricultural Products* | *Value of Import (Rs. Lakh) 1999-2001* |
|---|---|---|---|---|
| Group II | Inadequate Rate | 30 | 0.32 | |
| Group III | Sufficient | 365 | 3.86 | |
| Group IV | Unbound (UB) or Higher Bound Rate (BR) | 167 | 1.76 | |
| | Total (Sensitive Items) | 562 | 5.94 | 1401657 (2.18)** |
| | All non-agricultural products | 9467 | | 64210945 |

* Based on 8-digit lines of HS-1996.

** Represent % share to total imports of non-agricultural items.

Table 1.4 shows that there are 5.9 per cent of total lines (at 8-digit HS level) covered under non-agriculture, which should not be subject to a significant cut or should remain unbound. These items belong to the above-mentioned Group II (Bound Items—Inadequate Rate), Group III (Bound Items—Sufficient Rate), and Group IV (Unbound Item—High Binding Rate). The value of imports of these lines during 1999-2001 comes to 2.18 per cent of the total value of the corresponding imports of non-agricultural products (defined at 8-digit level of HS 1996).[10]

Hence the original proposal of special and differential treatment with 5 per cent tariff lines as unbound items (with 5 per cent of import values) in post-DDA should be the minimum flexibilities.

## III. Hong Kong Declaration

Just a month before the Cancun Ministerial Conference, the EC-US-Canada came up with a proposal, in which the pure Swiss formula served as the core modality i.e. on 11 August 2003. To take stock of the progress made in the non-agriculture market access negotiations, the Cancun Ministerial which took place in September 2003, collapsed later. The Ministerial Draft circulated in Cancun on 13 September 2003 accommodated the non-linear type formula as the core modality for market access negotiations. This draft was completely silent on the formula that should be adopted. Since the formula to be adopted is a non-linear one so it could be Swiss or modified Swiss or anything else also.

Ten months later the Chairman of the World Trade Organization released a draft in July 2004 also known as July Framework with the objective of bringing back these talks on track. This July Package was nothing but old wine in a new bottle since there was no difference between the 'Cancun Draft' and the 'July Package' for NAMA negotiations except the newly-added first paragraph. The text stuck at the adoption of the non-linear formula to be applied on each tariff line for further reduction. As per the July 2004 Framework Agreement the Negotiating Group was supposed to concentrate on:

"...... *a non-linear formula* applied on a *line-by-line* basis which shall take fully into account the *special needs and interests* of developing and least-developed country participants, including through *less than full reciprocity* in reduction commitments". (WTO, 2004)

Soon after this document was released the discussion with regards to the formula (core modality) to be used for tariff reduction got initiated. Later in Dalian, China a WTO Mini Ministerial was conducted on 12-13 July 2005 where intense discussions regarding the formula to be adopted, flexibilities, sectoral treatment of unbound lines, NTB's, etc. were held but nothing concrete came out of it. Till the Hong Kong Ministerial Conference various types of non-linear formulae were under discussion.

### *III.1 Formulae*

The Hong Kong Ministerial Conference took place in December 2005.The text released on the last day i.e. on 18 December 2005, laid down the following formula for the non-agriculture market access (WTO, 2005f).

"We adopt a Swiss Formula with coefficients at levels which shall *inter alia*:

- Reduce or as appropriate eliminate tariffs, including the reduction or elimination of tariff peaks, high tariffs and tariff escalation, in particular on products of export interest to developing countries; and
- Take fully into account the special needs and interests of developing countries, including through less than full reciprocity in reduction commitments.

We instruct the Negotiating Group to finalize its structure and details as soon as possible."

This brief excerpt of the Ministerial Text makes obvious the adoption of Swiss Formula for negotiating access in the markets of WTO member nations. The two variations of this formula are as follows:

#### *III.1.1 Swiss Formula by Application of Limited Number of Coefficients*

US (Third World Network, 2005), Norway (WTO, 2005b) and Pakistan (WTO, 2005d) had proposed the use of two different coefficients in the formula. Also as Chile, Columbia and Mexico

(WTO, 2005a) has suggested the number of these coefficients can rise up to four in the same formula for example.

$$t_1 = [B_i \times t_0] / [B_i + t_0] \quad \text{...(2)}$$
$$i = 2 \text{ or } 4$$

*III.1.2 Swiss Formula with Multiple Coefficients*

These coefficients may vary from one member nation to another. Proposals submitted by NGMA (WTO, 2004), Argentina-Brazil-India (WTO, 2005c) (ABI) and Caribbean (Bridges, 2005) countries also fall in this category, for example:

$$t_1 = [B_i \times t_0] / [B_i + t_0]$$
$$i = 1, 2, \ldots\ldots, n;$$

where

***n*** is number of countries

$B_i$ can vary from country to country. It can depend upon tariff averages, etc. $B_i$ can be written in a somewhat general form as:

$$B_i = [\ (A + C_{i)} \times t_a], \quad \text{...(3)}$$

where

$t_a$ = Average bound rate of member countries,

$C_i$ = Constant values which will change from country to country, based on level of development (higher the development level, lower the co-efficient). This is suggested by Caribbean countries,

= 0, for Argentina-Brazil-India proposal, and

$A$ = a constant number.

The Swiss formula using multiple coefficients has various advantages from the perspective of developing countries like India. The coefficient value can take care of the structure and average level of tariff rates of individual member countries. That means, the higher the tariffs the greater would be the decline. The Swiss formula tackles the high tariffs, peak tariffs and tariff escalation of member countries. But the rate of decline is dependent on the value of coefficient *B*. Hence by using higher coefficients in the formula for developing countries as compared to that of developed countries, a lesser percentage reduction in the tariffs of the former can be caused than that of the latter. Therefore, the use of more than one coefficient in this formula is necessary. Figure 1.3 shows the impact of the Swiss formula with different values of *B* on member countries' tariffs.

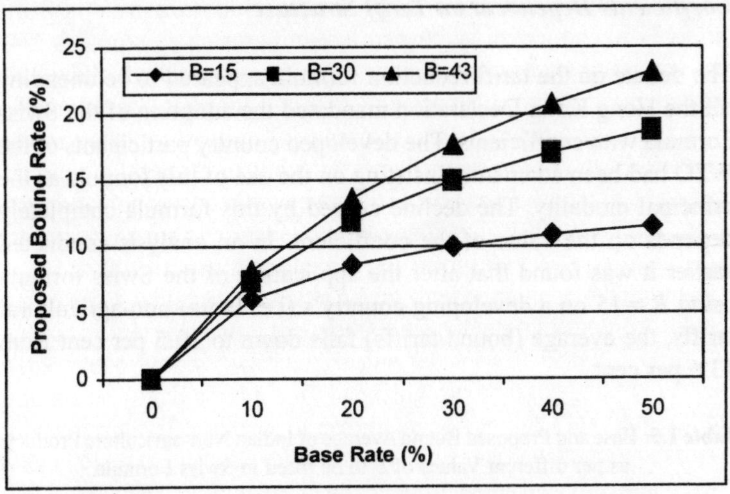


**Fig. 1.3:** Impact of Swiss Formula with Different Co-efficients on Member Countries' Tariffs

Argentina-Brazil-India and Caribbean countries had proposed in their respective submissions that the value of the coefficient should vary from country to country depending upon the structure of the tariffs and the levels of their development.

The main characteristics of the ABI formula are:

- The 'formula' would apply to tariff lines that are bound,
- The coefficient '*B*' will be varied according to the ambitions in other relevant market access areas being discussed in these negotiations, and
- Also, it proposes a separate formula for unbound tariffs to be applied only to their marked-up average and not on a line-by-line basis. This would permit developing countries to maintain high tariffs on items that are of domestic and strategic concern to them. They have to just ensure that the average tariff does not pass the allowed level.

The formula in the Caribbean countries' proposal counts various elements relevant to the developmental concerns of developing countries and adds them as credit to the base coefficient.

### *III.2 Debate: Swiss with Two/Four Coefficients or Multiple Coefficients Dependent on Tariff Structure*

The debate on the tariff reduction formula appeared to be unending till the Hong Kong Declaration mandated the adoption of the Swiss Formula with coefficients. The developed country participants of the WTO had been adamantly insisting on the use of this formula as the principal modality. The decline caused by this formula completely depends on the value of the coefficient. In an analysis conducted earlier it was found that after the application of the Swiss formula using $B = 15$ on a developing country's (i.e. India) non-agricultural tariffs, the average (bound tariffs) falls down to 10.5 per cent from 43.6 per cent.

**Table 1.5:** Base and Proposed Bound Average of Indian Non-agriculture Products as per different Values of *B* to be fitted in Swiss Formula

| B | Base Average (%) | Proposed Average (%) |
|---|---|---|
| 15 (Used in Tokyo Round) | 43.6 | 10.5 |
| 30 (Proposed by Pakistan) | 42.3 | 16.5 |
| 32 (ABI—Bound Items) | 33.2 | 15.8 |
| 22.9 (ABI—Unbound items) | | 22.9 |

*Source*: Author's calculations.

Table 1.5 gives the base and proposed bound average of Indian non-agricultural tariffs as per different values of *B* used in the Swiss formula. As compared to other values, i.e. 30, or 32, etc. the value of 15 would cause a maximum decline in developing country tariffs. This number 15 would bring the entire tariff profile below that number. As it can be noticed in Table 1.6 with the use of $B = 15$ in the formula, the entire Indian (bound) tariff profile falls in the range of 0-15 per cent. Hence, the tariff reduction would be very significant by use of this formula, using a lower value of the coefficient.

Although there would be more than one coefficient with a higher value to be used for developing countries and a lower one for developed countries, but still this formula can hurt developing countries' tariffs if the value of the coefficient used in the formula is lower than the present level of the applied MFN average. Like India's present level of applied MFN average for non-agricultural goods for the year 2006-07 is 12.2 per cent[11] which is above the proposed bound average as attained by the application of Swiss formula with $B = 15$, i.e. 10.4 per cent.

**Table 1.6:** India: Frequency Distribution of Proposed Bound Rates as per Swiss formula with $B = 15$ for Bound Non-agriculture Products

| *Base Rate-% (Final Bound Rate as on 1.1.2001)* | *Proposed Bound Rates-% (B = 15)* |
|---|---|
| 0 | 0.00 |
| 3 | 2.50 |
| 5 | 3.75 |
| 10 | 6.00 |
| 20 | 8.57 |
| 25 | 9.38 |
| 30 | 10.00 |
| 35 | 10.50 |
| 40 | 10.91 |
| 50 | 11.54 |
| 55 | 11.79 |
| 60 | 12.00 |
| 70 | 12.35 |
| 100 | 13.04 |
| 150 | 13.64 |
| 210 | 14.00 |
| **Average = 43.5** | **10.4** |

*Source*: Mehta, R. and P. Agarwal, (2005). "Non-agriculture Market Access—A Balancing Act for South Asia", *South Asian Yearbook of Trade and Development 2005*, Centad, October 2005.

The two coefficients that Pakistan has suggested in their proposal for the Swiss formula, i.e. 6 for developed and 30 for developing country members is possibly somewhat feasible for developing countries. As it can be seen from Table 1.5, India's bound average, using 30 as the coefficient, would arrive at 16.5 per cent which is not a bad option given India's present level of applied MFN average. Although developed countries have expressed their displeasure over the huge difference in the coefficients in the past, this option is still worth considering keeping in mind the developmental needs and concerns of developing countries.

However, it should not be forgotten that some developing countries have their average tariff at more than 30.

If the values of the fixed coefficient are fitted as per the proposal of ABI then the Swiss formula would reduce India's (bound) average tariff from 33.2 per cent to 15.8 per cent. The proposed average for unbound lines as given in Table 1.1 would be 22.9 per cent. It is only the Swiss formula with a co-efficient $B = 15$ which seems to contradict the development concerns of some developing countries.

### III.3 Flexibilities to be given to Developing Countries

The Doha mandate clearly highlights the development needs and concerns of the developing countries in the NAMA negotiations. Para 16 states that,

> 'We agree to negotiations ... to reduce or as appropriate eliminate tariffs, ...as well as non-tariff barriers, in particular on products of *export interest to developing countries*. ... The negotiations shall take fully into account the *special needs and interests* of developing and least-developed country participants, including through *less than full reciprocity* in reduction commitments' (emphasis added), (WTO, 2001b).

Evidently, the three aspects of the mandate are:

1. Tariff and non-tariff barrier elimination or reductions on products of *export interest to developing countries.*
2. Taking care of *special needs and interests* of developing and least developed countries.
3. *Less than full reciprocity* in reduction commitments.

The second aspect outlined for developing countries was contained in paragraph 8 of the July 2004 Framework Agreement (WTO, 2004) also known as paragraph 8 flexibilities. This includes longer implementation periods for tariff reduction, applying less than formula cuts and exclusion of some tariff lines. The market access interests of developing countries and the principle of less than full reciprocity (LTFR) are two different and separate issues of the Doha mandate. Although there are no talks relating to the former issue but as regards the inclusion of the principle of LTFR in the reduction commitments there are two conflicting opinions between the developing and developed countries.

Developed countries are continuously advocating (SUNS#5879, 2005) that flexibilities in paragraph 8 of the NAMA July Framework are not 'given' but should be connected to the core modality of tariff reduction i.e. the use of a single coefficient or multiple coefficients, different for developed and developing countries in the tariff reduction formula. If there are two or more coefficients in the formula then developing nations should not be given paragraph 8 flexibilities. On the other hand, developing country participants are insisting on treating the reduction through the core-modality and S&D flexibilities as two different concepts (WTO, 2005c). In a communication (WTO, 2005e) submitted by certain developing countries they have clearly opposed the developed nations' efforts to install more conditions on the use of the paragraph 8 flexibilities. But developed countries are quite rigid in their opinion that a lower reduction rate in the formula or a longer implementation period or no cuts in a few items automatically means flexibilities for developing countries.

These flexibilities are very important for developing countries to protect their domestically sensitive and strategic sectors. These flexibilities should be considered as completely different from the concept of less than full reciprocity. The principle of less than full reciprocity needs to be incorporated within the formula by applying a higher coefficient for developing countries compared to that for developed countries. This would lead to a higher percentage decline in the developed country's tariffs as that of developing countries'. There can be no linkage between less than full reciprocity in reduction commitments and "Para 8 flexibilities".

### *III.4 Unbound Lines*

The mandate of the Doha Declaration under the non-agriculture market access (NAMA) negotiations clarifies that all the participant countries have to necessarily bring their entire product line on the negotiating table. That means that no commodity would be left unbound.

Table 1.7 shows the binding coverage, final bound duties, the MFN applied average tariff and import value of bound and unbound items for the select WTO member nations. As can be seen from Table 1.7 most of the developed nations like Australia, Canada, EU, Japan and USA have already bound almost their entire non-agriculture product lines. Also newly acceded members like Nepal and China have bound all of their products. The issue of binding coverage is more important for developing and least developed countries. A certain proportion of the non-agricultural products of many of these countries was left unbound in the Uruguay Round. All of these unbound product

**Table 1.7:** Some Comparative Indicators for Bound and Unbound Tariff Lines of Select WTO Member Nations (MFN applied duties and imports refer to 2001 unless indicated otherwise)

| *Member* | *Bound tariff lines* | | | | *Unbound tariff lines* | |
|---|---|---|---|---|---|---|
| | *Binding coverage* | *Final bound duties* | *MFN applied duties* | *Imports* | *MFN applied duties* | *Imports* |
| | *In %* | *Average* | | *Mill US $* | *Average* | *Mill US $* |
| Australia | 96.5 | 11.0 | 4.5 | 572,923 | 7.1 | 697 |
| Bangladesh (1999) | 3 | 35.7 | 12.9 | — | 22.0 | — |
| Canada (2000) | 99.7 | 5.3 | 4.4 | 213,698 | 12.6 | 10,061 |
| China | 100 | 9.1 | 14.5 | 231,726 | ++ | ++ |
| Egypt | 98.7 | 28.3 | 21.2 | — | 16.6 | 84 |
| European Union | 100 | 3.9 | 4.3 | 729,799 | ++ | ++ |
| Hong Kong, China | 37.5 | 0.0 | 0.0 | 110,314 | 0.0 | 83,413 |
| India | 69.8 | 34.3 | 28.7 | 29,131 | 34.4 | 18,457 |
| Japan | 99.5 | 2.3 | 2.7 | 265,532 | 7.0 | 42,547 |
| Malaysia | 81.2 | 14.9 | 8.6 | 61,417 | 5.8 | 6,410 |
| Mauritius | 5.3 | 19.5 | 9.2 | 126 | 19.5 | 1,575 |
| Myanmar | 4.7 | 22.3 | 3.4 | — | 5.2 | — |
| Nepal (2002) | 99.3 | 23.7 | 13.4 | — | 68.7 | — |
| Pakistan | 37.0 | 35.3 | 20.2 | — | 19.7 | |
| Singapore | 64.5 | 6.3 | 0.0 | 80,047 | 0.0 | 30,560 |
| Sri Lanka | 28.3 | 19.3 | 6.8 | 1,979 | 6.6 | 2,690 |
| Suriname | 15.1 | 17.0 | — | — | — | — |
| Thailand | 70.9 | 24.2 | 15.3 | — | 11.5 | — |
| Togo | 0.9 | 80.0 | 12.0 | 2 | 11.7 | 244 |
| Uganda | 3 | 50.8 | 6.9 | — | 8.6 | — |
| United States (2000) | 99.98 | 3.2 | 3.9 | 1,057,962 | 0.3 | 52,288 |
| Zimbabwe | 9 | 11.0 | 14.7 | — | 17.3 | — |

*Note*: — Data not available.
++ Not applicable.

*Source*: "Statistical indicators related to unbound tariff lines", Note by secretariat, TN/MA/S/14, WTO 2005.

lines would be now negotiated under the NAMA negotiations. Before the Hong Kong Ministerial there were many proposals suggesting many ways for the treatment of unbound items. Out of those options, the Hong Kong Declaration had proposed the adoption of a non-linear mark up approach to establish base rates. The main objective of this method would be to keep high bound rates for sensitive items.

All this can be done by adding a mark up of some percentage points to the base rate. For example, as Pakistan (WTO, 2005d) has suggested a mark up of 30 percentage points should be added to the base rate. After addition that rate can be subjected to the proposed Swiss Formula for reduction. In this case there can be two possibilities. The percentage that has to be added to all the base rates of unbound lines of all member countries can either be kept constant or can vary from country to country (and/or commodity by commodity). In adding these points, the criterion should be the higher the applied rate the lower would be the mark up. Another way of providing a mark up can be achieved by binding these tariffs at an average level of 25 per cent with a ceiling of 40 per cent as Malaysia (Sen, 2005) had suggested in their proposal earlier.

All the tariff lines of developed countries are already bound so they demand the same from developing countries in order that they can easily cut them. Given the above suggestions and tariff structure of unbound items, the most suitable for the developing countries unbound tariffs would be to add a higher mark up to lower tariffs and *vice versa*.

## IV. Summary and Concluding Remarks

Market access for non-agriculture products has been one of the principal items in the agenda of WTO negotiations. The basic mandate in the Doha Declaration under the category 'tariff and trade of industrial products' is both broad and comprehensive. The developing countries should concentrate on reduction in peak/high tariffs and tariff escalation. It should also be a demand that all the countries should define their binding rates in the form of *ad valorem* rates, because it has been noticed that the *ad valorem* equivalence of non-*ad valorem* duties are very high.

After the adoption of the Doha agenda a number of proposals relating to the 'modalities' were submitted by member countries to NGMA. The Chairman of NGMA submitted a draft proposal of modalities on 16 May 2003, which proposed a modified Swiss Formula, after a series of formal and informal consultations carried on for one and a half-year. The core modality/formula suggested by NGMA-CD takes into account most of the concerns of the developing countries, i.e. (i) tariff peaks, (ii) tariff escalation, and (iii) non-*ad valorem* duties. The NGMA-CD formula can take care of: (i) reduction of tariffs, (ii) peak and high tariff, and (iii) structure of pre-development round binding rates. In other words, if the average tariff of a country is low the declining rate of peak tariff will be substantial. This formula is sensitive to the co-efficient value of *B*. In case *B* = Average bound (or base) rate, India's average applied rate will decline by around 51.8 per cent. The rate of decline of India's average bound rate will be 81 per cent, 67 per cent and 35 per cent, for *B* = one-fourth, half and two times of the average bound (or base) rate, respectively. Keeping this factor in mind India and the developing countries should adopt this proposal with *B* = average bound (or base) rate.

The Hong Kong mandate calls for the adoption of the Swiss formula for reduction of tariffs, which would be using different coefficients. For reduction of tariffs, developing countries should demand a very high value of fixed coefficient and the lowest for developed countries to be fitted in the proposed Swiss formula. The average value of the coefficients for developing countries should be minimally 6 times higher than that of developed countries.

The core modality adopted should not be linked to flexibilities of the SDT provided to developing countries. Special and differential treatment (SDT) for developing countries, and less than full reciprocity (LTFR) should be considered as two different concepts. The treatment of unbound items should not be contained in the core modality. The proposed non-linear mark up should be lower for high rates and vice versa. The main objective of this methodology should be to keep bound rates at higher levels for sensitive items.

The participation of developing nations in a sector-by-sector approach should be voluntary. The emphasis should be laid on eliminating tariffs of those sectors bringing which are of major export interests to the developing countries like India.

As far as non-tariff barriers are concerned, not much progress has been accomplished in NAMA negotiations on this issue. Developing countries must stress that the modalities for reduction and elimination of tariffs and non-tariff barriers (Mehta, 2005) should be inter-connected and solved simultaneously. The Hong Kong Mandate had also called for bringing a balance between the market access of agriculture and non-agriculture sector. Developing countries should try to achieve a maximum possible market access in agriculture in developed countries' markets.

## NOTES

1. Amount of value per unit of imported commodity.
2. A number of proposals have been submitted by different countries. Among these proposals three submissions have been made by India.
3. All products not covered by the WTO Agreement on Agriculture.
4. Credit may be given for autonomous liberalization provided that the items were bound on an MFN basis in the WTO since the conclusion of Uruguay Round. Thus, in the following cases, credit will accrue by using the base rate that was in place before the autonomous liberalization took place, and the formula reduction would be applied to this higher basis. In the case of items that were not previously bound, two times the MFN applied rate or the new bound rate, which ever is higher, for the year the liberalization took place would be the basis. It is noted that in the cases of the Ministerial Declaration on the Expansion of Trade in Information Technology Products, further initiatives in the Pharmaceutical zero-for-zero sector, and certain other individual initiatives, the bound rate was reduced to zero and through the application of the formula, credits would not be relevant. Thus, for the remaining items, credit could be given for the tariff lines noted in the following WTO documents which have been given legal effect through certifications: European Communities (WT/Let/178), Hungary (WT/Let/441), India (WT/Let/374), Korea (WT/Let/302), Pakistan (WT/Let/424), Sri Lanka (WT/Let/398), and the United States (WT/Let/182).
5. When the MFN applied rate in the base year is less than 2.5 per cent, 5 per cent shall be used as the basis.
6. If members so desire, they may commence with the HS2002 nomenclature if the corresponding concordance tables are provided.
7. All numbers used in the formula will be calculated to one significant decimal point.
8. The Uruguay Round led to increases in tariff escalation particularly for products in which developing countries have export potential. See, Mehta and Mohanty (2001) and UNCTAD (1999-2000), among others.
9. In the Hong Kong meeting, it was decided that participation in sectoral tariff elimination process is voluntary. Further, the discussion, at present, is going on for more than seven sectors.
10. This analysis has been conducted at the 8-digit HS level, because sensitive items have been identified at the 8-digit level. In case we define sensitive

items at the 6-digit level (containing all the expositions of items identified at 8-digit), the percentage share of sensitive lines will significantly increase. The details of the 6-digit analysis is presented in report, *Identification of Possible Items Sensitive to Indian Imports at 6-digit and 8-digit HS Level*, RIS/WTO-NAMA/Job 3/Revision1, November 2003, submitted to Ministry of Commerce.

11. Authors calculations based on data from Goyal, Arun (2006) *BIGs Easy Reference Customs Tariff 2006-07*, Silver Jubilee 25th Budget Edition, ABS.

## REFERENCES


Bacchetta, M. and Bora B., (2003). 'Industrial Tariff Liberalization and the Doha Development Agenda', WTO Discussion Paper.

Bridges (2005). Year 9, Number 6-7. June-July. Available at: http://www.ictsd.org/monthly/archive.htm

Mehta, R. (2001). 'WTO, Liberalisation and Industrial Sector: The Case of Market Access', RIS Occasional Paper No. 63.

——— (2003). 'Indian Industrial Tariffs: Towards WTO Development Round Negotiations', RIS.

——— (2005). 'Non-Tariff Barriers Affecting India's Exports', RIS Discussion Paper No. 97, June.

——— and S.K. Mohanty, (2001). 'WTO and Industrial Tariff: An Empirical Analysis for India', Reprint, RIS.

Sen, A. (2005). 'Status of Negotiations', Presentation at Regional Conference on the *Agenda for WTO Hong Kong Ministerial Challenges for South Asia*, organized by RIS-FICCI-IUCN, New Delhi: August.

SUNS#5879 (2005). 'Trade: WTO members still far apart in NAMA negotiations', September.

*Third World Network* (2005). 'North Onslaught on South's Industrial Tariffs in NAMA', Available at http://www.twnside.org.sg/title2/twninfo195.htm.

UN (1998). 'Market Access since UR, Implications, Opportunities and Challenges', Report prepared by UNCTAD and WTO, May.

UNCTAD (1998a). CDROM *TRAIN.* Winter.

——— (1998b). *TRAINS,* Winter.

——— (1999-2000). 'The Post-UR Tariff Environment for Developing Countries: Tariff Peaks and Tariff Escalation', TD/B/COM/1/14/Rev/1. September.

——— (2003). 'Back to Basics: Market Access Issues in the Doha Agenda', UNCTAD/DITC/TAB/Misc.9.

WTO (2001a). *US Trade Policy Review*. Geneva.

——— (2001b). Ministerial Declaration. 2001. WT/MIN (01)/DEC/W/1, 14 Nov. Doha, 9-14, November.

——— (2003a). 'Formula Approaches to Tariff Negotiations, Note by the Secretariat', Revision, TN/MA/S/3/Rev.2. April.

——— (2003b). 'Draft elements of modalities for negotiations on non-agriculture products', TN/MA/W/35. May.

——— (2003c). 'Draft elements of modalities for negotiations on non-agriculture products', TN/MA/W/35, Rev.1. August.

——— (2004). Paragraph 4. Annex. B, WT/GC/W/535, Page B-1, July.

——— (2005a). 'Squaring the circle of ambition plus flexibility: Providing options for developing countries', Communication from Chile, Colombia and Mexico, TN/MA/W/50, February.

——— (2005b). 'A Proposal for a Simple Non-Linear Formula with Credits', Communication from Norway, TN/MA/W7/Add.1, March.

——— (2005c). 'Communication to the Negotiating Group on Non-Agricultural Market Access from Argentina, Brazil and India', TN/MA/W/54, April.

——— (2005d). 'The Way Forward', Communication from Pakistan, TN/MA/W/60, July.

——— (2005e). 'Flexibilities for Developing Countries', Communication from Argentina, Bolivarian Republic of Venezuela, Brazil, China, Egypt, India, Indonesia, Namibia, Pakistan, Philippines and South Africa, TN/MA/W/65, November.

——— (2005f). 'Draft Ministerial Declaration', WT/MIN (05)/W/3/Rev.2, Para.14, p. 4,18 December.

# Chapter 2

# India and GATS: A Paradox

VEENA JHA[†]

*Assistance was provided by Dr Rashmi Banga*[**] and *Ms Swapna Nair*[**]

## I. Introduction

The GATS established the first ever set of multilateral, legally enforceable rules covering international trade in services. It covers all service sectors and all forms of trade in services. Current negotiations on services take place at a time when this sector is undergoing a profound transformation, which has considerably expanded the tradability of services. Technological developments, budgetary pressures and regulatory changes have greatly expanded the range and scope of trade in services. They have introduced competition into sectors formerly considered to be natural monopolies (e.g., telecommunications, energy); created additional possibilities for cross-border trade (e.g., business and computer services); and increased private sector participation in services where, in many countries, the public sector had traditionally played a major role (e.g., health, education, environmental services). The growth in services trade is also underpinned by the widespread liberalization of FDI regimes over the past decade, a trend which accelerated during this decade in the face of diminishing FDI inflows (UNCTAD, 2003). However, with stalled negotiations in the Doha Round, India may be unable to push an ambitious agenda of negotiations on services. In

[†] India Programme Coordinator, UNCTAD, New Delhi.

[**] Economists, UNCTAD—India Programme, UNCTAD, New Delhi.

addition, India may be able to go perhaps further with bilateral and even unilateral liberalization in services in a milieu of stalled negotiations at the WTO. India is therefore faced with a paradox, how much should it push for multilateral negotiations on services if it has to give up some of its crucial, poverty related interests in agriculture. Linked to this tradeoff is whether multilateral liberalization will deliver more or better gains than bilateral and unilateral liberalization, or rather whether WTO is the best forum to get gains in terms of services exports.

Many developing countries are highly specialized in services and have concrete—and growing—export interests to pursue in the Doha Round. Developing countries have increased their exports of services nearly four-fold in the last decade (faster than goods exports), increasing their share of the global market place from 14 per cent (1985-1989) to 18 per cent (1995-1998). The figures for 2005-2006 show that India alone occupies 2.8 per cent of the global services market. While developed countries still dominate trade in services, twenty-one developing countries feature in the list of top 40 services exports for 2003-2006 (excluding intra-EU trade), with five (China, Hong Kong, Korea, Singapore and India) ranked in the top. Developing countries enjoy a clear comparative advantage in labour intensive services in a growing number of areas and high skilled services.

India has received requests from around 25 countries (including all major developed and developing countries) in a large number of sectors such as distribution, telecommunication, energy, environmental, financial, education, tourism and travel, computer and related services, and business services. The horizontal request mainly focused on Modes 3 and 4. Horizontal requests under Mode 3 covered transparency in domestic regulation, administrative procedures, clarification of criteria (such as clarification of criteria for licensing), various definitional issues etc. The horizontal requests under Mode 4 have focused on expanding the scope and coverage to include more categories of high skilled service providers, elimination of economic needs test, improvement of transparency in visa and administrative procedure and extension of duration of stay for certain categories of service providers such as business visitors and intra-corporate transferees. The sectoral requests to India emphasized on broadening the coverage to include more sectors/sub-sectors such as energy, environment, education, distribution, accountancy and architecture.

For each sector, most countries have asked for full commitments under Modes 1, 2 and 3 stressing on removal/relaxation of Mode 3 restrictions.

India's exports of services witnessed one of the fastest rates of growth in the world—over 17 per cent per annum in the 1990s—and grew two and a half times faster than the domestically focused part of the services sector (World Bank, 2004). The rate of growth of India's service exports was more impressive during 1995-2000—23.2 per cent compared to the world rate of 3.7 per cent.

The growing importance of the service sector to the Indian economy, 52.4 per cent in 2004-05, compared to 46.6 per cent in 1998-99 of the GDP, also points to the importance of negotiations on market access for services. This sector has also recorded growth rates higher than that of the overall GDP.[1] Viewed over a longer time horizon, during the 1990s, the service sector in India grew at an average annual rate of 9 per cent, contributing to nearly 60 per cent of the overall growth rate of the economy (World Bank, 2004). It may, therefore, be correct to state that there has been a structural shift in the economy in which "services have assumed a dominant position in the production structure and is the key driver of growth" (*RBI Bulletin*, 2005).

Gordon and Gupta have found that while factors such as high income elasticity of demand and increased input usage of services by other sectors have played an important part in elevating services growth, other factors such as economic reforms and the growth of services exports also played an important role in accelerating services growth in the 1990s. Their findings also suggest that there is considerable scope for further rapid growth in the Indian service economy (Gordon and Gupta, 2003).

A liberal Doha agenda in services is attractive for India for a number of reasons. First, unilateral liberalization, though important has not been spread equally across all services and modes of supply of interest to India. Significant barriers remain, particularly in areas such as movement of natural persons to supply services under Mode 4, and in computer related services under Mode 1. In addition India has some sectoral market opening interests, which it wants to pursue in these negotiations. Second, given that domestic politics and vested interests can make reforms difficult to sustain, GATS negotiations offer scope to pursue domestic policy reforms by offsetting pressures for protection with pressure from those who gain from increased exports. Tradeoffs within the services sector would include domestic defensive interests, which are couched in terms of crowding out of domestic service providers with domestic regulatory reform that would deliver significant gains to consumers, e.g telecommunications liberalization in India. Third, in the mercantilist world of trade negotiations, preparedness by developed countries to lock in services reforms in GATS commitments can generate the leverage to push for the necessary movements in NAMA and agriculture on India's part. In fact, India's offensive interests in the entire Doha negotiations have been defined by its interest to gain meaningful market access in services.

Pursuing this agenda is however not easy. In general, barriers to international trade in services are more complex than those on trade in goods. They often take the form of regulatory measures, varying between and within sectors, some preventing market entry, others restricting the scope of operations within the market. For instance, in many countries, provision of professional services is restricted to nationals. Market access barriers in services can also limit the entry of new domestic suppliers into the market, restricting both domestic and foreign competition, especially in sectors where there are public or private monopolies, e.g telecommunications, insurance, environmental services, transport, banking and retail. Domestic regulatory barriers are very important in sectors such as accountancy. Available evidence suggests that developing countries have more restrictive barriers than developed countries, in key infrastructure services such as telecommunications and financial services. Developed countries may have higher barriers in other sectors, such as education, maritime, professional and distribution services. India has a key interest in opening markets for professional services where developed countries have a number of barriers (OECD, 2003).

Barriers to Modes 1 and 4 are of special concern to India. During the Uruguay Round, many Mode 1 entries were left "unbound (meaning that no commitment has been taken by the country in question) due to lack of technical feasibility" for services which are now tradable. While in practice it can be hard to prevent supply by this mode, WTO Members place a range of restrictions on it, including nationality and residency requirements, authorization and local authentication requirements (OECD, 1999). There is a fear of reversal of liberalization on this mode through some of the new legislation which is being debated in developed countries. Commitments on

*Mode 4* (temporary movement of people to supply services) are the fewest of any of the modes and the most restrictive, e.g burdensome visa formalities, stringent quotas, discriminatory taxes and standards. They are specially restrictive for unskilled personnel (Chanda, 2004).

With stalled WTO negotiations on the Doha Round, India may need to engage in bilaterals and plurilaterals to the extent possible for pursuing its trade agenda in services. It is also important to understand that despite the underlying hiatus in the negotiations, services exports have been growing rapidly reaching 2.8 per cent of global trade in the last fiscal year 2005-2006.

Against this background, this paper tries to identify the offensive and defensive interests of India in the Doha negotiations. Section II analyses the macro economic gains and losses that could accrue to India through liberalization of services in general. Section III focuses on trends in overall exports of services. Section IV focuses on cross cutting barriers to liberalization especially in pursuing an offensive agenda. Section V lists some of the main conclusions of this paper.

## II. Developmental Aspects of Services Liberalisation

Services today account for 20 per cent of global trade and 5 per cent of global GDP (UNCTAD, 2005). Services are a high employment generating sector and employ as high as 40 per cent and 70 per cent of the workforce in developing and developed countries respectively. Although large OECD countries dominate global trade in services, developing countries top the list of countries that are most specialized in (and dependent on) services exports as a source of foreign exchange. Many developing countries have carved a niche for themselves in particular service exports. For instance, India and Philippines have become major exporters of BPO (Business Processing Outsourcing) services. Moreover, developing countries have also become important destination markets for investment in services like insurance, transport, telecommunication and retail trading by the developed countries.

In line with the global trend, the services sector in India is also growing rapidly. In 2000-01 the share of services in the country's GDP was 52.4 per cent, up from the 51.5 per cent recorded in 1998-99[2]. More significantly, this sector accounted for around a quarter of India's trade flows in the same period. High growth of service exports explain higher share of India in global service trade: 1.4 per cent compared to 0.9 per cent in case of global merchandise trade (Chanda,

2004). The service sector has also played an important role in attracting foreign capital, with key producer services accounting for a growing share of foreign direct investment (FDI) inflows into the Indian economy. India exhibits a strong revealed comparative advantage in services vis a vis goods. Between 1996 and 2000, while the RCA index for services increased by 74 per cent, that of goods increased only by 15 per cent (World Bank, 2004).

The year 2004/05 was especially very encouraging in terms of service export growth. It saw services exports doubling to $ 51.3 billion from $ 24.9 billion in 2003-04—an astounding growth of 105.7 per cent (*Times of India*, 27th July 2005). Data on service-wise break-up of exports is not available, but indirect evidence reveals that there was substantial growth in value-added services in communication, construction, financial, news agency, royalty, copyright, licence fee and management. Exports of these services categorised as "miscellaneous services" (excluding software) are believed to have increased more than four-fold to $ 22.5 billion in 2004-05 from $ 4.7 billion in 2003-04. In comparison to the doubling of services exports achieved in one year 2004-05, it had taken as many as six years for services exports to double from $ 9.4 billion in 1997-98 to $ 20.8 billion in 2002-03. The highest growth in service exports was in the miscellaneous services category. Software exports went up by 41.8 per cent to $ 17.3 billion in 2004-05, the highest increase in the last four years. According to a report by NASSCOM and McKinsey exports of IT related services from India are expected to increase to US$ 57 billion by 2008/09. Another study by Deloitte Research shows that the global market for off-shore financial services could be as large as US$ 356 billion by 2008/09, of which a large share should go to India.

The growth and dynamism of the service sector in India is fuelled by its export potential, though domestic growth of the service sector is also a robust 9 per cent. India's main source of comparative advantage in services is its labour endowment. India's global competitiveness in this regard is striking. In recent years, the country has accounted for 70 per cent of all speciality occupation (H-1B) visas granted by the US in computer services. Overall, Indian professionals across services as diverse as accountancy, engineering, consulting, medical, and management accounted for nearly half of all H-1B visas granted to foreigners in the US in the late 1990s (Chanda, 2004).

India is also an important source country for low and semi-skilled service providers in services like construction, domestic work, and transport operations. It also has the potential to export labour-intensive services through technology-enabled data, voice, and information flows, i.e., cross-border supply (Mode 1 of GATS).

The country is ranked as the leading global outsourcing destination in services. In all, 60 per cent of the Fortune 500 companies are outsourcing services to India, ranging from simple back office services like processing and billing, to intermediate services like technical help and systems design, to specialised services, like research and development and technical analysis (Chanda, 2004). The cost-quality advantage in labour-based services combined with its high quality institutions has also enabled the country to considerably diversify its service exports to emerging areas, like health care, research and development, and educational services. Thus, the range of activities, modes, and markets where India has global export opportunities is vast. However, there are numerous barriers that constrain India's service exports.

Services liberalization provides three main sources of gains: it removes the bottlenecks in infrastructure services, it lowers prices in liberalized services; and it improves the range and quality of services provided. This has been for example the experience of India with respect to telecommunications. Because much of services liberalization is via FDI, services imports bring in flows of capital, know-how and technology—all severely constraining factors in the development of India. Moreover, the presence of foreign services firms often creates additional demand, including for other services, in the domestic economy.

The poverty attenuating effects of the services sector would work out through the following channels:

1. Services liberalisation itself leads to growth which in turn reduces poverty.
2. Direct poverty alleviation effects through increase in employment in this sector.
3. The increased access to some of these services as a result of liberalisation of this sector would in itself be meeting an MDG, e.g education, health, telecommunications.

### *Services Liberalisation, Growth and Poverty Alleviation*

According to an IMF study, growth in services averaged at 7.5 per cent per annum thus providing a valuable support to industry and agriculture which grew at 5.8 per cent and 3.1 per cent respectively in the decade of the 1990's (Gordon and Gupta, 2003). In order to arrive at a rough estimate of the contribution of this sector's exports to growth, the value added component of these exports have been estimated by the IMF at 60 per cent. Based on this estimation services exports contributed 0.6 per cent percentage points to the total growth of this sector. Using the following formula:

$$Po = Sg \times Es \times Sgdp \times Pe$$

where,

*Po* = Percentage reduction in poverty
*Sg* = Services growth = 7.5 per cent (IMF)
*Es* = Value added from exports of services to services growth = 0.6 of 1 per cent (IMF)
*Sgdp* = Share of services in total GDP = 0.5 (Economic Survey, GOI)
*Pe* = Poverty elasticity of growth = 0.27 (Ravallion and Dutt's survey of 2000)
*Po* = 7.5*0.006*0.5*0.27

This would imply that poverty would reduce by approximately 0.06 per cent with the current rates of growth of exports of the services sector. Given that it is estimated that there are about 300 million below poverty line, which would imply 1.6 million would be moved out of poverty per year. The direct effects through employment would be larger (Jha, Gupta, Nedumpara and Karthikeyan, 2005).

Most of the poverty reduction effects of export growth of the services sector can be however attributed to the indirect multiplier effects, rather than direct employment growth. The employment survey estimates the growth poverty elasticity of the services sector to be considerably higher than either agriculture or manufacturing (Jha, Gupta, Nedumpara and Karthikeyan, 2005).

A study (World Bank, 2004) by World Bank has shown that the more liberalized sectors in India have attracted more FDI and have shown far higher growth than less liberalized services. The study shows that the segments that have been aggressively liberalized i.e –

telecommunication, computer and related services, other business services (management consultancy, R&D, advertisement, etc) and hotels and restaurants—have experienced higher employment growth than other sectors which are relatively less liberalized. Other service sub-sectors, which have registered a fast growth rate, include communication services, financial services, tourism, hotel and restaurants, and distribution (Gordon and Gupta, 2003). The above studies indicate that the high-income elasticity of demand for services and increased input usage are likely to provide further impetus to growth in the services sector.

A study by FICCI (2003) shows that employment in the services sector has increased from 20 per cent to 26 per cent in the decade of the 1990's. This increase in employment would have directly reduced poverty as some estimates show that nearly 2/3rd of the employment in some service sectors is that of unskilled and semi-skilled labour, e.g telecommunications. According to a CGE simulation by NCAER and the University of Michigan, a 33 per cent reduction in service trade barriers would increase wages roughly by 0.17 per cent per annum in India. Economic welfare would increase by 0.5 per cent per annum and returns to capital by 0.2 per cent per annum (Chadha, Brown, Dearndoff and Stern, 2003). It is to be noted that the increase in wages is almost as much as the increase in returns to capital, which goes against the general trend in India where returns to labour are falling much faster than returns to capital. This also reiterates the high potential of this sector for attenuating poverty.

In some sectors, such as telecommunications, computers and related services, as well as health services, the provision of these services, would by themselves achieve the goals of MDGs. In some cases, such as telecom liberalisation, a significant impact on the provision and pricing of these services can be observed in the case of India. This has made these services accessible to a large section of the population, including the poor. For example, tele-density and internet usage has risen significantly in the post-liberalisation era along with an increased role of the private sector.

It is considered that even fully liberal cross-border trade in goods and services will leave significant global efficiency gains unrealised unless there is due recognition of factor movements (Mattoo and Subramaniam, 2003). Dani Rodrik has noted that the income gains that arise from international trade, rise with the square of price differentials across national markets (Rodrik, 2002). The wages of similarly qualified individuals in the advanced and low-income countries differ by a factor of 10 or more.[3] Rodrik concludes that a multilaterally negotiated visa scheme that allows expanded entry into advanced nations of mixed skill and unskilled workers from developing countries would create income gains that are larger than all of the items on the WTO negotiating agenda taken together (Rodrik, 2002). Despite this impressive reason for labour movement, unskilled and semi-skilled services were largely excluded from GATS, both because the subject matter was not covered, and physical movement of the service provider being the mode of delivery by which these services may be traded (Trachtman, 2003). In the context of GATS, the movement of natural persons were, in practice, linked to Mode 3, namely commercial presence. Such commitments were of limited value and interest to developing and other low-income countries who have limited share in foreign direct investment. Thus there is a need to de-link negotiations on Mode 4 with Mode 3.

The poverty links with Mode 4 can be traced to the following factors:

1. Income from remittances which increase the level of well-being of a particular society.
2. Skill upgrading which increases efficiency and hence growth with its accompanying poverty alleviation effects.
3. Direct poverty alleviation of economic migrants whose opportunity cost in their home countries may be low.

Even in the absence of any international framework for facilitating movement of labour, India has been able to derive substantial foreign remittance and has been the top recipient for a long time (Buktchevicine, 2003). In terms of foreign exchange earnings, foreign remittances come close to the contribution of the country's entire textiles and clothing industry in India. However, the benefits could be even more substantial in terms of temporary movement of natural persons (TMNP), encompassed under Mode 4, if it achieves moderate degree of success in the negotiations.[4]

Notwithstanding the benefits of liberalization, there would be some trade adjustment costs also associated with liberalization. Workers in India continue be skeptical about services liberalization. Although services rose from 42 per cent to 48 per cent of GDP during the 1990s, the employment share of services actually declined by about one percentage point during the decade. Thus, while output generation has shifted to services, employment creation in services has lagged far behind. India's relatively jobless service sector growth is unlike the experience of other countries, where the service sector has also tended to gain a larger share of employment over time. India, in fact, has an exceptionally low share of services employment, when compared with other countries (Gordon and Gupta, 2003). Labour productivity in Indian services has been increasing over time. Factors, which have led to an increase in labour productivity, include the growth of services being concentrated in sub-sectors that are more dependent on skilled labour than on unskilled labour or capital. This trend has no doubt been reinforced by technological improvements, as well as by efficiency gains resulting from liberalization (RBI, 2002). The relatively jobless nature of growth in India's services sector further underscores the need for growth in employment through both agriculture and manufacturing. This situation may have changed somewhat in this decade because of the big jump in services export and the consequent indirect creation of jobs through multiplier effects. Anecdotal evidence suggests that one person employed by BPOs in India create jobs for two to three additional people.

Other concerns relate to the legacy costs of public sector service providers who would find it difficult to compete with foreign and new domestic service providers. This would mean that there would be pressure on public sector employment, which constitutes a major part of the employment of the organized sector. For example in the financial services sector, public sector banks are saddled with excessive labour and non-performing assets relative to both new private sector banks and foreign banks. The geographical and sectoral concentration of employment in urban services also makes retrenchment consequent to liberalization particularly painful. Seven out of ten Indians in urban areas are currently employed in services whereas only two of ten are in rural areas (World Bank, 2004). Thus most of the trade adjustment costs would have to be borne by a vocal and organized urban India, leading to tough political decisions. Sectors which would be particularly vulnerable to higher trade adjustment costs are likely to include retail, road transport, construction, where the bulk of the labour force is poor and unskilled.

The provision of public services to the poor through cross subsidization is also a common practice of public sector companies. However, liberalization may make this practice difficult as was witnessed by the difficulties in implementing the Universal Service Obligation in the case of the telecommunications sector of India.

Another feature of the services sector in India has been that it has been focused on only a few sub-sectors and there has been little diversity. This would make exports from this sector particularly vulnerable to trends in target markets and limit the employment and poverty gains from the liberalization in this sector. Efficient and diversified services sector is critical for development. Be it efficient transport links or business services to enable trade, or health and education to build human capital, services have a major influence upon economic development. Low quality, costly or inefficient services act as a brake on the entire economy: inefficiencies in roads, railways, power and water alone cost an estimated US$ 55 billion a year in losses in the early 1990s—an amount equal to 1 per cent of the GDP of developing countries or twice the annual budget for financing infrastructure in the developing world (UNDP, 2004). Losses from inefficient services have spillover effects and are not one-time—they hamper economic growth on an on-going basis by lowering the profitability of existing investment and discouraging further investment (Hodge, 2002).

Openness in services can also influence long run growth performance. After controlling for other determinants of growth, countries that fully reformed the financial services sector grew, on average, about one percentage point faster than other countries. An even greater impetus on growth comes from fully reforming (liberalization plus regulatory reform) both the telecommunications and financial services sectors; countries, which fully liberalized both sectors, grew, on average, about 1.5 percentage points faster than other countries (World Bank, 2000).

Services are used intensively in the production of all goods and services, making up around 10-20 per cent of production costs in both industry and agriculture. The price and quality of services are critical in determining the cost of all other products and services in the economy. In fact, according to some estimates by the World Bank and IMF, inadequacy of infrastructural services, costs an Indian producer approximately 18 per cent per unit of production of industrial goods (Gordon and Gupta, 2003). Much of what is required to trade—telecommunications, transport, banking and insurance and distribution—is services. For agricultural exporters, integration of the agriculture sector within and between economies depends upon access to transportation services (Limao and Venables, 2001). Inadequate transport and distribution links result in considerable post-harvest losses, wastage and over-charging by middlemen—all problems particularly acute in relatively remote areas (World Bank, 2005).

Recognising the importance of services in the Indian economy, it is presumed that international negotiations can help further the benefits that India can obtain from market access in this sector. Trends in growth in services indicate that despite a hiatus in international negotiations, it is possible to increase trade in services. The next sections analyses these trends and some of the underlying causes.

### *Trends in Services*

The aggregate services sector witnessed a phenomenal growth in the decade of 1990s. During 1980s, services sector output grew at the rate of 6.6 per cent per annum, while during 1990s the growth rate increased to 7.5 per cent per annum. In the last ten years (1994-2004), we find that services sector in India has grown on an average by 7.9 per cent per annum (as seen in Fig. 2.1). In contrast to this, we find that in other countries like Thailand, Indonesia and China agriculture sector has grown at an average annual growth of 1.5 per cent, 1.9 per cent and 3.8 per cent while manufacturing sector has grown at the rate of 7.2 per cent, 6.6 per cent and 12.2 per cent respectively. Corresponding growth in services sector has been 3.9 per cent, 4.5 per cent and 8.9 per cent.

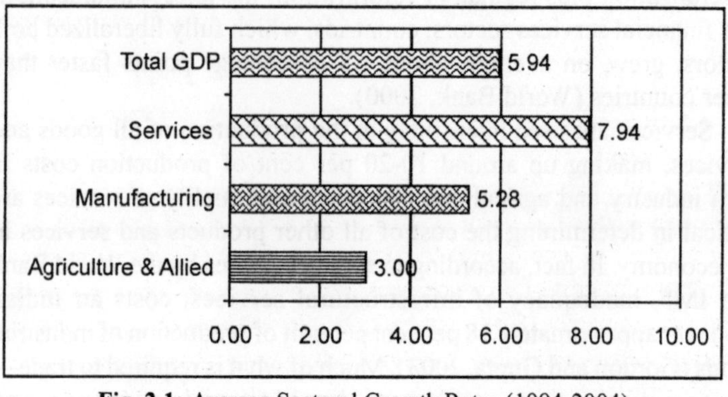


**Fig. 2.1:** Average Sectoral Growth Rates (1994-2004)

*Source*: Author's estimates using CSO.

### *Share in GDP*

A striking feature of India's growth performance is that in the four decade period, 1950 to 1990, agriculture's share in GDP has declined by about 25 percentage points, while industry and services have gained equally. The share of industry has stabilised since 1990 and consequently the entire subsequent decline in agriculture has been picked up by the services sector (Fig. 2.2). During the 1990s, the contribution of service sector to the growth rate of GDP was almost 60 per cent in contrast to 54 per cent in middle income countries, 43 per cent in least developed countries and 34 per cent in China. High share of services in GDP is a unique feature of the Indian economy as in other developing countries decline in agricultural sector's share has been followed by growth in manufacturing sector's share and the shift towards services sector has occurred only in the final stages of growth.

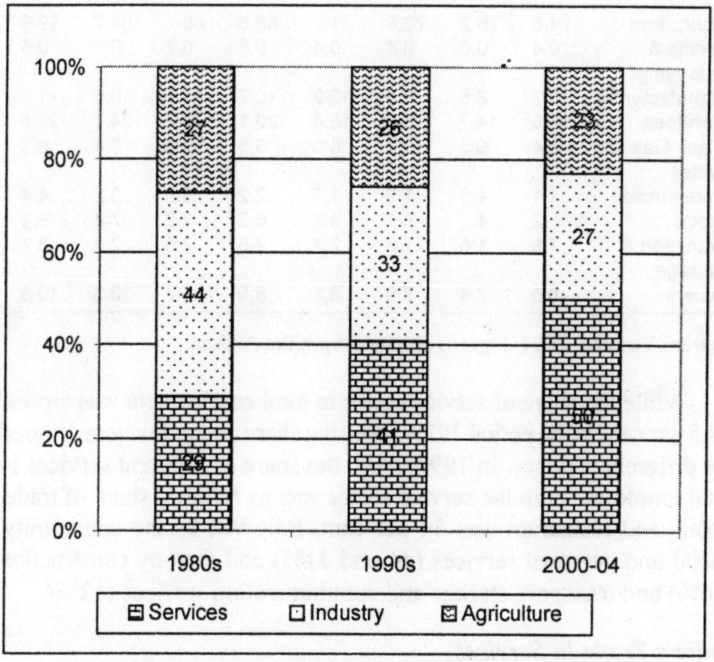


**Fig. 2.2:** Average Sectoral Contribution to GDP

*Source*: National Accounts Statistics.

### *Share in Employment*

Growth in the share of service sector in GDP is often followed by a corresponding growth in the share of service sector in total employment in the economy. However, in India we find that though there has been a phenomenal growth in the service sector, this growth has not been followed by a corresponding high growth in employment in the 1990s. And this rise in the share of services in employment has been much slower than the decline in the share of agriculture and manufacturing in total employment (*see* Table 2.1). In the year 1999 services contributed around 28.5 per cent of total employment in contrast to 30 per cent in middle income countries, 70 per cent in Singapore and around 39 per cent in Indonesia.

**Table 2.1:** Industrial Distribution of Total Workforce in India

| | *1951* | *1961* | *1972-73* | *1977-78* | *1983* | *1987-88* | *1993-94* | *1999-2000* |
|---|---|---|---|---|---|---|---|---|
| Agriculture | 74.6 | 76.2 | 73.9 | 71 | 68.6 | 65 | 64.7 | 59.9 |
| Mining & Quarrying | 0.4 | 0.5 | 0.4 | 0.4 | 0.6 | 0.7 | 0.7 | 0.6 |
| Manufacturing | 8.2 | 8.6 | 8.8 | 10.2 | 10.7 | 11.1 | 10.5 | 11 |
| **Services** | 16.8 | 14.7 | 16.9 | 18.4 | 20.1 | 23.2 | 24.1 | 28.5 |
| Elect, Gas and Water | 0.4 | 0.3 | 0.2 | 0.3 | 0.3 | 0.3 | 0.4 | 0.3 |
| Construction | 1.1 | 1.3 | 1.9 | 1.7 | 2.2 | 3.8 | 3.2 | 4.4 |
| Trade | 5.2 | 4.1 | 5.1 | 6.1 | 6.2 | 7.2 | 7.4 | 9.4 |
| Transport & Storage | 1.5 | 1.6 | 1.8 | 2.1 | 2.5 | 2.6 | 2.8 | 3.7 |
| Others | 8.5 | 7.4 | 7.9 | 8.1 | 8.9 | 9.3 | 10.3 | 10.8 |

*Source*: Virmani, 2004. Figures obtained from the Author.

While the share of service sector in total employment was around 28.5 per cent in the period 1999-2000, the share of employment differed for different services. In 1999-2000, the share of different services in total employment in the service sector was as follows: share of trade, hotels and restaurant was 34 per cent, followed by the community, social and personal services (around 31%) and then by construction (16%) and transport, storage and communication services (13%).

### *India's Trade in Services*

India's share in world merchandise exports was 0.8 per cent, the corresponding share in world commercial services was 1.9 per cent.

India's share in world markets for IT software and services (including BPO) increased from 1.7 per cent in 2003-04 to 2.3 per cent in 2004-05 and an estimated 2.8 per cent in 2005-06 (Economic Survey, 2005-06).

Due to the phenomenal rise in India's export of services in the 1990s, India' share in total world exports of services has increased overtime (*see* Table 2.2). We find that services exports have always been higher than services imports in India.

**Table 2.2:** India's Share in World Services Exports

| *Year* | *Exports of India's Services in (USD bn)* | *Imports of India's Services in (USD bn)* | *India's Share in World Exports of Services* |
|---|---|---|---|
| 1998-99 | 13.0 | 11.02 | 0.99 |
| 1999-2000 | 18.0 | 11.64 | 1.20 |
| 2000-01 | 20.0 | 16.39 | 1.40 |
| 2001-02 | 21.0 | 16.08 | 1.30 |
| 2004-05 | 46.0 | 37.9 | 1.80 |

*Source*: Reserve Bank of India, 2003.

*At the disaggregated level,* we find that exports of services like communications, computer and information, and financial services have gone up substantially in the period 2000 to 2003. But these are services with low employment potential. Imports of these services have also witnessed a rise except for financial services. Construction services, business services and royalty and licensing, on the other hand, witnessed a fall in their exports and a corresponding rise in their imports. These are services with high employment potential.

**Table 2.3:** India's Exports and Imports of Disaggregated Services: 1990-2003

| | *Exports (US Million Dollars)* | | | | | |
|---|---|---|---|---|---|---|
| | *1990* | *1995* | *2000* | *2001* | *2002* | *2003* |
| Communications | — | — | 598.8 | 1103.9 | 779.4 | 1065.9 |
| Construction | — | — | 501.9 | 65.1 | 231.4 | 284.1 |
| Insurance | 123.3 | 170.2 | 257.0 | 282.0 | 331.9 | 408.9 |
| Financial | — | — | 276.0 | 306.1 | 598.2 | 392.1 |
| Computer & Information | — | — | 4727.4 | 7407.4 | 8889.3 | 11365.7 |
| Royalities & Licence Fees | 1.3 | 1.4 | 82.6 | 37.2 | 20.2 | 25.2 |
| Other Business Services | 1967.1 | 2119.7 | 4147.8 | 2349.0 | 2699.1 | 2601.0 |
| Personal, Cultural & Recreational | — | — | — | — | — | — |
| Government, N.I.E | 15.4 | 11.5 | 653.7 | 537.9 | 352.9 | 305.1 |

(*Contd.*)

**Table 2.3** (*Contd.*)

| | *Imports (US Million Dollars)* | | | | | |
|---|---|---|---|---|---|---|
| | *1990* | *1995* | *2000* | *2001* | *2002* | *2003* |
| Communications | — | — | 104.8 | 266.8 | 1002.6 | 610.5 |
| Construction | — | — | 127.1 | 470.3 | 601.0 | 1208.9 |
| Insurance | 343.9 | 558.8 | 813.2 | 810.9 | 892.6 | 1168.9 |
| Financial | — | — | 1277.2 | 1780.1 | 1434.3 | 488.0 |
| Computer & Information | — | — | 576.8 | 910.9 | 905.3 | 659.3 |
| Royalities & Licence Fees | 72.5 | 90.3 | 282.5 | 317.0 | 345.2 | 420.8 |
| Other Business Services | 1715.0 | 2713.8 | 4320.7 | 3732.5 | 4084.0 | 8088.1 |
| Personal, Cultural & Recreational | — | — | — | — | — | — |
| Government, N.I.E | 147.0 | 205.7 | 290.4 | 306.9 | 262.9 | 199.2 |

*Source*: RBI, 2005.

## *Direction of India's Services Trade*

With regard to India's trading partners in services, we find that the most important trading partners of India with respect to services are: US, U.K, Germany, Japan and France.

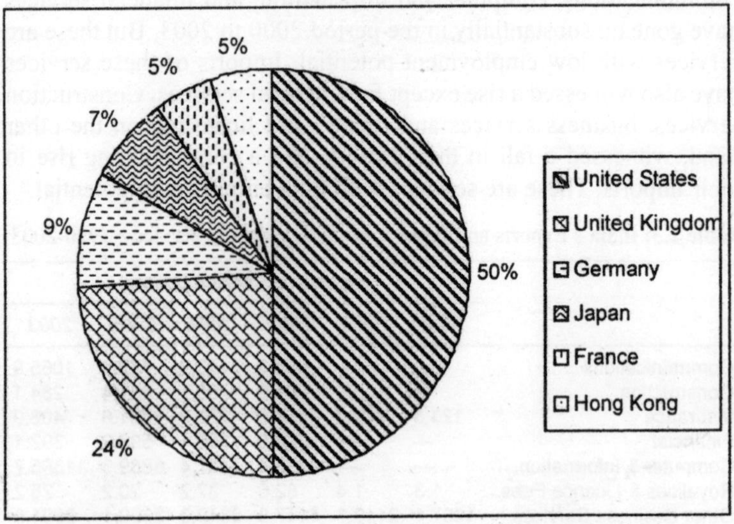


**Fig. 2.3:** Top Services Trading Partners (Average of 2000-2003)

*Source*: Services Statistics on International Trade, OECD. www.sourceOECD.org/database/services.

About 29 per cent of India's total services trade is with EU 5, i.e., U.K., France, Germany, Italy and Austria. As far as exports are concerned, amongst the top five trading partners the maximum exports i.e., around 74 per cent go to U.S. and U.K.

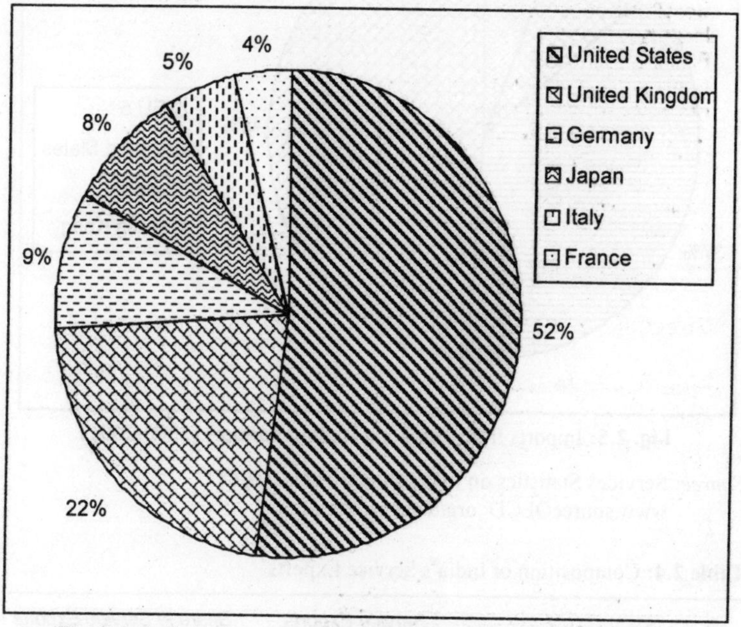


**Fig. 2.4:** India's Exports of Services to Top Five Trading Partners: Average 2000-2003

*Source*: Services Statistics on International Trade, OECD. www.sourceOECD.org/database/services.

However, with respect to imports of services, we find that EU 5 is an important partner and imports from EU 5 are almost 50 per cent of the total imports from top four trading partners. The other countries that have a share in trade in services of India are Australia, Canada, Netherlands and Austria.

*At a disaggregated level*, in percentage terms, software services constitute around 50 per cent of total exports while travel and transportation services constitute around 30 per cent. Together these three services constitute around 80 per cent of India's exports of services (Table 2.4).

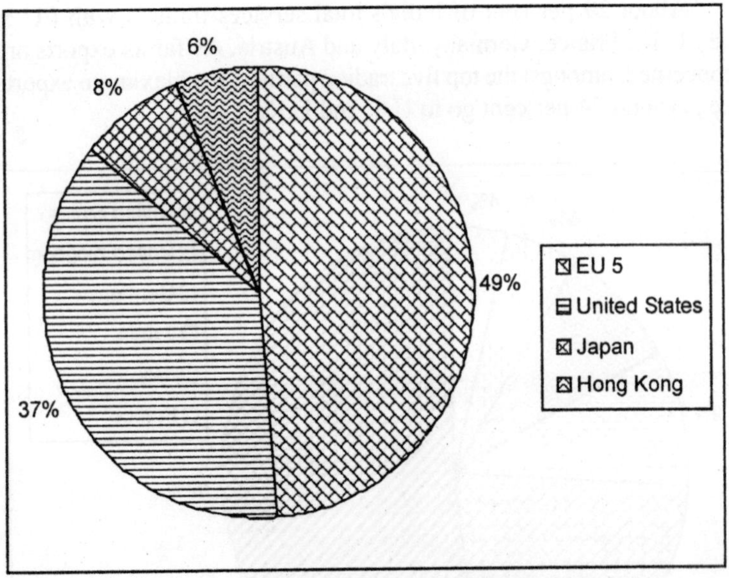


**Fig. 2.5:** Imports from Top Four Trading Partners (2000-2003)

*Source*: Services Statistics on International Trade, OECD. www.sourceOECD .org/database/services

**Table 2.4:** Composition of India's Service Exports

| | *Service Exports (million US $)* | | *Share in Service Exports (per cent)* | |
|---|---|---|---|---|
| | *2000-01* | *2003-04* | *2000-01* | *2003-04* |
| Travel | 3497 | 4122 | 22 | 17 |
| Transportation | 2046 | 3260 | 13 | 13 |
| Insurance | 270 | 420 | 2 | 2 |
| Communication Services | 1138 | 1047 | 7 | 4 |
| Construction Services | 536 | 465 | 3 | 2 |
| Financial Services | 347 | 315 | 2 | 1 |
| Software Services | 6341 | 12,200 | 41 | 49 |
| News Agency Services | 114 | 59 | 1 | 0 |
| Royalties, Copyright, and Licence Fees | 60 | 24 | 0 | 0 |
| Management Services | 334 | 1354 | 2 | 5 |
| Other Services | 934 | 1401 | 6 | 6 |
| **Total** | **15,617** | **24,667** | **100** | **100** |

*Source*: Calculations Based on RBI, 2005.

## III. Services as a Driver of the Indian Economy

India's trade openness is largely services driven. Its share in services trade is higher than that in manufacturing trade. In fact, the employment elasticity of agriculture and manufacturing has been relatively lower than services and has been declining over time, with the exception of textiles and apparel.

The service sector boom in India in the post-UR period shows that India has a competitive advantage in several of these service sectors. Its contribution to GDP has risen to over 50 per cent in the period 2001-2004. India's exports of services have displayed one of the fastest growth rates in the world, i.e., over 17 per cent per annum in the 1990s (the world average being 5.6 per cent). In 2004-05, gross earnings from invisibles stood at almost US$ 77.5 billion, just US$ 2 billion short of merchandise export earnings of US$ 80.8 billion (RBI, 2005). India is now the largest recipient of inward remittances in the developing world. As lower skill categories get vacated for white-collar workers and technical specialists, and as the Western world faced with greying populations allows freer movement of labour, such remittances will only increase.

Among the three sub-sectors of services, 'trade, hotels, transport and communication services' continued to lead by growing at double-digit rates for the third successive year. Impressive progress in expanding railway passenger network and production of commercial vehicles, and fast addition to existing stock of telephone connections, particularly mobiles, played key roles in such growth. Growth in financial services (comprising banking, insurance and real estate services), which after dipping in 2003-04 had bounced back in the following year, maintained the momentum with progressive maturing of Indian financial markets and the on-going construction boom.

NASSCOM has calculated that India is home to 28 per cent of the suitable talent available across all global sourcing locations and 80 of the world's 117 software companies that have attained the highest global quality standard are from India (Accenture, 2005).

Further there has also been a new trend in movement of foreign patients to India for medical treatment. A study by the Confederation of Indian Industry (CII), and McKinsey consultants estimated "medical tourism" could be worth 100bn rupees (£1.21bn) by 2012 (Guardian, 2005). Low cost and effective treatment is attributed to

**Table 2.5:** Trade in Invisibles

| | Item | Rupees crore | | | Us $ million | | |
|---|---|---|---|---|---|---|---|
| | | 2003-04 R | 2004-05 PR | 2005-06 P | 2003-04 R | 2004-05 PR | 2005-06 P |
| | (1) | (2) | (3) | (4) | (5) | (6) | (7) |
| I. | Non Factor Services, net | 46,381 | 63,519 | 98,437 | 10,144 | 14,199 | 22,265 |
| | Receipts | 1,23,175 | 2,06,082 | 2,68,706 | 26,868 | 46,031 | 60,610 |
| | Payments | 76,794 | 1,42,563 | 1,702,69 | 16,724 | 31,832 | 38,345 |
| | Travel, net | 6,520 | 4,361 | 6,085 | 1,435 | 985 | 1,368 |
| | Receipt | 23,054 | 29,105 | 34,580 | 5,037 | 6,495 | 7,789 |
| | Payments | 16,534 | 24,744 | 28,495 | 3,602 | 5,510 | 6,421 |
| | Transportation, net | 4,026 | 1,163 | –4,980 | 879 | 269 | –1,117 |
| | Receipts | 14,714 | 21,526 | 27,816 | 3,207 | 4,798 | 6,277 |
| | Payments | 10,688 | 20,363 | 32,795 | 2328 | 4,639 | 7,394 |
| | Insurance, net | 250 | 835 | 221 | 56 | 187 | 57 |
| | Receipts | 1,922 | 4,084 | 4,606 | 419 | 909 | 1,042 |
| | Payments | 1,672 | 3,249 | 4,385 | 363 | 722 | 985 |
| | G.N.I.E., net | 129 | 304 | -773 | 28 | 67 | -175 |
| | Receipts | 1,105 | 1,476 | 1,356 | 240 | 328 | 305 |
| | Payments | 976 | 1,172 | 2,129 | 212 | 261 | 480 |
| | Miscellaneous, net | 35,456 | 56,856 | 97,884 | 7,746 | 12,701 | 22,132 |
| | Receipts | 82,380 | 1,49,891 | 2,00,349 | 17,965 | 33,501 | 45,197 |
| | Payments | 46,924 | 93,035 | 102,465 | 10,219 | 20,800 | 23,065 |
| II. | Income, net | -20,708 | -17,157 | -24,969 | -4,505 | -3,814 | -5,599 |
| | Receipts | 17,909 | 20,436 | 25,076 | 3,904 | 4,547 | 5,651 |
| | Payments | 2,633 | 1,797 | 2,031 | 574 | 400 | 458 |
| III. | Private Transfers, net | 99,165 | 90,744 | 1,06,830 | 21,608 | 20,253 | 24,095 |
| | Receipts | 1,01,798 | 92,541 | 1,08,861 | 22,182 | 20,653 | 24,553 |
| | Payments | 2,633 | 1,797 | 2,031 | 574 | 400 | 458 |

(*Contd.*)

**Table 2.5** (*Contd.*)

| Item | Rupees crore | | | Us $ million | | |
|---|---|---|---|---|---|---|
| | 2003-04 R | 2004-05 PR | 2005-06 P | 2003-04 R | 2004-05 PR | 2005-06 P |
| (1) | (2) | (3) | (4) | (5) | (6) | (7) |
| IV. Official Transfers, net | 2,531 | 2,650 | 809 | 554 | 591 | 181 |
| Receipts | 2,531 | 2,792 | 2,961 | 554 | 623 | 667 |
| Payments | 0 | 142 | 2,152 | 0 | 32 | 486 |
| V. Invisibles, net (I to IV) | 1,27,369 | 1,39,756 | 1,81,107 | 27,801 | 31,229 | 40,942 |
| Receipts | 2,45,413 | 3,21,851 | 4,05,604 | 53,508 | 71,854 | 91,481 |
| Payments | 1,18,044 | 1,82,095 | 2,24,497 | 25,707 | 40,625 | 50,539 |

R: Revised. PR: Partially Revised. P: Preliminary. GNIE: Government Not Included Elsewhere.

be the main reason for this emerging trend. Table 2.6 provides a comparison of treatment costs in India, UK, France and the US depicting India's comparative advantage in costs.

**Table 2.6:** A Comparison of Treatment Costs in India, UK, France and US depicting India's Comparative Advantage in Costs

| | *India* | *UK* | *France* | *US* |
|---|---|---|---|---|
| Heart Bypass | £ 4,300 | £ 15,000 | £ 13,000 | £ 13,250 |
| Hip Replacement | £ 3,180 | £ 9,000 | £ 7,600 | £ 15,900 |
| Cataract Operation | £ 660 | £ 2,900 | £ 1,000 | £ 2,120 |

*Source*: Compiled from the Guardian, Tuesday February 1, 2005

There is also an increasing trend among US corporations in medical outsourcing towards countries such as India. Many US corporations are examining outsourcing as a health care option for their employees instead of health insurance coverage due to the vast differences in treatment costs between the US and countries such as India, Singapore and Thailand. As an incentive for supporting this option employees are provided up to 25 per cent of savings garnered from outsourcing. Health care procedures in these countries have been found to cost only 20 per cent to 25 per cent as much as comparable ones in the US. Comparing the costs in these countries it can be seen that India has a clear comparative advantage as is depicted in Table 2.6. The table also provides a comparison with the US insurance costs.

India is also fast emerging as a major center for cutting-edge research and development (R&D) projects for global multinationals such as Microsoft and Motorola as well as Indian firms. Microsoft in January launched its third international research center in India. Intel has 800 India-based engineers working on software and hardware designs for its communication and semiconductor product lines. More and more companies in industries ranging from IT and telecommunications through pharmaceuticals and biotech are setting up ambitious R&D projects, in part to serve the Indian market, but also with an eye to delivering new generations of products faster to the global market (Knowledge @ Wharton, 2005). For instance Dr Reddy's Laboratories (DRL), a leading Indian drug firm, entered into agreements in 1997 and 1998 with global pharmaceutical giant Novo

Nordisk to license molecules for further development. India's largest pharmaceutical company, Ranbaxy, also licensed its technology for an innovative drug delivery system for ciprofloxacin, named Cipro-OD, to Germany's Bayer, which owned the patent to the drug. Tata Motors has a $ 0.2 billion expenditure programme on improving its R&D capabilities.

**Table 2.7:** A Comparison of Treatment Costs in the US, India, Thailand, and Singapore Depicting India's Comparative Advantage in Costs (In US Dollar Terms)

| *Procedure* | *U.S. Insurer's cost* | *U.S. Retail price* | *India* | *Thailand* | *Singapore* |
|---|---|---|---|---|---|
| Angioplasty | 25,704 to 37,128 | 57,262 to 82,711 | 11000 | 13000 | 13000 |
| Gastric bypass | 27,717 to 40,035 | 47,988 to 69,316 | 11000 | 15000 | 15000 |
| Heart bypass | 54,741 to 79,071 | 122,424 to 176,835 | 10000 | 12000 | 20000 |
| Heart-valve replacement (single) | 71,401 to 103,136 | 159,326 to 230,138 | 9500 | 10500 | 13000 |
| Hip replacement | 18,281 to 26,407 | 43,780 to 63,238 | 9000 | 12000 | 12000 |
| Hysterectomy | 9,591 to 13,854 | 20,416 to 29,489 | 2900 | 4500 | — |
| Knee replacement | 17,627 to 25,462 | 40,640 to 58,702 | 8500 | 10000 | 13000 |
| Mastectomy | 9,774 to 14,118 | 23,709 to 34,246 | 7500 | 9000 | 12400 |
| Spinal fusion | 25,302 to 36,547 | 62,778 to 90,679 | 5500 | 7000 | 9000 |

*Sources*: Subimo (U.S. rates, including at least one day of hospitalization); Planet Hospital (international rates). As cited in TIME, May 29, 2006 (Outsourcing Your Heart).

India is a leading producer of films and in 1999 produced about 150 more feature films than the United States. In value terms, sales by the Indian film industry are only around 1 per cent of the world total, but production costs are much lower than in other parts of the world. Further India has significant potential for expanding exports to countries/regions with high non-resident Indian and South Asian concentration and since the Indian products cater to a niche audience,

India does not face any direct competition from major players such as the US (Mukherjee, 2002).

## IV. India's Offensive Interests in Services

While India has defensive interests in agriculture and NAMA, its edge is mainly in services. Unlike many developing countries, it has, in fact, taken offensive positions in this area as it has export interests in information technology (Mode 1). The country also seeks greater access to EU and US in terms of the movement of natural persons or what is termed as Mode 4 in cross-border supply of services. Indications are that there was only limited movement on this matter at the Hong Kong Ministerial. Lack of movement in Mode 4 due to opposition by the US and EU, may affect India's ability to offer much in other modes of services.

From India's point of view, services present a different picture than agriculture and industrial tariffs. As an emerging global power in IT and business services, the country, in fact, is a demandeur in the WTO talks as it seeks more liberal commitments on the part of its trading partners for cross-border supply of services, including the movement of natural persons to developed countries or what is termed as Mode 4 for the supply of services. With respect to Mode 2 also, India has an offensive interest. The last thing it needs at this juncture is pressure to be defensive in an area where it can afford to be more aggressive.

In sharp contrast, the interest of the EU and US is more in establishing a commercial presence in developing countries. Accordingly, Mode 3 of supply is accompanied by requests for more liberal policies on foreign direct investment in sectors like insurance. These developed countries are lukewarm to demands for a more liberal regime for the movement of natural persons because of the high unemployment in their economies.

India has received many plurilateral requests for opening of a number of services, however, while the demandeurs have high ambitions in terms of the market access they want, they are not willing to open up their own economies to the same degree. Whilst the EC is fully committed to the plurilateral process, the US continues to indicate the high importance they give to the bilateral request-offer, possibly because the US is unable to move at all in the Mode 4 plurilateral request.

### *India's Pro-Active Role in GATS and Current Status of Negotiations*

India has been a forerunner in the Doha Round of multilateral trade negotiations under GATS and has pursued an offensive strategy in trade liberalization of services, especially under Mode 1 and Mode 4. Being the largest recipient of inward remittances in the developing world, India's interest lies in pushing forward trade through Mode 4 i.e., temporary migration of workers. Further, having competitive strength in information technology and BPO, India wants to lower barriers and commitments in cross-border supply in services (Mode 1).

In the Hong Kong Ministerial Meeting India played a pivotal role in inclusion of Annex C into the main draft, which emphasizes three main points:

(a) Commitments under Mode 1 should include removal of existing requirements of commercial presence, which had hitherto militated against developing country suppliers who find it difficult and expensive to establish companies in the country where the service is being supplied.

(b) There should be new or improved commitments in Mode 4 on the categories of contractual services suppliers, independent professionals and others, again delinked from commercial presence, to reflect *inter alia* removal or substantial reduction of economic needs tests. These had been the demands of several developing countries, including India.

(c) Commitments on enhanced levels of foreign equity participation as well as "allowing greater flexibility on the types of legal entity permitted."

Inclusion of Annex C has implicitly changed the structure of negotiations in GATS, which had hitherto been based on voluntary unilateral commitments or bilateral requests and offers in the various modes. The request-offer negotiations can now also be pursued on a plurilateral basis. India submitted its initial offer in on-going services negotiations under GATS in January 2004. The offer indicated India's commitment to liberalise its economy in certain modes of supply in sectors such as professional businesses, engineering, tourism and transport. India's services offer focused primarily on mode one (cross-border supply), two (consumption abroad) and four (movements of natural persons). The offer contained various horizontal limitations on Mode 3 (commercial presence). More specifically, the offer improved market access and national treatment commitments in sub-sectors like accounting and book-keeping services; construction and engineering services; computer services; medical and dental services; financial services; tourism services; and maritime transport services.

However, market access limitations were retained in these sectors under Mode 3, including limits on ownership of Indian firms. Also, in many cases no commitments were undertaken in Mode 3, in terms of national treatment commitment. With regard to Mode 4, there were almost no limitations for certain professions including business visitors, intra-corporate transferees, managers, executives, specialists and employees of foreign companies for short periods of stay (less than one year).

In the *Revised Offer* submitted in August 2005 by India, there has been a substantial improvement, which reflects India's aggressive approach towards trade liberalization in services. The Revised Offer covers eleven sectors and 94 sub-sectors are covered in as opposed to seven sectors and 47 sub-sectors in the Initial Offer. In Mode 3 (commercial presence), India's Revised Offer covers commitments in many new services. Commitments on FDI levels have also been enhanced in existing sectors such as computer related services, engineering, R & D, technical testing, telecom, financial services, construction and related engineering services, and tourism services. The major sectors in which restriction on foreign investment remains are: legal, auditing and accounting, and postal services. However, with respect to retailing the government has now allowed 51 per cent FDI in single brand retailing though no formal commitment has been undertaken in GATS.

Under Mode 4, at the Initial Offer stage itself, India had made substantial improvements in its commitments. In the Revised Offer, further improvements have been made in the sectoral coverage of both contractual service suppliers and independent professionals.

So far, 30 countries including India have submitted their Revised Offers. A number of Initial and Revised Offers are still pending. However, in terms of quality of offers the Revised Offers have provided few commercial opportunities and even with two rounds of offers there has been no substantial improvement, especially in areas of interest to India and other developing countries viz., movement of natural persons (Mode 4) and cross-border supply (Mode 1).

India's efforts, along with other developing countries, have been to get binding commitments in cross-border supply of services (Mode 1) and movement of natural persons (Mode 4). A number of negotiating proposals were tabled at the WTO in furthering India's objectives. With respect to Mode 4, India has been pushing for issues such as removal of the Economic Needs Test (ENT), clear prescription of the duration of stay, provisions of extension, etc. It has often been noticed that domestic regulations create barriers for India's service providers even when the trading partners have taken firm commitments. Disciplining such domestic regulations is necessary to impart effective market access for Indian service providers, especially in Mode 4.

With respect to Mode 3, India has received many plurilateral requests for opening of a number of services. The US and the EU have made requests under Mode 3 asking for greater commercial presence rights in more than 10 sectors including telecommunication, financial services, construction and energy. However, while the demandeurs have high ambitions in terms of the market access they want, they are not willing to open up their own economies to the same degree. Moreover, whilst the EC is fully committed to the plurilateral process, the US continues to indicate the high importance they give to the bilateral request-offer, possibly because the US is unable to move at all in the Mode 4 plurilateral request India *et al.* are now preparing.

## V. Conclusions

The GATS commitments by India should be leveraged to expand market access for India's exports of labour and skill intensive services. India has a huge potential for cross-border supply of various professional services, especially through back-office and outsourced activities and via electronic delivery. In addition, substantial liberalization of Mode 4, which is movement of natural persons, would be beneficial. Negotiations should include relaxation of visa procedures, recognition of professional qualifications, and removal of discriminatory standards or burdensome licensing requirements in sectorals as well as in Mode 4. However as pointed earlier, it is not merely WTO negotiations but unilateral liberalization and negotiated contracts with individual countries that could deliver the maximum gains. Whether it is the WTO, bilateral or unilateral liberalization, there are some salient regulatory issues that India would need to address to get the maximum gains from trade in services.

India should achieve progressive liberalisation without exclusion of any sector/mode; however, special attention may be given to sectors/modes of export interest to India, such as Computer and Related Services; Professional Services; Health Related and Social Services; Hospitality, Tourism and Travel Related Services; Educational Services, Transport Services; Other Business Services; Construction and Related Engineering Services and Media, Entertainment and Audio-visual Services.

On the sectoral front, there are several issues that need to be considered in pursuing a liberalisation agenda. Liberalisation of infrastructural sectors such as financial services, telecom services, health and education creates significant benefits for the domestic financial entities through transfer of knowledge and technology. This includes knowledge on best practices. India should negotiate for targeted technical assistance to facilitate percolation of such knowledge transfer in these sectors. Opening should be linked to better domestic regulatory capacity and the necessary transfer of skills from foreign firms. Equally regulation on universal service obligations can be placed on all market participants, and can include incentives for implementation. For instance, funds for universal service can be pooled and allocated through competitive tender to the firm that offers to provide the necessary service or infrastructure at the least cost.

With liberalization of financial sector, there would be more ICT interface for online services across the border and speedy clearances. This would generate more opportunities for software development and outsourcing. India, having considerable strengths, in ICT as well as outsourcing, could ensure a win-win situation for both these sectors.

Liberalisation in the telecom sector is far greater than the commitments undertaken. This should be leveraged to gain market access in other sectors. Liberalisation of other infrastructure sectors such as health and education also require a comprehensive regulatory framework which will help India leverage the benefits of liberalization.

Issues on professional services are intrinsically linked to liberalization of Mode 4 and Mode 2. The question is whether granting access to foreign professionals and firms will help to create a more competitive services market, or will it lead to the crowding out of nascent Indian firms, none of which has a place in the top 50 firms (in terms of revenue) in the world.

Sound domestic regulation—prudential regulation in financial services, consumer protection in professional services and pro-competitive regulation in a variety of infrastructural services—is critical to realizing the benefits of liberalization. Credible regulatory frameworks are also important for attracting investors, especially in infrastructure services often characterized by large sunk investment costs (i.e., those costs that produce a stream of benefits over a long horizon but can never be recouped).

Designing, sequencing and enforcing reforms can be extremely complex. Regulatory thinking and economic analysis are still evolving rapidly, especially for network industries and solutions which have proved successful in some countries or some sectors may not be readily transferable to others. Careful assessment of the implications of alternative types of regulation is required to determine which options might be most appropriate for India. This situation has an important consequence for the Doha negotiations: it argues for a degree of caution in making binding commitments in areas where significant regulatory experimentation is still underway, as well as caution in GATS rule-making with regard to regulation.

Nonetheless, liberalisation will have positive effects as well. Liberalisation could lead to foreign investment, transfer of skills, increased efficiency and other distributional benefits. It could also lead to better prospects for skilled professionals. However there is a greater need to ensure that liberalisation does not lead to market failures and other socio-economic problems. With or without the Doha Round, India should pursue a careful agenda of opening markets and improving its share in global trade in services.

## END NOTES

1. Website of the Office of the Economic Adviser Ministry of Commerce and Industry, Department of Industrial Policy and Planning http://eaindustry.nic.in/mesout.htm
2. Federation of Indian Export Organisations (FIEO). 'India's Growing Services Sector' downloaded from http://fieo.org/service.html
3. For examination of the wages differences of software service personnel in various countries see, Rubin, H. (1999), '*Global Software Economics*',

New York: Hunter College, Department of Computer Science, and Rubin System, Inc.

4. Under TMNP, workers enter a country temporarily to carry out particular jobs and provide labour inputs. In such a situation there is no shift in residence, which is associated with international migration. However, its direct economic consequences can be thought of as those of migration. See Winters, A. (2001), '*The Economic Case for Labour Mobility*, Paper presented in the Joint WTO—World Workshop held in Geneva', April 11-12, 2001

## REFERENCES


'Beyond the Call Centre—Mastering India's Growth Dynamics' (2005). New Delhi: Accenture Policy and Corporate Affairs Publication. 2005. Downloaded from: http://www.accenture.com/Global/Research_and_Insights/Policy_And_Corporate_Affairs/BeyondIndiaDynamics.htm.

Buktchevicine, J. (2003). 'Increasing the Participation of Developing Countries through Liberalization of Market Access in GATS Mode 4 for Movement of Natural Persons Supplying Services', UNCTAD, 18 June.

Chadha, R., D. Brown, A. Dearndoff and R. Stern (2003). 'Computational Analysis of the Impact on India of the Uruguay Round and the Forthcoming WTO Negotiations' in A. Mattoo and R. Stern (eds.), *India and the WTO: A Strategy for Development*, The World Bank in collaboration with Oxford University Press, Delhi: Oxford University Press.

Chanda R. (2004). 'Use GATS Talks to Reform Domestic Economy', FE Insight, *The Financial Express*, Friday, October 8.

FICCI (2004). 'FICCI's Economic Agenda for the next five years'.

Gordon, J. and P. Gupta, (2003). 'Understanding India's Services Revolution', presented in an IMF-NCAER Conference on *A Tale of Two Giants: India's and China's Experience with Reform*, New Delhi

——— (2004). 'Understanding India's Services Revolution', IMF Working Paper WP/04/171, September.

Government of India, 2005-06. *Economic Survey of India*. Ministry of Finance, Economic Division.

Hodge J. (2002). 'Liberalization of Trade in Services in Developing Countries', in B. Hoekman, A. Mattoo, and P. English (eds.), *Development, Trade and the WTO—A Handbook*, pp. 226. World Bank.

Human Development Report (2004). 'Cultural Liberty in Today's Diverse World'. Downloaded from http://hdr.undp.org/reports/global/2004/?CFID = 304154&CFTOKEN=76740844.

Jha, V., S. Gupta, J. Nedumpara and K. Karthikeyan (2005). *Trade Liberalisation and Poverty in India*. New Delhi: Macmillian India Ltd.

Kher U., (2006). Outsourcing Your Heart, 2006. *TIME*, May 29. Available at: http://www.time.com/time/magazine/article/0,9171,1196429,00.html

Knowledge@Wharton (2005). 'What's Driving India's Rise as an R&D Hub?', November 21. http://knowledge.wharton.upenn.edu/index.cfm?fa=SpecialSection& special Id=40.

Limao, N. and A.J. Venables (2001). 'Infrastructure, Geographical Disadvantage, Transport Costs and Trade', *World Bank Economic Review* 15(3): 451-479.

Mattoo, A. and A. Subramaniam (2003). 'What Would a Development—Friendly WTO Architecture Really Look Like?'. IMF Working Paper. WP/03/153

———and R. Rathindran (2001). 'Measuring Services Trade Liberalisation and Its Impact on Economic Growth: An Illustration', Policy Research Working Paper Series 2655, The World Bank.

Mukherjee, A. (2002). 'India's Trade Potential in Audio-visual Services and the GATS', Indian Council for Research on International Economic Relations (ICRIER), Working Paper No. 81, April. Downloaded from http://www.eldis.ids.ac.uk/static/DOC11154.htm.

Munshi, P.R.D. (2005). 'Services exports grow 106%', *Times of India*, Wednesday, 27th July.

OECD. Services Statistics on International Trade, available at www.sourceOECD.org/database/services

OECD Policy Brief (2003). 'Opening up trade in Services—Opportunities and Gains for Developing Countries'.

Ramesh, R. (2005). 'This UK patient avoided the NHS list and flew to India for a heart bypass. Is health tourism the future?', *Guardian*, Tuesday February 1.

Reserve Bank of India (2003). *Handbook of Statistics on Indian Economy*, Downloaded from http://www.rbi.org.in/scripts AnnualPublications.aspx?head=Handbook%20of%20Statistics%20on%20Indian%20Economy.

————Bulletin, (2005). March.

Rodrik, D. (2002). 'Feasible Globalizations', Kennedy School of Government, Working Paper Series RWP02—029. July.

Rubin, H. (1999). 'Global Software Economics', New York: Hunter College, Department of Computer Science, and Rubin System, Inc

Trachtman, J.P. (2003). 'Legal Aspects of a Poverty Agenda at the WTO: Trade Law and 'Global Apartheid'', *Journal of International Economic Law*, 6(1): 3-21, March.

UNCTAD (2003). 'FDI Policies for Development: National and International Perspectives', *World Investment Report*.

———— (2005). 'Trade in Services and Development Implications', 16th March.

Virmani, A. *et al.* (2004). 'Impact of Tariff Reforms on Indian Industry: Assessment Based on A Multi-Sector Econometric Model' Working Paper Number 135, ICRIER

Winters, A. (2001). 'The Economic Case for Labour Mobility', Paper presented in the Joint WTO—World, Workshop held in Geneva', April 11-12.

World Bank (2004). 'Sustaining India's Services Revolution', World Bank Group, South Asia Region: India.

————(2005). 'From Competition at Home to Competing Abroad: A Case Study of India's Horticulture', Draft, June.

————South Asia, (2004). 'Trade in Services: Access to Foreign Markets, Domestic Reform and International Negotiations', Draft, June. http://eaindustry.nic.in/mesout.htm

*Chapter* 3

# TRIPS Patent System and Doha Declaration—Implementation by India

B.K. KEAYLA*

## I. Introduction

TRIPS Agreement expects WTO member countries to adopt minimum standards on patent laws as stipulated therein[1]. Doha Ministerial Conference Declaration on TRIPS Agreement and Public Health (November 2001) recognizes[2] the gravity of public health problems afflicting the poor countries, especially those resulting from HIV/AIDS, tuberculosis, malaria and other epidemics. The Declaration also stipulates[3] that in applying the customary rules of interpretation of public international laws, each provision of TRIPS Agreement should be read in the light of object and purpose of the Agreement as expressed, in particular in its objectives and principles. These are contained in Articles 7 and 8 of the TRIPS Agreement. For core areas of concern the Declaration also provides[4] that each member country has the right to grant compulsory licences and the freedom to determine the grounds upon which such licences are granted. In the background of the flexibilities and freedom available as stated, the amended national legislation on patent laws[5] should ensure that there is co-relation of the national patent system with the National Health Policy and the Pharmaceutical Policy so that the objectives of these policies are fully accomplished. This would also help in realisation

* Convenor, National Working Group on Patent Law and Trustee and Secretary General of Centre for Study of Global Trade System and Development.

of the Constitutional right of 'right of life'[6], which incorporates also 'right to health' which is guaranteed to the citizens of the country. In fact International Human Right Laws[7] also guarantee such rights. It is for the nation states to ensure that such rights are fully protected in its laws and policies

In order to conform the Indian Patents Act 1970 with the TRIPS provisions the Act has been amended thrice:

(i) Patents (Amendment) Act, 1999.
(ii) Patents (Second Amendment) Act, 2002.
(iii) Patents (Amendment) Act, 2005.

The Government has also introduced procedural improvements through the Patents Rules to make the Patents Act user friendly and simple. The flexibilities as clarified in the Doha Declaration[8] have provided enormous possibilities to strengthen public interest provisions in the patent laws. There are two major components of the patent system, which should have been carefully formulated. They relate to the scope of patentability and working of patents through compulsory licensing system. Transfer of technology, parallel imports and export of patented products are other important provisions. All these provisions have been suitably dealt within this Chapter.

**II. Scope of Patentability**

To comply with TRIPS requirement, during the transitional period India amended its Patents Act 1970 through Patents (Amendment) Act 1999 and incorporated sub-section (2) under Section 5. This incorporation provided for Mail Box facility from 1.1.1995 for receiving product patent applications for pharmaceuticals and agro-chemical products. It is observed that over 8500 applications have been received under this stipulation for the Mail Box. As against this the new molecules in the pharmaceutical field which are being invented in the world and which should only qualify for patentability through Mail Box are averaging between 40 to 50 per annum.

Article 27 of the TRIPS Agreement deals with the 'patentable subject-matter'. Under this Article the patent rights are enjoyable without discrimination as to the field of technology. However, the Doha Declaration on TRIPS Agreement and Public Health has recognized gravity of the public health problems afflicting many developing and least developed countries. In order to promote easy access to medicines for all as stipulated in the Declaration, the inventions relating to pharmaceutical products could be singled out for special emphasis.

In order to implement the scope of patentability aspects of the patent system, the following three Sections should have been carefully formulated:

(i) *Section 5*: Patentable subject-matter in the area of pharmaceutical and other inventions;
(ii) *Section 2*: Definitions and interpretation of technical patent terms; and
(iii) *Section 3*: Inventions not patentable.

The Pharmaceutical Research and Development Committee headed by Dr R.A. Mashelkar, Director General CSIR and Secretary to the Government of India suggested as part of intellectual property right strategies[9] that for the pharmaceutical sector there is a need to amend section (2) (1) (1) of the Patents Act 1970 to provide for New Chemical Entity (NCE)/New Medical Entity (NME) only to be patentable. However, this recommendation was ignored.

While debating the Patents (Amendment) Bill 2005 in Parliament, the Commerce Ministry promised to set up an expert group to examine this aspect. An Expert Technical Group was established in April, 2005 with the following terms of reference to re-examine:

❖ *Section 2*: *Definition*—Clause (ta)

"Pharmaceutical substance means any new entity involving one or more inventive steps."

❖ *Section 3*: *Inventions not Patentable*—Clause (j)

"Plants and animals in whole or any part thereof other than micro-organism but including seeds, varieties and species and essentially biological process for production or propagation of plants and animals."

We have recommended[10] that Patentable subject-matter should be as follows:

❖ *Section 5*: "Patents shall be available for pharmaceutical substances and any other inventions as defined in section 2, whether products or processes, in all fields of technology, provided they are new, involve an inventive step and are capable of industrial application".

The pharmaceutical substance from patentability point of view may be defined as follows:

"Pharmaceutical substance means new drug molecular entity with significant therapeutic advancement involving inventive steps".

It is relevant to point out that patent applications are filed only when the researchers reach the stage of 'new medical entity' or 'new chemical entity' which would satisfy the stipulated criteria for patentability viz. novelty, inventive step and capable of industrial application. The production and marketing of formulations in pharmaceuticals and agro-chemicals fields are the 'use' aspects of the patented product and should not be considered as part of protectable subject-matter.

**Definitions of Patent Terms**

There are certain important patent terms, which should have been carefully defined in the amended National Patents Act. It is important to do so to avoid representations or disputes due to casual interpretations in the patent laws.

The suggested[11] definitions are as follows:

(a) Invention may be defined as:

"Invention means a new basic product including machine, apparatus or other article or process including chemical process involving inventive step and capable of industrial application".

(b) New or novelty may be defined as follows:

"New or novel invention means any invention or technology which has not been anticipated by publication in any document or used in the country or elsewhere in the world before the date of filing of patent application with complete specification i.e.

the subject matter has not fallen in public domain or that it does not form part of the state of the art".

(c) Inventive step may be defined as follows:

"Inventive step means a feature of an invention that involves an important technical advance as compared to the existing knowledge which makes the invention not obvious to a person skilled in the art".

(d) Capable of industrial application may be defined as follows:

"Capable of industrial application in relation to an invention, means that the invention is capable of being made or used in any industry".

If above suggestions are accepted then there will be minor amendments to the existing provisions in the Act.

***Inventions not Patentable***

Exclusion of inventions from scope of patentablility is another important feature[12] of the national patents legislation. All frivolous claims such as formulation of known or new drugs should be specifically excluded. Article 27 (2) and 3 of TRIPS Agreement also stipulate inventions, which should be excluded from scope of patentability. Discoveries are not inventions and as such should not be patentable. Research tools particularly related to biotechnology inventions should also be specifically deleted, otherwise biotechnology research could be in jeopardy. It is estimated that over 70 per cent of the turnover of the drugs and pharmaceuticals in the coming future would be produced through biotechnology route and the use of these technologies being new will also qualify for process patent term of twenty years.

Further there is no decision as yet on the mandated review of Article 27(3)(b) of the TRIPS Agreement on patenting of 'micro-organisms and non-biological and micro-biological processes' which was initiated in WTO in 1999. As such there should be no need to make any provision on their patenting and also on any other life-form. Patenting of life form is a critical issue and should not be routinely implemented. Inventions which do not strictly meet the criteria of industrial application e.g. onco mouse, stem cell, partial gene fragments, PCR technique, machine based embedded bio-informatics software, genomic information and data bases should also be excluded. Thus exclusion of invention from scope of patentability is also quite important.

## III. Working of Patents

Working of patents in the country which grants exclusive rights on the relevant products is important to ensure easy availability and containing of prices of patented products through competitive environment. Article 27 of TRIPS Agreement has absolved the patent holders from the obligation of working their patents as 'patent rights are enjoyable *whether products are imported or locally produced*'. However, working of patent through the domestic enterprises must be ensured under the system of grant of compulsory licenses. Presently there are over 20,000 pharmaceutical manufacturers registered in the country and hundreds of enterprises are producing the same product and competing among themselves and meeting the country's requirements. This phenomenon cannot be equated to the working of patent through imports by the patent holder. Extensive involvement of domestic enterprises in the production and availability of patented products is absolutely necessary in India.

### *Compulsory Licensing System*

Compulsory licensing system is the back-bone of the patent laws. The question of constraints which would have emerged after the implementation of TRIPS had been a subject of serious concern and discussed in the TRIPS Council of WTO during the year 2001. The issue was further hotly debated in the Doha Ministerial Conference held in November 2001. The result was the Doha Declaration on TRIPS Agreement and Public Health, which clarified that sufficient flexibilities and freedom to determine the grounds upon which compulsory licences can be granted are available to member countries. It is now for the member countries to exercise their right and make suitable provisions in their national legislations. While enacting the Patents (Second Amendment) Act 2002, this aspect did not receive the due consideration even when the Indian delegation was the major player in the adoption of Declaration on TRIPS Agreement and Public

Health. There are nine possibilities of structuring the grant of compulsory licences arisitng from TRIPS Agreement and Paris Convention. These are:

(i) Voluntary Licence;
(ii) Authorisation for meeting the government requirements;
(iii) Compulsory Licence due to abuse of patent rights by the patent holder;
(iv) Compulsory Licence for reason of unsuccessful attempt by an enterprise to obtain voluntary licence directly from the patent holder;
(v) Compulsory Licence due to National Emergency;
(vi) Compulsory Licence due to circumstances of extreme urgency (Health Emergency, Environmental Emergency, etc);
(vii) Compulsory Licence in cases of public non-commercial use;
(viii) Compulsory Licence to remedy anti-competitive practices;
(ix) Second patent for an invention involving important technical advance of considerable economic significance over the existing patents.

If all the above possibilities are suitably provided in the national patent laws it would be possible to develop competitive environment about the availability of drugs and pharmaceuticals in the country. In the Patents (Second Amendment) Act 2002 certain possibilities have, neither been incorporated nor adequately provided. The framing of appropriate provisions on this subject is suggested hitherto.

***Voluntary Licence***

The Amended Patents Act 1970 does not provide for voluntary licensing system. This provision should be available in the Patents Act to meet the needs of the patentees who may not themselves like to promote their patented products in the markets due to certain limitations. They would, however be interested that their products are sold in the country and they realize royalty. The provisioning of voluntary licence in the Patents Act would help in meeting this need. To encourage this the Act could also provide for certain incentives for those patent holders who may like to avail of this provision.

### *Authorisation for Meeting Government Requirements*

Article 31 of TRIPS Agreement clearly provides for use of patented substances for meeting government requirements through government undertakings or other private enterprises authorized by the government to produce and supply. There will be no need to consult the patent holder while authorizing use of the patented product for meeting government requirements. Appropriate provision does exist in our amended Patents Act.

### *Compulsory Licence Due to Abuse of Patent Rights by the Patent Holder*

Article 8 of TRIPS Agreement and Article 5 of the Paris Convention deal with the abuse of patent rights by the patentees. These Articles provide that suitable steps could be taken by the government to remedy the abuse. The abuses arise when the patentee is charging high price for his patented product and that the relevant product is not available in sufficient quantities to meet the domestic demands either through imports or domestic production by the patentee. The grounds could be stipulated as follows:

(a) that the reasonable requirements of the public with respect to the patented invention have not been satisfied, or
(b) that the patented invention is not available at a reasonably affordable price, or
(c) that the patented invention is not being worked in the different regions of the country.

The terms and conditions for grant of compulsory licence for any of the reasons stated would be settled by the Controller of Patents in consultation with the patent holder. There is also no need of approaching the patent holder first by the intended enterprise to justify abuse. This stipulation in our law needs, to be suitably modified.

### *Compulsory Licence for Reason of Unsuccessful Attempt to Obtain Voluntary Licence*

Article 31 (a) and (b) of TRIPS Agreement provides for compulsory licence due to unsuccessful attempt by a domestic enterprise to obtain voluntary licence on commercial terms and conditions from the patent holder. The requirement is that the patent holder should be directly approached first by the interested enterprise offering commercial terms and conditions. If these efforts are unsuccessful then only he could approach the Controller of Patents for grant of compulsory licence after a reasonable period of waiting for response from the patent holder. The Controller shall grant the licence on such terms as he may deem desirable. This is an important provision for involving domestic enterprises and must be incorporated in the Patents Act.

The TRIPS Agreement in Article 31(b) deals with the contingencies of national emergency or other circumstances of extreme urgency or cases of Public non-commercial use together. The contingencies arise under different circumstances and should have been dealt with under different Articles in the Patents Act as suggested hitherto.

### *Compulsory Licence Due to National Emergency*

Under the circumstance of national emergency notified by the government the formulation of provision in the Patents Act could be as follows:

> "In the circumstance of notification of the national emergency by the government, the Controller of Patents may issue authorization of right at any time during the national emergency for working of any patent in the country on application by any enterprise interested to use the patent on such terms and conditions as the Controller of Patents may deem appropriate".

### *Compulsory Licence Due to Circumstances of Extreme Urgency (Health Emergency, Environment Emergency, etc.)*

Under circumstances of extreme urgency the contingency could arise because of health or environmental considerations. The formulation of provision in the Patents Act could be as follows:

> "In the circumstances of extreme urgency as notified by the Health authorities which may arise as the case may be including prevention or control of HIV/AIDS, malaria, tuberculosis or any other epidemic among human beings or animals and control of crisis relating to pollution of air or water or soil as notified by the concerned authorities in the Government. The urgency may

> be for the country as a whole or any region of the country. The Controller of Patents shall issue authorization of rights on relevant patented products to any enterprise interested on such terms and conditions as he may deem appropriate".

### *Compulsory Licence in Cases of Public Non-Commercial Use*

The circumstances of public non-commercial use are totally different from other contingencies. The formulation in the Patents Act could be as follows:

> "At any time after the expiration of three years from the date of sealing of a patent any enterprise may make an application to the Controller of Patents for grant of compulsory licence for using the patented substance to produce finished formulations for distribution/sale on public non-commercial basis i.e. on no profit no loss basis; that the concerned enterprise shall furnish a certificate to the Controller of Patents at the end of each year that the product has been used for public non-commercial purposes; that the term of the licence will be as may be requested by the applicant and may extend to the term as available to the patentee. The royalty payable to the patentee shall be decided by the Controller of Patents in consultation with the patentee".

### *Compulsory Licence to Remedy Anti-Competitive Practice*

Article 31 (k) of TRIPS provides for procedure for remedying anti-competitive practice. Where the situation of resorting to anti-competitive practice by the patentee has been determined after judicial or administrative process and that the need to remedy the practice has been notified by the Government in the official gazette, the Controller of Patents will issue compulsory licence to remedy the situation. The terms and conditions of the compulsory licence will be decided by the Controller of Patents.

### *Second Patent for an Invention Involving Important Technical Advance*

Where an important technical advance of a considerable economic significance over the first patent has been justified by an interested enterprise to the satisfaction of the Controller of Patents, compulsory licence may be granted to that enterprise in consultation with the first patent holder on such terms and conditions as may be settled by the Controller of Patents.

## IV. Transfer of Technology

Doha Declaration on TRIPS Agreement and Public Health in Para 5(a) stipulates that "the provision of the TRIPS Agreement shall be read in the light of the object and purpose of the agreement as expressed, in particular, in its objective and principles". The objectives and principles of TRIPS Agreement are stated in Articles 7 and 8. Article 7 provides for: "The protection and enforcement of intellectual property rights *should* contribute to the promotion of technological innovation and to the transfer and dissemination of technology". Article 8 provides for: "Appropriate measures may be needed to prevent the abuse of intellectual property rights by the right holders or the resort to practices which unreasonably restrain trade or adversely affect the international transfer of technology". The provisions contained in these two Articles cannot be regarded as "best endeavour" commitments as they form part of the "General Provisions and Basic Principles" just as Articles 3 and 4 relating to National Treatment and Most Favoured Nation Treatment are mandatorily enforced. Provisions of Articles 7 and 8 should also be equally mandatorily enforceable about transfer of technology.

Similarly, the reading of the stipulations in the Doha Declaration on TRIPS Agreement unambiguously provide that the patent legislation could have incorporated a provision for transfer and dissemination of technology and it should be one of the obligations for the patent holder to be fulfilled on issue of compulsory licences within a stipulated period. Similarly, there is also provision that appropriate measures could be taken if international transfer of technology is adversely affected for some reason or the other. If the patent holder does not cooperate in the transfer and dissemination of technology the issue of appropriate measures could be considered by the designated authority. Patents Act should be explicit on all aspects of transfer of technology.

## V. Parallel Imports

The need for parallel imports arises when availability of the patented product is not sufficient to meet the domestic demand. This type of contingency can arise similar to the situation as it arose in USA about the availability of 'Anthrax' drug, availability of HIV/AIDS drugs in African countries and the drugs needed for phenomena of SARS in China and Hong Kong, Dengue fever in Indian cities or drugs for bird flue etc. To meet such a contingency it is important that the Patent Act must provide for a clear cut provision so that no constraint is raised when parallel imports are authorized. Similarly, it should also be possible to import patented products if they are available in the foreign markets at prices lower than the prices at which the same are being marketed by the patent holders in the country. According to Doha Declaration on Public Health the member countries are free to establish their own regime for such exhaustion of right without challenge, subject to National Treatment and Most Favoured Nation Treatment under provisions of Articles 3 and 4 of the TRIPS Agreement. Accordingly, provision should be made in the Patents Act for parallel imports stating the circumstances under which parallel imports would be authorized. Such imports could be made from authorized sources producing patented product under compulsory licence or from the authorized traders of the patent holder or the licensee. Since, the imported price would include the element of royalty, no additional royalty should be payable on imports as stipulated under Section 90(3) of our Act.

## VI. Export of Patented Product

The compulsory licence granted should have clear right to produce the patented products predominantly for the domestic market and also some quantity for exports when required. The spirit of Article 31(f) of TRIPS Agreement on the use of word 'predominant' permits production mainly for domestic markets as well as for other markets. Even Article 8 of TRIPS Agreement also provides that appropriate measure could be provided to prevent resort to practices, which unreasonably restrain international trade. Exports are possible only when provision for parallel imports (under doctrine of exhaustion) is available in the importing countries in their national patent laws. For India it is important to have suitable provisions in its Patents Act for exports as domestic industry has strong potential to produce enough to meet both domestic demand as well as exports. Only the compulsory licence holder producing for domestic demand can meet the export orders. Similarly the importing countries should also have specific provision for parallel imports. The spirit of Para 6 of Doha Declaration on Public Health can be accomplished only when exporting and importing countries stipulate appropriate provisions in their Patent laws. The procedure as advocated by USA on the problem stated in Para 6 of the Doha Declaration has certain practical difficulties, which needs to be resolved.

## VII. Conclusions

International Human Right Law is becoming a focus issue in relation to implementation of TRIPS Agreement on many basic and fundamental rights of human being. These rights relate to right to health and right to food. In relation to monopolization factor under the TRIPS Agreement these issues are becoming crucial and are being debated worldwide. Patents to protect innovation could be supported, but the system should not be a device to restrict competition and allow creation of monopolies under any special circumstances. The originators of inventions should get their just reward by way of suitable royalties and there should be no grudge in providing the same. The doors should be opened for obligatory licensing involving the domestic enterprises in the production of patented drugs. The suggestions made in this Paper are within the frame-work of the TRIPS Agreement. Judicious and careful implementation of TRIPS was needed for its smooth application and balancing of rights and obligations of the patent holder in a manner conducive to social and economic welfare as stipulated in Article 7 of TRIPS Agreement.

## END NOTES

1. Article 1 of TRIPS Agreement, WTO, 1994.
2. Paragraph 1 of Declaration on the TRIPS Agreement and Public Health issued at Doha during fourth session of Ministerial Conference held on November 14, 2001.
3. Paragraph 4 of Declaration on the TRIPS Agreement and Public Health issued at Doha during fourth session of Ministerial Conference held on November 14, 2001.
4. Paragraph 5(b) of Declaration on the TRIPS Agreement and Public Health issued at Doha during fourth session of Ministerial Conference held on November 14, 2001.

5. Amended Patents Act. 1970.
6. Article 21 of the Constitution of India.
7. International Human Rights Laws issued by UNO.
8. Doha Declaration on TRIPS Agreement and Public Health, Paragraph 4.
9. Paragraph 6, Page 20 of the Report of Pharmaceutical Research and Development Committee, 1999.
10. Peoples' Commission Report (October 2004) on Review of Legislation Amending Patents Act, 1970, pp. 24-25.
11. Peoples' Commission Report (January 2003) on Patent Law for India, pp. 114-115.
12. Amended Patents Act, 1970 Section 3.

## REFERENCES

Constitution of India (1950). 'Article 21: Protection of Life and Personal Liberty'.

Government of India (GoI) (2005). 'The Amended Patents Act, 1970', Ministry of Law and Justice, Government of India, New Delhi.

Report Pharmaceutical Research and Development Committee (1999). 'Transforming India into a Knowledge Power', Paragraph 6, p. 20.

WTO (1994). 'Agreement on Trade-Related Aspects of Intellectual Property Rights', Article 1.

——— (2001). 'Doha Declaration on TRIPS Agreement and Public Health'.

# Chapter 4

# TRIPS and Public Health

C. NIRANJAN RAO*

Patents are supposed to be a means of encouraging investment in Research and Development (R&D) by private sector firms. There are inter-industry differences in how they are dependent on the patent system (Taylor and Silberston, 1973). Pharmaceutical industry is particularly dependent on the patent system because of two reasons. One that the technology is easy for reverse engineering and the other the entry barriers to the industry are low. This is the reason why most of the debate concerning patents has centered on pharmaceutical industry.

During the Uruguay Round negotiations the pharmaceutical firms from developed countries especially the US have been very vocal in claiming that 'lesser' level of patent protection in developing countries is distorting trade, enabling firms from these countries to copy the technology and that such actions are having an adverse impact on their ability to recoup the expenditure on R&D.

The discussions at the Uruguay Round also pertained to how a 'higher' level of patent protection will affect pharmaceutical prices and technological capability of developing countries. The TRIPS agreement stipulates that product patents have to be granted for pharmaceutical inventions, the duration of patent protection should be twenty years from the date of application and the compulsory licensing system should be narrowly defined.

In contrast the then Indian patent system under the Patents Act, 1970 granted only process patents for pharmaceutical inventions, had

* Fellow, Centre for Economic and Social Studies, Hyderabad.

a duration of seven years from the date of application or five years from date of grant whichever was shorter, and had a comprehensive 'licences of rights' system three years from date of grant. Among all these provisions the duration of seven years from the date of grant was the most important. The first effect it had was that the number of applications from foreign countries for pharmaceutical inventions came down in the immediate post-1972 period (Rao, 2002). Those foreign patents, which were taken out in India, expired within seven years of application. This enabled Indian pharmaceutical firms to copy the technology, use that technology in production, accumulate production experience and in some cases improve the process of production. By the time the patent expired in developed countries the Indian pharmaceutical firms were ready to export to these countries. The Indian pharmaceutical industry, which was virtually non-existent in 1970, came to occupy an important place in Indian economy by the late 1990s (Dhar and Rao, 2002). The most important indication of its success was ironically its excellent export performance (both bulk drugs and formulations) in the 1990s.

## Article 31 of the TRIPS Agreement

In the twentieth century compulsory licensing has been the public policy response to tackle problems relating to abuse of patent monopoly. Penrose (1951) illustrates how the compulsory working requirement has gradually transformed into compulsory licensing during the late nineteenth and early twentieth centuries. Paris convention has a provision for compulsory licensing to check abuse of patent monopoly, as an example of which non-working is cited.

During 1975-86 developing countries tried to revise the Paris convention to reflect their interests. One of the demands of the developing countries was to permit exclusive compulsory licences to make them attractive to prospective licensees. During these negotiations the nomenclature of compulsory licensing was changed to 'non-voluntary licenses'. By the time the TRIPS agreement was concluded in 1994 the article which resembled any thing like compulsory licensing was 'Article 31: Other Use Without Authorization of the Right Holder', making it sound positively criminal. For sake of economy of words we will continue to use the phrase 'compulsory licence'. We will exclude public non-commercial use, government use, revocation of patents, etc. from our analysis.

A reading of Article 31 conveys the impression that so called compulsory licences under this Article will be extremely rare. Because if there is any relationship between trade and patents, then compulsory licences create the most distortion to trade. One of the provisions, which make compulsory licences unattractive, is Article 31 (g), which says that the license has "to be terminated if and when the circumstances which led to it cease to exist and are unlikely to recur". This introduces such an uncertainty that no prospective licensee will come forward to ask for a compulsory licence.

Article 31 (c and k) seems to be most unambiguous in the case of anti-monopoly (or anti-trust) actions. This is very natural as the US was the largest user of compulsory licences through anti-trust decrees or settlements. The developing countries should explore ways of developing anti-trust institutions and legal structures to make effective use of compulsory licences.

Article 31 (along with clarifications in the Doha Declaration) seems to suggest three ways of granting compulsory licences. These are: (1) emergency situations, (2) non-emergency (for lack of a better word) situations[1], and (3) anti-trust cases. In the case of national emergency as in cases of public health crisis like epidemics or pandemics, granting of compulsory licences will be easier. In the cases of non-emergency situations there is a need to establish grounds, procedures to follow and terms and conditions to settle. It is in these situations that compulsory licensing should work properly. In our interpretation of Article 31 this is not easy.

While emphasizing that patent systems of member countries should not discriminate against any technology field [Article 27 (1)], Article 31 introduces discrimination against pharmaceutical inventions by indicating public health crises as national emergencies, and makes issue of compulsory licences much easier.[2] This is inevitable.

Many commentators have suggested that TRIPS has flexibility especially under Article 31[3]. Many of these commentators who on the one hand say that TRIPS agreement is a disaster for the developing countries go on to say that it offers flexibility.

While the emergency compulsory licensing provisions seem to be less controversial (especially after the Brazilian and South African experience) there is still some controversy on the non-emergency compulsory licensing provisions of Article 31 of the TRIPS agreement. One controversy is how to interpret Article 31 in the grant of compulsory licences in a non-emergency situation.

Chaudhuri (2002) argues that Article 31 does not lay grounds for the issue of compulsory licences but only prescribes some conditions, which need to be fulfilled. According to him the ground on which a compulsory licence can be issued should be that the patentee refused to give a licence on reasonable terms within a reasonable time. This according to Chaudhuri is subject to four conditions under Article 31, viz., (i) that it should be on individual merits [Article 31 (a)], (ii) that the licensee should have made efforts to get a licence [Article 31 (b)], (iii) that the licence will be terminated when the conditions are no longer there and unlikely to recur [Article 31 (g)], and (iv) that this is subject to judicial or other review [Article 31 (i)]. He says that the above ground can be made subject to all the conditions listed above. One interesting thing about Chaudhuri's proposal is that it makes a condition viz., Article 31 (b) (which is basically a procedural requirement) into a ground. Article 31 (b) says "such use may only be permitted if, prior to such use, the proposed user has made efforts to obtain authorization from the right holder on reasonable commercial terms and conditions and that such efforts have not been successful within a reasonable period of time".

Is this a correct interpretation of the TRIPS agreement? Chaudhuri's suggestion will make a compulsory licence under TRIPS more powerful than 'licences of right' system under the pre-amended act. Under 'licences of right' (all pharmaceutical inventions came under 'licences of right' automatically three years after grant) the patentee cannot refuse to grant a licence but can have a disagreement with the licensee on the amount of royalties. In such cases the Controller will settle the dispute. Even under 'licences of right' the licensee has to make an effort to contact the patentee. Under Chaudhuri's scheme of compulsory licensing, all that the licensee has to do is to approach the patentee and any disagreement between the patentee and the licensee will result in compulsory licensing.

## Brazil and South African Cases

The way Brazil and South Africa confronted the question of the conflict between the TRIPS Agreement and the public health crisis in the form of HIV/AIDS epidemic posed many challenges to the TRIPS agreement, hence the need for Doha Declaration. But it is interesting to see that neither Brazil nor South Africa issued any compulsory licence to produce any drug locally either under emergency or non-emergency provisions.

### *Brazil*

Brazil abolished product patents for pharmaceutical inventions in 1945 and process patents for pharmaceutical inventions in 1969. In 1988 while the Uruguay Round negotiations were going on, the US took unilateral sanctions under its Special 301 provisions saying that lack of patent protection for pharmaceutical inventions in Brazil is resulting in losses to its industry. Brazil chose not to opt for the ten-year transition period allowed under TRIPS, and brought in a product patent regime for pharmaceutical inventions in 1996.[4]

This law in its Article 68 (1) stipulates a local working requirement, which states that a patent shall be subject to compulsory licensing three years after the grant of the patent, if the subject-matter of the patent is not "worked" in the territory of Brazil. The other grounds on which compulsory licensing can be issued are: (1) abuse of patent rights; (2) abuses of economic power, and (3) failure of the patent holder to meet the requirement of the market. Apart from these non-emergency compulsory licensing provisions the Brazilian patent law in its Article 71 provides for compulsory licensing of drugs in cases of public health crisis.

During the year 2000 Brazil facing a public health crisis in the form of HIV/AIDS epidemic started a program called 'Free Distribution of AIDS Drugs for All Programme'. Under this programme 12 drugs under combination therapy were distributed. Seven of these drugs were not under patents in Brazil (but were under patents elsewhere) and were manufactured in Brazil. Five of the drugs were imported, two of which (Efivirenz of Roche and Nelfivanir of Merck) were under patents in Brazil. These two drugs accounted for 36 per cent of total cost of providing the combination therapy. The Brazilian government while conducting R&D in its public laboratories for the possible production of these two drugs, negotiated with these drug companies for reduction of prices for importing these drugs. The Brazilian government was successful in reducing the import prices of these drugs. The Brazilian government is cautious of increased prices of combination therapy in the future, once new drugs under patents become part of it. Interestingly in this case no compulsory licence was issued.

The US had taken Brazil to the Dispute Settlement Panel in 2001 for the provision of 'local working' being a ground for the issuance of compulsory licensing. This dispute was later withdrawn on the understanding between these two countries that the Brazilian government will notify the 'US-Brazil Consultative Mechanism' if the Brazilian government is contemplating using Article 68 and such use involves US firms. This amounts to back tracking by the Brazilian government. It would have been interesting to see how the WTO Dispute Settlement Mechanism would have interpreted Article 68 of Brazilian patent law.

### *South Africa*

The patent law in force is the Patents Act, 1978 (last amended in 1996). Its Section 56 provides for compulsory licensing and the grounds on which such a licence can be issued are, (1) the patent is being not worked in South Africa, (2) the market is not being met, and (3) the market is being met through importation and the price is excessive. This seems to cover the non-emergency compulsory licensing provisions. There does not seem to be any emergency compulsory licensing provisions in its patents law.[5]

'Medicines and Related Substances Act, 1965' (as amended in 1997) covers parallel imports. Section 15C of this Act authorizes the Minister of Health to prescribe conditions for the supply of more affordable medicines in conditions of need to protect the health of the public.[6] The relevant section is as follows:

"Measures to ensure supply of more affordable medicines

> Section 15C The Minister may prescribe conditions for the supply of more affordable medicines in certain circumstances so as to protect the health of the public, and in particular may—
>
> (a) Notwithstanding anything to the contrary contained in the Patents Act 1978 (Act No. 57 of 1978) determine that the rights with regard to any medicine under a patent granted in the Republic shall not extend to acts in respect of such medicines which has been put onto the market by the owner of the medicine or with his or her consent; and
>
> (b) Prescribe the conditions on which any medicine which is identical in composition, meets the same quality standard

> and is intended to have the same proprietary name as that of another medicine already registered in the Republic, but which is imported by a person other than the person who is the holder of the registration certificate of the medicine already and which originates from any site of manufacture of the original manufacturer as approved by the council in the prescribed manner, may be imported; …".

Section 15C (a) allows international exhaustion, which will enable South Africa to permit parallel imports. Section 15C (b) allows parallel imports to protect public health.

The Pharmaceutical Manufacturers Association of South Africa (which is an association of MNC drug manufacturers of South Africa) and thirty-nine pharmaceutical companies challenged this law in the Pretoria High Court in 1998. After a lot of negative publicity the pharmaceutical firms withdrew the case in April 2001. Hence an opportunity was lost on judicial pronouncement on the TRIPS compliance of the South African law.

**Doha Declaration**

The issue of "TRIPS and Public Health" was raised by Zimbabwe on behalf of the African Group in the TRIPS Council meeting of April 2001. At this meeting it was decided to hold a special discussion "on the interpretation and application of the relevant provisions of the TRIPS Agreement with a view to clarifying the flexibilities to which Members are entitled to and, in particular, to establish the relationship between intellectual property rights (IPRs) and access to medicines" (WTO, 2001a).

In the "Special Discussion on Intellectual Property and Access to Medicines" of the TRIPS Council held on June 20, 2001, the developing countries were asking for "clarifying the flexibilities to which Members are entitled to...". For example, India emphasised that if there is a clash between public health and the TRIPS Agreement, the issue of public health will be given preference (WTO, 2001b). This was followed by a discussion in the TRIPS Council during September 2001 and culminated in the Doha Declaration of November 2001.

The nature of discussions at the TRIPS Council are so structured that it is not easy to discuss substantive issues such as, TRIPS and public health.[7] In fact till April 2001 no discussion had taken place at the TRIPS Council on TRIPS and public health. It was at the April 2001 session of the TRIPS Council that Zimbabwe on behalf of the African Group raised the issue of TRIPS and public health and asked for a discussion at the TRIPS Council. India supported this request.

The TRIPS Council at its June 2001 session discussed what was called "Special Discussion on Intellectual Property and Access to Medicines". India was in the group of countries which circulated a note on 'TRIPS and Public Health' just prior to this meeting (WTO, 2001a). This note forcefully put forward the proposition that if there is a conflict between TRIPS agreement and public health goals, the latter should take precedence. It reiterated the primacy of Articles 7 and 8 of the TRIPS Agreement. The options it identifies in this context are parallel imports and compulsory licences.

In the 'Special Discussion', India's intervention also dealt with similar issues, especially that public health should have the priority. But one thing is striking both in India's as well as other countries' interventions in this discussion. While arguing that the TRIPS agreement offers 'flexibility'[8] these countries ask for elaborations and clarifications mostly from developed countries to make this 'flexibility' apparent! India specifically asked for clarifying that members could decide grounds for licences under Article 31.

In its intervention at the TRIPS Council meetings of September 2001 India made the very important point that the future Ministerial Declaration should concern TRIPS and public health in general and not confine itself to epidemics like HIV/AIDS only. After the Doha Declaration there was no substantive discussion on TRIPS and public health at the TRIPS Council except discussion on Para 6 of the Doha Declaration.

Apart from trying to clarify Article 31 'flexibilities' the need for the special discussion was prompted by the HIV/AIDS crises in Brazil, South Africa and other countries. These public health crises posed an early challenge to the TRIPS Agreement as a whole and more importantly to Article 31. The developed countries were not in a position to pose any challenge to the Doha Declaration.

The Doha Declaration has clarified many provisions of Article 31 of the TRIPS Agreement. According to us this is the case for emergency compulsory licensing provisions. The majority of the articles of Doha Declaration viz., 1, 2, 3, 4, 5 (a) and 5 (c) deal with emergency compulsory licensing provisions. Article 5 (b) seems to have general implications, while Article 5 (d) deals with parallel imports. According to us the two most important provisions of the Doha Declaration are:

> "4. We agree that the TRIPS Agreement does not and should not prevent Members from taking measures to protect public health. Accordingly, while reiterating our commitment to the TRIPS Agreement, we affirm that the Agreement can and should be interpreted and implemented in a manner supportive of WTO Members' right to protect public health and, in particular, to promote access to medicines for all".

This fulfils an important lacuna in the TRIPS Agreement and states that public health policies are paramount.

> "5. Accordingly and in the light of paragraph 4 above, while maintaining our commitments to the TRIPS Agreement, we recognize that these flexibilities include: (a) In applying the customary rules of interpretation of public international law, each provision of the TRIPS Agreement shall be read in the light of the object and purpose of the Agreement as expressed, in particular, in its objectives and principles".

Articles 7 and 8 are important provisions of the TRIPS Agreement, which many feared would remain as 'good intention' clauses. This Article makes it clear that other provisions have to be read in light of Articles 7 and 8.

**Amendments to the Patents Act, 1970**

Patents (Amendment) Act, 2002: In this sub-section we will discuss the provisions relating to compulsory licences in the Patents (Amendment) Act, 2002. The original Patents Act, 1970 had provisions for both compulsory licences and licences of right. The grounds under which compulsory licences could be issued were, unreasonable prices, the domestic market not being met, not being produced in India and export market not being met. Food, drug, medicine and chemical patents come under licenses of right at the end of three years from date of grant. The compulsory licensing and licences of right provisions of the Act were very comprehensive.

The procedure for the grant of compulsory licence was that the prospective licensee has to approach the patentee, and if he fails to get a licence, then approach the Controller for a compulsory licence. In India during 1972-2002 there were 28 applications for compulsory licence out of which two have been granted. While this figure is low, we have to be cautious of interpreting it as a failure of compulsory licensing provisions because of pharmaceutical inventions were not under compulsory licences. In the new TRIPS consistent patent regime we do not expect too many Indian firms to be applying for compulsory licences. Indian companies seem not to displease the MNCs, because they are technologically dependent on them.

As far as pharmaceutical inventions was concerned 'licences of right' was not important because of the duration of seven years from date of grant. By the time they were examined and granted it was three years, when 'licence of right' became operational three years after grant (which might be six years from date of grant) only one year was left in the life of the patent! But the experience of chemical inventions, which had duration of fourteen years and came under 'licences of right', was not very good. Only four applications came to the Controller General of Patents to adjudicate the royalties. In one case the Controller gave his ruling, in the case of two applications the patentee went to court and the cases were not decided till the patents expired and another application was withdrawn.

The revision of the Patents Act, 1970 to make it consistent with the TRIPS Agreement involved removal of the ground for compulsory licences, which says that the demand for the patented article is being met by imports. All the other grounds for issue of compulsory licences were retained.[9] The procedure remained the same. Another important departure was to make the compulsory licencing temporary, by incorporating the provision that "the circumstances which led to it cease to exist and are unlikely to recur" the compulsory licence can be withdrawn. The 'licence of right' provisions have been completely removed.

According to Chaudhuri (2002) India could have fulfilled all the obligations under TRIPS if it stipulated that refusal of the patentee to issue a voluntary licence on 'reasonable royalty' and within a 'reasonable period' could be made a (or the) ground for issuance of compulsory licences. This seems to be an ingenious but very strange argument because such a system would be stronger than 'licences of right' system, which was supposed to be violating the TRIPS

Agreement. The procedural requirement that the prospective licensee should approach the patentee first was made to make sure that the patentee could have issued a licence in which case he need not approach the Controller. Refusal to licence was never a ground for issuance of compulsory licences anywhere. This will rule out any case of a genuine reason for the patentee to refuse a licence. [10]

*Patents (Amendment) Act, 2005*: This amendment paved the way for acceptance of patent applications and grant of product patents for pharmaceutical, food and agricultural chemicals. This was done through the removal of Section 5(1) of the Patents Act, 1970 which provides for process patents in this field and also by removing the definition of food [Section 2(1) (g) of the earlier Act]. This will mean that from January 1, 2005 product patent applications will be accepted and examined.

**Possible Impact**

During the Uruguay Round discussions the developing countries argued that stronger IPRs will have adverse effect on the technological development of developing countries. The developed countries on the other hand argued that higher IPR protection would not only result in better technology transfer but also stimulate technological development in developing countries.

The developing countries did not want that TRIPS should be a part of GATT/WTO. But the TRIPS Agreement entailed them to give intellectual property protection at a very high level and also introduce many new intellectual property rights. Our own interpretation is that the TRIPS Agreement does not give much leeway for developing countries to counteract the monopoly elements in intellectual property rights.

Patents is not a fine tuned but a blunt instrument. It takes a long time to either feel the negative or positive effects. A lot of factors have to work themselves out before the impact is felt. We can discern two types of effects, one short-term and the other long-term. The short-term effect will be on prices and the long-term effect will be on technological capability.

Patents are means to give a temporary legal monopoly to inventors so that they can charge extra normal profits. These extra normal profits are supposed to encourage investments in R&D. Hence patents will result in increase in prices for those products, which are under patents. Patents without price increases are meaningless.

Technological development in developing countries will see the most negative impact of the strengthening of the patent system. The differences in patent protection across countries are because of the differences in perception of different countries on the role that the patent system plays in technological development. All the countries (even developed) started with a low level of patent protection and increased the patent protection as their technological capacity grew. There is no country in the world, which started with low technological development and achieved technological capability through a strong patent system. The impact of the TRIPS Agreement will be to restrict the maneuverability of these countries to have a weak patent system and gain technological capability. We can expect more technological dependence of developing countries on developed countries.

There are a few studies, which tried to estimate the effects of stronger patent protection on developing countries. The most notable of this set of studies is Deardorff (1992). Deardorff (1992) comes to the conclusion that the welfare of non-inventing countries will fall once they introduce a strong patent system. An important reason for the differences in developed and developing countries is the technology gap. One way of preserving this technology gap is the TRIPS Agreement (Dhar and Rao, 1996).

## Impact on Public Health

It is interesting to see the complaints of developing countries that stronger patent protection leads to a rise in prices. It means that they were not convinced by the developed country arguments that a higher level of patent protection world-wide will be beneficial to both developed and developing countries. The criticism of price increases shows that while the inventions will continue to take place in the developed countries, the burden of price increases fall on developing countries. The question is even if there is a short-term impact on prices, will the long-term impact be positive.

The most immediate impact of a stronger patent system will be on pharmaceutical prices. The Indian experience has been that in the pre-1972 period (when the Patents Act, 1911) was in force the prices of pharmaceutical products were high and technology transfer in this sector was low. This prompted the Indian Government to enact the Patents Act, 1970. In the post-1972 period when the original Patents Act, 1970 was in force the prices of pharmaceuticals were low. The advent of a product patent regime with a twenty-year patent term, will have a negative impact both on the prices of pharmaceuticals and the growth of the Indian pharmaceutical industry. Subramanian (1994) and Maskus and Eby-Konan (1994) have estimated the likely change in prices after the introduction of product patents in India. The assumptions of the model relate to the market structure before and after the introduction of product patents and the demand elasticity. Subramanian (1994) estimates the price rise to be a maximum of 67 per cent and a minimum of 5 per cent. Maskus and Eby-Konan (1994) estimate the rise in prices to be in the range of a maximum of 67 per cent and a minimum of -7 per cent.

The immediate impact of increases in prices of pharmaceuticals will be on public health. The seriousness of the impact will depend on the importance of patented products in total pharmaceutical production after about 10 years from 2005. We expect that if chemical based pharmaceuticals holds sway as at present and the number of new chemical entities is small the impact of the introduction of product patents will be comparatively less. If the importance of biotechnology based pharmaceuticals increases and all of them happen to be under patents then the impact on prices will be higher and consequently will have a negative impact on public health.

One interesting fact, which is often quoted while suggesting that product patent regime will not affect drug prices, is that many drugs on the 'WHO Essential Drugs' list are not under patents. While it could be looked at as a positive feature it could be looked at as negative feature too. This shows that drugs, which are 'essential drugs', are not the focus of R&D and hence no patented essential drugs are emerging.

Another issue, which arose out of the debate on public health and product patents, is the lack of R&D in diseases affecting the poor in developing countries. The reason why drugs important for developing country poor are not developed is that they are not profitable. The strength of the patent system does not make much difference in this context. But what is more important in India is that the Government and the public sector failed to develop drugs for the poor. It is ironic that the debate on TRIPS and public health is focusing on this issue. Some have suggested that a higher level of patent protection by developing countries will encourage firms from developed countries to focus their R&D efforts on the diseases prevalent there. But this may not come true because it is not the lack of patent protection that firms do not spend their R&D efforts on diseases prevalent in developing countries but the lack of purchasing power of the poor in developing countries. The other aspect overlooked by commentators is that it increases the technological dependence of developing countries on firms in developed countries.

When we are on the topic of public health we have to keep in mind the changes, which are occurring in the public health scenario in India, and not related to patents. These are:

1. decline of government funding for public health;
2. increasing privatisation of health care;
3. increasing emphasis on insurance which will be available to only persons within certain income groups;
4. withdrawal of public sector in pharmaceutical industry; and
5. withdrawal of drug control and its replacement by a supposedly more responsive system etc. All these measures are having a negative impact on public health scenario in India. For example the withdrawal of price control on TB is supposed to have increased its incidence in India.

**Impact on Pharmaceutical Industry**

The long-term impact of the strengthened patent system will be on technological capability of countries. This is not only long-term but very difficult to measure. Except a few instances of countries and in particular industries, technological development seems to be concentrated in developed countries. Developing countries are dependent on developed countries for their technology. The TRIPS Agreement may increase this technological gap between developed and developing countries rather than decrease it. While the TRIPS Agreement gives much more incentive for developed country firms to invest in R&D and recoup their expenditure through a strong worldwide patent system which includes all countries, it prevents developing country firms from copying and learning independently, develop technological capabilities and try to generate technology on their own. This avenue seems to have been closed for developing countries. They can now hope to get technology only through developed country firms.

The Patents Act, 1970 had a two-fold impact on the Indian pharmaceutical industry. First, the process patent regime adopted by

India encouraged reverse engineering and development of alternative processes for the products patented in other countries. Secondly, the duration of patent term being seven years from the date of application, coupled with the fact that the Patents Office took on an average three years to grant a patent, and these inventions coming under 'licences of right' three years after grant meant that the patentee did not enjoy patent monopoly for more than a year.

It was therefore quite clear that the Patents Act, 1970 was intended to restrict the rights of the patent holders especially in the area of pharmaceuticals. With a 'weak' patent regime the foreign inventors had very little incentive to take out patents in India. There was a decline in the number of foreign drug patents in India ever since Patents Act, 1970 became effective. This might have had a negative impact on technology transfer. But it also left the Indian firms free to produce alternative processes for the drugs, which were not under patent protection in India. In this manner Patents Act, 1970 became a useful tool in the hands of the Indian enterprises to make an entry into the previously uncharted territory. Those patents, which were taken out because of their short patent life, came on to public domain, which were free to be used by Indian pharmaceutical firms. While the Indian firms were not very successful in inventing new chemical entities, they were successful in applied inventions such as, new drug delivery systems. They have also developed and mastered processes for the production of known drugs.

The positive impact of the process patent regime was felt starting in late 1970s through the 1980s. The Indian pharmaceutical industry started producing bulk drugs, exporting formulations and later exporting bulk drugs to developed country markets. The Patents Act, 1970 enabled them to reverse engineer the products and be ready for exporting to the developed country markets when the patents expired there (Dhar and Rao, 2003).

In the chemical based pharmaceutical industry the impact will be much less because of the less number of inventions taking place. As the impact on the industry will depend on the number of inventions under patent protection, the less number under patents will mean less impact on the industry. The impact on generic pharmaceutical industry will not be immediate. The Indian firms can still continue to produce these products. But they will not be able to produce those inventions, which have been made after January 1, 1995 and for which product patents have been applied for in India. The time when these patented products will become a large part of the production of the pharmaceutical industry is way far into the future. The impact of the new product patent regime is not in terms of closure of Indian pharmaceutical firms, it is the much more subtler question of acquiring and developing technological capabilities. The industry witnessed consolidation in anticipation of product patent regime. The industry is long tailed, with a small number of large firms dominating the industry and a large number of small firms. This market structure is likely to change. The patent regime along with foreign investment policies reduced the dominance of foreign firms in this industry during late 1970s. This is likely to change and the importance of foreign firms in this industry will grow.

The Government of India has not taken any long-term measures to mitigate the negative impact of a stronger patent protection on pharmaceutical industry. While it would have been necessary to have a price control mechanism given the disparities in income in India, the Government is reducing the number of drugs, which are under price control. The strategy of the Government seems to be to give encouragement for R&D in this sector (GoI, 2000). But encouragement of R&D laudable in itself is a long-term goal and does not mitigate the short-term problems. The other factor is that the technological and financial capabilities of Indian firms in this sector are not enough to make any impact on new drug discovery. A re-focusing of the drug discovery programme to cater to the health problems of Indians may be an alternative.

The other industry where one can foresee a negative impact will be the biotechnology industry. Biotechnology has a vital role to play in two most important sectors viz., agriculture and pharmaceutical industry. The development of this industry will see a negative impact of the strengthening of the patent system. The development of this industry needs a weak patent system, which helps them in imitating and developing technological capabilities. But with the advent of a strong patent system this may not be possible. Without imitation the industry in developing countries may not develop.

Internationally the pharmaceutical industry has gone through two stages in the pre-molecular biology era. These can be broadly classified as "random drug discovery" (this approach entails screening of natural or chemically derived compounds for possible therapeutic activity) and "drugs by design" (advances in knowledge in pharmacology and cell biology etc. led to more sensitive screening mechanisms) (Henderson *et al.*, 1999). Henderson *et al.* (1999) while studying the impact of molecular biology on the pharmaceutical industries in US, Europe and Japan come to the conclusion that firms which have graduated from "random drug discovery", to "drugs by design" were found to move on to molecular biology than the firms which did not. The Indian pharmaceutical firms if they were into new drug invention at all seem to be in the "random drug discovery" mode. In such a case we cannot expect India to take advantage of molecular biology in medicine. By the time it gets ready the field may be fenced by a ring of patents. The other major problem area seems to be the lack of any important medical biotechnology industry in India. The industry is not taking any initiatives and the projects of the Government do not seem to achieve its objectives. The introduction of biotechnology patents will hinder in the acquisition of technological capability in this area through imitation.

On the one hand while stronger protection may facilitate technology transfer to occur, it may also result in technology transfer not occurring. While the patentee will be in a stronger position to determine whether technology transfer occurs by contractual licences, the developing countries do not have any mechanisms (like compulsory licensing) to see to it that technology transfer occurs. Even if any technology transfer occurs the outflow of resources on account of technology transfer will be considerable. World Bank (2001) estimates that technology related payments on the implementation of TRIPS for developing countries could be $ 20 billion. With the TRIPS Agreement strengthening intellectual property protection it would have been necessary to agree upon something similar to "Code of Conduct on Technology Transfer" [discussed in United Nations Conference on Trade and Development (UNCTAD) in the 1980s] to reduce the negative impact.

The Indian generic companies can continue to produce off-patent drugs in the foreseeable future. They will be affected only when the importance of patented drugs becomes substantial in overall drug production. But at any given time there will be off-patent drugs. The Indian drug firms should continue their practice of doing R&D and reverse engineering on new drug discoveries. If they can come up with better processes for their production, they can apply for a patent and either take licence from the product patentee or ask for compulsory licence as dependent patent. They should also continue to emphasise on good manufacturing practices and make process improvement all the time. They should be ready when the patent expires in the host countries, with the export of generic equivalent. They should use Bolar provisions [Section 107A (b) of the Patents Act, 1970] to experiment on bio-equivalence and get market approval.

## END NOTES

1. While in India under the 2002 amendment to the Patents Act, 1970 non-emergency compulsory licenses are granted under Section 84 emergency compulsory licenses are issued under Section 92. Similarly in Brazil non-emergency compulsory licenses are issued under Section 68 and emergency compulsory licenses are issued under Section 71.
2. Article 8 Principles states "Members may, in formulating or amending their laws and regulations, adopt measures necessary to protect public health and nutrition".
3. "..the in-built flexibility found in TRIPS", Cullet (2002); "flexibility is available within its framework of the TRIPS Agreement" Lalitha (2002); "..to take advantage of the possible safeguards that have been incorporated into the TRIPS Agreement", Roychaudhury and Gurbani (2002) and "TRIPS has inbuilt flexibilities available to developing countries", Savirimuthu (2003).
4. Industrial Property Law (Law No. 9279 of 14 May 1996), effective May 1997.
5. Contrary to the popular perception the South African case is not confined to or related exclusively to HIV/AIDS epidemic.
6. According to the then Foreign Minister of South Africa this measure was not only to respond to emergencies relating to public health but to make all medicines affordable (South Bulletin, March 20, 2001). South Africa refused to declare national emergency regarding AIDS epidemic.
7. In fact in a Communication dated October 6, 2000 India called for interpreting the TRIPS Agreement giving due weight to Articles 7 and 8 [WTO (2000)].
8. 'We are informed that there is some flexibility inherent in the TRIPS Agreement on this particular issue. Whether there is adequate flexibility or not will become apparent only when we clarify the existing flexibility to the fullest possible extent, so that Members are clear what they can do to protect public health.' India [WTO (2001b) p. 23].
9. The ground under the original Patents Act, 1979 were: (1) the price is high; (2) the domestic market is being not met; (3) the export market is not being met; (4) the patented article is not being manufactured in India; and (5) the working of the patent in India is being hindered by its importation among others.

10. Chaudhuri, (2002). Shows how the system of compulsory licensing and licenses of right under the original Patents Act, 1970 worked. But he overemphasizes the procedural hurdles, pp. 3358-3359.

## REFERENCES


Chaudhuri, S. (2002). 'TRIPS Agreement and Amendment of Patents Act in India', *Economic and Political Weekly*, 37(32): 3354-3360.

———— (2005). *The WTO and India's Pharmaceutical Industry: Patent Protection, TRIPS and Developing Countries*. New Delhi: Oxford University Press.

Chaudhury, R.R. and N.K. Gurbani (2002). 'The TRIPS Agreement: Implications for Access to Drugs in Developing Countries', *Journal of Health Management*, 4(1): 11-18.

Cullet, P. (2002). 'Amended Patents Act and Access to Medicines after Doha', *Economic and Political Weekly*, 37(24): 2278-2280.

Deardorff, A.V. (1992). 'Welfare Effects of Global Patent Protection', *Economica*, 59(233): 35-51.

Dhar, B. and C.N. Rao. (1996). 'Trade Relatedness of Intellectual Property Rights: Finding the Real Connections', *Science Communication: An Interdisciplinary Social Science Journal*, 17(3): 304-325.

——— (2002). '*Transfer of Technology for Successful Integration in the Global Economy: A Case Study of Pharmaceutical Industry in India*', United Nations Conference on Trade and Development, New York, (UNCTAD/ITE/IPC/Misc.22).

——— (2003). 'A Case Study of the Pharmaceutical Industry in India', in United Nations Conference on Trade and Development (UNCTAD), *Transfer of Technology for Successful Integration into the Global Economy*, United Nations, New York, (pp.87-140), (UNCTAD/ITE/IPC/2003/6).

Government of India (GoI). 1970. 'The Patents Act, 1970', Government of India, New Delhi.

————(2000). '*Transforming India into a Knowledge Power: Report of the Pharmaceutical Research and Development Committee*', Ministry of Chemicals and Fertilizers, Department of Chemicals and Petrochemicals, New Delhi.

Henderson. R, L. Orsenigo and G.P. Pisano (1999). 'The Pharmaceutical Industry and the Revolution in Molecular Biology: Interaction Among Scientific, Institutional, and Organizational Change', in D.C. Mowery and R.R. Nelson (eds.), *Sources of Industrial Leadership: Studies of Seven Industries*, pp.267-311. Cambridge: Cambridge University Press.

Lalitha, N. (2002). 'Indian Pharmaceutical Industry in the WTO Regime: A SWOT Analysis', *Economic and Political Weekly*, 37(34): 3542-3555.

Maskus, K.E. and D. Eby-Konan. 1994. 'Trade-Related Intellectual Property

Rights: Issues and Exploratory Results' in A.V. Deardorff and R.M. Stern (eds.), *Analytical and Negotiating Issues in the Global Trading System*, pp. 401-446. Ann Arbor, MI: University of Michigan Press.

Penrose, E.T. (1951). 'The Economics of the International Patent System', Baltimore, MD: Johns Hopkins Press.

Rao, C.N. (2002). '*Patents and Technological Progress in Developing Countries: A Case Study of India*', Ph.D. Thesis, New Delhi: Jawaharlal Nehru University.

Savirimuthu, J. (2003). 'The Corporate Pharmaceutical Model and the Legacy of Doha: Whither a Global Consensus on Public Health Governance?', *South Asia Economic Journal*, 4(1): 73-98.

Subramanian, A. (1994). 'Putting Some Numbers on the TRIPS Pharmaceutical Debate', *International Journal of Technology Management*, 10(2-3): 252-268.

Taylor, C.T. and Z.A. Silberston (1973). *The Economic Impact of the Patent System: A Study of the British Experience*. Cambridge: Cambridge University Press.

World Bank (2001). *Global Economic Prospects*, Washington DC: World Bank.

WTO (2000). *Clarifying TRIPS: A Confidence Building Measure*, Communication from India, WTO, Geneva, (IP/C/W/214).

——— (2001a). *TRIPS and Public Health*, Submission by the African Group, Barbados, Bolivia, Brazil, Cuba, Dominican Republic, Ecuador, Honduras, India, Indonesia, Jamaica, Pakistan, Paraguay, Philippines, Peru, Sri Lanka, Thailand and Venezuela, WTO, Geneva, (IP/C/W/296).

——— (2001b). *Special Discussion on Intellectual Property and Access to Medicines*, WTO, Geneva, (IP/C/M/31).

——— (2001c). *Minutes of Meeting Held in the Centre William Rappard on 19 and 20 September 2001*, WTO, Geneva, (IP/C/M/33).

——— (2001d). Declaration on the TRIPS Agreement and Public Health, WTO, Geneva, (WT/MIN(01)/DEC/2).

*Chapter 5*

# Traditional Knowledge and Intellectual Property Rights

NIRMAL SENGUPTA*

## The Background

According to the World Bank[1], Traditional Knowledge (hereafter TK) is an underutilized resource in the development process. Its dissemination can help to reduce poverty. At an estimate, two-thirds of the world's population could not survive without foods provided through indigenous knowledge of plants, animals, insects, microbes and farming systems (UNDP, 1994). According to the World Health Organization (WHO), up to 80 per cent of the world's population depends on traditional medicine for its primary health needs[2]. In eleven States of India a half or more of surface irrigation come from traditional sources (Sengupta, 1993). The Chinese Government has used extensively, traditional technology, knowledge, know-how and practices for combating desertification and for improvement of ecosystems and the environment[3]. These are just some examples[4]. Traditional knowledge, innovations and creativity, including "folklore", have received increasing attention in numerous policy areas, ranging from food and agriculture, the environment, health, human rights, and cultural policy, to trade and economic development. International agencies that have already adopted one or the other programmes for TK are: UNEP, CBD, UN Convention to Combat Desertification, UNESCO and WIPO, FAO, The UN Working Group

* Professor, Indira Gandhi Institute of Development Research (IGIDR), Mumbai.

for Indigenous Affairs, The World Bank, ILO, WHO, UNCTAD, WTO, and UNDP.

Commercial importance of TK is immense and fast increasing. Global market for herbal products, which include medicines, health supplements, herbal beauty and toiletry products, is estimated at around US $ 62 billion, and has been growing at a rate of 10 per cent to 15 per cent per annum. The market for herbal medicine alone is estimated at around US $ 5 billion and is expected to reach US$ 16 billion by 2005. The medicinal plants related trade in India alone is approximately Rs. 5.5 billion (Exim Bank, 2003). The current size of Ayurvedic drugs in global herbal market is about Rs.50,000 crores (US$ 10 billion) (Bhaumik, 2001). The market is rapidly increasing. In 1978, the WHO recognised the use of Traditional Medicine for use in Primary Health Centres. In wealthy countries, growing numbers of patients rely on alternative medicine for preventive or palliative care. Expenditure on alternative medicines in U.S.A. reached $ 13.7 billion in 1994. Over 300 companies worldwide have programmes of screening and drug development on traditional systems of medicine. With forty per cent of the pharmaceutical patents due to expire by 2006 and with the advent of biotechnology and pharmacogenomics, biotech firms are trying to discover and develop new active ingredients from traditional medicine (Mathur, 2003).

In certain countries with strong IPR regimes and strong presence of indigenous communities, the uses of TK in different fields were protected for quite some time. For over thirty years the copyright law of Australia extends community rights of the indigenous Australians in artistic creations. In the U.S., Indian Arts and Crafts Act, 1935, adopted criminal penalties for selling goods with misrepresentations—i.e. when they misled people into believing that they were (American) Indian produced. Essentially, TK protection in these cases is a domestic issue. Others include (WIPO, 2002) the use of copyright protection in Canada to protect tradition-based creations including masks, totem poles and sound recordings of Aboriginal artists; the use of industrial designs to protect the external appearance of articles such as head dresses and carpets in Kazakhstan and the use of geographical indications to protect traditional products such as liquors, sauces and teas in Venezuela and Vietnam. The matter is not confined to traditional design and folklore (current term "expressions of culture"). In 1998, the San people of South Africa threatened to move against the Council for Scientific and Industrial Research of the country for patenting a traditional knowledge of theirs, the appetite-suppressing element of *Hoodia cactus*. The total value of the aboriginal art market in Australia is around A$ 200 million per year. Half of the sales are related to the tourism market and of the total aboriginal art trade, A$ 50 million is estimated to reach the aboriginal producers directly. In an article we exposed the despicable situation we have in India where designs created by our craft persons and artisans are imitated without any second thought (Bhagirathy and Sengupta, 2003). In absence of any protective mechanism the creators are deprived of benefits actually brought out by their creations.

Patent laws require innovators to establish novelty of their innovations to qualify for a patent. However, there have been instances, where patents have been granted for TK already in the public domain or where, knowledge of the communities was used without any provision for sharing of benefits from commercialisation. Misuse of IP in general, is not confined to domestic arena. In case of TK the international dimension is far greater. I will not repeat here the widely discussed cases of biopiracy. This background has necessitated international protection. International frameworks for recognition and protection of traditional knowledge include:

- 1981: WIPO and UNESCO adopted a model law on folklore.
- 1989: The concept of Farmers' Rights was introduced by the FAO into its International Undertaking on Plant Genetic Resources.
- 1992: Convention on Biological Diversity (CBD) highlighted the need to promote and preserve traditional knowledge.[5]
- 2001: WTO in its Ministerial Conference at Doha in 2001, mandated[6] that as part of the agenda of the TRIPS Agreement, in the course of the review of Article 27.3 (b)[7], the relationship between the TRIPS Agreement and the CBD and protection of traditional knowledge (TK) and folklore is examined.

As I have indicated already, TK is important for several other reasons, like meeting basic needs, biodiversity conservation or supporting expressions of culture (folklore), although the biopiracy and drug discovery aspect of TK is more well-known. A satisfactory IPR system has to meet the requirements of at least, some of these dimensions than being single-mindedly responding to the requirements of the pharmaceutical sector. In 2000, the WIPO established an Intergovernmental Committee on Intellectual Property Rights to deal together (a) Genetic Resources, (b) Traditional Knowledge, and (c) Folklore.

The CBD Article 8(j) refers to *knowledge, innovations and practices of indigenous and local communities embodying traditional lifestyles*[8]. By far this is the most precise description, but too long. Shorter terms that developed as offshoots of the CBD are of two types. One stream picks up the term 'traditional' and uses expressions as: *traditional knowledge, innovations and practices*[9] *traditional knowledge, innovations and creativity*[10], *biodiversity and traditional knowledge*[11] etc. Another stream picks up the term 'indigenous' and uses *indigenous knowledge*[12, 13]. This is only about the term. A legal definition of the term/terms has not been agreed as yet.

## Available Options and the State of Debate

As yet, the CBD is the only international binding instrument that explicitly refers to the protection of TK. The famous Article 8(j) lay down:

- due attitude to TK relevant for the conservation and sustainable use of biological diversity,
- principles governing access to genetic resources and the associated TK, and
- sharing of benefits arising from such access.

The CBD did not prohibit further use of TK and genetic resources. It acted as a facilitator by identifying acceptable conditions. CBD stipulated that access to genetic resources can occur if based on *mutually agreed terms* and with *prior informed consent* (PIC). The Article 8(j) is "subject to national legislation". But CBD did not specify the means by which national governments would draw up national legislations to reflect these intents. Several different means have been suggested later and tried, IPR being only one of them. Also, it is noted that national legislations are not enough to contain transboundary violations of the intent. Complementary international agreements are required. Unfortunately, even after 10 years of intense debate no agreement has yet been reached.

"The institutional arrangements discussed in relation to allocation and production of knowledge and information goods are similar to solutions to the problem of allocation of public goods" (Bhagirathy, 2003). "In the case of public goods there are three kinds of solutions—subsidies, governmental production and regulated monopoly. Similarly, in relation to knowledge commodities, there are three kinds of institutional arrangements, often classified as prizes, research contracts (including government procurement) and intellectual property rights. Each of these systems has particular advantages and shortcomings as incentives for R&D and specific conditions under which one may be chosen." Bhagirathy (2003) listed several proposed and implemented institutional arrangements for intellectual property protection of TK:

1. Making use of the existing IPR system to protect and promote TK.
2. Developing *sui generis* systems[14] for protection of biodiversity and associated traditional knowledge.
3. Resource rights of indigenous people[15].
4. Benefits sharing contracts between pharmaceutical companies and TK holders.
5. Prizes and Awards.

Whether IPR is the best or even a desirable system for protection and promotion of TK is still under debate. In this paper, I will confine discussions to IPR. Patent system is only one of the IPR systems suggested for protection of TK. Others are:

- use of copyright,
- utility model protection or petty patents,
- plant variety legislation,
- use of geographical indications,
- trade secrets,
- unfair competition rules, and
- the international protection accorded to the Red Cross and Red Crescent symbols.

In assigning property rights—IPR in this case—to TK five main issues must be answered (Sampath, 2003):

(i) Subject-matter of IPR i.e. information categories that could be called traditional knowledge.
(ii) Identification of beneficiaries.
(iii) Contribution to biodiversity conservation and appropriate institutional mechanism for that
(iv) Specific attributes of any chosen system of IPR like duration, enforcement mechanism etc.
(v) Implementation mechanism.

On each of these issues there are numerous suggestions and some experiences. As yet, there is no clear consensus on any one issue. But this is unavoidable till we have enough applications to judge their merits. National legislations are made on the basis of intense debate but without the aid of much functional data. In the next section I will discuss IPR efforts of Indian legislations.

Efforts to arrive at International agreements are going on at three levels: CBD, WIPO and WTO. At the Sixth Meeting (May, 2002), the Conference of the Parties of CBD adopted a Guideline for Access and Benefit Sharing[16]. Discussions at WIPO's Intergovernmental Committee on Intellectual Property and Genetic Resources, Traditional Knowledge and Folklore focused mainly on two possible approaches: (a) asking patent applicants to disclose the origin of genetic resources and/or associated TK in related patent applications[17], (b) to improve the availability of public domain traditional knowledge to patent examiners to prevent improper awards. Two possible ways have been suggested for the latter: (i) to provide an inventory of publications that regularly document TK, and (ii) to compile databases of public domain traditional knowledge like the Traditional Knowledge Digital Library (TKDL) of India. In order to facilitate the use of the database the WIPO has extended the International Patent Classification Union system to include a Traditional Knowledge Resource Classification (TKRC) consisting of several additional categories and keywords.

At the WTO several countries[18] including India jointly submitted a paper to the Council for TRIPS in June 2002 asking amendment of TRIPS Agreement along the Bonn Guidelines, emphasizing that the onus of (a) disclosure of source of origin, (b) evidence of PIC, and (c) fair and equitable benefit sharing should be placed on the patent applicant. Proposals relating to compulsory disclosure of genetic resources and associated TK in patent applications have weak, medium and strong forms (Dutfield, 2002). The weak form is that such disclosure would be encouraged or even expected but not required and its omission would not disqualify the patent from being granted. The medium form is that disclosure of origin would be mandatory. The strong form goes beyond disclosure in the patent specification and requires that patent applicants submit official documentation from provider countries proving that genetic resources and associated TK were acquired through PIC and benefit sharing arrangements. Applications that are unaccompanied would automatically be returned to the applicants for re-submission with the relevant documentation.

The European Union Directive on the Legal Protection of Biotechnological Inventions (1998) adopted the weak version. The International Chamber of Commerce too supports this version. A Colombian proposal at the meetings of Patent Law Treaty of WIPO, for linking patent filing with access and benefit sharing regulations was supported by developing countries like India but opposed by the United States, the European Community, Japan and Korea. Dutfield argues that the way countries like Japan and Europe define and assess novelty-defeating prior art suggests that many so-called biopiracy cases could not be legally challenged despite the promising European legal interpretations. The TK databases will make little difference. He argues that action should be addressed at improving patent quality in the developed countries. Most controversial patents are granted mainly in the United States and to a lesser extent in Europe and Japan.

Some business associations like the European Chemical Industry Council (CEFIC), the International Chamber of Commerce and the Biotechnology Industry Organization have adopted liberal stand and issued constructive public statements. Otherwise, industry tends to be overly defensive and makes few if any constructive proposals of its own. In sum, industry's contribution to the debate has mainly been limited to restating its support for the CBD, pointing out what it considers to be the unfeasibility of proposals that others have made, and warning against over-regulation in national and regional access regimes[19] (Dutfield, 2002).

Currently, higher level of protection is given to wines and spirits under Articles 22 and 23 of the TRIPS Agreement relating to geographical indications. This is to be extended to other products as well and was a subject to be discussed at Cancun. Several countries called upon the TRIPS council to start informal consultations on this issue identifying target date, or various stages of the negotiations, just as for agriculture and services Agreements. But Argentina, Australia, Brazil, Canada, Chile, Mexico, New Zealand, and the US opposed it. They contested that unlike in agriculture and services, there is no mandate to negotiate expanded coverage of multilateral notification and registration system for geographical indications.

**TK and IPR in India**

In a short period India has introduced or amended several Acts that address TK issues: Geographical Indications of Goods (Registration & Protection) Act (1999), Protection of Plant Varieties and Farmers Rights Act (2001), Amendment of Patents Act, 1970 (2002) and Biological Diversity Act (2002). Besides, it has initiated a massive work on TKDL for facilitating global patent examination. Documentation of genetic resources and traditional knowledge by Government organizations and NGOs is another important aspect of Indian IPR scenario. This activity has assumed gigantic proportion. We will briefly discuss the merits and limitations of these steps.

In the Patents (Second Amendment) Act (2002) a significant new item is added to the list of things that are not inventions within the meaning of the Act: "an invention which, in effect, is traditional knowledge or which is an aggregation or duplication of known properties of traditionally known component or components." Section 10 (contents of specification) of the Amended Act provides that the applicant must disclose the source and geographical origin of any biological material deposited in lieu of a description. Also Section 25 (opposition to grant of patent) as amended allows for opposition to be filed on the ground that "the complete specification does not disclose or wrongly mentions the source or geographical origin of biological material used for the invention". Apart from this ground, patents may be revoked also on the ground "that the invention so far as claimed in any claim of the complete specification was anticipated having regard to the knowledge, oral or otherwise, available within any local or indigenous community in India or elsewhere." In his scale discussed earlier, Dutfield (2003) classifies Indian disclosure clause as of medium form.

On the negative side, the amended Act does not specify that "increment to traditional knowledge" is eligible for patents. This may divert patent applications outside the country. It has been suggested (Vasudeva, 2003) that this is one of the reasons why Central Institute of Medicinal and Aromatic Plants and Go-Vigyan Anusandhan Kendra have jointly obtained a US patent on a drug composition that has cow's urine distillate. The therapeutic properties of cow urine are well known in rural India, and therefore, is not patentable here. In contrast, as much as 86.6 per cent of the OTC drugs approved by the Chinese government in June 2001, was processed Chinese medicine[20]. Another weakness is that the amended Act prevents biopiracy but does not talk of benefit sharing, although there is a safeguard elsewhere. The Bio diversity Act addresses issues of access and benefit sharing and clearance from the Biodiversity Authority has been made necessary, where applicable, for patent application. But one has to wait to find whether this mechanism will actually be applied. India did not adopt cost-effective soft-forms like utility-model protection or petty patent systems which might have helped SMEs.

The Plant Varieties and Farmers' Rights Act allows four types of varieties to be registered reflecting the interests of actors: New Variety, Extant Variety, Essentially Derived Variety and Farmers Variety. The provision for protecting *farmers variety* and *extant varieties* in Indian law has no parallel. It was an ingenious use of the *sui-generis* clause in TRIPs. The third draft (1997) of a Bill originally drafted in 1993/94 added the words Farmers Rights in the title. To allow the farmers to register varieties, the definition of extant variety found in the previous drafts was expanded. Farmers Variety is a variety which has been traditionally cultivated and evolved by the farmers in their fields; or is a wild relative or land race of a variety about which the farmers possess the common knowledge. The legislation also establishes various other provisions for protecting traditional varieties such as benefit sharing and a National Gene Fund. Unquestionably, the Act recognises the role of farmers as cultivators and conservers and the contribution of traditional, rural and tribal communities to the country's agrobiodiversity. The ability of farmers to actually register their varieties would depend on the definition of distinctness, uniformity and stability (DUS) that would be adopted in practice.

The Biodiversity Act provides for protection of knowledge of local people relating to biodiversity through measures such as registration of such knowledge and development of a *sui-generis* system. Anybody seeking any kind of intellectual property right on a research based upon biological resources or knowledge obtained from India would need to obtain prior approval of the National Biodiversity Authority (NBA). The NBA may also take measures to oppose the grant of IPRs in any country outside India on any biological resource obtained from India or knowledge associated with such biological resource. However, this Act adopted a *limited sui-generis* system[21] for protection of traditional knowledge. It focuses its attention on the regulation of access by foreigners but does not have a strong framework for regulating access within the country. Also, the application of the principle of geographical indicator in the Biodiversity Act would prevent the species from being taken out of the country but would not prevent (traditional) knowledge being taken out. Hence its coverage of TK is also partial.

The Plant Varieties Protection Authority and National Biodiversity Authority, set up under the corresponding Acts, will approve and determine the amount of benefit sharing by taking into consideration several criteria. The full effect of these is yet to be experienced. Ramanna (2003) noted an area of ensuing complexity. In the past few years the process of documenting genetic resources and traditional knowledge already in public domain, has taken on an enormous momentum. Many of these documents enable parties to apply for registration under the Plant Variety and Farmers Rights Act with claims for benefit sharing. Unfortunately these registers are being developed in an ad hoc manner, and there is a great deal of duplication of efforts and overlap not only in terms of resources but also by regions covered. This may result in multiple ownership claims between different types of protection systems (e.g. patents, plant breeders rights, farmers varieties, etc.) as well as between different claimants of rights over the same product (Ramanna, 2003). Organizations with best intentions may make claims of rights and benefits on IP on behalf of different communities and agencies they identified as the holders of a particular TK. This is the kind of undesirable consequence that IPR regimes bring about. Organizations like *Farm Rights Information System* (FRIS) maintained by the M.S. Swaminathan Foundation or *HoneyBee data base* established by SRISTI were formed with the intent of preventing possible future patents based on the innovations using TK. Towards this end they have been systematically disclosing the innovations compiled in their TK-databases.

In the field of medicinal plants the Govenment of India has set up an electronic database called Traditional Knowledge Digital

Library (TKDL), which can be accessed from all over the world. India is a keen proponent of such databases all over the world and moved this proposal in WIPO. No country involved in the WIPO IGC has opposed the idea in principle, although there have been some differences of opinion on whether TK databases should be made publicly available only or provided for the exclusive use of patent offices. The lack of agreement "reflects a fundamentally different view among the delegates about whose interests they are advancing. In countries like India, the predominant view is that the nation itself is the "victim" of biopiracy. For Africa, the perception seems to be that the continent as a whole is prey to the biopirates. But in the Americas, Australia and New Zealand, the victims are seen generally as indigenous peoples who usually—though not always—represent minority populations" (Dutfield, 2002).

But would TK databases actually be useful? They could certainly stop patents like the turmeric one from being granted. It is by no means certain that they would have prevented the many other controversial patents (Dutfield, 2003).

As early as 1999 India enacted the Geographical Indications Act. This IPR provision may become a real safeguard for products like Basmati rice. But global protection can be obtained only through a multilateral system of notification and registration in WTO, recognising Basmati as a product based on geographical origins eligible for Geographical Appellations clause of the TRIPS Agreement. Until then each single case of IPR theft has to be contested by India. Although India has won a case, there are several others. There is also a move, primarily in US but also by some rice growers of the EC, to declare that Basmati is a generic name not a geographical indication. Two issues have to be faced in the WTO when the claim of Basmati as a GI is raised. First, India and Pakistan have to be joint owners of the right for which sufficient ground has to be prepared. Also, they may be asked to explain why they did not take action against the gradual adoption of generic status of Basmati over the last couple of decades. India did not lodge a formal protest when the US Federal Trade Commission formally declared Basmati generic. India is waiting to claim GI status for several products apart from Basmati.

Copyright Act 1957 as amended later, has implications for TK. However, very little is realised as yet because of lack of awareness (Bhagirathy and Sengupta, 2003).

## Beyond IPR

The burgeoning market of traditional medicine is mostly, out of the purview of IPR regime. Currently, this industry gets its raw material from traders who show little concern for biodiversity protection and access and benefit sharing with the local communities. Wild and destructive collections are rampant. Recently, the Department of Indigenous Systems of Medicine of the Health Ministry has suggested regulatory measures to prevent wanton biopiracy of herbs from the wild. These include captive cultivation by the user industry, community participation in collection, marketing and profit sharing of the plants and their parts (Exim Bank, 2003). Another suggestion pending with the Government was the setting up of a Medicinal Plants Conservation Board funded by external agencies and the industry to finance family-level enterprises in farming, collection and scientific storage.

Natural product research is one of several competing approaches to drug discovery. Chemists have created 10 million new molecules since the nineteenth century, and at present they can make 25,000 variants of the same molecule[22]. Bioprospecting is not the only way for drug discovery. On the other hand, the earlier belief that pharmaceutical prospecting would generate sufficient revenues for conservation of medicinal plants has gone a full circle starting from the 'Magic Well' picture that changed drastically as studies showed 'vanishingly small' values derived from prospecting of medicinal plants. Currently, the debate is again at a more optimistic lead (Bhagirathy, 2003). TK is seen as the crucial factor for economic viability of discoveries led by bioprospecting. However, IPR for TK is designed essentially as a system of protection. This may be the Achilles' heel. Conventional IPR systems protect the monopoly rights of private inventors. Though the critics argue that knowledge is best utilized if it is in public domain, IPR supports investment in invention by grant of temporary monopoly rights for a short period. Its availability free of charge may insure optimal utilization of information but provides no incentive for investment in research (Arrow, 1962). In other words, if it does not lead to additional benefit, expenses on IPR is wastage from the investors' point of view and inefficient from social welfare considerations. It is imperative therefore, to note that the emerging legislative framework and TK regime, though intended largely to contain biopiracy, has considerable potential for promoting investment in TK research with a goal of increasing production. The TKDL for example, has used up a quarter of a million dollars. Unless such registers also lead to scientific investigation into the traditional remedies, including trials in animals and humans, the cost will be incurred merely for preventive purposes. On the other hand, searchable databases along with clear norms of benefit sharing with the right holders may support incentives for investigations and development. A public debate must be started about the right to access databases like TKDL.

With increasing interest in TK and its widespread commercialisation, the need for quality maintenance has increased considerably. Traditional or complementary medicine for example, is a victim not only of uninformed sceptics but also of uncritical enthusiasts. Its increasing popularity has given rise to concerns of safety. Problems have occurred even out of incorrect use of traditional therapies. For instance, the herb *Ma Huang* (ephedra) is traditionally used in China to treat short-term respiratory congestion. In the United States, the herb was marketed as a dietary aid, whose long-term use led to at least a dozen deaths, heart attacks and strokes. In Belgium, at least 70 people required renal transplant or dialysis for interstitial fibrosis of the kidney after taking the wrong herb from the Aristolochiaceae family, again as a dietary aid. In May 2002 the WHO has launched a global plan to assist countries to regulate traditional or complementary/alternative medicine (TM/CAM) and to make its use safer. Or consider the case of Basmati rice. Although US companies are trying to cut into this area their success is limited. In Saudi Arabia, the major importer of Basmati—it is understood as the rice coming from India and Pakistan; Texas grown rice is not accepted as Basmati. In this situation geographical indication protection or patent protection are unimportant for securing sub-continental market. But questions of quality maintenance can impinge on the market. Some US Companies have been aggressively advertising their products as of consistently high quality unlike the imports from India and Pakistan. Unless the exporters of the sub-continent take timely steps they may waste the image that was developed over years. IPRs cannot create market. Product merit is fundamental.

## END NOTES

1. www.worldbank.org/arf.ik
2. WHO/IUCN/WWF, *Guidelines for the Conservation of Medicinal Plants*, Gland, Switzerland.

3. Source: *The China National Committee for the Implementation of the UN Convention to Combat Desertification (CCICCD).*
4. For more, see Nirmal Sengupta (ed.), *Economic Studies of Indigenous and Traditional Knowledge*, edited, Indian Economic Association Trust for Research and Development and Academic Foundation, 2006.
5. Article 8(j) of CDB provides that "Members should respect, preserve and maintain knowledge, innovations and practices of indigenous and local communities embodying traditional lifestyles relevant for the conservation and sustainable use of biological diversity and promote their wider application with the approval and involvement of the holders of such knowledge, innovations and practices and encourage the equitable sharing of the benefits arising from the utilization of such knowledge, innovations and practices".
6. Paragraph 19 of the Doha Ministerial Declaration, Document WTO/MIN(01)/DEC/1.
7. Article 27.3 (b) deals with the patentability/non-patentability of plant and animal inventions and the protection of plant varieties. As required by the TRIPS Agreement, Article 27.3(b) is one of the Articles that is being reviewed by the TRIPS Council.
8. CBD.
9. UNCTAD.
10. WIPO.
11. WTO, submission by India, 14th July 2000.
12. The Indigenous Knowledge (IK) Programmes of the World Bank, http://www.worldbank.org/afr/ik/
13. Draft Declaration on the Rights of Indigenous Populations.
14. Need arises because "Protection provided by the conventional IPR regime is limited by operation factors—lack of adequate education, awareness and resources, for example—and, most importantly, by conceptual factors, since certain aspects of the knowledge produced in most traditional communities are not necessarily within the scope of the TRIPS Agreement. Traditional knowledge is often held collectively, which makes it difficult to determine its title holders. It may also be intergenerational, which may not fit adequately the requirement of novelty. Dissemination of traditional knowledge is often made orally, which makes it difficult to constitute documented prior art."(*WTO Submission by Brazil,* WTO/IP/C/W/228). A *sui-generis* system is one that overcomes these difficulties and assigns rights automatically. Essential difference with IPR is that products that exist *in-situ* as genetic resources for which medical uses are not known as well as traditional knowledge concerning the use of such resources may be protected within national boundaries (Until and unless international recognition to national *sui-generis* systems are offered) under this system. This is separate from a *sui-generis* system for the protection of plant varieties called for in Article 27(3)(b) of the TRIPS Agreement. (Wilder, 2001).

15. Can also be considered as a *sui-generis* system.
16. The Bonn Guidelines on Access to Genetic Resources and Fair and Equitable Sharing of the Benefits Arising out of their Utilization were officially adopted in Secretariat of the Convention on Biological Diversity (2002), "Report of the Sixth Meeting of the Conference of the Parties to the Convention on Biological Diversity" [UNEP/CBD/COP/6/20].
17. The US delegation stated that such requirements would conflict with TRIPS by creating another substantive condition on patentability beyond those already provided by the latter.
18. Submitted by Bolivia, Brazil, Cuba, Dominican Republic, Ecuador, India, Peru, Thailand, Venezuela, to World Trade Organization—TRIPS Council (2002) [IP/C/W/403].
19. For details, *see* Dutfield, 2002.
20. As per Hong Kong Trade Development Council, WTO Accession Monitor, March 2002.
21. *See* note No. 14.
22. Bensaude-Vincent, B., and I. Stengers (1996), *A History of Chemistry*, Cambridge and London: Harvard University Press, at 255. cited by Dutfield (2003).

## REFERENCES

Bhagirathy, A. (2003). '*Intellectual Property Rights for Traditional Knowledge—Economic Analysis of an Incentive System*', SANDEE Project Report (unpublished).

————and N. Sengupta (2003). "Surviving in a globalizing world", *Seminar*, No. 523, pp. 58-62, March.

http://www.india-seminar.com/2003/523/523%20aparna%20bhagirathy%20&%20nirmal%20sengupta.htm#top

http://www.mq.edu.au/hoa/briefhistory.htm (for Australia)

http://www.state.gov/p/wha/rt/oas/20827.htm (for US situation)

Bhaumik. T.K. Senior Advisor, CII, in session on 'Indian System of Medicine and Homeopathy: Export Opportunities", organised by Confederation of Indian Industry, (CII), Mumbai, March 27, 2001.

Commission of Intellectual Property Rights, (2002). '*Report on Integrating Intellectual Property Rights and Development Policy*', DFID.

Cullet, P. (2001). 'Property Rights over Biological Resources—India's proposed Legislative Framework', *Journal of World Intellectual Property*, 4(2): 211-230 March.

Dutfield, G. (2002). 'Sharing the benefits of biodiversity: is there a role for the patent system?', *Journal of World Intellectual Property*, 5(6): 899-931, November.

———— (2003). 'Protecting Traditional Knowledge and Folklore: A Review of Progress in Diplomacy and Policy Formulation', UNCTAD-ICTSD

Project on IPRs and Sustainable Development, International Centre for Trade and Sustainable Development (ICTSD), Geneva, Issue Paper No 1.

Exim Bank (2003). *Exporting Indian Healthcare.*

Kenneth J.A. (1962). 'Economic Welfare and the Allocation of Resources for Invention', in R.R. Nelson (ed.), *The Rate and Directions of Inventive Activity: Economic and Social Factors*, pp. 616-617. New York: Princeton University Press.

Mathur, A. (2003). '*Who Owns Traditional Knowledge?*', Working Paper No. 96, Indian Council for Research on International Economic Relations (ICRIER), New Delhi.

Proceedings and Resolutions of the *Workshop on Traditional Knowledge—Appreciation for Policy-Making*, India International Centre, March 2002 (Unpublished).

Ramanna, A. (2003). '*India's Plant Variety and Farmers Rights Legislation: Potential Impact on Stakeholder Access to Genetic Resources*', EPTD Discussion Paper No. 96, International Food Policy Research Institute, Washington, D.C.

Sampath, P.G. (2003). '*Defining an Intellectual Property Right on Traditional Medicinal Knowledge: A Process-oriented Perspective*', Discussion Paper, INTECH, Maastricht: United Nations University.

Sengupta, N. (1993). *User-Friendly Irrigation Designs*, pp. 14-16. New Delhi: Sage Publication.

———— (2006). (ed.), *Economic Studies of Indigenous and Traditional Knowledge*, Indian Economic Association Trust for Research and Development and Academic Foundation.

UNDP (1994). '*Conserving Indigenous Knowledge: Integrating Two Systems of Innovation*', Rural Advancement Foundation International, New York.

Vasudeva, P.K. (2003). 'Amend law to patent traditional knowledge', *The Tribune*, Chandigarh, India, August 25. (http://www.tribuneindia.com/2003/20030825/agro.htm)

Wilder, R. (2001). '*Protection of Traditional Medicine*', Paper No. WG 4: 4, Commission on Macroeconomics and Health (WHO) Working Paper Series also published as ICRIER Working Paper No. 66.

WIPO Reviews of Existing Intellectual Property Protection of TK and Folklore (WIPO Document No. WIPO/GRTKF/IC/3/7) 25 March 2002.
http://www.wipo.org/eng/meetings/2002/igc/doc/grtkfic3_7.doc)
(WIPO Document No. WIPO/GRTKF/IC/3/10) 25 March 2002.
http://www.wipo.org/eng/meetings/2002/igc/doc/grtkfic3_10.doc).

# Chapter 6

# Social and Economic Aspects of Agricultural Biotechnology

SUMAN SAHAI*

## Introduction

Genetic Engineering is perhaps the only technology developed in food and agriculture, which is overwhelmingly controlled by private companies. Other technologies have been largely publicly owned and used for public good. The last major technology in agriculture, the high yielding varieties which formed the basis of the Green Revolution, was fully in the public domain and accessible to everyone. In the case of GM (genetically modified) technology, multinational companies rooted in the agro-chemical sector, control the research, the genetic materials and methodologies used in that research, the field testing of the varieties created from GM research, seed production from those varieties as well as the commercialization and sale of GM crops. This control is now extending increasingly to the downstream products made from those crops. A scenario is emerging of control from the farmers' field to products in the markets. Most importantly, the transnational companies exercise immense control on the policies of regulation, sale of GM crops and intellectual property rights regimes relevant to GM crops in almost all countries of the world.

This control enables the companies to determine the direction the technology is taking. On offer are herbicide resistant varieties so

* Convenor, Gene Campaign, New Delhi.

that the company (with its agro-chemical roots) can sell a variety tailored to be resistant to only its own herbicide. Monsanto is selling the Roundup Ready soybean and Roundup herbicide to the farmer as a package. It would appear that GM technologies are being developed less to solve important agricultural problems, than to tie up a profit route in selected crops through patents and the consequent monopoly sales. Although some efforts have been made, like the virus resistant cassava developed in Kenya by Monsanto and the Bt maize developed by Syngenta for Malawi[1] by and large the private sector has shown little interest in developing crops of interest to poor farmers.

In an unfortunate development, public research institutions are failing to match the output of the corporations because of the vast difference in financial capacity. Added to this is the serious problem of access to research materials and methodologies since the companies increasingly patent these. As though giving up on this unequal struggle, public research institutions have done the very thing they should not have, drastically reduced their investment in research. This has created the situation that when the companies decide not to do a line of research, the public institutions cannot do that pro-poor research because of diminished funds (Nuffield Council on Bioethics, 1999). The result is that agricultural research overall is addressing more and more the crops of interest to the commercial, mechanized farmer of industrial nations rather than the small farmers in developing countries who could benefit from new technologies to improve agricultural productivity. In fact there is little in GM technology at present that could be of use to farmers in risk prone, diverse and integrated agricultural systems.

Given the dominance of the US in this field and their economic and political stake in transgenic crops, the public debate on the regulation of GM crops is led by the US and its agencies, particularly the State Department. One of the most aggressive electronic list serves promoting agricultural biotechnology, is supported by the US State Department[2]. The inclusion of the TRIPS (Trade Related Intellectual Property Rights) in the Uruguay GATT Round in 1986 is a reflection of the US interest in Agbiotechnology. TRIPS demands for the first time, that patent laws must be harmonized across countries as diverse as Nepal, Sri Lanka and the US and that biological material are brought under the purview of patents (Sahai, 2000).

US agencies are setting standards and sending teams to train developing country regulators. Thus US standards are being adopted by most developing countries. The low levels of technical skills in these countries make the situation worse, and not enough public pressure to develop better suited, indigenous regulatory systems. Official US policy is to create a regulatory environment that will encourage the spread of GM technologies being developed by US based companies. Regulation is not intended to be a neutral exercise but is supposed to aid this goal. This approach is not likely to result in regulatory systems appropriate for agriculturally sensitive regions with small farmers and centers of origin and diversity of crop plants.

Because of these developments and the generally declining standards of agricultural research, developing countries are becoming the consumers of GM technologies that were not developed for them. Apart from this, the entry of these GM products does not always follow established safety norms. Companies entering the market in developing countries neglect to follow the kind of stringent procedures they do in their home countries. Compliance with established norms for field trials, like the informed consent of farmers in the region; adequate containment and safety measures are disregarded, usually with the complicity of local officials. Ethical conduct would require that if corporations want to enter developing country markets, they should do so with the best, most relevant technologies and technical practices even if the current local laws and regulations are less rigorous.

Plant genomics and Ag-biotechnology may have the potential to contribute to solving agricultural and food security challenges but at the moment, this hope stands belied. People are questioning who stands to benefit and who may end up paying the costs of accidents and unintended consequences, as the GM revolution forges ahead (Benbrook, 2000). People are also suspicious of the view that all kinds of problems in agriculture, ranging from production, pest resistance, nutritional enhancement or salinity tolerance, in short, all problems arising in farmers' fields can be fixed by genetic modification. Those knowledgeable about agriculture in developing countries are alarmed at this overly simplistic presentation of agricultural systems. Molecular biologists familiar with the cutting and pasting of genes rarely have any clear notion about how crops grow in the field, especially in the complex and dynamic agro-ecosystems that operate in developing countries.

Genetic improvement either through the transgenic or classical route will not result in better crops unless there are accompanying skills in farm management and optimal management of resource inputs which are many times not plentiful in developing countries. This over expectation from any one agent of change, genetic, biological or chemical is not likely to deliver solutions.

The approach of using agricultural genomics as a 'techno-fix', also makes people nervous because its practical impact is so hard to predict. Ag-biotech is moving rapidly and the capacity to shift genes across species barriers has developed much faster than the understanding of gene function and the ways in which genetic modification is likely to affect functions at the various levels from the genome to the organism and the ecosystem.

Developing countries are adopting GM technology with no real grip on what should be an appropriate regulatory regime under their conditions. Regulation is heavily influenced by the US and a developed country paradigm, which is being adopted under pressure. The patent/IPR regimes surrounding GM technology is emerging as a legal minefield and has begun to limit the free exchange of germplasm, research data and research tools. Genetically Modified Organisms (GMOs) have emerged as a contentious, controversial area and are at the heart of the tensions between good, independent science and trade and commerce.

Farmers in developed countries can take risks that developing country farmers cannot, where small farmers have virtually no risk taking capacity. Given the failure of the few crop insurance schemes that there are, the poor access to credit, leading to dependence on moneylenders at usurious rates of interest, the small farmer in most developing countries is very vulnerable. GM technology should be very cautiously assessed for its utility in such situations before taking a decision to introduce it. It becomes the moral responsibility of those introducing GM technology to ensure that farmers get the best possible seeds and any variety approved for their use is thoroughly tested by the best institutions under the best possible conditions. In addition, an effective liability regime should be put in place to ensure that farmers are protected and the seller of seeds that do not perform is held accountable.

## GM Crops and Hunger

Is GM technology going to feed the world or increase food supply as the Ag-biotech industry claims? There is little evidence today to suggest that this might be the case. Although the technology has the potential to create crops that could be more relevant to the needs of the poor, it is not doing so at present. Apart from that, hunger is a complex issue. It is not just about food production, it is also about international trade policies, access to water, soil quality, the size of land holdings, the nature and extent of agricultural subsidies, the availability of easy credit, the availability of good quality agricultural inputs and so on. Safe and meaningful GM technology could play a role but other factors will remain overwhelmingly important.

A dispassionate appraisal will indicate that all crop varieties that are important for food security are still emerging from conventional breeding. Comparing investments in the two technologies, it is clear that conventional breeding has been more effective and productive and has offered greater number of varieties of both food and cash crop compared to GM technology. If the same amount of money and resources that have been invested in GM technology were to be invested in conventional breeding and in crops and traits of importance to developing countries then it is likely we could see increases in food production and the emergence of crop varieties of direct relevance to the poor.

### GM Crops and Sustainable Food Production

Being an expensive technology, GM technology could exacerbate the inequalities in agriculture, both between the North and South as also between large and small farmers. This technology threatens to marginalize small farmers further and establish the dominance of corporations in the seed and food sector. This has serious implications for the self-reliance in agriculture and food production that developing countries have been striving for. By aggressively marketing its few varieties, the entry of GM crops is going to accelerate genetic erosion further.

The importance of genetic diversity for agriculture and food security cannot be underestimated (Sahai, 2004). Any technology which results in a loss of genetic diversity is a technology that goes against long-term food security and sustainable agricultural production. It is the diversity of genetic material that enables the stability and viability of farming systems because it is possible for farmers to plant a wide range of crops and therefore insure against biotic and abiotic stress. It is genetic diversity that can tide through adverse conditions. Genetic resources are like money in the bank, which can be used when the need arises. When the agro-climatic conditions change, as would appear to be happening with global warming, these genetic resources will come in handy to breed new crops, to again stabilize agriculture.

**Socio-Economic Issues**

The socio-economic impact of using biotechnology to replicate or substitute products, on which livelihoods are based, can be considered an ethical question. Many crops of developing countries have a global value because of the special chemical compounds they contain like aromatic or other oils. If biotechnology will modify common, commodity crops to produce these higher value chemicals, it will lead to displacement of the developing country products from such niche markets from where they can earn incomes. This will lead to economic deprivation.

Ag-biotech is targeting the special oils produced in coconut and creating GM canola to produce the same oils (Nichterlein, 1997). Coconut provides high value oil used for edible and for industrial purposes. The main advantage of this oil is the high lauric acid that it contains. The US alone imports upwards of US$ 350 worth of coconut and palm oil annually (Bannet, 1999). Genetic modification has enabled the production of lauric acid containing oil in rapeseed. Calgene has produced a high lauric acid rapeseed by using genes from the California bay tree. This rapeseed will ultimately displace the coconut and palm kernel oil and deprive Asian farmers of revenues. The loss of the coconut oil income, the farmers' principal revenue opportunity, will inflict great economic hardship. This has to be understood in the context of the very limited opportunities for alternative or additional income sources in rural parts of Asia.

**Intellectual Property Rights**

There has been a major consolidation of the plant biotechnology industry in the last few years. As part of the overall trend of corporate globalization, there are now six mega corporations (Monsanto, Syngenta, Bayer Crop Science, DuPont, DOW and BASF Plant Science) that exercise near total monopoly on the Ag-biotech sector. This situation makes it very difficult for developing countries or public sector institutions to access the technologies or enter the field. Most of the basic technologies of genetic modification are patented and the larger companies own these patents. These companies are reluctant to license them to developing country organizations at an affordable cost. Patent laws do not require them to do so they are not obliged to grant any licenses, preferring instead to exercise complete control over the technology. It is worth recalling the case of Hoffman La Roche, which holds the patent on the PCR (Polymerase Chain Reaction) technology, one of the most fundamental technologies, used in genetic laboratories. The company actually demanded licence fees from all university research laboratories using PCR but had to withdraw in the face of united opposition by research laboratories.

The patenting of GMOs (Genetically Modified Organisms), of DNA and genes and of basic technologies used in genetics research is an instrument of corporate monopoly and cause for concern. Patent holders often refuse to license patents with broad claims to key technologies, to scientists and even to public sector institutions. Companies often seek patents not necessarily to conduct research themselves but to prevent research in areas that would threaten their monopoly. It is of equal concern that to keep pace with the corporations, pubic research institutions are also getting into the patenting of plant technologies and research tools, further restricting access to genetic material and research data that are needed to cross complement research efforts (OECD, 2002).

Broad claim patents are an issue in themselves. They violate the ethical intent of patent law, which is to balance private gain with public good while leaving the way open for further innovation. Excessively broad claims like the one claimed by Agracetus (Bijamin, 1994) on all types of genetic transformation in cotton are contrary to the original intention of patent law. They are monopoly instruments restricting useful research and therefore diminishing social welfare.

Most developing countries are at a disadvantage when negotiating licence terms from patent holders, not having learnt to bargain and being vulnerable to pressures (Nuffield Council on Bioethics, 1999). Licensing the technology is expensive and subject to the company's protectionist policies. The ownership of the technology also results in the corporations determining the direction of research. Commercial rather than social objectives dominate research, even in the publicly funded research institutions. Corporatisation has led to an increasing trend to capture and privatize scientific knowledge as intellectual property, with unhappy implications for public science and research.

The agro-chemical giants have invested heavily in genome sequencing programs, for example Syngenta in rice and DuPont-pioneer in Maize. This has led to the alarming prospect of patents being granted on ESTs (Expressed Sequence Tags) or partial gene sequences of unknown function. There is concern that such EST patents will create a binding dependency or 'reach through' on subsequent patent applications on full DNA sequences of known function. Through licensing agreements, the patent holder of an EST could acquire a right in later patents and downstream development of products. This will lead to further consolidation in the hands of a few players who have entered the field early, effectively blocking the way for new entrants, especially in developing countries.

Advocates of IPR as a necessary precondition for technology transfer will do well to recall the tenuous link between the two. The most successful commercialization and technology transfer is driven by market demand, not IPR status. Hundreds of products cloaked in patents sit on laboratory shelves and never reach the market. If a good variety is in demand because it offers a real life solution to the farmer, it will be a runaway success with or without IPR. On the other hand, it is equally important to remember that the hungry in many parts of the developing world were fed in an era when there was no IPR. The Green Revolution, with all its drawbacks, increased food production in certain regions because it came unfettered by patents and the seed moved freely through farmers' fields. Agricultural production was increased and more food was produced precisely because there was no IPR. So the IPR issue, like much else in the GM story, is tailored for the corporations, not the farmers. It is an instrument that works against food and livelihood security and there is little evidence it can contribute to increasing the production of food and removing poverty.

## Introducing Equity into IPR Regimes

When a transgenic variety is created, there are many more players involved than is acknowledged. The transgenic construct is only one part of a GM crop variety; on its own it is of no use for farmers. There are a series of plant varieties that are involved in the breeding process using the gene construct that will ultimately yield a product of interest to the farmer. In the creation of this product, varieties bred by the farmers or public research institutions are used. When a company claims to have a 'proprietary' variety, that is a variety on which it has a patent, it needs to be reminded that this variety was bred using other varieties, including farmers' varieties and land races. The companies take the position that they do not use farmer varieties or land races. This is a falsehood. Farmers and scientists in public research institutions base plant varieties that companies are using to make GM or non-GM varieties, on varieties that have been created.

It needs to be remembered that farm women and men have not only created several thousand varieties of food and cash crops, they have also identified valuable genes and traits in these crops and maintained them over generations through a highly sophisticated system of crossing and selection. Communities have developed complex systems of pest management and biological control; they have identified and managed a series of genes conferring valuable traits for commercial and domestic needs. So it is that genes for traits as diverse as disease resistance, high salt tolerance, resistance to water logging and drought tolerance have been maintained in the repertoire of communities. This work of genetic selection, maintenance and cross-breeding is the result of innovative and creative scientific experimentation in the field.

If credit had to be apportioned for the breeding of a new crop variety, then it should be shared perhaps as 80:20 between the farming and scientific communities. In other words, if the breeding of a crop variety entailed 100 steps, then farming communities have contributed the first 80 steps and laboratory science the next 20 steps. It stands to reason therefore that credit, reward and recognition for a new variety should be shared keeping these facts in mind. (Sahai, 2003b)

Improvements in agricultural production in all parts of the world has been possible because the free access to landraces and farmers varieties, enabled their valuable genes to be incorporated into modern varieties. For example, the wheat variety *Marquis* that is grown in about 90 per cent of the acreage under spring wheat in North America, originated from a cross between the Indian landrace *Hard Red Calcutta* and the European variety *Red Fife*. Similarly, the winter wheat breeding programmes in Europe have relied on a variety of landraces from various countries (FAO, 1996 and 1999).

The patent system, which allows the patent holder to appropriate the entire variety for making only one of many contributions, is therefore iniquitous and unjust. Equity and justice demand that an

IPR regime acknowledges Farmers Rights along with Breeders' Rights. This is what the Indian law on plant variety protection, the Plant Variety Protection and Farmers Rights Act, 2001, attempts to do (Sahai, 2003b). The law acknowledges that farmers are also breeders. It has provisions that if farmer varieties are used in the breeding of other varieties, a certain amount of money will be paid for the use of the farmer variety, into a National Gene Fund, which will be used by farmers. The Indian law has also banned the use of the GURT (Gene Use Restricting Technology) technologies because these would totally negate the rights of farmers by denying them access to seeds in the creation of which they have played a significant role (Sahai, 2003a).

## The Need for Transparency

The manner in which GM technology is being handled in developing countries, especially India, would constitute a textbook case of how not to implement a technology. There is a shroud of secrecy surrounding the research, the location of field trials, the results of safety tests and the results on the basis of which commercial approvals are granted. When GM crops are field-tested, farmers in the region are not informed, nor is their consent sought for holding trials in their areas.

It is important to create open and transparent systems and have a public debate on risks and benefits. Data from trials should be accessible to the public. The testing regimes for transgenic plants should be standardized and designed in open consultation with scientific experts from various disciplines. There should be a consultation with the broader scientific community before setting a research agenda. At present, companies come with their own agenda and pursue it.

Consultations should be done with the farming community about their most pressing needs so that research goals can target these. Consultations with farming communities, especially women, assume particular significance in light of two developments in developing countries. One, the extension services have broken down practically everywhere, so there are now no avenues through which the technical and economic problems faced in the field goes back to researchers. Second, urban migration in search of jobs has led to the increasing feminization of agriculture, resulting in a large number of farming households being headed by women. Women will have different perspectives and needs and research programmes should address these.

Independent experts reporting in a public forum should do the evaluation of field trials and regulatory agencies should consist of neutral, independent experts who do not have a direct stake in the outcome of tests. Regulators should make public the scientific data and the rationale for their decisions. Research results emanating from GM crops should be subjected to critical peer review before any decisions are taken.

## Corporate Control and GM Technology

One of the key reasons why GM foods have raised hackles across the world is because of the unprecedented corporate control over this technology. Young people protesting on the streets against GM foods are as concerned about the safety of their food as the corporate take over of their lives. Had this technology come from universities and public research institutions, it is unlikely to have generated such deep-seated antagonism. The aggressive stance of corporations riding roughshod over the concerns voiced by the public has had the predictable backlash. Monsanto's attempts to acquire and use the GURT technology led to a dramatic scaling up of the public's antagonism and Monsanto as a company became synonymous with everything the public found reprehensible about greedy corporate.

There is distrust of the manipulations of the industry and the way it turns the jargon and semantics of the debate on biotechnology. Discusses the use of the 'science based' argument by promoters of biotechnology, pointing out that 'science' is defined by those scientists who are in political and financial control of science policy, not the larger scientific community, the philosophers of science and the experts in various fields. He places this in his larger argument that 'scientific' assessment of safety of GM crops does not include experts from scientific disciplines like ecology or evolutionary sciences, but only scientists directly involved in the creation of transgenic crops.

The enormous resources of the industry are routinely used to influence national and international policies. It is no secret that the American biotechnology lobby continues to play a major role in the WTO agreements on Intellectual Property Rights, Agriculture and others. The US refusal to ratify the largely pro-developing country Convention on Biological Diversity is also attributed to the power of the biotechnology lobby, which wants to ensure continued access to biological materials from the south, without paying for them.

Lobbyists and corporate strategists are active at the level of those shaping policy within the biotech community and within governments, legislators and even the judiciary. Two years ago, a group of such corporate lobbyists held seminars in India to educate the judges of the Supreme Court about the benefits of biotechnology. The influence of the corporate sector in the corridors of power is no secret and their proclivity for 'buying influence' is not unknown either. In Asian nations like India, Thailand and Indonesia, GM policy is being practically formulated by the multinationals, excluding the views even of concerned scientists and certainly of other stakeholders.

The extent of industry influence in fixing regulatory systems is most visible in the US. The manipulation of the FDA (Food and Drug Administration) has been exposed in a set of correspondence between the scientists of the FDA. This correspondence was obtained by a public interest group in the USA, Alliance for Biointegrity, under the Freedom of Information Act[3].

The correspondence reveals the concerns expressed by FDA scientists about the technology and the ultimate FDA decisions, which clearly favoured the industry. During the formulation of the "Statement of Policy: Foods from Genetically Modified Plants", the document that set regulatory guidelines, FDA scientists had expressed concern about the internal manipulations which were forcing a conclusion that there was no difference between plants modified by conventional breeding and genetic transformation, when in fact technical evidence points that there is.

Scientists in FDA had expressed their unhappiness about the incomplete scientific analysis on which conclusions were being based and the selective use of language, saying the word 'risk' was deliberately avoided. In fact the genesis of the 'science based' approach can be found in the FDA documents where internal experts have questioned how safety was assumed for these GM foods, charging that decisions were being taken by molecular biologists, chemists and toxicology experts, without the involvement of experts in risk analysis. Even supporters of biotechnology criticize the aggressive promotion by the biotech lobby of this selective 'science based' approach. It has become a smokescreen preventing a comprehensive and honest appraisal of GM technology and its overall impact on the environment and human and animal health.

The FDA's aggressive pro-industry position has set the tone for regulatory systems elsewhere in the world, perpetrating a similar mindset and bias, with regrettable consequences. In countries like India, this has resulted in an atmosphere where decisions are taken in the interest of companies, not the farmers.

## Consumer Concerns in Developing Countries

Consumer concerns are a big issue in the West where consumers have rightly demanded the right to know what their food contains and the right to have a choice to refuse GM food. This is the basis for the legitimate demand to label GM foods, so fiercely resisted by the US. Consumers in developing countries have the same positions. However in developing countries, the issues are more vexed. What does labelling mean to large sections of rural people, without adequate access to information? And when food is not packaged as for the super markets but sold loose in wholesale and retail stores, how would one implement labels? Large sections of the consumers and shopkeepers in developing countries would be illiterate and even when literate, unaware of the concerns around GM foods. How does one offer a choice to them? What form should labelling take? In any case, without large-scale awareness generation and public education about the process of genetic engineering and how it creates the food on offer to them, any label or presentation of choice would be meaningless.

Labelling, identity preservation, traceability etc. will pose a major challenge in developing countries and a suitable system will have to be developed if GM crops are to be grown there. Labelling and identity preservation etc. will have to be done in a way that ordinary people can comprehend it and make an informed choice. It would be grossly unethical to introduce genetically engineered foods into the market without taking adequate steps to present the consumers a choice in a manner they comprehend and can deal with.

## Cultural and Ethical Views

There are deep-seated ethical concerns about eating GM foods. The thought of a human gene in the food that they are eating fills many people with revulsion because they associate it with cannibalism. The biotech lobby's 'science based' approach is as misplaced here as in many of its other arguments. The 'scientific' argument that genes are neither human, nor vegetarian or non-vegetarian, is meaningless in the face of deeply held religious and cultural beliefs. It would be revolting to most Hindus to eat GM food containing genes from a cow or for Muslims to eat food modified with a pig gene.

These civilisation influences and taboos are deep seated and have to be respected (Burke, 2002). It was observed in a survey that Christians were divided in their opposition to GM foods whereas Jews were more comfortable with the notion. Hindus and Muslims were greatly opposed, as were animal rights groups and vegetarians. All groups questioned were worried that today there may be only one, for example, human gene in the sheep they might eat but tomorrow there could be a situation of half the genes being human and the other half sheep. Everyone wanted these details put on the label of foods so that people could avoid food-containing genes they wished to avoid. If food with ethically sensitive transgenes is to be marketed for human use, these must be clearly labelled to allow informed choice.

## END NOTES

1. *See* www.africabiotech.com, www.syngentafoundation.com, and www.monsantoafrica.com
2. *See* AgBioView, www.AgBioWorld.org
3. *See* Alliance for Biointegrity, www.biointegrity.org

## REFERENCES

Benbrook, C. (2000). 'Who Controls and Who Will Benefit from Plant Genomics', The 2000 Genome Seminar: Genomic Revolution in the Fields: Facing the Needs of the New Millennium, AAAS Annual Meeting. Washington, D.C.

Bennet, D.J. (1999). 'Ethical Aspects of Agricultural Biotechnology', European Federation of Biotechnology Task Force Report on Public Perception of Biotechnology, pp.46-47.

Bijamin, J. (1994). 'Agracetus: Patenting all Transgenic Cotton', *Biotechnology and Development Monitor*, 21: 8-9, December. www.biotechmonitor.nl/2105.htm

Burke, D. (2002). 'The UK Regulatory Process in Practice, GM Crops Understanding the Issues', UK Agricultural Biotechnology Industry, pp.61-68.

FAO. (1996). Background Documentation prepared for the International Technical Conference on Plant Genetic Resources. Leipzig, Germany, 17-23 June 1996.

——— (1999). Rome, in Ethical Aspects of Agricultural Biotechnology, Bennet, D.J., (ed): pp.53.

Nichterlein, K. (1997). 'Biotechnology Advances in Oil Crops Affecting Coconut Production', BINAS News, 3: 2-4

http://www.bdt.fat.org.br/binas/News/97issue34/1.html

Nuffield Council on Bioethics, (1999). 'Genetically Modified Crops: The Ethical and Social Issues', Medical Research Council, Nuffield Foundation and Wellcome Trust.

OECD, (2002). 'Genetic Inventions, IPR and Legal Licensing Practices Evidence and Policies', UN Organisation for Economic Co-operation and Development.

Sahai, S. (2000). 'GATT/WTO and the TRIPS Agreement and South Asia', *South Asia Economic Journal*.1(2): 25-41.

——— (2003a). 'Importance of Indigenous Knowledge', *Indian Journal of Traditional Knowledge*, 2(1): 11-14.

——— (2003b). 'India's Plant Variety Protection and Farmers' Rights Act', 2001 *Current Science*, 84(3): 407-412.

——— (2004). 'Strategies for Sustainable Increase in Food Production, National Food Security Summit', New Delhi, February.

*Chapter 7*

# The Substantive Patent Law Treaty: What It Means for India[1]

BISWAJIT DHAR*

## Introduction

The issue of harmonisation of national and regional patent laws has been a contentious one for many decades now, primarily because of the differing interests and priorities of developed and developing countries. The former set of countries has consistently argued for several decades now that national patent laws need to be harmonised, which in other words implies that there should be a "one size fits all" international patent system[2]. On the other hand, the latter set of countries has argued that the international patent system should have adequate flexibilities to enable developing countries adopt patent laws suited to their development needs. The developing countries have made their arguments quite persuasively in the backdrop of the on-going negotiations for the review of the Agreement on the Trade Related Aspects of Intellectual Property Rights (TRIPS) as a part of the work programme of the World Trade Organization (WTO). The main aim of these countries is to introduce additional flexibilities in the structure of the patent system provided for in the TRIPS Agreement.

While the WTO has been looking for ways to resolve the widely differing perceptions of its members over the framework for patent

* Professor and Head, Centre for WTO Studies, Indian Institute of Foreign Trade, New Delhi.

protection that must be accepted, the World Intellectual Property Organization (WIPO) has been engaged in a parallel process of negotiations for harmonisation of patent laws in order to develop an international patent system[3]. The WIPO process, in fact, pre-dates the Uruguay Round negotiations that led to the adoption of the Agreement on TRIPS. Negotiations on a draft "Treaty Supplementing the Paris Convention as far as Patents are Concerned", more commonly known as the Patent Harmonization Treaty, were initiated in 1985. A Diplomatic Conference held in Hague in 1991 considered the draft Patent Harmonization Treaty, which was inconclusive. This draft included proposals by both developing and developed countries, which could be used for setting globally acceptable norms and standards for the patent protection.

The framework proposed in the draft Patent Harmonization Treaty of 1991 included both substantive and the formal aspects of the patent law. According to the WIPO, some of the provisions of the draft Treaty "for instance those on patentable subject-matter, rights conferred, term of protection and reversal of burden of proof of process patents, were incorporated into the Agreement on Trade Related Aspects of Intellectual Property Rights, concluded in 1994"[4]. This acknowledgement by the WIPO that it played a key role in the adoption of the TRIPS Agreement assumes importance in the present context when substantial review of the Agreement is taking place. It reflects the inevitable influences that the WIPO and TRIPS processes have on each other.

As stated earlier, the review of the TRIPS Agreement is considering the possibilities of improving the flexibilities currently available to WTO members for enacting national legislations. WIPO's Harmonization Treaty, which was revived in 1995 in the form of the Patent Law Treaty (PLT), on the other hand, aims at removing the major differences that exist between the patent laws of countries. In the first phase of this renewed initiative by the WIPO harmonisation of patent formalities were taken up, the culmination of which was the adoption of the PLT in 2000. Immediately following the adoption of the PLT, the Standing Committee on the Law of Patents of the WIPO took up the issue of harmonising the norms and standards of the patent laws in respect of some of the key elements, which were to form the basis of a Substantive Patent Law Treaty (SPLT). Elements of the SPLT for furthering patent law harmonisation have been considered in the successive sessions of the Standing Committee on the Law of Patents of the WIPO, a process that has produced the draft SPLT.

This paper analyses some of the key provisions of the draft SPLT that is before the Standing Committee in the Law of Patents (WIPO, 2003c). The focus of the paper is on the nature of obligations that are likely to arise if the draft SPLT were to be adopted and the implications that such obligations would have for India. A key question that needs to be examined in this context is whether harmonisation of patent laws through the adoption of the SPLT, marks a step towards introducing a TRIPS-plus patent regime in terms of the obligations that it would bring on the signatory countries.

## Multilateral Initiatives at Harmonisation of Patent Laws

The first major attempt at harmonisation of patent laws across countries was the Paris Convention for the Protection of Industrial Property adopted in 1883, which has subsequently been amended several times, the most recent of these being the Stockholm Act of 1967. In 1974, the World Intellectual Property Organization (WIPO) was established as a specialised agency under the United Nations, with the purpose of monitoring international treaties on intellectual property. Efforts towards enhancing the level of harmonisation between patent laws of the Paris Convention members began in earnest under the aegis of the WIPO in the first half of the 1980s, which, as indicated earlier in the paper, turned out to be inconclusive. This was primarily because of severe differences between the negotiating countries, including the fact that, at that stage, even for countries such as the United States, it would have been inexpedient to harmonise substantive issues of patent laws. The United States was reluctant to support substantive harmonisation, given the wide range of changes that the proposed Patent Harmonization Treaty would have forced on its Patent Act[5].

From the mid-1980s, the issue of intellectual property rights (IPRs) began to be discussed in the GATT as a part of the Uruguay Round of multilateral trade negotiations primarily because of the initiative taken by the industrialised countries. The negotiating mandate adopted at *Punta del Este* in 1986 for the launch of the Uruguay Round negotiations for the inclusion of IPRs as a part of the GATT discipline stated that the "negotiations shall aim to clarify GATT provisions and elaborate as appropriate new rules and disciplines" so as to promote effective and adequate protection of intellectual property rights. Quite clearly thus, the Uruguay Round negotiations were aimed at developing norms and standards for intellectual property protection, which could be enforced on all the Contracting Parties to the GATT. Developing countries opposed the inclusion of intellectual property rights (IPRs) in the GATT negotiations, arguing that this issue be dealt with by the United Nations and its specialized agencies like the WIPO and the UNCTAD. These arguments however proved ineffectual and in 1994, a significant step towards harmonisation of intellectual property laws was taken with the conclusion of the Agreement on TRIPS as part of the Uruguay Round Agreements establishing the World Trade Organisation.

The basic objective of the TRIPS Agreement was to set minimum standards for patent protection across countries[6]. The controversial aspects of substantive harmonisation that had made the WIPO processes inconclusive were not addressed in the TRIPS. Instead, the focus was on elevation of standards of patentability across all countries. A significant aspect of the TRIPS Agreement is that it establishes a link with the major international conventions for the protection of intellectual property that are in force. Article 2.1 of the TRIPS Agreement provides that the WTO Members shall comply with the Articles 1-12 and 19 of the Paris Convention for the Protection of Intellectual Property, as amended in 1967[7]. Furthermore, Article 2(2) of the Agreement provides that substantive parts of the TRIPS Agreement relating to the basic principles of IPRs, the setting of the norms and standards, the enforcement of IPRs and their acquisition and maintenance would not "derogate from existing obligations that Members may have to each other under the Paris Convention, the Berne Convention, the Rome Convention and the Treaty on Intellectual Property in Respect of Integrated Circuits". Besides, the WTO and the WIPO have established a working relationship through the agreement that they entered into in 1996[8].

But even as the TRIPS Agreement was being established as the basis for global harmonisation of patent laws, WIPO revived discussions on patent law harmonisation. With the United States remaining an unwilling partner to negotiate a treaty that aimed at substantive harmonisation of patent laws[9] till as recently as the mid-1990s, the WIPO Director General proposed that a new approach be adopted for promoting harmonisation of patent laws; one that "focuses entirely on the formalities of national and regional patent applications"

(WIPO, 1997). This formed the basis for the negotiations for the adoption of the Patent Law Treaty (PLT) in 2000. However, from the first session of the Standing Committee on Law of Patents (SCP), the forum which has been conducting the PLT negotiations, several WIPO Members and participating organisations from the intellectual property community, made it clear that substantive harmonisation of the patent laws had to be the eventual outcome and that the PLT was but the initial step[10].

Support for negotiations for substantive harmonisation of patent laws was lent by the Industry Advisory Commission of WIPO, which adopted a Resolution calling for "work, in the medium term, on a treaty on the harmonisation of substantive patent law, with a view to facilitating greater mutual recognition of search and examination results by Patent Offices." (WIPO, 2000a) In addition, the Policy Advisory Commission of WIPO made several recommendations at its meeting of June 15, 2000, which among other things stated, "that efforts should be made towards further substantive harmonisation in the field of industrial property law, in particular, patent law."

The adoption of the PLT in 2000 thus paved the way for "deep harmonisation of a number of issues relating to the grant of patent rights as well as the validity of patents" through the negotiations for the adoption of a Substantial Patent Law Treaty (SPLT)(WIPO, 2002c). The SCP decided that the draft SPLT should address a number of issues relevant to the grant and validity of patents. It was suggested that at least the following basic issues underlying the grant of patents, which are of particular importance from the point of view of further developing of the international patent system, could be included in the discussions of the SCP. These include, definition of prior art, novelty, inventive step (non-obviousness) and industrial applicability (utility); sufficiency of disclosure; and the structure and interpretation of claims [WIPO (2000b), WIPO (2002b) and WIPO (2003c)]. This approach suggested by the SCP was in fact consistent with the recommendations of the United States that WIPO's patent law harmonisation efforts "begin with fewer issues, concentrating on deep harmonisation of those concerned with the drafting, filing and examination of patent applications". It was further emphasised that "genuine harmonization" of the issues selected should be the objective, which would ensure that there would be "*no exceptions* to the result-oriented standards agreed to"(Godici, 2001) (emphasis added).

A formal proposal to conclude "a more limited substantive patent law treaty" was made jointly by the US and Japan. In the statement to the WIPO General Assembly in 2004, the two countries argued in favour of "a revised approach that limits the work of the SCP to an initial package of priority items" that include prior art-related issues like definition of prior art, novelty and non-obviousness/inventive step (WIPO, 2004).

The initiative to commence negotiations on the SPLT had two interesting dimensions. In the first place, the initiative received the backing from all the major developed countries, including the United States, which, as discussed earlier, was opposed to the substantive harmonisation of patent laws, and a range of associations representing the intellectual property community. The second dimension was that by initiating a work the Fourth Session of the SCP brought back the 1991 Patent Harmonisation Treaty onto the agenda of the WIPO, which may be seen as the stepping-stone towards the adoption of an international patent system.

The latter dimension was in fact reinforced by the Policy Advisory Committee of the WIPO, which gave the mandate to the organisation "[T]hat efforts towards further substantive harmonization of patent law, and PCT reform, should be pursued in a coordinated manner, consistent with the objectives of the *global patent system*" (emphasis added). In keeping with this mandate, the WIPO Director General outlined Agenda for Development of the International Patent System, which was envisaged as the strategic framework for the future development of the international patent system (WIPO, 2001b).

It may well be a few years before the SPLT negotiations are able to produce what would be the blueprint of the international patent system. As was mentioned in the foregoing, the fact that United States Patents Act would have to undergo some fundamental changes, and that the Members of the European Union would also have problems with harmonisation of patenting standards, would make negotiation of the SPLT a difficult process. Some concerns of developed countries which led to the failure of The Hague Diplomatic Conference on the Patent Harmonisation Treaty in 1991, remain unresolved. It was pointed out for instance, that the provisions of Directive 98/44/EC on the Legal Protection of Biotechnological Inventions might be affected by the SPLT negotiations, particularly "those relating to industrial application and those relating to the deposit of a biological material with a recognised institution"[11]. It is however becoming increasingly evident that these positions of the United States and the Members of the European Union notwithstanding, the industry and the intellectual property community are keen to push ahead with patent law harmonisation. Besides insisting that the governments (that of the United States in particular) should be more engaged in the SPLT negotiations[12], some industry associations have even suggested the way forward. The Biotechnology Industry Association (BIO) has stated in its position on the global patent law harmonisation that a "more realistic short-term target is a treaty that achieves "true harmonisation" of those elements of patent systems that are necessary to create a streamlined global patent granting system". "True harmonisation" according to BIO would take place through "a treaty that imposes identical standards on substantive patentability among all treaty signatories, rather than a treaty that accommodates a range of options". In view of BIO, "patent systems based on such a treaty should capture the best elements of the *US, European and Japanese patent systems*"[13] (emphasis added). The above-mentioned positions of the interest groups in the United States clearly indicate that the SPLT negotiations could result in the harmonisation of patent laws in conformity with the standards prevailing in the developed countries.

In light of the above, the challenges before the developing countries as they engage themselves in the SPLT negotiations are two-fold. First, the position they have taken in the review of the TRIPS Agreement that opposes harmonisation of the patent laws involving some of the key elements, could be undermined. As was indicated earlier, developing countries have been arguing in favour of expanding the flexibilities that must be available under national patent laws. Emphasising this point in the discussions in the Standing Committee on the Law of Patents, Brazil, on behalf of the Group of Friends of Development[14], stated that the SPLT should include, *inter alia*, provisions on the transfer of technology, on anti-competitive practices, on the safeguarding of public interest flexibilities, as well as specific clauses on principles and objectives (WIPO, 2005a).

The second set of challenges that the developing countries face stems from the fact that they have, in general, not been effectively engaged within the WIPO in setting the intellectual property agenda. The PLT and the SPLT negotiations have been dominated largely by developed countries and NGOs representing corporations and patent lawyers' interests. There are no NGOs representing the interests of developing countries.[15] It is from this perspective that the developments centring on the SPLT assume importance.

## SPLT and TRIPS Agreement: Where They Differ and Why That Matters

The discussion in the previous section pointed to the fact that the SPLT negotiations have been considering several issues relating to the grant of patents. More critical from the point of view of their implications for national patent laws are the following issues: (i) setting standards in respect of conditions of patentability, (ii) sufficiency of disclosure of the invention for which the patent is sought, and (iii) the definition of prior art. The following discussion critically examines the proposals in respect of each of the issues mentioned above, particularly in light of the standards that have been set in the Agreement on TRIPS. The discussion would take into consideration the interventions that have been made by some of the key countries as well as the stakeholders from the intellectual property community who have been more active in the SPLT negotiations.

### *(i) Conditions of Patentability*

Article 12 of the draft SPLT, which defines the conditions of patentability, has two substantive parts. In the first instance, it attempts to define the subject-matter eligible for patent protection. Secondly, it proposes alternative formulations for standards regarding the three criteria used for assessing whether or not inventions are patentable. These are: (i) novelty, (ii) non-obviousness or inventive step, and (iii) industrial application or usefulness. The inclusion of these issues in the harmonisation exercise is significant since it marks a major departure from the framework that the Agreement on TRIPS has introduced as has been elaborated in the following section.

#### *(a) Limiting Exclusions Under National Laws*

The discussion below highlights some of the more glaring areas of conflict between the TRIPS Agreement and the proposed SPLT that could have implications for countries like India. The areas of conflict arise primarily because the SPLT is aimed at expanding the scope of protection available to the inventors well beyond that currently provided by the TRIPS Agreement.

Article 12 of the draft SPLT states that patentable subject-matter shall include products and processes that can be used in any *field of activity*. A set of narrowly defined exclusions from patentability has been proposed. Article 12 also seeks to define the three criteria for patentability, viz. novelty, inventive step and industrial applicability. The actual scope of each of these criteria is being debated threadbare. These provisions proposed in the draft SPLT have two major differences with the framework provided in the Agreement on TRIPS. First, Article 27.1 of the TRIPS Agreement provides that patents shall be available for any inventions, whether products or processes, *in all fields of technology*, provided that they are new, involve an inventive step and are capable of industrial application (emphasis added). At the same time, however, the Agreement also provides some significant exceptions. The second point of departure between the TRIPS Agreement and the proposed SPLT is that while the former grants the freedom to national patent offices to adopt standards for the three patentability criteria, the latter seeks to set uniform standards across countries. The implications of these differences are elaborated below.

The TRIPS Agreement requires WTO Member countries to provide patent protection to products and processes in "all fields of technology", barring a set of exceptions. It may be pointed out that by so defining the patentable subject-matter the TRIPS Agreement itself marked a major departure from the past when many developing countries excluded several areas from the ambit of their respective patent laws[16]. Article 27.2 of the TRIPS Agreement, however provides for exclusions from patentability when it is necessary to prevent commercial exploitation of certain inventions which is necessary to protect *ordre public* or morality, including those that are essential for the protection of human, animal or plant life or health or for avoiding serious prejudice to the environment. More significant are the exclusions from patentability that are provided in Article 27.3, which include, (a) diagnostic, therapeutic and surgical methods for the treatment of plants; (b) plants and animals, and (c) essentially biological processes for the production of plants and animals. In contrast, the exceptions to patentability proposed under SPLT are limited to mere discoveries, abstract ideas, scientific and mathematical theories, laws of nature and purely aesthetic creations[17]. The SPLT could therefore severely restrict the flexibility of developing countries in designing exclusions to patentability. For instance, most developing countries have not been extending patent protection to higher forms of life, which they can under the patent regime underlined by the TRIPS Agreement. However, this flexibility would not be available under the proposed SPLT.

The move under SPLT seems to be to expand the TRIPS subject matter limitation through removal of the phrase "fields of technology"[18]. Dropping the term 'fields of technology' could potentially expand the scope of the patent system. The country rooting for the SPLT wording for patentable subject-matter in any field of activity was the United States, supported by NGOs representing interests of the industry. Their argument was the standard of patentability should be such that an invention need only provide for a practical application having a useful, concrete and tangible result[19]. Their argument was also that the inclusion of a 'technical' or 'industrial' requirement would result in a step backwards[20]. The ostensible objective of the United States' stand seems to be to incorporate liberal rules for patentability of software, business methods and research tools, each of which is not considered patentable today under laws of many countries, including that of India. Software, for instance, is currently protected under copyright laws. The concern with extending patent rights over software is that this would place greater control and rights in favour of the patent holder, and nullify public interest benefits, such as 'fair use' that is currently available under copyright laws.

Whether an invention should show a 'technical character' in order to be patentable has long been an issue of concern for both developing countries and the European Communities. These countries have argued that the TRIPS language of 'fields of technology', and 'industrial use' should be retained under the SPLT[21]. The current SPLT draft has taken the step of introducing, in brackets, the term "in all fields of technology"[22]. The implication of a phrase being in brackets is that no consensus has yet been reached regarding its usage. In fact, opinions expressed by the participating countries have been so fractured that a decision was taken in the Eighth Session of the SCP in 2002 to postpone discussion on the issue of patentable subject-matter.

This development has not diminished the importance of the SPLT negotiations as far as its role in defining patentable subject matter is concerned. We would try to argue in the following section that harmonisation of the criteria for patentability, in particular the assessment of whether or not an invention stands the test of industrial applicability or utility, could introduce commitments to extend the scope of patentability beyond that provided in the TRIPS Agreement.

*(b) Setting the Standards for Criteria to be Adopted*

The attempt being made in the SPLT to set the standards in respect of the three essential criteria of patentability, viz., novelty, inventive step or non-obviousness and industrial applicability or utility, could have ramifications for the structure of the patent laws in the WIPO member countries. Harmonisation of the criteria to be adopted is yet another step that the SPLT proposes to take which goes beyond the standard setting exercise that the TRIPS Agreement has undertaken. As was indicated earlier, Article 27 of the TRIPS Agreement merely states that inventions on which patent rights are claimed must meet the three criteria mentioned above, thus implying that the TRIPS Agreement grants freedom to the patent granting authorities in the Member countries to define each of these requirements. By so doing, the TRIPS Agreement recognises the widely varying approaches adopted by countries while applying the three criteria used for examining patent applications.

The implications of harmonisation of criteria for patentability can be far reaching. The discussion below would try to highlight that setting the uniform global standards in respect of the criteria of industrial application can, for example, influence the patentable subject-matter.

Three alternative formulations on industrial application/utility were proposed in the draft SPLT by the Standing Committee on the Law of the Patents, which the Tenth Session considered in May 2004 (*See* Annex 7.2). The first formulation provided that an invention would be considered industrially applicable if it "can be made or used for exploitation in any field of [commercial] [economic] activity". The second formulation stated that industrially applicable inventions would be those that could be made or used in any kind of industry. It was elaborated that "the term industry shall be understood in its broadest sense, as in the Paris Convention". And, finally, the third formulation stated that industrially applicable inventions should have a specific, substantial and credible utility.

In the context of the proposals contained in the draft SPLT, it needs to be pointed out that while most countries adopt industrial applicability of an invention as a criterion, United States, Canada and Australia are among the more prominent countries, which use the criterion of utility instead[23]. The present discussion would confine itself to an examination of the definitions of "industrial application" adopted in the different national laws of select industrialised countries.

The patent laws of several countries provide for a broad definition of what constitutes "industrial application". The European Patent Convention, for instance, states the following in respect of industrial application in its guidelines for examination of a patent claim: "An invention shall be considered as susceptible of industrial application if it can be made or used in any kind of industry, including agriculture".[24]

Germany, France and Austria are among the countries, which have adopted very broad definitions of "industrial application". In case of Germany, industry within the meaning of "industrial applicability" was a continuing, independent, authorized activity geared towards profit, including primary production, such as agriculture, forestry and horticulture. The condition of industrial applicability adopted by France requires that the invention could be exploited (made or used) in the industry at large, including commerce and agriculture. Although the Austrian Patent Law does not contain any definition of the term "industrial applicability," it was understood in a very broad sense that the invention must be able to be made or used in any kind of industry, including agriculture. Among the developing countries, Argentina also follows an approach similar to that mentioned above. According to Article 4 of Law No. 24481 (T.O. 1996), industry should be understood as including agriculture, forestry, livestock breeding, fisheries, mining, processing industries in the strict sense and services.

This approach of adopting broad definitions of industry for applying the criteria of industrial application, one that has been followed by a host of countries, could leave its imprint on the process of harmonisation that the SPLT negotiations have initiated. Countries in the developing world, many of which have taken hesitant steps towards expanding the scope of patentable subject-matter while fulfilling their obligations under the TRIPS Agreement, need to take a careful look at the progress of the work on harmonisation.

An area where the criteria of industrial application would have an extremely important role to play would be patenting of biotechnological inventions, more specifically, of inventions concerning, for example, a sequence or a partial sequence of a gene.

In what has become a generally followed practice in respect of biotechnological inventions, an applicant has to indicate the manner in which the claimed invention satisfies the possibility of industrial application in the description unless it is clear to a person skilled in the art from the nature of the claimed invention. For instance, Article 5.3 of the Directive 98/44 of the European Parliament and of the Council on the legal protection of biotechnological inventions stipulates that the industrial application of a sequence or a partial sequence of a gene must be disclosed in the patent application. Furthermore, the Guidelines for Examination in the EPO, Part C, II, 4.12 regarding EPC Rule 27(1)(f) provide that the description should indicate explicitly the way in which the invention is "capable of exploitation in industry," if it is not obvious from the description or from the nature of the invention. Based on this understanding the EPO has refused to grant patent rights on an invention that was able to show only its potential rather than actual uses[25].

The approach of EPO as regards biotechnological inventions seems to have been endorsed by the United States Patent and Trade Marks Office (USPTO) and the Japanese Patent Office (JPO) as the three patent offices have found common ground in relation to DNA sequence patents. Mere determination of a DNA sequence is not enough for patentability. But where the inventor is the first to identify a gene and its useful function, to isolate and clone the gene and thereby make synthetic copies of the gene (or more often a modified form of the natural gene) that are available for use in diagnosis or therapy, these offices accept that this is not mere discovery but the kind of invention for which a patent can be granted (OECD, 2002).

Harmonisation of the criteria of industrial application that is consistent with the common approach of the USPTO, the JPO and the EPO can have implications for the patenting of biotechnological inventions in WIPO member countries. Thus, even if the SPLT does not explicitly consider harmonisation of patentable subject-matter, harmonisation of the criteria of industrial application using the standards prevailing in the United States, Europe and Japan could result in the expansion of patentable subject-matter. Developing countries that have been against extending patent protection to life forms would therefore have to renege on their position taken in the review of the TRIPS Agreement if the SPLT takes shape.

As regards India, the Patents Act, 1970[26] includes several elements that would be out of sync with the practices in the developed countries.

The most significant of these arises from the definition of "invention" adopted by the Act, which reads as follows: "invention means a new product or process involving an inventive step and capable of industrial application". Further, Section 3 provides a detailed rendering of what are "not inventions". Among others these include "mere discovery of a new form of a known substance which does not result in the enhancement of the known efficacy of that substance or the mere discovery of any new property or new use for a known substance or of the mere use of a known process, machine or apparatus unless such known process results in a new product or employs at least one new reactant"[27]. This definition of what does not constitute an invention under the Indian Patents Act has immense significance in the area of pharmaceuticals where India has tried to restrict patenting of drugs that are minor improvements of existing drugs. Responding to the arguments of the public interest groups, in particular, the government has adopted the above-mentioned definition to prevent patents on formulations and new use of known drugs to ensure that the prices of drugs are kept in check. This is in sharp contrast to the practice in the US, where the patent system has allowed patenting of formulations and new use of known substances, which has often led to "ever-greening" of patents.

### *(ii) Prior Art*

"Prior art" is generally used to refer to "the entire body of knowledge which is available to the public before the filing date, or if priority is claimed, before the priority date, of an application for certain industrial property titles, principally patents, utility models and industrial designs" (WIPO, 2001c). Although the definition of "prior art" seems quite unambiguous, patent offices across countries have adopted widely differing approaches for determining what constitutes "prior art" while examining patent claims.

According to the EPC, "state of the art ("prior art") shall be held to comprise everything made available to the public by means of a written or oral description, by use, or in any other way, before the filing of the European patent application"[28]. This definition is elaborated further in the Guidelines for Examination: "[t]he width of this definition should be noted. There are no restrictions whatever as to the geographical location where, or the language or manner in which the relevant information was made available to the public;

also no age limit is stipulated for the documents or other sources of the information."[29] But while the EPC considers a very broad canvas for determining "prior art", the United States considers a rather narrow canvas. Two sets of indicators are considered by the USPTO: "(a) the invention was known or used by others in this country, or patented or described in a printed publication in this or a foreign country, before the invention thereof by the applicant for patent, or (b) the invention was patented or described in a printed publication in this or a foreign country or in public use or on sale in this country, more than one year prior to the date of the application for patent in the United States".[30] This narrowly defined canvas for determining "prior art" excludes a range of knowledge in a foreign country that is either in use and/or is existing in oral tradition, is not considered by the USPTO while examining patent claims.

The TRIPS Agreement is silent on the definition and explanation of how 'prior art' is to be determined while examining a patent application. There is, therefore, space for the national patent offices to use their own standards to determine 'prior art'. The formulation that has been proposed in the SPLT, on the other hand, defines 'prior art' as "information, which has been made available to the public anywhere in the world in any form". The draft SPLT includes a provision that states that information made available to the public in any form, such as in written form, in electronic form, by oral communication, by display or through use, shall qualify as prior art.

Harmonisation of prior art standards is a contentious issue, since this would eliminate the flexibilities that patent offices in individual countries have been exercising while examining patent claims. For instance, in the United States, an isolated and purified form of a natural product (such as a pre-existing biological resource that was unknown to the public at large) is patentable. The rationale for this is that the concept of 'new' under the novelty criterion for patentability does not mean 'pre-existing', but that there was no 'prior art'. Such a conclusion could well be arrived under the SPLT on a reading of Article 8 on 'Prior Art' with Article 12 definition of 'novelty'.[31] Under the Indian Patents Act, 1970, discovery of any living thing or non-living substance occurring in nature, are excluded from the purview of patentability[32]. The draft SPLT, if adopted, could potentially restrict this flexibility available under Indian Patent Act, since the emphasis is not on the act of 'discovery', but on whether there was 'prior art' available on the concerned subject-matter.

It could however also be argued that the emphasis in the draft regulations to the SPLT that information made public by whatever means, including oral communication, could actually prove beneficial for a country like India where the traditional knowledge associated with much of our biological resources exists in oral form. If such oral knowledge was considered by the patent offices in every country for determining prior art, it could reduce the instances of frivolous patents, such as the one given for the wound healing properties of turmeric which India won after challenging its grant, may not be granted in the first place[33].

***(iii) Disclosure Norms***

Patenting of inventions that utilise biological resources and/or associated traditional knowledge has been an issue that has been at centre of much controversy during the past several years. The core of the controversy is that while the Convention on Biological Diversity (CBD) recognises the rights of the States over their genetic resources as well as those of the traditional communities over their knowledge; the patent laws, which, in most countries are consistent with the TRIPS Agreement, do not take into consideration the above-mentioned rights recognised by the CBD. Developing countries have been seeking a resolution of this conflict between the Agreement on TRIPS and the CBD as a part of the mandated review of the TRIPS Agreement. In recognition of the arguments that this regard, the WTO's Doha Ministerial Declaration the relationship between the TRIPS Agreement and the Convention on Biological Diversity, the protection of traditional knowledge and folklore. Based on this, several developing countries, including India submitted a paper to the TRIPS Council in June 2002[34], with the recommendation that members shall require that an applicant for a patent relating to biological materials or to traditional knowledge shall provide, as a condition to acquiring patent rights:

(i) Disclosure of the source and country of origin of the biological resource and of the traditional knowledge used in the invention;

(ii) Evidence of prior informed consent through approval of authorities under the relevant national regimes; and

(iii) Evidence of fair and equitable benefit sharing under the national regime of the country of origin.

The rationale for imposing the above-mentioned conditions on the patent applicant, according to the submission, was that these conditions would play a significant role in preventing biopiracy and misappropriation of traditional knowledge.

One of the controversial aspects of the SPLT is that members cannot impose any additional conditions on patent applicants, other than those envisaged in the SPLT. Article 5 of the draft SPLT provides that no additional requirements relating to the form or contents of national patent applications can be introduced, which do not favour the patent applicants or the patentees[35]. This, in other words, pre-empts the moves that the developing countries have taken in the WTO TRIPS Council for strengthening the disclosure norms in case of inventions that use biological resources and/or associated traditional knowledge. Furthermore, Article 10 of the draft SPLT, which lays down the norms for disclosure provides that the claimed invention should be disclosed in a manner sufficiently clear and complete for the invention to be made and used by a person skilled in the art. These conditions regarding disclosure essentially correspond with the conditions that have been set out in Article 29 of the Agreement on TRIPS. The approach followed in the SPLT would thus directly conflict with the proposals being made by the developing countries to the TRIPS Council regarding the disclosure of origin of biological and genetic material, which, as the proposing countries have argued, should be introduced as an amendment or clarification to the TRIPS provision.

A resolution of this issue was sought by several developing country delegations arguing that the SPLT should contain a requirement on source and country of origin of a biological or genetic resource and the associated traditional knowledge used in a patent claim[36]. In contrast, developed countries, including the EU, US, Japan, the Russian Federation, Switzerland, Czech Republic and Bulgaria have held the view that the appropriate forum for discussion of this issue is the WIPO's Intergovernmental Committee on Intellectual Property and Genetic Resources, Traditional Knowledge and Folklore (IGC), which was established in the year 2000 and not the SPLT[37].

It is to be noted in this regard, that the IGC was established by the WIPO after the Patent Law Treaty (PLT) negotiations failed to consider aspects relating to Traditional Knowledge and IPRs in 2000. At the time of conclusion of the PLT, a proposal was made by the Colombian Delegation to include aspects of origin of biological material in the treaty. However, the PLT was adopted by the WIPO in June 2000, without any reference to the Colombian proposal. The WIPO Secretariat instead recommended formation of the IGC as a separate forum to consider issues of Traditional Knowledge and IPRs. The implications of this development is that concerns of developing countries regarding patents based on biological material and TK would not be addressed in the SPLT negotiations, even when these have a direct bearing on conditions on patent applicants.

In this context, the proposal made by the Delegation of Switzerland in the Ninth Session of the Standing Committee on the Law of Patents needs to be considered. Switzerland had proposed that the Patent Cooperation Treaty (PCT)[38] could be amended to include the explicit requirement to disclose the source and country of origin of genetic resources as well as traditional knowledge that may have been used in an invention for which patent rights were sought[39]. It was argued that since Article 5 of the draft SPLT provides that any condition that is imposed on the patent applicants through the PCT would be allowed, an amendment to the PCT would result in obligations being brought on the Contracting Parties of the SPLT.

As regards the definition of the terms "source", Switzerland proposed that the broadest possible definition could be adopted. It was clarified that term "not only includes other terms used in this context such as "origin," "geographical origin," "country of origin of genetic resources" or "Contracting Party providing genetic resources," but also any other source such as publications in scientific journals or books, databases on traditional knowledge, or *ex situ* collections of genetic resources".

At least three sets of issues arise from the proposal made by Switzerland. The first is that the amendment was not proposed as a binding commitment on PCT Contracting Parties. The amendment would "apply if the national law of a Contracting Party of the PCT requires patent applicants submitting an international patent application to declare the source of genetic resources and/or knowledge, innovations and practices, in their patent applications". Given that most developed countries have not been keen to accept any condition to be imposed on the patent applicant requiring disclosure of source and country of origin of genetic material and/or traditional knowledge, the approach suggested by Switzerland would make the proposed amendment a non-starter[40]. Secondly, the scope of application of the condition on the patent applicants would be narrow since the PCT applicable only to the so-called "international" applications and not to all applications. And, finally, although the definition of what can be considered as the "source" appears quite comprehensive, it does not include an important element, viz. oral tradition, which is a key depository of traditional knowledge.

For reasons stated above, the proposal made by Switzerland would not result in an outcome that would be the most desirable manner from the point of view of developing countries. At the same time, however, it marks an important development in that the recognition of the importance of disclosing the source and country of origin of genetic resources and/or traditional knowledge in the patent applications has gone beyond the confines of the developing world. This may be a positive augury from a development country perspective in the on-going negotiations in the WTO.

## Conclusion

Enhancing the level of harmonisation of patent laws across countries has been on the agenda of the WIPO at least since the first half of the 1980s. During the past few years, moves have been afoot in the TRIPS Council to find ways of improving the flexibilities available in the Agreement to meet the concerns of the developing countries. The main objective of the TRIPS review process, in view of the developing countries, is to improve the available flexibility to allow developing countries to adopt TRIPS-consistent patent laws that would suit their development imperatives in the best possible manner. This process was given further impetus through the adoption of the Declaration on TRIPS and Public Health at the Doha Ministerial Conference in November 2001. The Doha Ministerial Declaration has taken some steps towards rebalancing the TRIPS Agreement, keeping in view the development needs and interests of developing countries. In addition to this, the Doha Ministerial Conference also asked for a time-bound resolution to the TRIPS-review process.[41]

However, the flexibilities that are currently available under the TRIPS Agreement could be considerably eroded if the processes of patent harmonisation initiated under the WIPO Patent Agenda move towards higher and stricter standards. In the ninth session of the SPLT negotiations held in May 2003, several of the aforementioned contentious issues were discussed. Because of the numerous outstanding issues on which consensus has not been achieved, it is likely that several more sessions would be required before the SPLT is signed and ratified. There is therefore some time that developing countries like India have at their disposal for making appropriate interventions.

Further, it is expected that SPLT would not limit the freedom of Member States to regulate matters, which are not currently included within its scope, such as exclusive rights conferred by the patent, exceptions to such rights, use of patented subject-matter without authorization of the right holder, exhaustion of patent rights and judicial procedures against acts infringing patent rights (WIPO, 2002d). These areas may however be considered in future negotiations, and developing countries would need to be prepared for the same.

A significant aspect to be underscored in this regard is that clear linkages between the TRIPS and SPLT negotiating processes have not been established either at the multilateral level or at the domestic level in the developing countries. Given this serious lacuna, it is incumbent on developing countries who have taken a proactive role in the TRIPS negotiations, to make its presence felt and concerns heard at the SPLT negotiations. There is an urgent need to review how the SPLT negotiations and the TRIPS review processes could be reconciled. This would also be imperative in view of the recognition in the Preamble to the TRIPS Agreement that there should be a mutually supportive relationship between the WTO and WIPO. It is also important to ensure coordination between the authorities at the national level who are engaged in the negotiations for the review of the TRIPS Agreement and the SPLT, so that consistent and complementary stands best suited to India's interests, can be taken in the two forums.

## ANNEX 7.1:
## DEVELOPMENTS LEADING TO NEGOTIATIONS ON SUBSTANTIAL PATENT LAW TREATY

*1967* : Stockholm Act of Paris Convention.

*1980* : Negotiations initiated under WIPO for the revision of the Paris Convention for the Protection of Industrial Property, resulting from pressures exerted by developing countries.

*1985* : Negotiations for Treaty Supplementing the Paris Convention as far as Patents are concerned, commonly known as the Patent Harmonisation Treaty.

*1991* : Draft of Patent Harmonisation Treaty considered at WIPO Diplomatic Conference. The proceedings were inconclusive.

*1994* : TRIPS Agreement concluded under the WTO negotiations. Sets minimum standards for patent protection across countries.

*1995* : Initiatives taken to revive the Patent Harmonization Treaty.

*1998* : Negotiations begin under WIPO's Standing Committee on Law of Patents for the conclusion of a Patent Law Treaty. Initial focus on harmonising procedural aspects only.

*1999* : Review of Article 27.3(b) of the TRIPS Agreement: Developing countries putting forth the view that the Agreement has to recognise their development concerns,

*June 2000*: Successful adoption of the Patent Law Treaty (PLT) under the WIPO, which harmonizes many aspects of patent procedure.

*November 2000*: The Fourth Session of WIPO's Standing Committee on the Law of Patents initiates work on "deep harmonisation" of a number of issues relating to the grant of patent rights as well as validity of patents.

*November 2001*: WTO Ministerial Conference at Doha. Doha Ministerial Declaration mandates the Member States to review the relationship between the CBD and the TRIPS Agreement and protection of traditional knowledge. Separate declaration on TRIPS Agreement and Public Health emphasizes "the TRIPS Agreement does not and should not prevent Members from taking measures to protect public health".

*May 2004*: Tenth Session of WIPO's Standing Committee on the Law of Patents considered the Draft Substantive Patent Law Treaty (SPLT).

## ANNEX 7.2: ALTERNATIVE FORMULATIONS FOR INDUSTRIAL APPLICATION/UTILITY

*Article 12(3)*: [*Industrial Applicability/Utility*] A claimed invention shall be industrially applicable (useful). It shall be considered industrially applicable (useful) if it

| *[Alternative A]* | *[Alternative B]* | *[Alternative C]* |
|---|---|---|
| can be made or used for exploitation in any field of [commercial] [economic] activity. | can be made or used in any kind of industry. "Industry" shall be understood in its broadest sense, as in the Paris Convention. | has a specific, substantial and credible utility. |

*Source*: WIPO (2003c).

## END NOTES

1. An earlier version of this paper was published in the *Economic and Political Weekly See*. Dhar, B. and Anuradha, R.V. 2005. 'The Substantive Patent Law Treaty: What It Means for India', *Economic and Political Weekly,* 40(13): 1346-1354.
2. The US President's Commission on the Patent System had stated as early as in 1966 that "the ultimate goal in the protection of inventions should be the establishment of a universal patent, respected throughout the world, issued in the light of, and inventive over, all of the prior art of the world, and obtained quickly and inexpensively on a single application, but only in return for a genuine contribution to the progress of the useful arts", quoted by James E. Rogan (2002).
3. This was one of the recommendations of the Policy Advisory Commission of the WIPO in 2001, *See* WIPO (2001a).
4. WIPO (2000a), p. 3.
5. Among the more significant changes that the United States would have had to bring about in its Patents Act (United States Code Title 35—Patents) if the Patent Harmonization Treaty was adopted are the following: (i) replacing

the first-to-invent system with a first-to-file system, and (ii) changing some elements of the patentability criteria. For details, see *Fryer* (1990).

6. Questions may however be asked whether the framework for patent protection underlined by the TRIPS Agreement was established on the basis on "minimum standards" since for an overwhelmingly large majority of Members of the WTO fulfilling the TRIPS commitments meant that their patent laws had to be significantly strengthened in favour of the patentee. More significantly, the term of patent provided under the TRIPS Agreement was longer than that existing in the country that has had the strongest patent law, viz. the United States.
7. Articles 1-12 of the Paris Convention (the Stockholm Act of 1967) provide the framework of protection that the member countries have to adopt in respect of patents, utility models, industrial designs, trademarks, service marks, trade names, indications of source or appellations of origin, and the repression of unfair competition. Article 19 of the Paris Convention states "that the countries of the Union reserve the right to make separately between themselves special agreements for the protection of industrial property, in so far as these agreements do not contravene the provisions of this Convention". In other words, Article 19 of the Paris Convention establishes the fact that the TRIPS Agreement is consistent with the provisions of the Paris Convention.
8. One of the objectives of this agreement is the following: "Desiring to establish a mutually supportive relationship between them and with a view to establishing appropriate arrangements for cooperation between them". *See* WTO (1996)
9. The United States delegation took the position that "substantive matters [in the context of harmonisation of patent laws] ... were beyond the mandate of the draft Treaty". Interestingly, the official stance of the United States remained strongly opposed to the substantive harmonisation of the patent laws despite the fact that the substantive patent community, in particular organisations like the American Intellectual Property Law Association (AIPLA), was in favour of substantive harmonisation. *See* for instance, Arriola (1995).
10. Prominent among the countries that concurred with this position were Japan, Canada, France and Austria from the developed world and China, Korea and Kenya from the developing world.
11. Commission of the European Communities, 2002, p. 11.
12. The AIPLA has suggested that the United States Patents and Trademarks Office (USPTO) should "stay on course in its efforts to negotiate in WIPO a treaty reflecting best practices ... and to resist the inclusion of destructive amendments such as those put forward by certain developing countries". *See*, AIPLA (2002).
13. Response of the Biotechnology Industry Association (BIO) to the USPTO questions pertaining to global patent law harmonization. *See* BIO (2001).
14. The following countries belong to the group: Argentina, Brazil, Bolivia,

Cuba, Dominican Republic, Ecuador, Egypt, Iran, Kenya, Peru, Sierra Leone, South Africa, Tanzania and Venezuela. *See* WIPO (2005b).

15. Correa & Mussungu (2002) point out that despite NGOs being granted only 'observer' capacity, they have played a significant role in the negotiations so far, making proposals or reservations, and supporting or opposing the positions of Governments.
16. For instance, the Indian Patents Act of 1970 did not allow the granting of product patents in the area of chemicals, which included pharmaceuticals. Some countries excluded pharmaceuticals from the ambit of their patent laws.
17. During the discussion, the US, supported by the Representative of BIO, opposed the inclusion of the exceptions contained in Articles 27.2 and 27.3 of the TRIPS Agreement at this stage, in particular with respect to plants and animals. *See* WIPO (2002a), paragraph 186.
18. This term is currently in square brackets.
19. WIPO (2002a). paragraph 185.
20. WIPO, (2002c). paragraph 171.
21. WIPO, (2002c). paragraph 159.
22. Article 12 of the Draft SPLT. *See* WIPO (2003c).
23. Under the Canadian Patent Act, the term "utility" means having industrial or commercial value in a manner that benefits the public. Thus defined, "utility" as criteria adopted by Canada, is, in effect, closer to that of industrial application.
24. Article 57 of the European Patent Convention states further the "industry" should be understood in its broad sense as including any physical activity of "technical character", i.e. an activity which belongs to the useful or practical arts as distinct from the aesthetic arts; it does not necessarily imply the use of a machine or the manufacture of an article and could cover e.g. a process for dispersing fog, or a process for converting energy from one form to another. Thus, Article 57 excludes from patentability very few "inventions" which are not already excluded by the list in Article 52(2) of the EPC. *See* European Patent Office (2006).
25. Decision of the Opposition Division of the European Patent Office dated June 20, 2001, ICOS Corporation/Seven transmembrance recepter (EP B 0630405), OJEPO 2002, 293. In this case, the Opposition Division decided that, as "potential uses of the invention are disclosed in the specification which however are based on a proposed function of the V28 protein as a receptor which is not sufficiently disclosed in the specification," "the potential uses disclosed in the application are speculative, i.e., are not specific, substantial and credible and as such are not considered industrial applications", quoted in WIPO (2003a).
26. As amended in 1999, 2002 and 2005 for making it consistent with India's obligations under the Agreement on TRIPS.
27. The Patents Act provides clarification of this clause in Section 3(d): "... salts, esters, ethers, polymorphs, metabolites, pure form, particle size,

isomers, mixtures of isomers, complexes, combinations and other derivatives of known substance shall be considered to be the same substance, unless they differ significantly in properties with regard to efficacy".

28. Article 54(2) of the European Patent Convention.
29. European Patent Office (2001), Part C, Chapter IV, paragraph 5.1.
30. United States Code Title 35—Patents, Section 102.
31. *See* WIPO (2003c). Article 8 defines 'Prior art' as consisting of all information which has been made available to the public anywhere in the world in any form before the priority date of the invention for which patent rights are sought. Article 12(2) while dealing with 'novelty' states that a claimed invention shall be considered novel if it does not form part of the prior art. Article 12 (3) further states that a claimed invention is considered to involve an inventive step (be non-obvious) if, having regard to the differences and similarities between the claimed invention and the prior art as defined in Article 8(1), the claimed invention as a whole would not have been obvious to a person skilled in the art.
32. Section 3 (c) of the Patents Act, 1970.
33. In the United States, for instance the existing patent law demands proof of prior art from other countries only in the form of 'printed publication'. This would limit the use of oral knowledge as evidence of prior art.
34. WTO (2003). This submission was made by Bolivia, Brazil, Cuba, Dominican Republic, Ecuador, India, Peru, Thailand and Venezuela. This was followed up by a series of submissions by this group of countries, which include WTO (2005a), WTO (2005b) and WTO (2006).
35. Article 5(1)(a) states: "...no Contracting Party shall require compliance with any requirement relating to the request, description, claims, drawings or abstract of an application different from or additional to the requirements relating to the request, description, claims, drawings or abstract which are provided for under the Patent Cooperation Treaty in respect of international applications". Article 5(1)(b) states: "A Contracting Party shall be free to provide for requirements which, from the viewpoint of applicants and patentees, are more favourable than the requirements referred to in sub-paragraph (a) in so far as they relate to the form or contents of an application".
36. Prominent among the countries were Argentina, Brazil, China, South Africa, Egypt and India. For details *see*, WIPO (2003b), paragraphs 46-48.
37. WIPO (2003b). paragraphs 41-43.
38. *See* WIPO (2003d). The Patent Cooperation Treaty allows inventors to apply patent protection for an invention simultaneously in a number of countries by filing an "international" patent application. This facility is available to the nationals or residents of a Contracting Parties to the Treaty.
39. The Swiss proposal read as follows: "The national law applicable ... may ... require the applicant:
    (i) to declare the source of a specific genetic resource to which the inventor has had access, if an invention is directly based on such a resource; if such source is unknown, this shall be declared accordingly;

(ii) to declare the source of knowledge, innovations and practices of indigenous and local communities relevant for the conservation and sustainable use of biological diversity, if the inventor knows that an invention is directly based on such knowledge, innovations and practices; if such source is unknown, this shall be declared accordingly." *See* WIPO (2003d), paragraph 21.

40. For instance, the United States has held the view that a system that requires patent applicants to disclose "the source of any genetic materials or traditional knowledge used in developing their claimed inventions ... *would be a legal and administrative nightmare for all involved* and would not ensure that those contributing such resources or knowledge would share in any benefits that might flow from commercialization of any product or process that might be developed from the resource or knowledge" (emphasis added). *See* WTO (2000).

41. Para 19 of the Doha Ministerial Declaration, states, *inter alia*: "In undertaking this work, the TRIPS Council shall be guided by the objectives and principles set out in Articles 7 and 8 of the TRIPS Agreement and shall take fully into account the development dimension." *See* WTO (2001).

## REFERENCES

AIPLA (2002). Recommendations for Achieving Additional Patent Law Harmonization, statement made in the USPTO Round Table on International Harmonization of Patent Laws, December.

Arriola M.T. (1995). Report of the First Session of the Committee of Experts on the Patent Law Treaty in Geneva, December 11 to 15, *CARIP Newsletter* (V311).

BIO (2001). Submission made to Mr Nicholas Godici, Acting Undersecretary of Commerce and Acting Director of the United States Patent and Trademark Office (www.bio.org/ip/action/ltr20020506c.pdf).

Commission of the European Communities (2002). Development and Implications of Patent Law in the Field of Biotechnology and Genetic Engineering: Report from the Commission to the European Parliament and the Council.

Correa, C. and S. Mussungu (2002). *The WIPO Patent Agenda: The Risks for Developing Countries*, South Centre, Geneva.

European Patent Office (2001). 'Guidelines for Examination in the European Patent Office', accessed from http://www.european-patent-office.org/legal/gui_lines/index.htm.

———— (2006). Convention on the Grant of European Patents (version as of 1 January 2006), accessed from http://www.european-patent-office.org/legal/epc/pdf / epc_2006_v5_bm_en.pdf.

Fryer, W.T. (1990). 'Patent Law Harmonization Treaty Decision is not far off—

What course should the US Take?' A Review of the current situation and alternatives available, in *IDEA: The Journal of Law and Technology*, pp. 309-354. http://www.idea.piercelaw.edu/articles/30/p309.Fryer.pdf

Godici, N.P. (2001). 'Progress Toward a World Patent: The view from the United States', paper presented in the International Symposium on Protecting IP Assets in the New Millennium, Paris.

Rogan, J.E. (2002). Under Secretary of Commerce for Intellectual Property, and Director of the U.S. Patent and Trademark Office before the WIPO Conference on the International Patent System, Geneva.

OECD (2002). *Genetic Inventions, Intellectual Property Rights and Licensing Practices: Evidence and Policies*, Paris.

WIPO (1997). 'The Protection of Inventions: Patents and other Titles of Protection', WIPO National Workshop for Patent Lawyers, organised jointly by WIPO and Government of Ethiopia, WIPO/IP/ADD/97/2, Geneva.

——— (2000a). Standing Committee on the Law of Patents, "Suggestions for the Further Development of International Patent Law", Fourth Session, SCP/4/2, Geneva.

——— (2000b). Standing Committee on the Law of Patents, Report, Fourth Session, SCP/4/6, Geneva.

——— (2001a). Policy Advisory Commission, Report, Geneva.

——— (2001b). 'Agenda for Development of the International Patent System: Memorandum of the Director General, Assemblies of the Member States of WIPO', Thirty-Sixth Series of Meetings, Geneva.

——— (2001c). Inter-governmental Committee on Intellectual Property and Genetic Resources, Traditional Knowledge and Folklore, *Progress Report on the Status of Traditional Knowledge as Prior Art*, Second Session WIPO/GRTKF/IC/2/6, Geneva.

——— (2002a). Standing Committee on the Law of Patents, "Report adopted by the Standing Committee", Sixth Session, SCP/6/9, Geneva.

——— (2002b). Standing Committee on the Law of Patents, "Draft Regulations and Practice Guidelines under the Substantive Patent Law Treaty", Seventh Session, SCP/7/4, Geneva.

——— (2002c). Standing Committee on the Law of Patents, Report, Seventh Session, SCP/7/8, Geneva.

——— (2002d). Standing Committee on the Law of Patents, "Proposals by the Delegations of the Dominican Republic and Brazil Concerning Articles 2, 13 and 14 of the Draft Substantive Patent Law Treaty", Eighth Session, SCP/8/5, Geneva.

——— (2003a). Standing Committee on the Law of Patents, "Industrial Applicability" and "Utility" Requirements: Commonalities and Differences, Ninth Session, SCP/9/5, Geneva.

——— (2003b). Standing Committee on the Law of Patents, "Report adopted by the Standing Committee", Eighth Session, SCP/8/9, Geneva.

——— (2003c). Standing Committee on the Law of Patents, "Draft Substantive Patent Law Treaty", Tenth Session, SCP/10/4, Geneva.

——— (2003d). Working Group on Reform of the Patent Cooperation Treaty (PCT), Proposals by Switzerland regarding the Declaration of the Source of Genetic Resources and Traditional Knowledge in Patent Applications, Fourth Session, PCT/R/WG/4/13, Geneva.

——— (2004). General Assembly, Thirty-First (15th Extraordinary) Session, "Proposal by the United States of America and Japan for establishing a new work plan for the Standing Committee on the Law of Patents (SCP)", Geneva.

——— (2005a). Standing Committee on the Law of Patents, "Statement received from Brazil", Eleventh Session, SCP/11/4, Geneva.

——— (2005b). Inter-sessional Inter-governmental Meeting on a Development Agenda for WIPO, Proposal to Establish a Development Agenda for WIPO: An Elaboration of Issues raised in document WO/GA/31/11, Geneva.

WTO, (1996). 'Technical Cooperation Handbook on Notification Requirements', Part VI, WT/TC/NOTIF/TRIPS/1, Geneva.

——— (2000). Council for Trade-Related Aspects of Intellectual Property Rights, "Review of the Provisions of Article 27.3(b): Further Views of the United States", IP/C/W/209, Geneva.

——— (2001). Ministerial Conference, 'Declaration on the TRIPS Agreement and Public Health', WT/MIN(01)/DEC/2, Doha.

——— (2003). Council for Trade-Related Aspects of Intellectual Property Rights, "The Relationship between the TRIPS Agreement and the Convention on Biological Diversity and the Protection of Traditional Knowledge", IP/C/W/403, Geneva.

——— (2005a). Council for Trade-Related Aspects of Intellectual Property Rights, 'The Relationship between the TRIPS Agreement and the Convention on Biological Diversity (CBD) and the Protection of Traditional Knowledge—Elements of the Obligation to Disclose Evidence of Benefit-Sharing under the Relevant National Regime: Submission from Bolivia, Brazil, Colombia, Cuba, Dominican Republic Ecuador, India, Peru and Thailand'.

——— (2005b). Council for Trade-Related Aspects of Intellectual Property Rights, "The Relationship between the TRIPS Agreement and the Convention on Biological Diversity (CBD) and the Protection of Traditional Knowledge: Technical Observations on the United States Submission IP/C/W449 by Bolivia, Brazil, Colombia, Cuba, India and Pakistan", IP/C/W/459, Geneva.

——— (2006). Council for Trade-Related Aspects of Intellectual Property Rights, "Submission in Response to the Communication from Switzerland (IP/C/W/446): Communication from Bolivia, Cuba, Ecuador, India, Sri Lanka and Thailand", IP/C/W/470, Geneva.

# Chapter 8

# Multilateral Framework on Investment under WTO: A Developing Country Perspective

DIPAYAN DATTA CHAUDHURI*

## 1. Introduction

The Final Act of the Uruguay Round included an Agreement on Trade Related Investment Measures (TRIMs). The General Agreement on Trade in Services (GATS) provided a framework for liberalization of trade in services including cross-border commercial presence which is akin to FDI. Even without waiting for the mandated review of TRIMs becoming due in 1999, developed countries attempted to widen the scope of multilateral regime on investment beyond what is covered in Agreements on TRIMs and GATS.

At the First Ministerial Conference of WTO in Singapore the EU and Canada proposed to create a Multilateral Framework on Investment (MFI) under the auspices of WTO. A Working Group on Trade and Investment (WGTI) was set up in WTO to study the issue.

Before the Working Group on Trade and Investment (WGTI) could complete its work, European Union with the support of other industrialized countries pushed the investment issue for negotiations at the Fourth Ministerial Conference of WTO held at Doha in November 2001. The Doha Declaration (Para 20) recognized "the

* Associate Professor, Department of Economics, Indian Institute of Management, Indore.

case for a multilateral framework to secure transparent, stable and predictable conditions for long-term cross-border investment, particularly foreign direct investment, that will contribute to the expansion of trade" and it was agreed that "negotiations will take place after the Fifth Session of the Ministerial Conference on the basis of a decision to be taken, by explicit consensus, at that session on modalities of negotiations". It further recognized (Para 21) "the needs of developing and least-developed countries for enhanced support for technical assistance and capacity-building in this area, including policy analysis and development so that they may better evaluate the implications of closer multilateral cooperation for their development policies and objectives, and human and institutional development". The Doha Declaration (Para 22) stated that the Working Group should focus on "scope and definition; transparency; non-discrimination; modalities for pre-establishment commitments based on a GATS-type positive list approach; development provisions; exceptions and balance-of-payments safeguards; consultation and the settlement of disputes between members". The issue of MFI has, however, been dropped from Doha Agenda work programme as per the July Package, 2004. But, this issue has raised an important question whether FDI inflows to any country are influenced by its economic policy. In this paper, we have tried to address this issue from the perspective of developing countries.

This paper is organized in the following manner: Section 2 outlines the broad objective of this paper. The major issues in the Working Group submissions on the relationship between trade and investment are summarized in Section 3. Section 4 deals with the survey of literature. Main features of the relevant Agreements namely, General Agreement on Trade in Services (GATS) and Agreement on Trade Related Intellectual Property Rights (TRIPS) are highlighted in Sections 5 and 6 respectively. Methodology for this paper is discussed in Section 7. Section 8 mentions the data sources. The results of the paper are analyzed in Section 9 and concluding observations are made in Section 10.

## 2. Objectives

The proponents of MFI argue that a MFI would help developing countries to attract larger inflows of FDI. This multilateral framework calls for policy liberalization on the part of WTO member countries.

In this paper we will analyse, based on the experiences of major developing countries, whether policy liberalization results in greater FDI inflows. Under WTO, FDI is contained in three agreements namely, General Agreement on Trade Related Investment Measures (TRIMs), General Agreement on Trade in Services (GATS) and Agreement on Trade Related Intellectual Property Rights (TRIPS). The central question is whether opening up the service sector and stronger protection of intellectual properties necessarily improve the attractiveness of a developing country to foreign investors.

## 3. Major Issues in the Working Group Submissions on the Relationship between Trade and Investment

A number of countries submitted Working Group reports on different aspects of trade and investment such as scope and definition, transparency, non-discrimination, pre-investment commitments etc. Here we will briefly highlight the broad differences among the member countries with regard to certain major issues of the MFI.

One of the most predominant issues for discussion in the Working Group was on the definition of the term "investment". Canada (WT/WGTI/W/113[1] and WT/WGTI/W/157[2]), United States (WT/WGTI/W/142[3]) and the Separate Customs Territory of Taiwan, Penghu, Kinmen and Matsu (WT/WGTI/W/128[4]) were in favour of "asset-based" definition of investment. This definition covers all types of foreign investment [direct investment (FDI) and indirect investment] and all forms of investment assets. On the other side, the countries like Japan (WT/WGTI/W/111[5]), Korea (WT/WGTI/W/114[6]), European Community (WT/WGTI/W/140[7]) and China (WT/WGTI/W/159[8]) argued for the need to restrict the scope of MFI to FDI which is the most stable form of capital.

The Secretariat Note (WT/WGTI/W/109[9]) highlighted the importance of "transparency" for creating a predictable, stable and secure climate for foreign investment. In the opinion of EC (WT/WGTI/W/110[10]) and Japan (WT/WGTI/W/112[11] and WT/WGTI/W/158[12]) greater transparency in international commercial treaties is likely to encourage higher inflows of FDI by reducing the investors' perception of risk. Many members, however, emphasized the need to strike an appropriate balance between pursuing transparency and avoiding the imposition of burdensome obligations on host country governments. China (WT/WGTI/W/160[13]) suggested that transparency obligations in any prospective investment agreement should apply to investors, home countries as well as host countries.

"Non-discrimination" is another core policy-making principle of international trade and investment agreements (WT/WGTI/W/118[14]). The two most widely used standards of non-discrimination are "most-favoured-nation" (MFN) and "national treatment" (NT). According to EC (WT/WGTI/W/121[15]), Korea (WT/WGTI/W/96[16] and WT/WGTI/W/123[17]), Mexico (WT/WGTI/W/132[18]) and the Separate Customs Territory of Taiwan, Penghu, Kinmen and Matsu (WT/WGTI/W/127[19]) the GATS approach provides a useful mode for addressing pre-establishment rules in a multilateral investment framework. India (WT/WGTI/W/149[20]) argued that there are many differences between the definition of investment in the MFI and in the GATS in which investment is defined as "commercial presence" which mainly focuses on the supply of services. Canada (WT/WGTI/W/130[21]) acknowledged that pre-establishment market access could not be permitted by the host country in all cases in all sectors. Canada, therefore, argued in favour of MFN/NT negative list kind of agreements, where, flexibility is implicitly embodied. In the NAFTA, for example, an annex also exists for Mexico which exempts several broad sectors such as petroleum, electricity, rail-roads and others from MFN, national treatment and other provisions in the agreement.

## 4. A Review of Literature

A brief survey of literature will indicate that there are studies on both for and against the issue of MFI. Low and Subramanian (1995) presented six main arguments in favour of multilateral rules on investment. First, international commitments help to support national commitments and make them harder to reverse. Second, common ground rules and purpose may give a fillip to liberalization. Third, a framework of international commitments offers greater certainty regarding policy continuity and therefore provides improved investment opportunities. Fourth, an international framework is required to ensure that regional investment agreements do not diverge in ways that fragment the international economy. Fifth, international cooperation could control wasteful competition among governments to attract foreign investment through fiscal and other incentives and sixth, a broad-based investment agreement would fill an illogical gap in existing multilateral rules. According to Das (2003) as there are about 1,600 plus bilateral investment treaties (BITs) in the world economy, multilateral rules under WTO would substantially reduce the transaction costs of abiding by multiple bilateral treaties and hence would ensure greater efficiency. Rules would also help to reduce wasteful and costly competition in terms of providing subsidies by potential host countries in attracting FDI.

In the opinion of Kumar (2001) an agreement on investment, beyond TRIMs, on the WTO agenda will not be in the interests of the developing countries. A trade-type regime is not appropriate for investment and there is a need for government regulation for better utilization of FDI inflows in developing countries. Singh (2001) argued that unless developing country governments can adequately regulate the timing, quality, and total amount of FDI, FDI can lead to short-and long-term financial fragility, making these countries prone to financial crisis. According to Hoekman and Saggi (2000, 2001) there is no urgent need for new multilateral rules for investment. Governments can achieve much of what is beneficial unilaterally by including the application of the principles of NT and MFN in national law. Kumar and Pradhan (2002) analyzed the relationships between FDI, growth and domestic investment for a sample of 107 developing countries for the 1980-99 periods. Panel data estimations in a production function framework suggested a positive effect of FDI on growth. However, tests of causality found that in a majority of cases the direction of causation is not pronounced and in a substantial number of cases the direction of causation actually runs from growth to FDI. Although FDI appears to crowd-out domestic investments in net terms, some countries have had favourable effect of FDI on domestic investments in net terms suggesting a role for host country policies. So, developing countries should try to retain their policy flexibility to influence the quality of FDI inflows in WTO negotiations.

In the opinion of Brooks *et al.* (2003), the establishment of a multilateral framework of rules can contribute to improvement of the investment climate in the long-run. Regardless of the outcome of the Doha Round of WTO negotiations, individual countries can adopt a policy framework that is beneficial to both foreign and domestic investors. Basic components of such policies should include transparency about investment rules and regulations, with clear identification of agencies responsible for issuing relevant licences, permits and approvals.

Kumar (2003) argued that WTO is not the right forum for handling investment. In his view WTO does not have the necessary expertise to deal with investment, which is more a subject, dealt by finance ministries or industry ministries and not by trade diplomats. So, there is a very little justification of including a full-fledged investment agreement in the multilateral 'trade' negotiations after taking care of possible trade distorting investment policies under TRIMs Agreement. In his view this 'one-size-fits-all' approach to FDI policy, which is likely to evolve through MFI in WTO, cannot serve the best interest of countries at different levels of development.

Nunnenkamp and Pant (2003) suggested that rather than engaging in a futile attempt to block multilateral negotiations on investment altogether, the developing countries should use the rule-based multilateral investment policy as a negotiating chip and, thereby, increase the pressure on the industrialized countries to agree to negotiations on labour mobility. Nicoletti *et al.* (2003) observed that despite extensive liberalization over the past two decades, there is scope for further reducing policy barriers in order to integrate with OECD markets. Further liberalization of trade, FDI and domestic product and labour markets will facilitate the process of integration. Lee and Mansfield (1996) observed a direct relationship between increased Intellectual Property Rights (IPR) protection and inflows of FDI. They found that the level of IPR protection in a country also affects the composition of FDI. Lesser (2001), on the basis of the study of 44 developing countries, concluded that the relationship between the IPR score and FDI is positive and significant at 10 percent level.

## 5. The General Agreement on Trade in Services (GATS)

GATS is the first and only set of multilateral rules governing international trade in services. It provides for market access to the foreign suppliers of the services for which market access commitments are undertaken. The agreement covers all internationally traded services—for example, banking, telecommunications, tourism, professional services, etc. It also defines four ways (or "modes") of trading services:

- Mode 1—*cross-border supply* which is defined as the supply of a service from the territory of one member into the territory of any other member, analogous to trade in goods; (e.g. banking or architectural services transmitted via telecommunications or mail, international telephone calls);

- Mode 2—*consumption abroad* which is defined as situations where a service consumer (e.g. tourist or patient) moves into another member's territory to obtain a service;
- Mode 3—*commercial presence* which implies that a service supplier of one member establishes a territorial presence, including through ownership or lease of premises, in another member's territory to provide a service (e.g. domestic subsidiaries of foreign insurance companies or hotel chains, analogous to foreign direct investment); and
- Mode 4—*movement of natural persons* consists of persons of one member entering the territory of another member to supply a service (e.g. accountants, doctors or teachers).

GATS is not an investment agreement in the same sense as most International Investment Agreements (IIAs). Its focus is on the ability to supply a service rather than on investment *per se*. Nonetheless, it has been noted that "commercial presence" in the GATS approximates to the notion of "investment" in an IIA, and in that context "service supplier" approximates to the notion of "investor". Thus, Mode 3 i.e. commercial presence relates to the delivery of services through foreign investment.

Individual countries' commitments appear in "schedules" that list the sectors being opened, the extent of market access being given in those sectors (e.g. whether there are any restrictions on foreign ownership), and any limitations on national treatment (whether some rights granted to local companies will not be granted to foreign companies). Obligations contained in the GATS may be categorized into two broad groups: 'general obligations' and 'specific commitments'. General obligations apply directly and automatically to all members and services sectors, as well as commitments concerning market access and national treatment in specifically designated sectors. Under General Obligations Article II and Article III deal with MFN Treatment and Transparency respectively.

Under Specific Commitments Articles XVI and XVII are concerned with Market Access and National Treatment respectively. Market Access is a negotiated commitment in specified sectors. It may be made subject to various types of limitations that are enumerated in Article XVI (2). For example, limitations may be imposed on the number of service suppliers, the total value of service transactions, the total number of service operations, the total number of natural persons, the legal form of service supplier or the participation of foreign capital. A commitment to National Treatment implies that the member concerned does not operate discriminatory measures benefiting domestic services or service suppliers.

Each WTO member is required to have *Horizontal* and *Specific* Commitments relating to market access and national treatment. The 'Horizontal Section' contains entries that apply across all sectors subsequently listed in the schedule. Horizontal limitations often refer to a particular mode of supply, notably commercial presence and the presence of natural persons. The 'Sector Specific Sections' contain entries that apply only to the particular service. For each service sector or sub-sector that is offered, the schedule must indicate, with respect to each of the four modes of supply, any limitations on market access or national treatment, which are to be maintained.

In the great majority of schedules the order in which the sectors are listed corresponds to the GATT Secretariat classification which lists twelve broad sectors as follows: (1) Business; (2) Communication; (3) Construction and Engineering; (4) Distribution; (5) Education; (6) Environment; (7) Financial; (8) Health; (9) Tourism and Travel; (10) Recreation, Cultural and Sporting; (11) Transport; and (12) Others.

## 6. Agreement on Trade Related Intellectual Property Rights (TRIPS)

The three main features of the TRIPS Agreement are *Standards*, *Enforcement* and *Dispute Settlement*:

- *Standards*: In respect of each of the main areas of intellectual property covered by the TRIPS Agreement, the Agreement sets out the minimum standards of protection to be provided by each member. The Agreement sets these standards by requiring, first, that the substantive obligations of the main conventions of the WIPO, the Paris Convention for the Protection of Industrial Property (Paris Convention) and the Berne Convention for the Protection of Literary and Artistic Works (Berne Convention) in their most recent versions, must be complied with. With the exception of the provisions of the Berne Convention on moral rights, all the main substantive provisions of these conventions are incorporated by reference and thus become obligations under the TRIPS Agreement between TRIPS member countries. The relevant provisions are to be found in Articles 2.1 and 9.1 of the TRIPS Agreement, which relate, respectively, to the Paris Convention and to the Berne Convention. Secondly, the TRIPS Agreement adds a substantial number of additional obligations on matters where the pre-existing conventions are silent or were seen as being inadequate. The TRIPS Agreement is thus sometimes referred to as a Berne and Paris-plus agreement.

- ❖ *Enforcement*: The Agreement lays down certain general principles applicable to all IPR enforcement procedures so that right holders can effectively enforce their rights.
- ❖ *Dispute Settlement*: The Agreement makes disputes between WTO members about the respect of the TRIPS obligations subject to the WTO's dispute settlement procedures.

The obligations under the Agreement will apply equally to all member countries, but developing countries will have a longer period to phase them in. The TRIPS Agreement is a minimum standards agreement, which allows members to provide more extensive protection of intellectual property if they so wish. Members are left free to determine the appropriate method of implementing the provisions of the Agreement within their own legal system and practice.

Articles 9.1 and 9.2 deal with copyrights and related rights in relation to the Berne Convention. Members are expected to comply with Articles 1 through 21 of the Berne Convention (1971). Article 9.2 confirms that copyright protection shall extend to expressions and not to ideas, procedures, methods of operation or mathematical concept as such. Article 10.2 states that databases and other compilations of data or other material shall be protected. According to Article 12 whenever the term of protection of a work, other than a photographic work or a work of applied art, is calculated on the basis other than the life of a natural person, such term shall be no less than 50 years from the end of the calendar year of authorized publication, or failing such authorized publication within 50 years from the making of the work, 50 years from the end of the calendar year of making.

For the protection of Trademarks, the basic rule contained in Article 15 is that any sign, or any combination of signs, capable of distinguishing the goods and services of one undertaking from those of other undertakings, must be eligible for registration as a trade-mark, provided that it is visually perceptible. The term of protection in the case of trade-mark is "no less than seven years" (Article 18).

The protection of geographical indication is dealt with in Article 22 of the TRIPS Agreement. Geographical indications are defined as indications which identify a good as originating in the territory of a member, or a region or locality in that territory, where a given quality, reputation or other characteristics of the good is essentially attributable to its geographical origin. Article 23 provides that interested parties must have the legal means to prevent the use of a geographical indication identifying wines for wines not originating in the place indicated by the geographical indication.

Article 25 is concerned with the requirements for protection of industrial design. Article 27.1 of the TRIPS Agreement requires member countries to make patents available for any inventions, whether products or processes, in all fields of technology without discrimination, subject to the normal tests of novelty, inventiveness and industrial applicability. It is also required that patents be available and patent rights enjoyable without discrimination as to the place of invention and whether products are imported or locally produced. Article 33 states that the term of protection available shall not end before the expiration of a period of 20 years from the filing date.

Article 35 of the TRIPS Agreement requires member countries to protect the layout-designs of integrated circuits in accordance with the provisions of the IPIC Treaty (the Treaty on Intellectual Property in Respect of Integrated Circuits), negotiated under auspices of WIPO in 1989. Article 39.1 states that members should protect undisclosed information and data submitted to governments or governmental agencies.

## 7. Methodology

Developing countries, which could attract larger FDI inflows, are selected for this study. Aggregate FDI inflows of the developing countries between 1991 and 2002 are deflated by the GDP figures of the respective countries for the year 2002. On the basis of values of FDI/GDP ratios we have selected twelve developing countries which are more successful in attracting FDI, namely, Argentina, Brazil, China

Mainland, Chile, Colombia, Malaysia, Mexico, Peru, Singapore, Thailand, Venezuela and India.

### *7.1 Methodology for GATS-Scoring*

We have quantified restrictions relating to the "limitations on Market Access" and "limitations on National Treatment" in the service sector in the selected developing countries. The methodology followed here for quantification of restrictions in the service sector is similar to that of Golub (2003). From the GATS sector—specific schedules it is possible to obtain two sets of measures of restrictions: (1) limitations on market access, and (2) limitations on national treatment. Restrictions on foreign ownership are the most obvious barriers to establishment for FDI. Obligatory screening and approval procedures can also be used to limit FDI through their constraining effects. Stipulations that foreign investors must show economic benefits are another barrier to the inflow of foreign capital. Prior approval of FDI can also limit foreign capital inflow. Pre or post-notification can have a negative effect upon FDI inflows. Stipulations that nationals or residents must form a majority of the board of directors make foreign owners hesitant to invest. Similarly, if regulations restrict the employment of foreign nationals, investors may feel that they cannot fully utilize their investment. Operational requirements may limit profits of foreign-owned corporations, and hence the amount of funds foreign investors are willing to commit. The GATS covers 12 broad sectors, which encompass 155 sub-sectors. Indices are calculated for 11 of these broad sectors (by calculating simple averages of sub-sector scores). Index values for the 'other services' sector are not calculated because the services included in this sector vary greatly across countries, making cross-country comparisons impossible.

Table 8.1 in Appendix presents the scoring system used to calculate the overall restrictiveness for each of the eleven sectors in the selected developing countries. The scale for scoring is between 0 and 1, 0 for no restriction (i.e. 'none') and 1 for full restriction. So, a completely open FDI regime can be assigned an index value of 0 while at the other extreme a complete ban on FDI can be assigned an index value of 1. Higher weights are given to equity restrictions since foreign ownership is a necessary and essential condition for FDI. Screening and limitations on management are generally less important. Similarly, requiring an investor to demonstrate economic benefits is much more stringent than an approval, which is more demanding than simple notification. Other restrictions include restrictions on the board of directors, restrictions on people (e.g. duration of residency), working manpower (e.g. magnitude of local workforce), licensing requirement and miscellaneous other restrictions. To derive the overall sector score, the sub-sector scores are summed, then this aggregate score is divided by the total number of sub-sectors. The implicit assumption is that all sub-sectors are of equal significance. The index numbers are calculated for individual GATS sub-sectors in individual economies. To get an overall FDI restrictiveness index for a country, sectors scores are needed to be added. But in this case the relative importance of sectors should be taken into consideration. The most obvious way to aggregate would be to weight each sector according to its share in the total value of service sector output in the country. This method of aggregation, however, could not be followed here since disaggregated services data are not always available. A problem with the GATS positive list is that information on many sectors is not provided, so assumptions have to be made. In this study the absence of a positive commitment in some sectors (i.e. non-scheduled sectors) is construed as a restriction and those sectors are assigned a very high restrictive score of 0.95. The index weights presented in Table 8.1 are assigned so as the maximum score for any sector is 1. To restrict the value of the index between 0 and 1, multiple restrictions of the same type are counted only once.

### 7.2 Methodology for TRIPS-Scoring

In this study an attempt is made to measure the strength of IPR protection for the selected developing countries. For this purpose, signatory countries of the Berne, Paris and Rome Conventions are noted as 1, otherwise 0.

Union for the Protection of New Varieties of Plants (UPOV) was established by the International Convention for the Protection of New Varieties of Plants. The objective of the Convention is the protection of new varieties of plants by an intellectual property rights. The mission of this Union is to provide and promote an effective system of plant variety protection, with the aim of encouraging the development of new varieties of plants for the benefit of society. Membership of UPOV (1, otherwise 0) is taken as an indicator of an existing system for plant variety protection.

Article 63.2 of the TRIPS Agreement obliges the WTO Members to notify the laws and regulations to the Council for TRIPS in order to assist the Council in its review of the operation of the Agreement. These notifications are expected to promote the transparency of members' policies on intellectual property protection. In the case of patent protection, countries certify their compliance with WTO in the IP/N/[3 letter country code]/P publication series[22]. Those which have certified compliance are noted with 1, 0 otherwise. Similarly, from these notifications it is possible to find out whether a member country has an Act for copyright protection or the protection of the trademark or on geographical indication or industrial design or on integrated circuit layout design. For each protection, if a country has passed an Act, it is coded as 1; otherwise 0. It is difficult to quantify the level of enforcement of intellectual property rights as the ranking of national legal systems, assessments of the competence of justices and the like are not available. For this purpose, USTR's *Special 301 Report* [23],2002 was used as a source of information. The level of enforcement was coded on a scale of 0 to 1. We have used a method of weighting since all criteria are not of equal importance. The level of enforcement, Patent Protection Act and Copyright Act each was allotted the highest weight (i.e.15), followed by Trademark Act (12), the protection of test data (9), geographical indication Act (7), protection for integrated layout design (6), industrial design (5), and convention membership (4 each). The relative scores for IPR protection of the selected countries are shown in Table 8.2.

## 8. Sources of Data

Countrywise FDI data were collected from various issues of *Balance of Payments Statistics*, published by International Monetary Fund. FDI consists of *equity capital, reinvested earnings and other capital.* Countrywise GDP data were taken from *World Development Indicators*, a World Bank publication. Information on sector-specific commitments was collected from GATS database [24]. Information about the protection of Intellectual Property Rights (IPR) in these countries were collected from various sources such as *Trade Policy Reviews* from WTO website, *United States Trade Review* (USTR) and US & Foreign Commercial Service, U.S. Department of State, 2001. Information on protection of test data submitted for obtaining marketing approval for pharmaceuticals and agro-chemicals was obtained from Correa (2002). USTR's *Special 301 Report*, 2002[25] was used as a source of information for enforcement of IPR in different countries.

**9. Results**

Figure 8.1 in Appendix shows inflows of FDI into the developing countries taken for this study between 1991 and 2002. There was a steady increase in FDI inflows till the year 1997 after that it declined in the year 1998 because of East-Asian financial crisis, recovered in 1999 but again it continued to decline in later years.

Table 8.3 shows sector-wise scores of each country relating to Mode 3. These scores indicate that there are significant differences among countries and across sectors in terms of openness of the service sector. There are only three sectors, namely, *business services*, *communication services* and *financial services* where all the developing countries have made commitments. Among these three sectors, financial services sector seems to be subject to the most stringent FDI control. Commitments are minimum in environmental services and in recreational, cultural and sporting services. Among 12 developing countries only China and Thailand made commitments in the Environmental Services Sector and Malaysia and Peru in the Recreational, Cultural and Sporting Services Sector. Most of the developing countries are not willing to open up these sectors. China made maximum number of commitments for 9 sectors, Malaysia, Mexico, Thailand each committed for 8 sectors, Peru and Brazil for 7 and 6 sectors respectively, and each of the remaining countries, namely, Argentina, Chile, Colombia, India, Singapore and Venezuela made commitments only in 5 sectors. The average score in Table 8.3 suggests that so far as the 'commercial presence' in the service sector is concerned, Chile, Thailand and Venezuela are highly restrictive, whereas, Peru, Mexico and Argentina are very liberal.

In the case of IPR protection, the weighted averages of scores indicate that there exist significant differences among the developing countries (Table 8.2). China provides the maximum IPR protection followed by Argentina, Singapore and India. On the other side, IPR protection is found to be very weak in Peru and in Brazil.

Table 8.4 shows the relative positions of the developing countries in terms of FDI/GDP ratios, GATS and TRIPS-scores. The rank correlation between FDI/GDP ratios and GATS-scores is negative but not statistically significant. The scatter diagram (Fig. 8.2) does not indicate the existence of strong associations between GATS-scores and FDI/GDP ratios. The country like Peru is found to be the least restrictive (i.e. ranked twelfth) so far as the opening up of the service sector is concerned. But it is not very successful (i.e. ranked sixth) in attracting FDI. There is no significant correlation between FDI/GDP ratios and TRIPS–scores (Table 8.4). FDI/GDP ratios of the countries such as Brazil, Peru, Venezuela, Colombia, Thailand and China are close to each other but there is wide variation among TRIPS-scores of these countries (Fig. 8.3).

## 10. Conclusion

The study of twelve major developing countries showed that opening up of the service sector or stronger IPR protection does not guarantee greater inflows of FDI. Many African countries that have liberalized their FDI policy as a part of structural adjustment programmes administered by the IMF and the World Bank during 1980s have failed to receive any significant FDI inflows. On the contrary, countries which pursued selective policies with respect to FDI, for instance, South Korea, Taiwan and China among other south-east Asian nations (for instance, in channeling FDI into export-oriented and high-technology activities) have had a greater success in achieving their developmental objectives with FDI inflow (Kumar, 2001). Empirical studies have shown that FDI inflows are largely driven by the factors such as market size, income levels, the extent of urbanization, geographical and cultural proximity with the major source countries of FDI and the quality of infrastructure. The policy factors play marginal role as far as FDI inflows are concerned (Correa and Kumar, 2003). So, MFI is unlikely to increase the level of FDI inflows for the developing countries. It is further believed that a multilateral regime will take away the ability of the host governments to direct FDI in accordance with their development policy objectives and the overall "quality" of any FDI inflows will suffer. The MFI is, however, excluded from Doha Work Programme through July, 2004 decision. But, the developed countries may bring back this issue in future in order to use it as a negotiating chip.

# Appendix

**Table 8.1:** GATS—Mode 3 ( Commercial Presence)—Scores on Restrictions

| *Type of Restriction* | *Scores* |
|---|---|
| *Foreign Equity Limits* | |
| No foreign equity allowed | 1 |
| 1 to 19% foreign equity allowed | 0.6 |
| 20-34% foreign equity allowed | 0.4 |
| 35-49% foreign equity allowed | 0.3 |
| 50-74% foreign equity allowed | 0.2 |
| 75-99% foreign equity allowed | 0.1 |
| *Screening and Approval* | |
| Investor must show economic benefits | 0.2 |
| Approval unless contrary to national interest | 0.1 |
| Notification (pre or post) | 0.05 |
| *Other Restrictions* | |
| Board of Directors/Managers/Shareholders | |
| Majority must be nationals or residents | 0.1 |
| Atleast 1 must be national or resident | 0.05 |
| Must be locally licensed | 0.025 |
| *Restrictions on People* | |
| No entry | 0.1 |
| Domicile for atleast 3 years | 0.075 |
| Domicile for atleast 2 years | 0.05 |
| Domicile for atleast 1year | 0.025 |
| *Restriction on Working Manpower* | |
| Local employees must be more than 50% | 0.1 |
| Any other | 0.05 |

*Source*: Golub, 2003

**Table 8.2:** TRIPS—Score—Country-wise

| | | Weights | Argentina | Brazil | Chile | China | Colombia | India | Malaysia | Mexico | Peru | Singapore | Thailand | Venezuela |
|---|---|---|---|---|---|---|---|---|---|---|---|---|---|---|
| 1. Whether the country is a member of UPOV? | Y = 1<br>N = 0 | 4 | 1 | 1 | 1 | 1 | 1 | 0 | 0 | 1 | 0 | 0 | 0 | 0 |
| 2. Whether the country is a signatory of the Berne Convention? | Y = 1<br>N = 0 | 4 | 1 | 1 | 1 | 1 | 1 | 1 | 1 | 1 | 1 | 1 | 1 | 1 |
| 3. Whether the country is a signatory of the Paris Convention? | Y = 1<br>N = 0 | 4 | 1 | 1 | 1 | 1 | 1 | 1 | 1 | 1 | 1 | 1 | 0 | 1 |
| 4. Whether the country is a signatory of the Rome Convention? | Y = 1<br>N = 0 | 4 | 1 | 1 | 1 | 0 | 1 | 0 | 0 | 1 | 1 | 0 | 0 | 1 |
| 5. Whether the country has revised its Patent Protection Act. Following the WTO Agreement on TRIPS? | Y = 1<br>N = 0 | 15 | 1 | 1 | 1 | 1 | 1 | 1 | 1 | 1 | 1 | 1 | 1 | 1 |
| 6. Whether the intellectual property Act. of the country includes provision for the protection of well-known trade-marks? | Y = 1<br>N = 0 | 12 | 1 | 0 | 0 | 1 | 0 | 1 | 1 | 0 | 0 | 1 | 1 | 0 |
| 7. Whether the country has passed an Act for copyright protection? | Y = 1<br>N = 0 | 15 | 1 | 1 | 1 | 1 | 1 | 1 | 1 | 1 | 1 | 1 | 1 | 1 |
| 8. Whether the country has passed an Act on Geographical Indication? | Y = 1<br>N = 0 | 7 | 1 | 0 | 1 | 0 | 0 | 1 | 1 | 0 | 0 | 1 | 0 | 0 |
| 9. Whether the country has passed an Industrial Design Act.? | Y = 1<br>N = 0 | 5 | 0 | 0 | 0 | 0 | 0 | 1 | 1 | 0 | 0 | 0 | 0 | 0 |
| 10. Whether the intellectual property law provides protection of test data? | Y = 1<br>N = 0 | 9 | 1 | 0 | 0 | 1 | 0 | 0 | 0 | 1 | 0 | 0 | 1 | 1 |
| 11. Whether the intellectual property law provides protection for integrated circuit layout design? | Y = 1<br>N = 0 | 6 | 0 | 0 | 0 | 1 | 1 | 1 | 1 | 1 | 0 | 1 | 1 | 0 |
| 12. Degree of Enforcement | Good = 0.8<br>Fair = 0.6<br>Bad = 0.4<br>V. Bad = 0.2 | 15 | 0.2 | 0.2 | 0.4 | 0.6 | 0.2 | 0.2 | 0.4 | 0.8 | 0.4 | 0.8 | 0.4 | 0.4 |
| Average Score | | | .77 | .49 | .59 | .78 | .55 | .71 | .74 | .73 | .48 | .75 | .67 | .57 |

*Source*: Explained in the Text (Sections 7.2 and 8).

**Table 8.3:** GATS (Mode 3)—Scores—Country-wise

| Sl. No. | Specific Commitments | Argentina | Brazil | Chile | China | Colombia | India | Malaysia | Mexico | Peru | Singapore | Thailand | Venezuela |
|---|---|---|---|---|---|---|---|---|---|---|---|---|---|
| 1. | Business Services | 0.1 | 0.438 | 0.52 | 0.461 | 0.154 | 0.25 | 0.362 | 0.457 | 0.438 | 0.112 | 0.55 | 0.264 |
| 2. | Communication Services | 0.11 | 0.075 | 0.533 | 0.663 | 0.358 | 0.318 | 0.418 | 0.392 | 0.075 | 0.221 | 0.721 | 0.28 |
| 3. | Construction & Engineering Services | 0.1 | 0.575 | 0.95 | 0.65 | 0.15 | 0.25 | 0.6 | 0.35 | 0.95 | 0.95 | 0.55 | 0.25 |
| 4. | Distribution Services | 0.95 | 0.075 | 0.95 | 0.438 | 0.95 | 0.95 | 0.95 | 0.95 | 0.075 | 0.95 | 0.55 | 0.95 |
| 5. | Educational Services | 0.95 | 0.95 | 0.95 | 0.6 | 0.95 | 0.95 | 0.95 | 0.5 | 0.95 | 0.95 | 0.55 | 0.95 |
| 6. | Environmental Services | 0.95 | 0.95 | 0.95 | 0.55 | 0.95 | 0.95 | 0.95 | 0.95 | 0.95 | 0.95 | 0.55 | 0.95 |
| 7. | Financial Services | 0.284 | 0.4 | 0.569 | 0.51 | 0.22 | 0.4 | 0.581 | 0.5 | 0.4 | 0.364 | 0.593 | 0.541 |
| 8. | Health Related & Social Services | 0.95 | 0.95 | 0.95 | 0.95 | 0.95 | 0.25 | 0.8 | 0.5 | 0.95 | 0.95 | 0.95 | 0.95 |
| 9. | Tourism & Travel Related Services | 0.1 | 0.95 | 0.5 | 0.675 | 0.15 | 0.95 | 0.675 | 0.26 | 0.125 | 0.11 | 0.95 | 0.25 |
| 10. | Recreational, Cultural & Sporting Services | 0.95 | 0.95 | 0.95 | 0.95 | 0.95 | 0.95 | 0.3 | 0.95 | 0.075 | 0.95 | 0.95 | 0.95 |
| 11. | Transportation Services | 0.95 | 0.2 | 0.5 | 0.6 | 0.95 | 0.95 | 0.367 | 0.54 | 0.2 | 0.1 | 0.806 | 0.95 |
| | Average Score | 0.581 | 0.592 | 0.756 | 0.641 | 0.612 | 0.652 | 0.632 | 0.577 | 0.472 | 0.601 | 0.702 | 0.662 |

*Source*: Explained in the text (Sections 7.1 and 8).

**Table 8.4:** Relative Positions of the Developing Countries

| Country | FDI/GDP (%) | Rank | GATS Scores | Rank | TRIPS Scores | Rank |
|---|---|---|---|---|---|---|
| Argentina | 6.5 | 2 | 0.581 | 10 | 0.77 | 2 |
| Brazil | 3.23 | 5 | 0.592 | 9 | 0.49 | 11 |
| Chile | 5.48 | 3 | 0.756 | 1 | 0.59 | 8 |
| China | 2.77 | 7 | 0.641 | 5 | 0.78 | 1 |
| Colombia | 2.47 | 9 | 0.612 | 7 | 0.55 | 10 |
| India | 0.4 | 12 | 0.652 | 4 | 0.71 | 6 |
| Malaysia | 4.07 | 4 | 0.632 | 6 | 0.74 | 4 |
| Mexico | 1.8 | 11 | 0.577 | 11 | 0.73 | 5 |
| Peru | 2.97 | 6 | 0.472 | 12 | 0.48 | 12 |
| Singapore | 10.06 | 1 | 0.601 | 8 | 0.75 | 3 |
| Thailand | 2.44 | 10 | 0.702 | 2 | 0.67 | 7 |
| Venezuela | 2.65 | 8 | 0.662 | 3 | 0.57 | 9 |
| Rank Correlation* | | | | -0.168 (-0.602) | | 0.231 (0.471) |

* Rank correlation is calculated with FDI/GDP rankings.

*Note* : Figures in brackets denote *t*-values.

*Source*: Computed from *Balance of Payment Statistics* (various issues), International Monetary Fund, *World Development Indicators* 2003, World Bank, Washington D.C. and Table 8.2 and Table 8.3

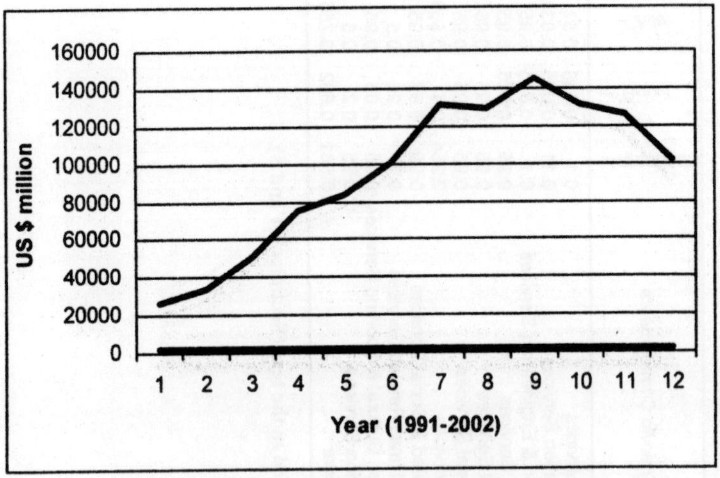


**Fig. 8.1:** FDI In flows into the Developing Countries

*Source*: *Balance of Payment Statistics* (various issues), International Monetary Fund.

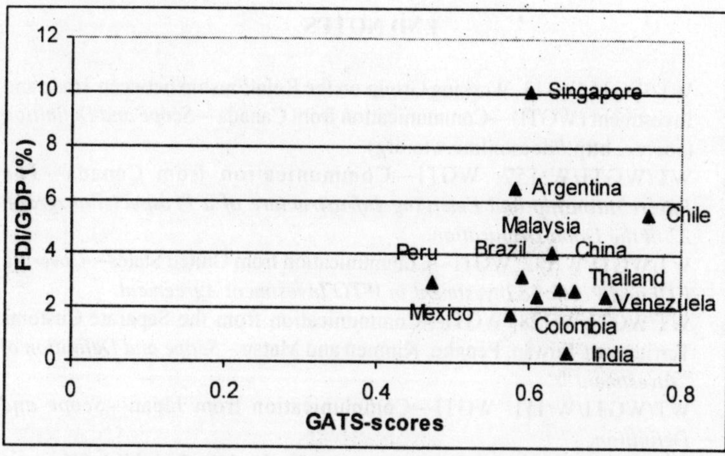


**Fig. 8.2:** FDI & GATS—Scores: Scatter

*Source*: Table 8.4.

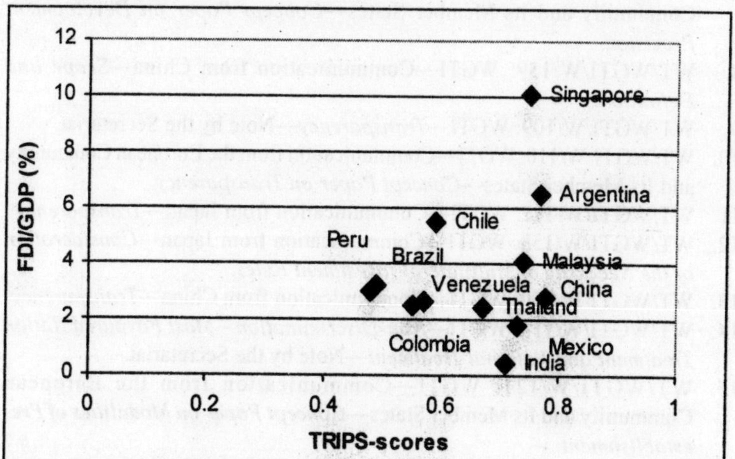


**Fig. 8.3:** FDI & TRIPS—Scores: Scatter

*Source*: Table 8.4.

---

*I am grateful to Dr. Paramita Dasgupta, Dr Biswajit Dhar, Shri S. Narayanan, Dr K. Krishnamurthy, and the participants of a workshop on " Major Issues in the WTO and Its Implications for India" held at ASCI, Hyderabad on April 30 & May 1, 2004 for their valuable comments and suggestions. Thanks are also due to Dr N. G. Satish, Librarian, ASCI for his extremely helpful support and co-operation. None of them are responsible for any error remaining in this study.*

## END NOTES

1. WT/WGTI/W/113: Working Group on the Relationship between Trade and Investment (WGTI)—Communication from Canada—*Scope and Definition* (*source*: http://docsonline.wto.org).
2. WT/WGTI/W/157: WGTI—Communication from Canada—*The Interrelationship and Emerging Infrastructure of a Prospect Paragraph 22 of the Doha Declaration.*
3. WT/WGTI/W/142: WGTI—Communication from United States—*Covering FDI and Portfolio Investment in WTO Investment Agreement.*
4. WT/WGTI/W/128: WGTI—Communication from the Separate Customs Territory of Taiwan, Penghu, Kinmen and Matsu – *Scope and Definition of "Investment".*
5. WT/WGTI/W/111: WGTI—Communication from Japan—*Scope and Definition.*
6. WT/WGTI/W/114: WGTI—Communication from the Republic of Korea—*Scope and Definition of "Investments".*
7. WT/WGTI/W/140: WGTI—Communication from the European Community and Its Member States—*Concept Paper on Development Provision.*
8. WT/WGTI/W/159: WGTI—Communication from China—*Scope and Definition.*
9. WT/WGTI/W/109: WGTI—*Transparency*—Note by the Secretariat.
10. WT/WGTI/W/110: WGTI—Communication from the European Community and Its Member States—*Concept Paper on Transparency.*
11. WT/WGTI/W/112: WGTI—Communication from Japan—*Transparency*
12. WT/WGTI/W/158: WGTI—Communication from Japan—*Consideration of the Necessity of Multilateral Investment Rules.*
13. WT/WGTI/W/160: WGTI—Communication from China—*Transparency*
14. WT/WGTI/W/118: WGTI—*Non-Discrimination—Most Favoured Nation Treatment and National Treatment*—Note by the Secretariat.
15. WT/WGTI/W/121: WGTI—Communication from the European Community and Its Member States—*Concept Paper on Modalities of Pre-establishment.*
16. WT/WGTI/W/96: WGTI—Communication from the Republic of Korea—*The General Agreement on Trade in Services & Its Implications for an Investment Agreement.*
17. WT/WGTI/W/123: WGTI—Communication from the Republic of Korea—*Non-Discrimination and GATS-type Approach for Investment*
18. WT/WGTI/W/132: WGTI—Communication from Mexico—*Non-Discrimination.*
19. WT/WGTI/W/127: WGTI—Communication from the Separate Customs Territory of Taiwan, Penghu, Kinmen and Matsu—*Pre-establishment Commitment.*

20. WT/WGTI/W/149: WGTI—Communication from India—*Non-Discrimination.*
21. WT/WGTI/W/130: WGTI—Communication from Canada—*Non-Discrimination and Modalities for GATS-type Positive List Approach.*
22. http://www.wto.org/
23. http://www.ustr.gov/Document_Library/Reports_Publications/2002/2002_Special_301_Report/Section_Index.html.
24. http://tsdb.wto.org/
25. Same as No.23.

## REFERENCES

Brooks, D.H., E.X. Fan and L. R. Sumulong, (2003). 'Foreign Direct Investment: Trends, TRIMs, and WTO Negotiations', *Asian Development Review*, 20(1): 1-33.

Correa, M.C. (2002). 'Protection of Data Submitted for the Registration of Pharmaceuticals: Implementing the Standards of the TRIPS Agreement', South Centre. Available at: http://www.who.int/medicines/areas/policy/wto_trips/en/index.html.

———— and N. Kumar, (2003). *Protecting Foreign Investment—Implications of a WTO Regime and Policy Options.* London: Zed Books.

Das, S.P. (2003). 'An Indian Perspective on WTO Rules on Direct Foreign Investment' in A. Mattoo and R.M. Stern (eds.) *India and the WTO*, World Bank, Washington, D.C. pp.141-167.

Golub, S.S. (2003). 'Measures of Restrictions on Inward Foreign Direct Investment for OECD Countries', *OECD Economic Studies*, 36(1): 85-116.

Hoekman, B. and K. Saggi (2000). 'Assessing the Case for Extending WTO Disciplines on Investment-Related Policies', *Journal of Economic Integration*, 15(4): 629-653.

———— (2001). 'From TRIMs to a WTO Agreement on Investment?' in B. Hoekman and K. Saggi (eds.), *Developing Countries and the WTO: A Pro-active Agenda*, Oxford: Blackwell. pp.201-214.

Kumar, N. (2001). 'WTO's Emerging Investment Regime-Way Forward for Doha Ministerial Meeting', *Economic and Political Weekly*, 36(33): pp. 3151 – 3158.

———— (2003). 'Performance Requirements as Tools of Development Policy: Lessons from Experiences of Developed and Developing Countries for the WTO Agenda on Trade and Investment', Discussion Paper No. 52, RIS, New Delhi.

———— and J. P. Pradhan (2002). 'Foreign Direct Investment, Externalities and Economic Growth in Developing Countries: Some Empirical Explorations and Implications for WTO Negotiations on Investment', Discussion Paper No.27, RIS, New Delhi.

——— and J. P. Pradhan (2002). 'Foreign Direct Investment, Externalities and Economic Growth in Developing Countries: Some Empirical Explorations and Implications for WTO Negotiations on Investment', Discussion Paper No.27, RIS, New Delhi.

Lee, J. Y. and E. Mansfield (1996). 'Intellectual Property Protection and U.S. Foreign Direct Investment', *Review of Economics and Statistics*, 78: 181-186.

Lesser, W. (2001). 'The Effects of TRIPS—Mandated Intellectual Property Rights on Economic Activities in Developing Countries', prepared under WIPO Special Service Agreements, Cornell University.

Low, P. and A. Subramanian (1995). ' TRIMs in the Uruguay Round: An Unfinished Business?', in W. Martin and L.A. Winters (eds.) The Uruguay Round and the Developing Economies, World Bank Discussion Paper 307.

Nicoletti, G., S.S. Golub, D. Hajkova, D. Mirza and K.Y. Yoo (2003). 'The Influence of Policies on Trade and Foreign Direct Investment', *OECD Economic Studies*, 36(1): 7-83.

Nunnenkamp, P. and M. Pant, (2003). 'Why the Economic Case for a Multilateral Agreement on Investment is Weak' in *Bridging the Differences: Analysis of Five Issues of the WTO Agenda*, CUTS Centre for International Trade, Economics & Environment, pp. 3-51.

Singh, A. (2001). 'Foreign Direct Investment and International Agreements: A South Perspective', South Centre, T.R.A.D.E. Occasional Papers.

# Chapter 9

# Competition Policy, Mergers and Acquisitions and the Relevance of a Multilateral Framework for India

PARAMITA DASGUPTA*

## Introduction

This paper examines the economic rationale for Competition Policy in developing countries and outlines the priorities for such a policy in India. Data with regard to mergers and acquisitions taking place in India is analysed and the requirements for a competition policy in India in the specific context of mergers and acquisitions taking place in India are outlined. In the light of the above analysis the relevance of a multilateral framework on competition policy for developing countries is assessed.

The paper consists of four sections. Section I examines the rationale and priority for a competition policy for developing countries. The issue of mergers and acquisitions in terms of creating a rationale for competition policy is examined in some detail in this section. Section II discusses in detail the issue of a competition policy in India with specific reference to Mergers and Acquisitions. Section III examines India's Competition Act and makes suggestions on it based on the preceding discussion and Section IV discusses whether there is relevance for a multilateral framework on competition policy for India.

* Dean of Training and Conferences and Director, Centre for Economics & Finance, Administrative Staff College of India, Hyderabad.

**A Background**

From the start of the negotiations in the WTO there was no agreement between the developed and developing countries regarding placing the 'new issues' or the 'Singapore Issues' on the negotiating agenda. At the first Ministerial Conference of the WTO in Singapore, the developed countries demanded that the four new issues, namely, Trade and Investment, Trade and Competition Policy, Trade Facilitation and Transparency in Government Procurement should be added to the negotiating agenda. On the other hand, developing countries resisted these demands since they were not keen to include these issues on a multilateral trade agenda. Finally Working Groups were set up at the WTO on investment, competition policy and transparency in government procurement to undertake study processes without any negotiating mandate. At Doha, the Singapore Issues were among the most contentious issues (Clarke and Evenett, 2003).

An examination of submissions made by different WTO member countries to the Working Group on the Interaction between Trade and Competition Policy after the Doha Ministerial indicates that there was no consensus in most of the areas. Submissions were made in the areas of core principles including transparency, non-discrimination and procedural fairness, hard core cartels, modalities for voluntary cooperation, capacity building and special and differential treatment. Consensus had only emerged with respect to the need to control hard-core cartels and a few other areas such as enhancing voluntary cooperation between national authorities providing technical assistance for developing countries. However, it may be mentioned here that even on these areas there was disagreement as to whether these issues should be dealt with within the WTO framework. [(Clarke and Evenett, 2003) and (WTO, Report of the Working Group, 2003)].

In fact as per the decision adopted by the General Council in August 2004, also known as the 'July Package' (WTO, 2004), three of the four Singapore Issues, including Trade and Investment, Trade and Competition Policy, and Transparency in Government Procurement are no longer a part of the Doha Work Programme. Thus no work towards negotiations on these issues will take place within the WTO framework. However Competition Policy remains an important policy issue in developing countries like India, as well as in developed countries, in the context of economic reforms and new and evolving market structures.

In this background, this paper discusses the economic rationale of competition policy in developing countries, the priorities of competition policy in India, particularly in the context of on-going mergers and acquisitions, India's Competition Act 2002 and the logic, if at all, of a multilateral framework on Trade and Competition Policy for India.

## SECTION I
## COMPETITION POLICY: AN ECONOMIC RATIONALE FOR DEVELOPING COUNTRIES

The major question that is asked in this section is 'Do developing countries need a competition policy at the domestic and international levels for promoting economic development'?

There has been a great deal of discussion in the Working Group on Trade and Competition Policy in the WTO regarding the role of competition policy in promoting economic development in developing countries. While developing countries are not convinced of the rationale for a multilateral framework on competition policy, there seems to be broad agreement regarding the need for a competition policy at the domestic level for promoting economic development and facilitating the economic reforms process. Studies undertaken on the subject point at the need to have a competition policy in developing countries to regulate anti-competitive practices of international firms like international cartels, which may lead to high import prices and adverse implications for exports from developing countries. Thus given the presence of international cartels, developing countries, which do not have a competition policy, may face adverse effects of these types of cartels [(Jenny and Anderson, 2002) and (Clarke and Evenett, 2003)].

Two major reasons that have been cited as creating the rationale for a competition policy in developing countries are (a) privatization and deregulation of industry at a domestic level, and (b) the global merger wave and liberalization of FDI in developing countries (Singh, 2003).

We examine these issues in some detail as below:

### Domestic Economic Reforms and Competition Policy

Most developing countries have been going through a period of structural reform over the past two decades including privatization and deregulation of industry. However for developing countries, it may not be possible to achieve improved economic performance just through deregulation or privatization. This is so because some of the public monopolies may simply be replaced by private monopolies that exploit the market. Hence there is need for an appropriate competition policy and efficient regulation to ensure competition on the market. [(Krueger, 1974), (Singh, 2002), (World Bank, 1997) and (UNCTAD, 1997)].

**The Global Merger Wave, Liberalization of Foreign Direct Investment and Competition Policy in Developing Countries**

Mergers and Acquisitions (M&As) have been very important in driving foreign direct investment (FDI) in the decade of the nineties. In 1996, the value of cross-border M&As stood at $ 275 billion. Transnational Corporations (TNCs) based in US and UK are the biggest players accounting for 40 per cent of the value of purchases in majority held mergers and acquisitions and 57 per cent of sales in 1996. In fact in contrast to the 50s and 60s when greenfield FDI was the most popular mode of entry into foreign markets, cross-border M&As have become the major mode of entry into foreign markets since the mid-80s. Most cross border inter firm agreements during 1990-95 involved firms from the EU, Japan and US. However developing countries are increasingly becoming involved in such agreements. The number of cross-border inter-firm agreements with developing country participation increased from around 440 in 1990 to around 2120 in 1994. The share of developing countries in the total number of cross-border inter-firm agreements increased from 27 per cent in 1991-92 to 35 per cent during 1993-95, (UNCTAD, 1997).

Given the above trends and the fact that almost all developing countries have undertaken liberalization of FDI policy, there is a need to formulate and strengthen competition policy in developing countries to ensure that the M&As do not lead to anti-competitive practices of firms, whether foreign or domestic. This was also emphasized by the UNCTAD Set adopted in 1980 (UNCTAD, 1980). In fact there is need to incorporate a merger review in the competition legislation of developing countries in order to enhance market efficiency through FDI liberalisation.

Among countries, which have adopted merger control regulations, four broad types of regulations can be identified: (UNCTAD, 1997)

- Regulations that apply only to locally registered companies.
- Regulations that cover acquisition of domestic firms by foreign firms.
- Regulations that cover acquisition of foreign firms by domestic firms.
- Regulations that cover M&As between foreign firms. In this case one of the merging firms may be present on the domestic market or the merger may have potential anti-competitive effects on local consumers.

**Effects of Mergers**

There is no agreement in literature regarding whether mergers lead to increased concentration or monopoly power. A particular view held by economists is that since the size of the markets have increased as a result of liberalisation; the monopoly effects of mergers are not significant (Singh, 2002). However, on the contrary, Tichy (2001) holds that concentration is a rapidly increasing problem as a result of the policy of large corporations.

Different types of scenarios relating to mergers and acquisitions (M&As) which lead to different types of issues relating to concentration and monopoly power across and within countries have been discussed in detail elsewhere. (UNCTAD, 1997).

The long and short of it is that there are a number of categories of cross-border M&As and joint ventures that can potentially lead to greater concentration on markets where such M&As are occurring. In such situations competition policy has a critical role to play to ensure that as a result of such M&As the competition situation in the host countries is not adversely affected.

Given the above arguments, the issue therefore is that with liberalization of foreign and domestic investment, privatization and the global merger wave, a competition policy and competition law are required to be put in place by countries to ensure that firms do not indulge in anti-competitive practices. For developing countries which have undertaken economic reforms in the decade of the nineties, it is important to put in place a competition policy to ensure that monopolies which may abuse their dominant positions are not created, combinations like M&As do not lead to increased concentration on markets and M&As involving multinational corporations do not lead to increased concentration and abuse of dominant positions vis a vis domestic companies (Singh, 2003). In fact, competition policy should be an important part of the policy framework alongside with trade policy and FDI policy to ensure, on the one hand, liberalisation of entry of investment and on the other to regulate and control anti-competitive practices.

The question now is what kind of competition policy do developing countries need? In this context it is useful to examine the different types of competition policies existing in developed countries.

In UK, in the late 19th and early 20th century, restrictive agreements were legal. Cartels were promoted by the State in the 1930s. Active prosecution of cartels began in UK only in the last fifty years. Even so, in the UK, emphasis is placed on "public interest". Promotion of competition was not a priority till the 80s. Efficiency was not a major objective. Different goals were given priority such as export promotion, full employment, balanced distribution of industry etc. In fact the multiple objectives of UK's competition policy had led to it being ineffective (Bhattacharjea, 2003). The new UK Competition Act of 1998 has adopted a clear focus on competition.

EU's competition law emphasizes a number of objectives relating to equity such as employment and measures that encourage cooperation between small and medium enterprises. It also gives priority to prevention of dominance by large firms. In the 70's the European Community encouraged cartels. In fact rationalisation agreements are even now covered by a block exemption in the EU and crisis cartels can be considered for exemption.

In the US, enforcement of competition law has increasingly focused on consumer welfare and economic efficiency (Khemani, 2002). But this was not always the case. The Sherman Act (1890) indicated an explicit preference for 'pluralism' in terms of diffusion of economic power. There was also a tendency towards protection of small business and local economies.

Among the developed countries, Japan has evolved its own approach to competition policy. Thus during 1950-73, industrial policy in Japan was dominant vis a vis competition policy. The emphasis of industrial policy during this period was on encouraging investment. Thus a variety of cartels were sponsored and there was active government intervention in the exit and entry decisions of firms. As

Singh (2002) says "Thus Japan followed a policy that promoted dynamic efficiency (in the sense of maximizing long-term growth of productivity) through an institutional structure that combined both cooperation and competition between firms".

Also a range of exemptions have been built into the competition policy across different countries. As succinctly summarized by Khemani (2002), exemptions to competition policy granted across countries fall into four categories:

- Exemptions aimed at balancing unequal economic or bargaining power.
- Exemptions aimed at addressing information, transaction costs and collective action problems.
- Exemptions that reduce risk and uncertainty.
- Special sector and interest group demands.

Thus competition policy in developed countries has evolved over a long period and there have been differences in the approach to competition policy among them. In fact, a clear-cut emphasis on efficiency and competition has developed only in the recent years in developed countries. Even now, there are exemptions built into competition policy.

As the foregoing discussion makes clear, developing countries do require a competition policy in the wake of economic reforms and the global merger movement. However the nature of competition policy would require to be different from developed countries primarily because the objectives are different. In particular, competition policy in developing countries needs to take into consideration development policy objectives that are specific to them [(Singh, 1999, 2000, 2002) and (Bhattacharjea 2001, 2003)].

## SECTION II
## COMPETITION POLICY IN INDIA—THE ISSUE OF MERGERS AND ACQUISITIONS

Similar to other developing countries, there is need for a competition policy in India at the current juncture because of significant structural and other changes as a result of economic reforms in the country and also the wave of global mergers. We focus on the issue of mergers in India in this sub-section.

Post-1990 the number of M&As in India has increased rapidly. We examine here data relating to M&As in India over the period 1999-2004 for selected industry and services sectors.

The basic objectives of this analysis are:

- To analyse the trend in domestic *vs.* foreign M&As in India in terms of numbers and value, for selected industry and service sectors.
- To analyse the trends in the concentration index for the selected industry and services sectors in order to derive some conclusions regarding the market structures in the selected sectors where a large number of M&As are taking place. The Herfindahl Index of Concentration as computed by the Centre for Monitoring the Indian Economy (CMIE) is used for the purpose of this analysis.

Table 9.1 presents data relating to 38 industry sectors and 6 service sectors on M&As in terms of numbers of M&As taking place with respect to Indian owned companies and foreign owned companies over the period 1999-2004. The table includes the concentration index for these sectors over the period 1997-98 to 2001-02. The sectors have been ranked in terms of the number of M&As taking place. The following observations can be made from this table:

- The number of acquisitions by Indian owned companies and the number of mergers with Indian owned companies are higher than the number of acquisitions by foreign owned companies and the number of mergers with foreign owned companies except for **seven** industry sectors.
- These seven sectors are:
  - *beer,* where the number of acquisitions by foreign owned companies are higher than the number of acquisitions by Indian owned companies and the number of mergers with foreign owned companies are larger than the number of mergers with Indian owned companies.
  - *machine tools* where the number of acquisitions by foreign owned companies are larger than the number of acquisitions by Indian owned companies. The number of mergers is the same for Indian and foreign owned companies.

- *dyes and pigments* where the number of acquisitions by foreign owned companies are larger than those by Indian owned companies.
- *refractories* where the number of acquisitions by foreign owned companies are higher than the number of acquisitions by Indian owned companies.
- *valves* where the number of acquisitions by foreign owned companies are higher than those by Indian owned companies and also the number of mergers with foreign owned companies are higher than those with Indian owned companies.
- *carbon black* where the number of acquisitions by foreign owned companies are larger than the number of acquisitions by Indian owned companies.
- material handling equipment where the number of acquisitions by foreign owned companies are larger than the number of acquisitions by Indian owned companies.

❖ For all the industry and services sectors in the table, the concentration index is low and is not changing at all significantly over the period 1997-98 to 2001-02.

Table 9.2 presents acquisitions in value terms for the same sectors as in Table 9.1 over the same time period with their concentration index. Ranks have been provided in terms of the value of acquisitions. The following observations can be made:

❖ For 18 out of 38 sectors in industry being studied, value of acquisitions by foreign owned companies is higher than the value of acquisitions by Indian owned companies. These sectors are:

- drugs and pharmaceuticals,
- tractors,
- material handling equipment,
- beer,
- dyes and pigments,
- machine tools,
- paints and varnishes,
- vegetable oils,
- motors and generators,

- bicycles,
- textile machinery,
- dry cells,
- sponge iron,
- refractories,
- chemical machinery,
- granite,
- valves, and
- caustic soda.

- In 20 out of 38 sectors in industry, value of acquisitions by Indian owned companies are higher than those by foreign owned companies.
- Of the 18 sectors mentioned above where the value of acquisitions by foreign owned companies is higher, in 8 sectors, there is a marginal *decline* in the concentration index. For the remaining sectors also there is no significant change.
- The concentration index is low and not changing over the reference period.
- For services, out of 6 sectors, in 3 sectors, namely, air transport, housing construction and road transport, value of acquisitions of foreign owned companies is higher than corresponding Indian owned companies. In the other 3 sectors, the trend is the reverse.

Table 9.3 presents M&As in numbers for the first 50 sectors, ranked in terms of total number of M&As taking place over the period April 1999-January 2004 in industry as well as service sectors. The following observations can be made:

- Among industry sectors, a large number of mergers and acquisitions have taken place in sectors such as machinery (1162), chemicals (914), electronics (755), computer software (483), food and beverages (462), especially food products (364), drugs and pharmaceuticals (310), textiles (262), metal and metal products (259).
- For industry sector taken as a whole, the number of acquisitions by Indian owned companies is higher than by foreign owned companies and the number of mergers with Indian owned companies are higher than the number of mergers with foreign owned companies.

- ❖ For the industry sector among the top 50 ranks, except for beverages and tobacco, beer and alcohol and other industrial machinery, in all the other sectors acquisitions by Indian owned companies are higher than acquisitions by foreign owned companies and mergers with Indian owned companies are higher than mergers with foreign owned companies.
- ❖ For beverages and tobacco, mergers with foreign owned companies are higher than mergers with Indian owned companies; for beer and alcohol, acquisitions by foreign owned companies are higher than acquisitions by Indian owned companies and mergers with foreign owned companies are also higher than mergers with Indian owned companies; for other industrial machinery, mergers with foreign owned companies are higher than mergers with Indian owned companies.
- ❖ For the services sector among the first 50 ranks, for all the sectors, acquisitions by Indian owned companies are higher than by foreign owned companies and mergers with Indian owned companies are higher than mergers with foreign owned companies.
- ❖ It is observed that for the industry sectors, the number of acquisitions are higher than the number of mergers for Indian owned and foreign owned companies.
- ❖ In the services sector, the trend is reversed for the investment services sector where the number of mergers are higher both for Indian owned and foreign owned companies.

Table 9.4 presents data on acquisitions in terms of value for the first 50 sectors ranked in terms of value of acquisitions in industry as well as services sectors. The following observations may be made:

- ❖ Overall in the industry sector, value of acquisitions by Indian owned companies is higher than the value of acquisitions by foreign owned companies.
- ❖ Of the top 50 ranks, which includes 28 industry sectors, in 12 sectors value of acquisitions by foreign owned companies is higher than the value of acquisitions of Indian owned companies.
- ❖ For services sector taken as a whole, among the top 50 ranks, which includes 19 services sectors, for 3 sectors, namely

banking services, transport services, and miscellaneous services, value of acquisitions of foreign owned companies are higher than Indian owned companies. For the remaining sectors, the trend is reversed.

Tables 9.5 and 9.6 present the average size of acquisitions for Indian owned and foreign owned companies respectively for industries and services for the first 50 ranks, ranked according to the average size of acquisitions.

The table shows that the average size of acquisitions for foreign owned companies is higher than for Indian owned companies.

Table 9.7 presents data on the concentration index for 40 industry sectors and 6 services sectors ranked according to the number of M&As in the sector and also provide the number of firms/units in each sector. The following observations may be made:

- For the top 100 ranks indicating a large number of M&As, the index of concentration is low and there is not much change indicated.
- This indicates that there is not much change in market structures as a result of increasing numbers of M&As.
- The reason for this may be that there are a large number of firms in these sectors.

From the above analysis of data presented in Tables 9.1 to 9.7, the following conclusions may be drawn:

- There has been a large number of M&As spread across a large number of industry and services sectors during the period 1999-04 in India. Acquisitions have been larger in number than mergers.
- Acquisitions and mergers by and among Indian companies are larger in number than for foreign owned companies in a majority of the industry sectors and in all the services sectors.
- In terms of value of acquisitions also, in 52 per cent of the industry sectors shown, value of acquisitions by Indian owned companies are larger than for foreign owned companies.
- There is not much change in the concentration index as a result of M&As taking place during the period under consideration. Market structures are therefore not changing

due to M & As. The number of companies are large. This may explain this phenomenon.

- ❖ The average size of acquisitions of foreign owned companies are higher than for Indian owned companies.
- ❖ A *limitation* of the data is that the concentration index is available from 'rank 18' onwards in terms of number of M&As. (see Table 9.1). Thus we are not able to analyze the concentration index of those sectors, which have ranks between 1-17 among the various industry and services sectors.

From the above data it appears that mergers and acquisitions are being used widely as a corporate strategy by Indian firms in the post reforms period. As a result of the opening up of the economy in 1991 domestic firms have had to face severe competition for which they were largely unprepared. Also, there were a number of policy changes in industrial, trade and financial sector policy. Thus corporate strategies have been changing and M&As have been used by industry as a corporate strategy to consolidate themselves and achieve objectives such as scale economies, cost reduction and enhancement of market shares. This process is still continuing.

Regarding the issue of efficiency effects of M&As versus anti competitive effects through enhanced concentration in industry, it is also apparent that there is no significant increase in industry concentration for the selected sectors in India.

We would like to emphasize that in the current post liberalization scenario, this process of restructuring through mergers and acquisitions among Indian firms possibly requires to continue so that Indian firms can effectively face competition on the market.

Keeping in mind the above arguments, from the point of view of Competition Policy in India therefore, domestic mergers should be exempted from merger reviews. However, even though industry concentration is not increasing, mergers and acquisitions involving foreign firms should be subjected to reviews and investigations. Our data (Table 9.3) shows that in at least 3 sectors, the number of M&As involving foreign owned companies are higher than Indian owned companies. It is also seen from Tables 9.5 and 9.6 that the average size of deals in acquisitions involving foreign owned firms is larger than those involving Indian owned firms. Keeping these trends in mind and also keeping in mind the developmental implications of

**Table 9.1:** Industries/Services experiencing Mergers/Acquisitions in India with Concentration Index ( April 1999-January 2004 )

| *Industry* | *No. of Acquisitions Indian-owned Companies* | *No. of Mergers with Indian-owned Companies* | *No. of Acquisitions by Foreign-owned Companies* | *No. of Mergers with Foreign-owned Companies in India* | *Grand Total* | *Rank* | *Herfindahl Index of Concentration* | | | | |
|---|---|---|---|---|---|---|---|---|---|---|---|
| | | | | | | | *1997-98* | *1998-99* | *1999-00* | *2000-01* | *2001-02* |
| Drugs & Pharmaceuticals | 173 (55.81) | 47 (15.16) | 79 (25.48) | 11 (3.55) | 310 | 18 | 0.01 | 0.01 | 0.012 | 0.013 | 0.016 |
| Steel | 60 (74.07) | 11 (13.58) | 10 (12.35) | 0 | 81 | 51 | 0.111 | 0.108 | 0.108 | 0.102 | 0.107 |
| Cement | 62 (80.52) | 7 (9.09) | 8 (10.39) | 0 | 77 | 53 | 0.043 | 0.049 | 0.047 | 0.051 | 0.055 |
| Sugar | 52 (88.14) | 6 (10.17) | 1 (1.69) | 0 | 59 | 68 | 0.003 | 0.002 | 0.003 | 0.004 | 0.005 |
| Tea | 34 (61.82) | 12 (21.82) | 8 (14.54) | 1 (1.82) | 55 | 72 | 0.062 | 0.086 | 0.068 | 0.081 | 0.082 |
| Paper | 42 (77.78) | 5 (9.26) | 6 (11.11) | 1 (1.85) | 54 | 75 | 0.01 | 0.009 | 0.011 | 0.014 | 0.016 |
| Beer | 15 (35.71) | 2 (4.76) | 20 (47.62) | 5 (11.91) | 42 | 92 | 0.152 | 0.092 | 0.074 | 0.117 | 0.103 |
| Machine Tools | 14 (38.88) | 2 (5.56) | 18 (50) | 2 (5.56) | 36 | 98 | 0.011 | 0.007 | 0.008 | 0.007 | 0.006 |
| Wires and Cables | 26 (74.29) | 4 (11.42) | 5 (14.29) | 0 | 35 | 101 | 0.033 | 0.029 | 0.029 | 0.028 | 0.025 |
| Dyes & Pigments | 9 (32.14) | 3 (10.72) | 15 (53.57) | 1 (3.57) | 28 | 110 | 0.036 | 0.026 | 0.023 | 0.02 | 0.02 |
| Motors and Generators | 15 (53.57) | 2 (7.14) | 11 (39.29) | 0 | 28 | 110 | 0.073 | 0.085 | 0.084 | 0.08 | 0.084 |
| Paints and Varnishes | 9 (39.13) | 3 (13.04) | 8 (34.79) | 3 (13.04) | 23 | 126 | 0.168 | 0.154 | 0.164 | 0.171 | 0.166 |
| Aluminium Products | 15 (65.22) | 6 (26.08) | 1 (4.35) | 1 (4.35) | 23 | 126 | 0.172 | 0.134 | 0.132 | 0.113 | 0.124 |
| Vegetable Oils | 10 (58.82) | 3 (17.65) | 4 (23.53) | 0 | 17 | 142 | 0.004 | 0.004 | 0.004 | 0.007 | 0.01 |
| Chemical Machinery | 7 (41.18) | 2 (11.76) | 7 (41.18) | 1 (5.88) | 17 | 142 | 0.212 | 0.267 | 0.556 | 0.18 | 0.2 |
| Transformers | 10 (62.5) | 3 (18.75) | 2 (12.5) | 1 (6.25) | 16 | 145 | 0.098 | 0.099 | 0.078 | 0.077 | 0.101 |
| Material Handling Equipment | 7 (46.67) | 0 | 8 (53.33) | 0 | 15 | 151 | 0.062 | 0.1 | 0.077 | 0.109 | 0.093 |
| Copper and Copper Products | 9 (75) | 2 (16.67) | 1 (8.33) | 0 | 12 | 165 | 0.049 | 0.089 | 0.129 | 0.173 | 0.212 |
| Caustic Soda | 7 (70) | 2 (20) | 1 (10) | 0 | 10 | 182 | 0.053 | 0.055 | 0.06 | 0.061 | 0.061 |
| Pig Iron | 7 (70) | 1 (10) | 1 (10) | 1 (10) | 10 | 182 | 0.103 | 0.095 | 0.097 | 0.077 | 0.081 |
| Ferro Alloys | 7 (70) | 1 (10) | 2 (20) | 0 | 10 | 182 | 0.08 | 0.067 | 0.05 | 0.051 | 0.059 |
| Tractors | 7 (70) | 0 | 3 (30) | 0 | 10 | 182 | 0.179 | 0.171 | 0.177 | 0.172 | 0.158 |
| Granite | 5 (55.56) | 1 (11.11) | 3 (33.33) | 0 | 9 | 190 | 0.037 | 0.036 | 0.036 | 0.043 | 0.049 |

*(Contd.)*

| Industry | No. of Acquisitions Indian-owned Companies | No. of Mergers with Indian-owned Companies | No. of Acquisitions by Foreign-owned Companies | No. of Mergers with Foreign-owned Companies in India | Grand Total | Rank | Herfindahl Index of Concentration | | | | |
|---|---|---|---|---|---|---|---|---|---|---|---|
| | | | | | | | 1997-98 | 1998-99 | 1999-00 | 2000-01 | 2001-02 |
| Storage Batteries | 5 (55.56) | 1 (11.11) | 3 (33.33) | 0 | 9 | 190 | 0.302 | 0.41 | 0.448 | 0.391 | 0.36 |
| Textile Machinery | 4 (50) | 1 (12.5) | 3 (37.5) | 0 | 8 | 196 | 0.027 | 0.027 | 0.039 | 0.049 | 0.034 |
| Coffee | 6 (85.71) | 1 (14.29) | 0 | 0 | 7 | 201 | 0.03 | 0.03 | 0.021 | 0.014 | 0.017 |
| Refractories | 1 (16.67) | 0 | 5 (83.33) | 0 | 6 | 203 | 0.084 | 0.079 | 0.087 | 0.085 | 0.086 |
| Valves | 2 (33.33) | 0 | 3 (50) | 1 (16.67) | 6 | 203 | 0.104 | 0.091 | 0.075 | 0.079 | 0.116 |
| Dry Cells | 3 (50) | 0 | 1 (1.67) | 2 (33.33) | 6 | 203 | 0.283 | 0.222 | 0.217 | 0.175 | 0.207 |
| Vanaspati | 5 (100) | 0 | 0 | 0 | 5 | 211 | 0.049 | 0.042 | 0.039 | 0.028 | 0.036 |
| Phosphatic Fertilisers | 3 (60) | 1 (20) | 1 (20) | 0 | 5 | 211 | 0.055 | 0.063 | 0.064 | 0.063 | 0.044 |
| Abrasives | 4 (80) | 1 (20) | 0 | 0 | 5 | 211 | 0.322 | 0.311 | 0.307 | 0.279 | 0.258 |
| Sponge Iron | 4 (80) | 0 | 1 (20) | 0 | 5 | 211 | 0.179 | 0.171 | 0.151 | 0.139 | 0.153 |
| Starch | 4 (100) | 0 | 0 | 0 | 4 | 221 | 0.069 | 0.074 | 0.08 | 0.084 | 0.076 |
| Acetic Acid | 3 (75) | 1 (25) | 0 | 0 | 4 | 221 | 0.153 | 0.149 | 0.149 | 0.171 | 0.127 |
| Bicycles | 3 (75) | 0 | 1 (25) | 0 | 4 | 221 | 0.215 | 0.243 | 0.262 | 0.273 | 0.285 |
| Carbon black | 1 (33.33) | 0 | 2 (66.67) | 0 | 3 | 228 | 0.191 | 0.211 | 0.235 | 0.252 | 0.299 |
| Printing machinery | 2 (100) | 0 | 0 | 0 | 2 | 231 | 0.008 | 0.046 | 0.059 | 0.078 | 0.061 |
| **Services** | | | | | | | | | | | |
| Production of TV serials/films | 38 (60.32) | 5 (7.93) | 19 (30.16) | 1 (1.59) | 63 | 62 | 0.144 | 0.107 | 0.114 | 0.078 | 0.083 |
| Shipping | 26 (76.47) | 2 (5.88) | 6 (17.65) | 0 | 34 | 104 | 0.316 | 0.272 | 0.241 | 0.201 | 0.191 |
| Housing Construction | 12 (48) | 12 (48) | 1 (4) | 0 | 25 | 119 | 0.123 | 0.1 | 0.099 | 0.107 | 0.126 |
| Road Transport | 3 (30) | 5 (50) | 1 (10) | 1 (10) | 10 | 182 | 0.117 | 0.09 | 0.079 | 0.073 | 0.082 |
| Air Transport | 3 (60) | 1 (20) | 1 (20) | 0 | 5 | 211 | 0.3 | 0.325 | 0.28 | 0.277 | 0.271 |
| Courier Services | 4 (80) | 0 | 1 (20) | 0 | 5 | 211 | 0.304 | 0.193 | 0.183 | 0.184 | 0.189 |

*Note*: ( i ) Mergers/Takeovers data pertaining to the period April, 1999-January, 2004.
( ii ) Figures in brackets denote percentages.

*Source*: Computed from CMIE data.

**Table 9.2:** Value of Acquisitions of Industry/Services in India with Concentration Index

| *Industry* | *Value of Acquisitions by Indian-owned Companies (Rs. Crore)* | *Value of Acquisitions by Foreign-owned Companies (Rs. Crore)* | *Grand Total* | *Rank* | *Herfindahl Index of Concentration* | | | | |
|---|---|---|---|---|---|---|---|---|---|
| | | | | | *1997-98* | *1998-99* | *1999-00* | *2000-01* | *2001-02* |
| Drugs & Pharmaceuticals | 2609.29 (47.22) | 2916.56 (52.78) | 5525.85 | 23 | 0.01 | 0.01 | 0.012 | 0.013 | 0.016 |
| Cement | 3497.15 (76.67) | 1063.92 (23.33) | 4561.07 | 31 | 0.043 | 0.049 | 0.047 | 0.051 | 0.055 |
| Steel | 1375.42 (65.23) | 733.24 (34.77) | 2108.66 | 58 | 0.111 | 0.108 | 0.108 | 0.102 | 0.107 |
| Paper | 1719.54 (92.26) | 144.25 (7.74) | 1863.79 | 64 | 0.01 | 0.009 | 0.011 | 0.014 | 0.016 |
| Copper and Copper Products | 990.64 (99.29) | 7.13 (0.71) | 997.77 | 82 | 0.049 | 0.089 | 0.129 | 0.173 | 0.212 |
| Tractors | 376.22 (42.59) | 507.1 (57.41) | 883.32 | 87 | 0.179 | 0.171 | 0.177 | 0.172 | 0.158 |
| Material Handling Equipment | 31.42 (3.56) | 851.28 (96.44) | 882.7 | 89 | 0.062 | 0.1 | 0.077 | 0.109 | 0.093 |
| Beer | 372.61 (42.68) | 500.5 (57.32) | 873.11 | 90 | 0.152 | 0.092 | 0.074 | 0.117 | 0.103 |
| Sugar | 729.79 (99.73) | 1.99 (0.27) | 731.78 | 97 | 0.003 | 0.002 | 0.003 | 0.004 | 0.005 |
| Tea | 319.09 (59.02) | 221.56 (40.98) | 540.65 | 112 | 0.062 | 0.086 | 0.068 | 0.081 | 0.082 |
| Wires and Cables | 440.42 (83.02) | 90.1 (16.98) | 530.52 | 113 | 0.033 | 0.029 | 0.029 | 0.028 | 0.025 |
| Dyes & Pigments | 62.95 (12.35) | 446.74 (87.65) | 509.69 | 115 | 0.036 | 0.026 | 0.023 | 0.02 | 0.02 |
| Machine Tools | 53.04 (18.50) | 233.63 (81.50) | 286.67 | 135 | 0.011 | 0.007 | 0.008 | 0.007 | 0.006 |
| Paints and Varnishes | 100.94 (36.10) | 178.71 (63.90) | 279.65 | 136 | 0.168 | 0.154 | 0.164 | 0.171 | 0.166 |
| Storage Batteries | 150.81 (79.53) | 38.82 (20.47) | 189.63 | 152 | 0.302 | 0.41 | 0.448 | 0.391 | 0.36 |
| Vegetable Oils | 41.84 (24.35) | 130 (75.65) | 171.84 | 156 | 0.004 | 0.004 | 0.004 | 0.007 | 0.01 |
| Motors and Generators | 20.33 (12.17) | 146.76 (87.83) | 167.09 | 158 | 0.073 | 0.085 | 0.084 | 0.08 | 0.084 |
| Bicycles | 61.56 (38.10) | 100 (61.90) | 161.56 | 160 | 0.215 | 0.243 | 0.262 | 0.273 | 0.285 |
| Pig Iron | 144.1 (90.72) | 14.74 (9.28) | 158.84 | 161 | 0.103 | 0.095 | 0.097 | 0.077 | 0.081 |
| Textile Machinery | 13.8 (9.02) | 139.26 (90.98) | 153.06 | 163 | 0.027 | 0.027 | 0.039 | 0.049 | 0.034 |
| Aluminium Products | 134.47 (97.66) | 3.22 (2.34) | 137.69 | 168 | 0.172 | 0.134 | 0.132 | 0.113 | 0.124 |
| Carbon Black | 57 (57.86) | 41.52 (42.14) | 98.52 | 182 | 0.191 | 0.211 | 0.235 | 0.252 | 0.299 |
| Ferro Alloys | 78.36 (98.06) | 1.55 (1.94) | 79.91 | 190 | 0.08 | 0.067 | 0.05 | 0.051 | 0.059 |
| Coffee | 61.35 (100) | 0 | 61.35 | 192 | 0.03 | 0.03 | 0.021 | 0.014 | 0.017 |

(*Contd.*)

| Industry | Value of Acquisitions by Indian-owned Companies (Rs. Crore) | Value of Acquisitions by Foreign-owned Companies (Rs. Crore) | Grand Total | Rank | Herfindahl Index of Concentration | | | | |
|---|---|---|---|---|---|---|---|---|---|
| | | | | | 1997-98 | 1998-99 | 1999-00 | 2000-01 | 2001-02 |
| Dry Cells | 16.78 (28.07) | 43 (71.93) | 59.78 | 195 | 0.283 | 0.222 | 0.217 | 0.175 | 0.207 |
| Transformers | 57.27 (100) | 0 | 57.27 | 196 | 0.098 | 0.099 | 0.078 | 0.077 | 0.101 |
| Sponge Iron | 19.9 (36.07) | 35.27 (63.93) | 55.17 | 197 | 0.179 | 0.171 | 0.151 | 0.139 | 0.153 |
| Refractories | 1 (2.22) | 43.96 (97.78) | 44.96 | 202 | 0.084 | 0.079 | 0.087 | 0.085 | 0.086 |
| Chemical Machinery | 10.3 (24.25) | 32.17 (75.75) | 42.47 | 203 | 0.212 | 0.267 | 0.556 | 0.18 | 0.2 |
| Granite | 11.23 (30.44) | 25.66 (69.56) | 36.89 | 206 | 0.037 | 0.036 | 0.036 | 0.043 | 0.049 |
| Abrasives | 32.98 (100) | 0 | 32.98 | 209 | 0.322 | 0.311 | 0.307 | 0.279 | 0.258 |
| Valves | 1.08 (3.72) | 27.99 (96.28) | 29.07 | 214 | 0.104 | 0.091 | 0.075 | 0.079 | 0.116 |
| Caustic Soda | 2.76 (9.94) | 25 (90.06) | 27.76 | 215 | 0.053 | 0.055 | 0.06 | 0.061 | 0.061 |
| Printing Machinery | 15.73 (100) | 0 | 15.73 | 219 | 0.008 | 0.046 | 0.059 | 0.078 | 0.061 |
| Acetic Acid | 6.85 (100) | 0 | 6.85 | 224 | 0.153 | 0.149 | 0.149 | 0.171 | 0.127 |
| Vanaspati | 4.87 (100) | 0 | 4.87 | 225 | 0.049 | 0.042 | 0.039 | 0.028 | 0.036 |
| Starch | 2.25 (100) | 0 | 2.25 | 230 | 0.069 | 0.074 | 0.08 | 0.084 | 0.076 |
| Phosphatic Fertilisers | 0.22 (100) | 0 | 0.22 | 231 | 0.055 | 0.063 | 0.064 | 0.063 | 0.044 |
| **Services** | | | | | | | | | |
| Production of TV serials/films | 3108.74 (60.51) | 2029.23 (39.49) | 5137.97 | 25 | 0.144 | 0.107 | 0.114 | 0.078 | 0.083 |
| Shipping | 1142.84 (91.39) | 107.64 (8.61) | 1250.48 | 72 | 0.316 | 0.272 | 0.241 | 0.201 | 0.191 |
| Courier Services | 185.93 (99.05) | 1.79 (0.95) | 187.72 | 153 | 0.304 | 0.193 | 0.183 | 0.184 | 0.189 |
| Air Transport | 18(19.35) | 75 (80.65) | 93 | 183 | 0.3 | 0.325 | 0.28 | 0.277 | 0.271 |
| Housing Construction | 35.62 (43.64) | 46 (56.36) | 81.62 | 188 | 0.123 | 0.1 | 0.099 | 0.107 | 0.126 |
| Road Transport | 0 | 4.2 (100) | 4.2 | 227 | 0.117 | 0.09 | 0.079 | 0.073 | 0.082 |

*Note* : (i) Mergers/Takeovers data pertaining to the period April, 1999-January, 2004
(ii) Figures in brackets denote percentages.

*Source*: Computed from CMIE data.

**Table 9.3:** Industries/Services experiencing Mergers & Acquisitions (numbers) in India during April, 1999-January, 2004

| *Industries* | *No. of Acquisitions by Indian-owned Companies* | *No. of Mergers with Indian-owned Companies* | *No. of Acquisitions by Foreign-owned Companies* | *No. of Mergers with Foreign-owned Companies in India* | *Grand Total* | *Rank* |
|---|---|---|---|---|---|---|
| Industry | 3373 (53.55) | 1263 (20.05) | 1466 (23.27) | 197 (3.13) | 6299 | 1 |
| Manufacturing | 2138 (58.51) | 465 (12.73) | 951 (26.02) | 100 (2.74) | 3654 | 2 |
| Machinery | 614 (52.84) | 116 (9.98) | 394 (33.91) | 38 (3.27) | 1162 | 5 |
| Chemicals | 513 (56.13) | 127 (13.90) | 248 (27.13) | 26 (2.84) | 914 | 7 |
| Electronics | 402 (53.24) | 81 (10.73) | 249 (32.98) | 23 (3.05) | 755 | 8 |
| Computer Software & Hardware | 301 (55.33) | 59 (10.85) | 168 (30.88) | 16 (2.94) | 544 | 9 |
| Computer Software | 263 (54.45) | 52 (10.77) | 153 (31.68) | 15 (3.10) | 483 | 10 |
| Food & Beverages | 255 (55.19) | 83 (17.97) | 102 (22.08) | 22 (4.76) | 462 | 13 |
| Food Products | 218 (59.89) | 74 (20.33) | 65 (17.86) | 7 (1.92) | 364 | 16 |
| Drugs & Pharmaceuticals | 173 (55.81) | 47 (15.16) | 79 (25.48) | 11 (3.55) | 310 | 18 |
| Textiles | 203 (77.48) | 35 (13.36) | 24 (9.16) | 0 | 262 | 20 |
| Metals & Metal Products | 162 (62.55) | 50 (19.30) | 39 (15.06) | 8 (3.09) | 259 | 21 |
| Non-electrical Machinery | 105 (50.72) | 12 (5.80) | 81 (39.13) | 9 (4.35) | 207 | 22 |
| Ferrous Metals | 126 (61.46) | 39 (19.02) | 33 (16.10) | 7 (3.42) | 205 | 23 |
| Electrical Machinery | 107 (52.97) | 23 (11.39) | 65 (32.18) | 7 (3.46) | 202 | 24 |
| Transport Equipment | 116 (60.10) | 17 (8.81) | 59 (30.57) | 1 (0.52) | 193 | 27 |
| Other Food Products | 88 (47.57) | 46 (24.87) | 45 (24.32) | 6 (3.24) | 185 | 30 |
| Non-Metallic Mineral Products | 128 (69.19) | 18 (9.73) | 37 (20) | 2 (1.08) | 185 | 30 |
| Miscellaneous Manufacturing | 99 (61.87) | 15 (9.38) | 43 (26.87) | 3 (1.88) | 160 | 33 |
| Other Electronics | 67 (50.76) | 16 (12.12) | 43 (32.58) | 6 (4.54) | 132 | 35 |
| Automobile Ancillaries | 77 (62.60) | 15 (12.20) | 31 (25.20) | 0 | 123 | 36 |
| Cotton Textiles | 94 (83.93) | 11 (9.82) | 7 (6.25) | 0 | 112 | 38 |
| Other Non-metallic Mineral Products | 66 (61.11) | 11 (10.19) | 29 (26.85) | 2 (1.85) | 108 | 40 |
| Beverages & Tobacco | 37 (37.76) | 9 (9.18) | 37 (37.76) | 15 (15.30) | 98 | 42 |
| Other Chemicals | 43 (44.33) | 13 (13.40) | 40 (41.24) | 1 (1.03) | 97 | 43 |
| Plastic Products | 66 (68.75) | 17 (17.71) | 13 (13.54) | 0 | 96 | 45 |

*(Contd.)*

| Industries | No. of Acquisitions by Indian-owned Companies | No. of Mergers with Indian-owned Companies | No. of Acquisitions by Foreign-owned Companies | No. of Mergers with Foreign-owned Companies in India | Grand Total | Rank |
|---|---|---|---|---|---|---|
| Other Textiles | 63 (66.32) | 21 (22.10) | 11 (11.58) | 0 | 95 | 46 |
| Beer & Alcohol | 33 (36.67) | 8 (8.89) | 34 (37.78) | 15 (16.66) | 90 | 47 |
| Other Industrial Machinery | 41 (48.80) | 3 (3.57) | 36 (42.86) | 4 (4.77) | 84 | 49 |
| Metal Products | 39 (46.99) | 18 (21.69) | 21 (25.30) | 5 (6.02) | 83 | 50 |
| **Services** | | | | | | |
| Services | 1024 (44.08) | 746 (32.12) | 457 (19.67) | 96 (4.13) | 2323 | 3 |
| Other Services | 631 (47.55) | 318 (23.97) | 329 (24.79) | 49 (3.69) | 1327 | 4 |
| Financial Services | 393 (39.46) | 428 (42.97) | 128 (12.85) | 47 (4.72) | 996 | 6 |
| Non-banking Financial Cos. (NBFCs) | 250 (53.53) | 135 (28.91) | 58 (12.42) | 24 (5.14) | 467 | 11 |
| Hire Purchase & Leasing Services | 250 (53.53) | 135 (28.91) | 58 (12.42) | 24 (5.14) | 467 | 11 |
| Misc. Services | 153 (33.26) | 147 (31.96) | 141 (30.65) | 19 (4.13) | 460 | 14 |
| Hire Purchase Financial Services | 219 (52.90) | 124 (29.95) | 49 (11.84) | 22 (5.31) | 414 | 15 |
| Investment Services | 49 (14) | 268 (76.58) | 13 (3.71) | 20 (5.71) | 350 | 17 |
| Trading | 133 (43.18) | 97 (31.50) | 56 (18.18) | 22 (7.14) | 308 | 19 |
| Business Consultancy | 76 (38.39) | 42 (21.21) | 74 (37.37) | 6 (3.03) | 198 | 25 |
| Communication Services | 114 (57.87) | 25 (12.69) | 56 (28.43) | 2 (1.01) | 197 | 26 |
| Telecommunications Services | 110 (57.29) | 25 (13.02) | 55 (28.65) | 2 (1.04) | 192 | 28 |
| Misc. Other Services | 54 (28.42) | 72 (37.89) | 58 (30.53) | 6 (3.16) | 190 | 29 |
| Other Telecommunication Services | 100 (61.73) | 21 (12.96) | 39 (24.07) | 2 (1.24) | 162 | 32 |
| Recreational Services | 92 (64.33) | 17 (11.89) | 30 (20.98) | 4 (2.80) | 143 | 34 |
| Real Estate | 107 (93.04) | | 8 (6.96) | | 115 | 37 |
| Hotels & Tourism | 84 (76.36) | 10 (9.09) | 15 (13.64) | 1 (0.91) | 110 | 39 |
| Hotels & Restaurants | 82 (78.85) | 10 (9.61) | 12 (11.54) | 0 | 104 | 41 |
| Construction | 44 (45.36) | 35 (36.08) | 18 (18.56) | 0 | 97 | 43 |
| Transport Services | 42 (49.41) | 14 (16.47) | 28 (32.94) | 1 (1.18) | 85 | 48 |

(Figure in brackets denote percentages)

*Source*: Computed from CMIE data.

**Table 9.4:** Value of Acquisitions of Industry/Services (April, 1999-January, 2004)

| *Industries* | *Value of Acquisitions by Indian-owned Companies (Rs. Crore)* | *Value of Acquisitions by Foreign-owned Companies (Rs. Crore)* | *Grand Total* | *Rank* |
|---|---|---|---|---|
| Industry | 89969.45 (59.24) | 61913.21 (40.76) | 151882.66 | 1 |
| Manufacturing | 51878.72 (60.40) | 34007.19 (39.60) | 85885.91 | 2 |
| Machinery | 10743.45 (43.87) | 13747.54 (56.13) | 24490.99 | 5 |
| Chemicals | 13865.86 (62.22) | 8420.75 (37.78) | 22286.61 | 6 |
| Electronics | 8757.74 (46.39) | 10122.55 (53.13) | 18880.29 | 7 |
| Computer Software & Hardware | 5800.64 (48.14) | 6249.73 (51.86) | 12050.37 | 11 |
| Computer Software | 5345.93 (46.72) | 6096.08 (53.28) | 11442.01 | 12 |
| Metals & Metal Products | 6948.85 (85.37) | 1190.47 (14.63) | 8139.32 | 14 |
| Diversified | 4743.16 (63.98) | 2670 (36.01) | 7413.16 | 15 |
| Electricity | 4893.78 (69.12) | 2186.32 (30.88) | 7080.1 | 16 |
| Electricity Generation | 4413.02 (66.87) | 2186.32 (33.13) | 6599.34 | 19 |
| Food & Beverages | 2752.29 (45.40) | 3310.59 (54.60) | 6062.88 | 20 |
| Transport Equipment | 3704.44 (61.13) | 2355.09 (38.87) | 6059.53 | 21 |
| Petroleum Products | 4815.5 (82.49) | 1022.11 (17.51) | 5837.61 | 22 |
| Drugs & Pharmaceuticals | 2609.29 (47.22) | 2916.56 (52.78) | 5525.85 | 23 |
| Non-metallic Mineral Products | 3945.62 (75.21) | 1300.55 (24.79) | 5246.17 | 24 |
| Non-ferrous Metals | 4890.63 (98.10) | 94.91 (1.90) | 4985.54 | 26 |
| Refinery | 4782.15 (98.01) | 97.4 (1.99) | 4879.55 | 27 |
| Mining | 596.56 (12.42) | 4208.04 (87.58) | 4804.6 | 28 |
| Food Products | 2131.88 (44.81) | 2625.7 (55.19) | 4757.58 | 29 |
| Automobile | 2438.35 (52.57) | 2199.82 (47.43) | 4638.17 | 30 |
| Cement | 3497.15 (76.67) | 1063.92 (23.33) | 4561.07 | 31 |
| Communication Equipment | 1660.36 (40.77) | 2411.94 (59.23) | 4072.3 | 36 |
| Non-electrical Machinery | 1015.05 (28.42) | 2556.56 (71.58) | 3571.61 | 39 |
| Polymers | 3170.14 (94.72) | 176.84 (5.28) | 3346.98 | 41 |

(*Contd.*)

| *Industries* | *Value of Acquisitions by Indian-owned Companies (Rs. Crore)* | *Value of Acquisitions by Foreign-owned Companies (Rs. Crore)* | *Grand Total* | *Rank* |
|---|---|---|---|---|
| Textiles | 2969.85 (91.70) | 268.95 (8.30) | 3238.8 | 42 |
| Ferrous Metals | 2058.22 (65.26) | 1095.56 (34.74) | 3153.78 | 43 |
| Thermoplastics | 3075.14 (99.44) | 17.36 (0.56) | 3092.5 | 44 |
| Miscellaneous Manufacturing | 2206.5 (74.80) | 743.19 (25.20) | 2949.69 | 45 |
| Passenger Cars & Multi-utility Vehicles | 1125.39 (38.89) | 1768.2 (61.10) | 2893.59 | 48 |
| Aluminium & Aluminium Products | 2772.12 (98.12) | 53.22 (1.88) | 2825.34 | 49 |
| Other Food Products | 737.47 (26.26) | 2070.35 (73.74) | 2807.82 | 50 |
| **Services** | | | | |
| Services | 29577.36 (59.14) | 20431.03 (40.86) | 50008.39 | 3 |
| Other Services | 21935.03 (59.55) | 14902.08 (40.45) | 36837.11 | 4 |
| Communication Services | 9242.78 (57.57) | 6812.52 (42.43) | 16055.3 | 8 |
| Telecommunication Services | 9056.85 (57.08) | 6810.73 (42.92) | 15867.58 | 9 |
| Financial Services | 7642.33 (58.02) | 5528.95 (41.98) | 13171.28 | 10 |
| Other Telecommunication Services | 5316.57 (59.90) | 3559.81 (40.10) | 8876.38 | 13 |
| Telephone Services | 3730.28 (53.43) | 3250.92 (46.57) | 6981.2 | 17 |
| Recreational Services | 4416.71 (66.07) | 2267.99 (33.93) | 6684.7 | 18 |
| Production of TV serials/films | 3108.74 (60.50) | 2029.23 (39.50) | 5137.97 | 25 |
| Non-banking Financial Cos. (NBFCs) | 2749.63 (65.47) | 1450.49 (34.54) | 4200.12 | 32 |
| Hire Purchase & Leasing Services | 2749.63 (65.47) | 1450.49 (34.54) | 4200.12 | 32 |
| Misc. Services | 1987.04 (47.72) | 2176.65 (52.28) | 4163.69 | 34 |
| Trading | 3290.13 ( 79.49) | 849.08 (20.51) | 4139.21 | 35 |
| Hire Purchase Financial Services | 2651.22 (65.21) | 1414.4 (34.79) | 4065.62 | 37 |
| Banking Services | 937.7 (24.91) | 2826.27 (75.09) | 3763.97 | 38 |
| Transport Services | 1192.3 (35.13) | 2201.65 (64.87) | 3393.95 | 40 |
| Real Estate | 2620.93 (89.04) | 322.54 (10.96) | 2943.47 | 46 |
| Financial Institutions | 2829.16 (97.49) | 72.98 (2.51) | 2902.14 | 47 |

(Figures in brackets denote percentages )
*Source*: Computed from CMIE data.

**Table 9.5:** Average size of Acquisitions of Indian Owned Companies

| *Industry Code* | *Industries* | *Value of Acquisitions by Indian-owned Companies (Rs. Crores)* | *No. of Acquisitions by Indian-owned Companies* | *Average size of Acquisition by Indian-owned Companies* | *Rank* |
|---|---|---|---|---|---|
| 010105020101 | Aluminium | 2637.65 | 7 | 376.81 | 2 |
| 010103140100 | Refinery | 4782.15 | 15 | 318.81 | 3 |
| 010105020200 | Other non-ferrous metals | 1127.87 | 5 | 225.57 | 5 |
| 010103140000 | Petroleum products | 4815.5 | 22 | 218.89 | 6 |
| 010107010200 | Passenger cars & multi utility vehicles | 1125.39 | 6 | 187.57 | 7 |
| 010301000000 | Electricity generation | 4413.02 | 31 | 142.36 | 9 |
| 010300000000 | Electricity | 4893.78 | 35 | 139.82 | 10 |
| 010105020000 | Non-ferrous metals | 4890.63 | 36 | 135.85 | 11 |
| 010105020100 | Aluminium & aluminium products | 2772.12 | 22 | 126.01 | 12 |
| 010302000000 | Electricity distribution | 480.76 | 4 | 120.19 | 13 |
| 010105020300 | Copper & copper products | 990.64 | 9 | 110.07 | 14 |
| 010109000000 | Diversified | 4743.16 | 48 | 98.82 | 15 |
| 010103120100 | Thermoplastics | 3075.14 | 32 | 96.10 | 16 |
| 010103120000 | Polymers | 3170.14 | 35 | 90.58 | 17 |
| 010107010300 | Two & three wheelers | 789.9 | 10 | 78.99 | 23 |
| 010103080000 | Soaps & detergents | 867.35 | 13 | 66.72 | 25 |
| 010107010000 | Automobile | 2438.35 | 39 | 62.52 | 26 |
| 010106030300 | Communication equipment | 1660.36 | 27 | 61.49 | 27 |
| 010103110200 | Carbon black | 57 | 1 | 57.00 | 28 |
| 010104010000 | Cement | 3497.15 | 62 | 56.41 | 29 |
| 010106010305 | Tractors | 376.22 | 7 | 53.75 | 30 |
| 010105000000 | Metals & metal products | 6948.85 | 162 | 42.89 | 35 |
| 010204000000 | Offshore drilling | 208.68 | 5 | 41.74 | 36 |
| 010108010100 | Paper | 1719.54 | 42 | 40.94 | 37 |

*(Contd.)*

| Industry Code | Industries | Value of Acquisitions by Indian-owned Companies (Rs. Crores) | No. of Acquisitions by Indian-owned Companies | Average size of Acquisition by Indian-owned Companies | Rank |
|---|---|---|---|---|---|
| 010108010000 | Paper & paper products | 1805.3 | 52 | 34.72 | 40 |
| 010103030300 | Other fertilizers | 425.35 | 13 | 32.72 | 42 |
| 010202000000 | Crude oil & natural gas | 324.59 | 10 | 32.46 | 43 |
| 010101010502 | Bakery & milling products | 287.61 | 9 | 31.96 | 45 |
| 010107000000 | Transport equipment | 3704.44 | 116 | 31.93 | 46 |
| 010103120200 | Plastic resins | 95 | 3 | 31.67 | 47 |
| 010104000000 | Non-metallic mineral products | 3945.62 | 128 | 30.83 | 48 |
| 010106020602 | Storage batteries | 150.81 | 5 | 30.16 | 49 |
| 010106030403 | Electronic components | 569.3 | 19 | 29.96 | 50 |
| | **Services** | | | | |
| 010402060101 | Telephone services | 3730.28 | 8 | 466.29 | 1 |
| 010401020100 | All india development institutions (DFIs) | 2031.46 | 9 | 225.72 | 4 |
| 010401020000 | Financial institutions | 2829.16 | 18 | 157.18 | 8 |
| 010401020300 | Other financial institutions | 797.7 | 9 | 88.63 | 18 |
| 010402060100 | Telecommunication services | 9056.85 | 110 | 82.34 | 19 |
| 010402020100 | Production of TV serials/films | 3108.74 | 38 | 81.81 | 20 |
| 010402060000 | Communication services | 9242.78 | 114 | 81.08 | 21 |
| 010402020500 | Amusement parks/entertainment centres/theatres | 475.25 | 6 | 79.21 | 22 |
| 010402020400 | Pre-recorded and recorded cassettes | 565.58 | 8 | 70.70 | 24 |
| 010402060102 | Other telecommunication services | 5316.57 | 100 | 53.17 | 31 |
| 010402020000 | Recreational services | 4416.71 | 92 | 48.01 | 32 |
| 010402060200 | Courier services | 185.93 | 4 | 46.48 | 33 |
| 010402050400 | Shipping | 1142.84 | 26 | 43.96 | 34 |
| 010402000000 | Other services | 21935.03 | 631 | 34.76 | 38 |
| 010401010000 | Banking services | 937.7 | 27 | 34.73 | 39 |
| 010402070100 | Commercial complexes | 598.86 | 18 | 33.27 | 41 |
| 010603000000 | Civil engineering | 256.22 | 8 | 32.03 | 44 |

*Source*: Computed from CMIE data

**Table 9.6:** Average size of Acquisitions of Foreign Owned Companies (Rs. Crores)

| *Industry Code* | *Industries* | *Value of Acquisitions by Foreign-owned Companies (Rs. crore)* | *No. of Acquisitions by Foreign –owned Companies* | *Average size of Acquisition by Foreign-owned Companies* | *Rank* |
|---|---|---|---|---|---|
| 010109000000 | Diversified | 2670 | 4 | 667.50 | 1 |
| 010204000000 | Offshore drilling | 1960 | 3 | 653.33 | 2 |
| 010202000000 | Crude oil & natural gas | 800 | 2 | 400.00 | 3 |
| 010200000000 | Mining | 4208.04 | 16 | 263.00 | 5 |
| 010101010501 | Cocoa products & confectionery | 1170.2 | 5 | 234.04 | 6 |
| 010106010305 | Tractors | 507.1 | 3 | 169.03 | 7 |
| 010107010200 | Passenger cars & multi-utility vehicles | 1768.2 | 11 | 160.75 | 8 |
| 010203000000 | Minerals | 1442.04 | 10 | 144.20 | 9 |
| 010300000000 | Electricity | 2186.32 | 16 | 136.65 | 10 |
| 010301000000 | Electricity generation | 2186.32 | 16 | 136.65 | 10 |
| 010104010000 | Cement | 1063.92 | 8 | 132.99 | 12 |
| 010103140200 | Lubricants, etc. | 924.71 | 7 | 132.10 | 13 |
| 010106010304 | Material handling equipments | 851.28 | 8 | 106.41 | 19 |
| 010106030300 | Communication equipment | 2411.94 | 23 | 104.87 | 20 |
| 010103130300 | Plastic films | 100 | 1 | 100.00 | 22 |
| 010107010402 | Bicycles | 100 | 1 | 100.00 | 22 |
| 010103080000 | Soaps & detergents | 687.64 | 7 | 98.23 | 24 |
| 010105010201 | Finished steel | 731.69 | 8 | 91.46 | 25 |
| 010103140000 | Petroleum products | 1022.11 | 12 | 85.18 | 27 |
| 010107010000 | Automobile | 2199.82 | 28 | 78.57 | 30 |
| 010105010200 | Steel | 733.24 | 10 | 73.32 | 33 |
| 010106010105 | Compressors | 134.35 | 2 | 67.18 | 34 |
| 010103130100 | Plastic tubes & pipes | 183.02 | 3 | 61.01 | 35 |
| 010108010200 | Paper products | 274.19 | 5 | 54.84 | 36 |
| 010103040000 | Pesticides | 797.23 | 15 | 53.15 | 37 |

(*Contd.*)

| Industry Code | Industries | Value of Acquisitions by Foreign-owned Companies (Rs. crore) | No. of Acquisitions by Foreign –owned Companies | Average size of Acquisition by Foreign-owned Companies | Rank |
|---|---|---|---|---|---|
| 010106010300 | Other industrial machinery | 1824.88 | 36 | 50.69 | 38 |
| 010105020101 | Aluminium | 50 | 1 | 50.00 | 39 |
| 010106010203 | Textile machinery | 139.26 | 3 | 46.42 | 40 |
| 010101010100 | Dairy products | 185.47 | 4 | 46.37 | 41 |
| 010101010500 | Other food products | 2070.35 | 45 | 46.01 | 42 |
| 010103110300 | Explosives | 271.42 | 6 | 45.24 | 45 |
| 010107010300 | Two & three wheelers | 175.5 | 4 | 43.88 | 47 |
| 010106020601 | Dry cells | 43 | 1 | 43.00 | 49 |
| 010000000000 | Industry | 61913.21 | 1466 | 42.23 | 50 |
| | **Services** | | | | |
| 010402060101 | Telephone services | 3250.92 | 12 | 270.91 | 4 |
| 010402060100 | Telecommunication services | 6810.73 | 55 | 123.83 | 14 |
| 010402060000 | Communication services | 6812.52 | 56 | 121.65 | 15 |
| 010401010000 | Banking services | 2826.27 | 25 | 113.05 | 16 |
| 010402020500 | Amusement parks/entertainment centres/theatres | 219 | 2 | 109.50 | 17 |
| 010402020100 | Production of TV serials/films | 2029.23 | 19 | 106.80 | 18 |
| 010402050500 | Transport support services | 2014.81 | 20 | 100.74 | 21 |
| 010402060102 | Other telecommunication services | 3559.81 | 39 | 91.28 | 26 |
| 010604000000 | Other construction activities | 557.01 | 7 | 79.57 | 28 |
| 010402050000 | Transport services | 2201.65 | 28 | 78.63 | 29 |
| 010402020000 | Recreational services | 2267.99 | 30 | 75.60 | 31 |
| 010402050300 | Air transport | 75 | 1 | 75.00 | 32 |
| 010602000000 | Housing construction | 46 | 1 | 46.00 | 43 |
| 010402000000 | Other services | 14902.08 | 329 | 45.30 | 44 |
| 010400000000 | Services | 20431.03 | 457 | 44.71 | 46 |
| 010401000000 | Financial services | 5528.95 | 128 | 43.19 | 48 |

*Source*: Computed from CMIE data

**Table 9.7:** Herfindahl Index of Concentration

| *Industry* | *1997-98* | *1998-99* | *1999-00* | *2000-01* | *2001-02* | *Rank* | *No. of Companies* |
|---|---|---|---|---|---|---|---|
| Drugs & pharmaceuticals | 0.01 | 0.01 | 0.012 | 0.013 | 0.016 | 18 | 552 |
| Steel | 0.111 | 0.108 | 0.108 | 0.102 | 0.107 | 51 | 368 |
| Cement | 0.043 | 0.049 | 0.047 | 0.051 | 0.055 | 53 | 133 |
| Sugar | 0.003 | 0.002 | 0.003 | 0.004 | 0.005 | 68 | 124 |
| Tea | 0.062 | 0.086 | 0.068 | 0.081 | 0.082 | 72 | 228 |
| Paper | 0.01 | 0.009 | 0.011 | 0.014 | 0.016 | 75 | 253 |
| Beer | 0.152 | 0.092 | 0.074 | 0.117 | 0.103 | 92 | 40 |
| Machine tools | 0.011 | 0.007 | 0.008 | 0.007 | 0.006 | 98 | 139 |
| Wires and cables | 0.033 | 0.029 | 0.029 | 0.028 | 0.025 | 101 | 186 |
| Dyes & pigments | 0.036 | 0.026 | 0.023 | 0.02 | 0.02 | 110 | 146 |
| Motors and generators | 0.073 | 0.085 | 0.084 | 0.08 | 0.084 | 110 | 90 |
| Paints and varnishes | 0.168 | 0.154 | 0.164 | 0.171 | 0.166 | 126 | 76 |
| Aluminium products | 0.172 | 0.134 | 0.132 | 0.113 | 0.124 | 126 | 112 |
| Vegetable oils | 0.004 | 0.004 | 0.004 | 0.007 | 0.01 | 142 | 342 |
| Chemical machinery | 0.212 | 0.267 | 0.556 | 0.18 | 0.2 | 142 | 57 |
| Transformers | 0.098 | 0.099 | 0.078 | 0.077 | 0.101 | 145 | 55 |
| Material handling equipment | 0.062 | 0.1 | 0.077 | 0.109 | 0.093 | 151 | 39 |
| Copper and copper products | 0.049 | 0.089 | 0.129 | 0.173 | 0.212 | 165 | 91 |
| Caustic soda | 0.053 | 0.055 | 0.06 | 0.061 | 0.061 | 182 | 39 |
| Pig iron | 0.103 | 0.095 | 0.097 | 0.077 | 0.081 | 182 | 23 |
| Ferro alloys | 0.08 | 0.067 | 0.05 | 0.051 | 0.059 | 182 | 51 |
| Tractors | 0.179 | 0.171 | 0.177 | 0.172 | 0.158 | 182 | 14 |
| Granite | 0.037 | 0.036 | 0.036 | 0.043 | 0.049 | 190 | 87 |
| Storage batteries | 0.302 | 0.41 | 0.448 | 0.391 | 0.36 | 190 | 16 |
| Textile machinery | 0.027 | 0.027 | 0.039 | 0.049 | 0.034 | 196 | 54 |
| Coffee | 0.03 | 0.03 | 0.021 | 0.014 | 0.017 | 201 | 50 |

(*Contd.*)

| Industry | 1997-98 | 1998-99 | 1999-00 | 2000-01 | 2001-02 | Rank | No. of Companies |
|---|---|---|---|---|---|---|---|
| Refractories | 0.084 | 0.079 | 0.087 | 0.085 | 0.086 | 203 | 46 |
| Valves | 0.104 | 0.091 | 0.075 | 0.079 | 0.116 | 203 | 71 |
| Dry cells | 0.283 | 0.222 | 0.217 | 0.175 | 0.207 | 203 | 11 |
| Vanaspati | 0.049 | 0.042 | 0.039 | 0.028 | 0.036 | 211 | 92 |
| Phosphatic fertilisers | 0.055 | 0.063 | 0.064 | 0.063 | 0.044 | 211 | 54 |
| Abrasives | 0.322 | 0.311 | 0.307 | 0.279 | 0.258 | 211 | 15 |
| Sponge iron | 0.179 | 0.171 | 0.151 | 0.139 | 0.153 | 211 | 25 |
| Starch | 0.069 | 0.074 | 0.08 | 0.084 | 0.076 | 221 | 18 |
| Acetic acid | 0.153 | 0.149 | 0.149 | 0.171 | 0.127 | 221 | 27 |
| Bicycles | 0.215 | 0.243 | 0.262 | 0.273 | 0.285 | 221 | 10 |
| Carbon black | 0.191 | 0.211 | 0.235 | 0.252 | 0.299 | 228 | 9 |
| Printing machinery | 0.008 | 0.046 | 0.059 | 0.078 | 0.061 | 231 | 15 |
| Phthalic anhydride | 0.22 | 0.23 | 0.269 | 0.264 | 0.277 | 238 | 6 |
| Soda ash | 0.272 | 0.252 | 0.301 | 0.233 | 0.199 | 238 | 9 |
| **Services** | | | | | | | |
| Production of TV serials/films | 0.144 | 0.107 | 0.114 | 0.078 | 0.083 | 62 | 60 |
| Shipping | 0.316 | 0.272 | 0.241 | 0.201 | 0.191 | 104 | 82 |
| Housing construction | 0.123 | 0.1 | 0.099 | 0.107 | 0.126 | 119 | 52 |
| Road transport | 0.117 | 0.09 | 0.079 | 0.073 | 0.082 | 182 | 64 |
| Air transport | 0.3 | 0.325 | 0.28 | 0.277 | 0.271 | 211 | 18 |
| Courier services | 0.304 | 0.193 | 0.183 | 0.184 | 0.189 | 211 | 19 |

*Source*: Computed from CMIE data.

M&As involving foreign firms (Kumar, 2000) the case for reviewing foreign owned M&As certainly deserves separate consideration.

In fact in the Working Group (WTO, Report of the Working Group 2003), India has been arguing that the principle of National Treatment i.e. non-discrimination between domestic and foreign suppliers cannot be extended to competition policy for developing countries like India. It was also pointed out that if such National Treatment is given, it would be the domestic firms, which will bear the brunt of investigations since it will be difficult for India to prosecute foreign firms. India also argued for a more liberal attitude towards domestic mergers in order to allow for domestic restructuring (Bhattacharjea, 2003)

However if we examine India's Competition Act 2002, these issues have not received the consideration required. Section 5 of the Act defines combinations in terms of thresholds, which focuses upon the large players. However Section 20(1) on Inquiry into combinations by the Commission, where criteria for determining adverse effects to competition by such combinations have been laid down, does not include any criterion for separating out 'domestic' combinations from 'foreign' combinations. Secondly, Clause 4(m) speaks about the criterion of contribution to 'economic development', which may provide a 'relative advantage' to even those combinations having an adverse effect on competition. As pointed out elsewhere (Bhattacharjea, 2003), this clause may exempt anti-competitive activities of a merger/amalgamation involving a large multinational corporation on a hazy ground like contribution to economic development.

Thirdly, although threshold limits are specified, no specific considerations in terms of exemptions or otherwise have been provided for domestic mergers and acquisitions in the Competition Act 2002.

Therefore there appears to be a contradiction existing between India's submission to the Working Group and the Competition Act 2002.

## SECTION III

### INDIA'S COMPETITION ACT 2002[1]

The Act and its implications have been discussed in detail elsewhere (Bhattacharjea, 2003). As discussed by Bhattacharjea, the Act has three major prongs, namely, prohibition of anti-competitive agreements which applies to the horizontal and vertical restraints applied between firms for restricting competition, prohibition of abuse of dominant positions which refers to the anti-competitive practices by a single firm by virtue of its 'dominant' position and regulation of combinations which refers to anti-competitive mergers and acquisitions. The three prongs are discussed below:

***Regulation of Combinations***

- Section 5 of the Act specifies minimum thresholds for mergers and acquisitions. However there is no distinction made between mergers and acquisitions where the dominant firm is an Indian firm or where the mergers/acquisitions are happening between Indian firms. Thus *de jure* National Treatment has been built into Section 5 and Section 20 of the Act.
- Our analysis of data relating to M&As shows that a large majority of M&As in India is occurring between Indian owned companies. According to our analysis this is happening for the purpose of corporate restructuring in the post-liberalisation scenario and is very critical for Indian industry. Given this situation, there should be an exemption or exclusion for domestic mergers vis a vis foreign mergers in terms of regulation.
- Also as per our study, the number of M&As involving foreign firms is sizeable, albeit lower than those involving Indian firms. M&As involving foreign firms require regulation given the different types of implications of such M&As for India's industrial sector including changing market structures, enhanced concentration and possible anti-trust implications. (Kumar, 2000).
- Clause 4(m) of Section 20 provides relative advantage to combinations, which contribute to economic development even though they may have adverse effects on competition. This provides an "escape route" for foreign owned M&As, which may have adverse effects particularly since " economic development" is a loose phrase for which no specific criteria are laid down.

***Prohibition of Abuse of Dominant Position***

In Section 19(4) of the Act, which lays down the criteria for determining abuse of a dominant position the following points may be noted:

- There is no distinction made between domestic and foreign firms which in fact should be made given the initial advantage that foreign firms enjoy in terms of economies of scale, cost structures, etc.
- Clause 4(l) in the same section refers to a "relative advantage by way of contribution to economic development". This would potentially allow an enterprise even though it may be a large multinational corporation to indulge in practices amounting to an abuse of dominant position, provided it is contributing to 'economic development'. Since specific criteria are not laid down for the latter, this clause may be misused and misinterpreted to the advantage of large corporations.
- *Anti-Competitive Agreements* as defined in the Competition Act 2002 in Section 3(1) is a fairly broad definition and would encompass all types of cartels, including domestic and international cartels. These are prohibited, with some exemptions provided under Section 3(5) and Section 54 of the Act. In particular, Section 3(5) provides exemptions for rights covered under the Copyright Act, the Patents Act, Trade Marks Act, Geographical Indications Act, Designs Act and the Integrated Circuits Layout Design Act. It also states that there will be no restrictions on agreements undertaken exclusively for the purpose of exports. Section 54 provides exemptions for enterprises if necessary for national security, any agreement undertaken to comply with an International Treaty, and enterprises, which performs a sovereign function on behalf of the Government.

It may be noted here that in the Working Group (WTO, Report of the Working Group, 2003), while a variety of views have been expressed regarding hard core cartels there was no consensus regarding passing a legislation banning hard core cartels in developing countries. Distinctions were pointed out between domestic and international cartels and it was noted that for developing countries only certain types of cartels e.g. bid rigging and price fixing cartels may have harmful effects. It was pointed out that other cartels may have positive efficiency effects and would need to be examined on a case-by-case basis. It was also opined that focus should be on banning of 'international cartels'. In fact while the EC proposals put forth proposals for a ban on hard-core cartels including both domestic and international cartels, India had argued in the Working Group in favour of a permissive attitude towards 'rationalization cartels'.

However in Section 3 of India's Competition Act 2002, there is no distinction made between domestic and international cartels, which in effect imply that *de jure* National Treatment has been provided to cartels. The Competition Act 2002 by prohibiting all types of cartels, with a few exceptions, therefore seems to be largely in tune with the EC proposals as far as hard-core cartels are concerned. (Bhattacharjea, 2003).

In view of the above, the following aspects should be incorporated into India's Competition Act:

- ❖ On regulation of combinations such as M&As, domestic mergers should be exempted given that most of the domestic mergers, which are currently taking place in India, are taking place for corporate restructuring and reorganization among Indian enterprises. M&As involving foreign companies should however be regulated. Providing de jure National Treatment to M&As is not desirable at the current juncture.
- ❖ On the issue of exemptions, Section 54 of India's Competition Act 2002 provides for exemptions on the grounds of security, any practice in accordance with an obligation under an international treaty and for any enterprise performing a sovereign function. Also Section 3(5) provides for exemptions for protection of Intellectual Property Rights as well as for export cartels. However, these require to be broadened. In Section 3 criteria such as size of enterprises, exemptions for particular sectors, extent of competition faced from imports by a particular sector, tariff protection for specific sectors, etc. need to be taken into consideration and adequate exemptions given (Bhattacharjea, 2002, 2003).

It may be noted in this connection that in many developed countries such as UK and France, restrictive agreements like cartels were legal till recently. In the EU, even now block exemptions are given for rationalization agreements and crisis cartels are allowed. EU also gives importance to criteria such as equity, employment etc. in granting exemptions within its competition policy. However India's Competition Act does not allow for exemptions for cartels on these grounds.

- There should also be a distinction made between domestic cartels and international cartels. International cartels should be prohibited but domestic cartels may actually have certain desired effects on the grounds of equity, scale economies and other considerations. Provisions should be made in the Act to accommodate these issues and there should be flexibility built into allow examination on a case-by-case basis.

## SECTION IV
## RELEVANCE OF A MULTILATERAL FRAMEWORK ON COMPETITION POLICY

Although the issue of Trade and Competition Policy is no longer a part of the Doha Work programme, it remains a major policy issue in the context of both developed and developing countries. Accordingly we discuss in this section the relevance of a multilateral agreement on competition policy.

Proponents of a multilateral framework like the EU and US among others, have argued that if anti-cartel enforcement is to be effective at an international level, then apart from prohibition of such cartels, other multilateral disciplines in the form of adoption of the core principles such as voluntary cooperation, procedural fairness and non-discrimination is also required in an interrelated fashion. For instance, issues such as prosecution of international cartels require information and documentation on cross-border cartels from other countries. For this, adoption of core principles such as voluntary cooperation between competition agencies in different countries is necessary. Also, adoption of core principles such as procedural fairness and non-discrimination is required so that foreign firms know of their legal obligations and rights and also know that they will be treated on a comparable basis with domestic firms. Absence of such an assurance may lead to a firm being reluctant to supply to another country (Clarke and Evenett, 2003).

However, as far as developing countries like India are concerned, as discussed in detail earlier, there is no consensus regarding adoption of a multilateral framework due to a variety of reasons.

We conclude that adopting a multilateral framework on the lines being suggested by developed countries is not advantageous for a country like India. This is because adoption of such a framework—

- will involve large costs, since it is largely opined that adoption of the core principles including transparency, non-discrimination, voluntary cooperation and procedural fairness will impose an unnecessary burden on developing countries in terms of resources and costs and also would be contrary to their developmental interests.
- would imply that domestic cartels, which may have social welfare implications and may be required in certain sectors may be adversely affected by the adoption of a multilateral framework as proposed.
- would imply that domestic mergers which may be essential from the point of view of domestic restructuring would be regulated and reviewed under the same norms as mergers involving large foreign firms. This may have potentially adverse implications for development since domestic mergers are a part of the restructuring process in a country like India. These are required in order that domestic industry may compete effectively with multinational corporations. Adoption of the principle of non-discrimination between domestic mergers and mergers involving foreign companies would thus be contrary to the developmental interests of developing countries like India.
- may not lead to an effective prosecution of international hard core cartels because developing countries would not readily have access to the kind of information required to prosecute such cartels especially if they are located in other developed countries.

## Concluding Observations

This paper basically examines the rationale for a competition policy for developing countries, and specifically India, with specific reference to mergers and acquisitions happening in India over a six-year period in selected industry and service sectors. On the basis of this analysis the paper discusses changes in India's Competition Act 2002. The relevance of a multilateral framework on Competition Policy for India is discussed and the paper concludes that while a competition policy at the domestic level is beneficial for India in terms of its developmental interests, a multilateral framework as suggested by its proponents within the framework of the WTO has no relevance and is not beneficial for India at the current juncture.

*The author would like to thank Dr Dipayan Datta Chaudhuri for his help in the data tabulation and analysis . Any errors that remain are solely those of the author.*

## END NOTE

1. Competition Commission of India (2003). 'The Competition Act, 2002', No. 12 of 2003, New Delhi.

## REFERENCES

Bhattacharjea, A. (2001). 'Competition Policy: India and WTO', *Economic and Political Weekly*, 36(51): 4710-13.

——— (2003). 'India's Competition Policy: An Assessment', *Economic and Political Weekly*, 38(34): 3561-74.

Clarke, J. L. and Evenett, S. J. (2003). 'A Multilateral Framework for Competition Policy', in Evenett S.J. and the Swiss State Secretariat of Economic Affairs (eds.) *The Singapore Issues and the World Trading System: The Road to Cancun and Beyond*. Available at http://www.evenett.com/chapters/wtoguidecompetition.pdf.

Competition Commission of India, (2003). 'The Competition Act, 2002', No. 12 of 2003, New Delhi.

Jenny, F. and Anderson, R. (2002). '*Competition Policy, Economic Development and the Multilateral Trading System: Overview of the Linkages and Current Proposals for an Agreement in the WTO*', World Trade Organization, Geneva, 19 March.

Khemani, R.S. (2002). 'Application of Competition Law: Exemptions and Exceptions' UNCTAD, United Nation, document UNCTAD/DITC/CLP/Misc., New York and Geneva.

Krueger, A. (1974). 'The Political Economy of the rent seeking society', *American Economic Review*, 64(3): 291-303.

Kumar, N. (2000). 'Mergers & Acquisition by MNEs: Patterns & Implications', *Economic and Political Weekly*, 35(32): 2851-58.

Singh, A. (1999). 'Competition Policy, Development and Developing Countries', Working Paper No. 50, ICRIER, New Delhi.

——— (2002). 'Competition & Competition Policy in Emerging Markets—International & Developmental Dimensions', ESRC Center for Business Research, University of Cambridge, Working Paper No. 246, December.

——— (2003). 'Multilateral Competition Policy & Economic Development—A Developing Country Perspective on the European Community Proposals', paper presented at Fifth Session of the Inter-governmental Group of Experts on Competition Law and Policy, Geneva, 2-4 July.

Tichy, G. (2001). 'What do we know about the Success and Failure of Mergers', Paper presented at UNIP Conference in Vienna, December.

UNCTAD, (1980). UNCTAD. 'The Set of Multilaterally Agreed Equitable Principles and Rules for the Control of Restrictive Business Practices'. Available at http://r0.unctad.org./en/subsites/cpolicy/docs/Cpset/cpset.htm

——— (1997). 'Transnational Corporations, Market Structure and Competition Policy', World Investment Report—1997, United Nations, New York & Geneva.

World Bank—OECD, (1997). World Bank and OECD. 'A Framework for the Design and Implementation of Competition Law and Policy', Paris.

WTO, (2003). 'Report (2003) of the Working Group on the interaction between Trade and Competition Policy to the General Council', Geneva, July.

——— (2004). 'Doha Work Programme—Decision adopted by the General Council on 1st August 2004', WT/L/579, August 2.

*Chapter* **10**

# Trade Facilitation Issue and India

NIRMAL SENGUPTA*

---

Trade facilitation is not a recent phenomenon. The exploration of new trade route by Vasco da Gama is an important landmark in trade facilitation (Staples, 1998). But requirements have changed over ages. Now that the trade routes are known, there are other priorities. Reopening the channels of international trade was one of the primary concerns of economic policy between the Wars. The League of Nations and the International Chamber of Commerce initiated the present trade facilitation activities. There are other reasons (Sengupta, 2006). The benefits of increased trade may not be realised by the economies whose customs houses and transportation infrastructures are ill-equipped to handle increased imports or are unable to clear exports with sufficient speed. A few percentage reductions in export prices may provide considerable competitive advantage to the exports of a trade facilitating country. Another argument for trade facilitation is related to the increasingly time-sensitive nature of production and trade in modern world. Countries that are unable to improve their policies towards trade facilitation deprive their national firms the competitiveness necessary to survive in this new form. Also, it discourages FDI associated with cross-border production networks.

## I. Trade Facilitation in India

What are the trade facilitation needs of India? India's foreign trade

* Professor, Indira Gandhi Institute of Development Research (IGIDR), Mumbai.

increased in value from about US $ 4,000 million in 1970 to 40,000 million in 1990, and is close to US$ 100,000 million at present. Total volume of trade has increased many times (*see* Fig. 10.1). However staggering it may appear, it is far less than what the country aspires. Indian share is only about 0.7 per cent of world trade[1]. The current target is to achieve 1 per cent share in world trade by 2007, and far more in future. The country should have enough capacity to handle international trade of this magnitude. This requires infrastructure and human resource capacity-building as well as more efficient capacity-utilisation. Trade facilitation for India entails this two-pronged task.

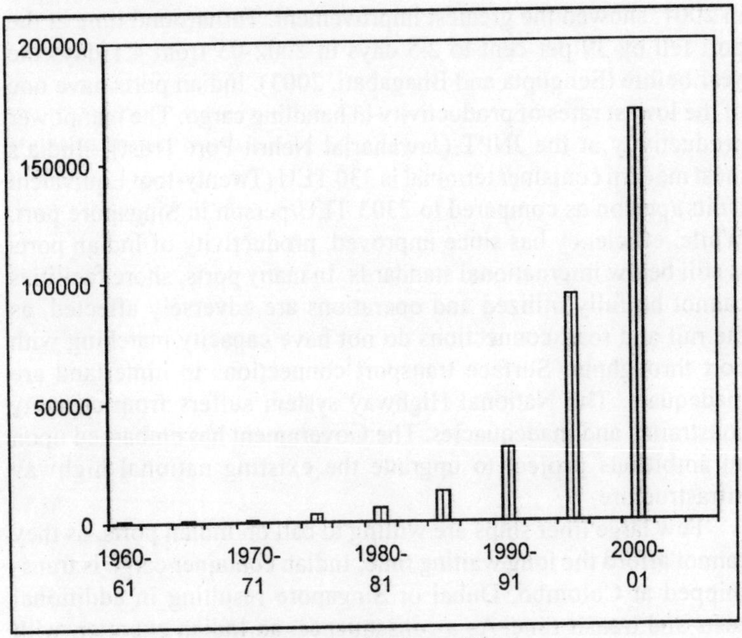


**Fig. 10.1**: Total Volume of Trade

Following liberalisation and opening up of the economy in the early nineties, there has been a significant increase in India's maritime trade. In this short time, considerable improvements of containerisation of general cargo, berthing capacity, etc. have been brought about at major ports. But, there are still large gaps between what is needed and what is in existence. Most major ports were originally designed to handle specific categories of cargo, but have not been able to adjust to the newer categories. There are thus several berths for traditional cargo, which are under-utilized and fewer for new cargo which are over utilised. Equipment is obsolete and poorly maintained. The major ports of India deal with traffic much in excess of capacity. As a result, in India ships have to wait for berths instead of berths having to wait for ships. The average vessel turn around time for Indian ports varies from 37-50 hours to 145 hours (2000) as compared to the international benchmark of 24 hours and less than 12 hours in Singapore (2000). However, in the period 2001-02 to 2002-03, the all India average for vessel turn around time has improved from 3.02 days to 2.6 days. Chennai, which got privatised in 2001, showed the greatest improvement. Turnaround time at the port fell by 39 per cent to 2.5 days in 2002-03 from 4.1 days the year before (Sengupta and Bhagabati, 2003). Indian ports have one of the lowest rates of productivity in handling cargo. The manpower productivity at the JNPT (Jawaharlal Nehru Port Trust)—India's most modern container terminal is 330 TEU (Twenty-foot Equivalent Units)/person as compared to 2303 TEU/person in Singapore port. While, efficiency has since improved, productivity of Indian ports is still below international standards. In many ports, shore facilities cannot be fully utilized and operations are adversely affected, as the rail and road connections do not have capacity matching with port throughput. Surface transport connections to hinterland are inadequate. The National Highway system suffers from capacity constraints and inadequacies. The Government has embarked upon an ambitious project to upgrade the existing national highway infrastructure.

Few large liner ships are willing to call on Indian ports, as they cannot afford the long waiting time. Indian container cargo is trans-shipped at Colombo, Dubai or Singapore resulting in additional costs and transit time. As a consequence, an Indian exporter, with rare exception, is not in a position to avail of "fixed-day-of-the week" services offered by the liner-industry at a time when manufacturing and trading companies abroad are increasingly selling and buying on "just-in-time" basis. Most Indian exporters are, therefore, operating on the basis of substantial buffer stocks, except probably a few who operate on "just-in-time" basis.

Substantial buffer stocks make Indian exporters less competitive. It has been estimated that the annual incidence of these factors such as demurrage charges, trans-shipment costs, pre-berthing delays and vessel turn-around time could be as high as US $ 1.5 billion per annum (Government of India, 1999). These costs have ultimately to be borne by the end users, raising the cost of India's exports in international markets and the prices of imports for the Indian economy. The Government recognises that additional port capacity to meet the increasing traffic cannot be met without the help of massive private investment. Accordingly, policy guidelines were issued in 1997 to enable the major ports to set up joint ventures with foreign ports, minor ports or private companies. The major Port Trust Act was amended to give effect to the guidelines issued in 1996 and 1997. An ambitious proposal (Sagar Mala Project) to give a facelift to the maritime sector with 2 new major ports and 50 minor ports coming up along the Indian coastline was ultimately dropped.

The government is planning to establish vessel traffic service (VTS) on the west and east coasts at a cost of Rs. 785 crore. One such system is coming up at the Gulf of Kutch and another is being planned at the Gulf of Khambat. Besides these, five more VTS on the either side of peninsula are also being planned in the next 10 years. VTS is a combination of radar, direction finder, satellite positioning system and various other sensors for effective control of traffic in waterways. Other systems being planned for improving navigation facilities include monitoring of lighthouses through remote control and automation system requiring an expenditure of Rs. 140 crore. Automatic identification system is also being planned to ensure collision free safe navigation.

International cargo at 5 major international airports, 6 newly declared international airports and at domestic airports increased by 13.4 per cent, 54.2 per cent and 48.7 per cent respectively in the period (April - January) 2002- 2003 vis-à-vis (April - January) 2001-2002. There has been a rise of 16.6 per cent in the total international cargo handled by the AAI during this period. The total cargo traffic handled in January 2003 has increased by 15.5 per cent as compared to January 2002, with international cargo traffic increasing by 14.2 per cent (Sengupta and Bhagabati, 2003). All the international airports in India have shortage of space in their air cargo complexes resulting in severe congestion, often making storage of goods on the tarmac unavoidable. Also, the limitations of space make it difficult to allocate spaces to other operators to facilitate competition. For courier services new and separate fully equipped courier terminals are required. State-of-the-art equipments for quick inspection of sealed containers are very costly and India cannot afford to purchase the adequate numbers.

India initiated modernisation and efficiency building measures almost immediately, after opening up. A new Shipping Bill format was introduced in the late nineteen eighties. India joined the EDI movement in 1992, when it became a member of the Asia Pacific Council for Facilitation of Procedures and Practices for Administration, Commerce and Transport (AFACT, earlier Asia EDIFACT Board). In a Vision Document published by the C.B.E.C. (Central Board of Excise and Customs) in 1998, trade facilitation was given the same thrust as realising revenue and combating duty evasion. In his Budget Speech for 1999-2000 the Union Finance Minister announced the formation of a High Powered Committee under the Revenue Secretary to go into the problems of transaction costs and to suggest measures/steps to reduce such costs on India's exports. The Committee made its recommendations in 1999, many of which have been pursued since then. Recently, the Task Force on Indirect Taxes (Kelkar Committee, Kelkar 2002) indicated the importance of the subject; and its Report outlined the basic reforms in Customs procedures and Trade Facilitation. In his Budget Speech 2003-2004, the Finance Minister recommended trade facilitation measures not only for customs but also for excise. The Medium Term Export Strategy announced by the Government of India in January 2002 in the EXIM (Export and Import) Policy 2002–07, and the modified EXIM Policy for 2003-04 have set broad policy directions for facilitating trade and for reducing transaction time and costs.

The procedure for movement of goods in coastal vessels has been simplified considerably. Special attention is given to the speedy handling of cargo for reducing its dwell time. An EXIM Bank sample survey of select firms followed by an update (EXIM Bank, 2003), show the *perceptions* of Indian exporters about the importance of transaction costs in different industries, expressed as percentage of export revenues. The two studies show that very remarkable improvements have been brought about in dwell time reduction, in just five years, between 1998 and 2003. It is claimed that approximately 80 per cent of daily air cargo shipments are assessed on the same day by Customs (subject to the condition that all the required documentation is complete). The Airports Authority has launched "Operation Instant Cargo" which envisages de-congesting of the Import Cargo Terminals by disposing of all unclaimed/uncleared cargo in consultation with Customs.

India is a natural hub for several of its neighbours. The goal of forging a South Asian Free Trade Area (SAFTA) Treaty has not yet been achieved. Trade between neighbours in SAARC region is facilitated by bilateral Agreements. To facilitate traffic from landlocked Nepal and third country, a transit traffic agreement between the governments of Nepal, India and Bangladesh was concluded in 1997. The transit traffic could move by road from Nepal to Bangladesh through India and avail a second port facility of Chittagong. Initially, the agreement was for six months but has been extended time and again. Customs and cross-border procedures are complex. Even though the SAARC countries have begun to liberalise trade, failure to address logistic inefficiencies not only compromises the extent and depth of other reforms, but also risks loss in market share. Excessive border dwell times are common. There is a proposal for construction of a 2600 km. pipeline (1600 km. from Iran to Sindh province in Pakistan and 1000 km. on to India) to transfer gas from Iran to India through Pakistan. India is hesitant.

However, infrastructure is a serious constraint. Along India's long border with neighbouring countries, the infrastructure for storage and movement of goods and vehicular traffic is highly inadequate. Even basic facilities like post offices, banks, vehicle parking, hotels, etc. are not available at all places. Customs organizational set up along the border is barely enough to cope with the present volumes. Conditions of roads leading to border stations are chaotic due to road traffic conditions and local law and order problems. From land border stations samples have to be brought over a long distance, e.g. the import of food articles from Myanmar involves testing of the items in laboratories located in Kolkata. Laboratories for testing of samples are a serious bottleneck in both import and export cargo. Moreover the ICDs/CFSs in the hinterlands often do not function well because of lack of requisite equipment and facilities.

India, a country of continental proportions, has some 60 major and minor ports, 8 customs airports, 5 international aircargo terminals, over 160 ICDs/CFSs, a very long border with its neighbouring countries with above 100 Land Customs Stations. For effective trade facilitation all personnel associated with trade, viz., licensing authorities, Customs officials, inspectors, scientists manning testing and quality control laboratories, banking and insurance staff should be present at each of these locations. This requires enormous cost and effort. Many ICDs/CFCs in the hinterlands or the land ports often did not function well because of non-availability of full complement of customs staff and other export inspection agencies. Also, the staffs of department/agencies at the grassroot level are not always aware of the extant provisions of policy, law and procedures (Sengupta and Bhagabati, 2003).

Last but not least is the problem of quality of human resources. The number or knowledge-base of the personnel are not the only factors. Many of the trade facilitation problems are also the result of a lack of positive approach and service orientation on the part of officers and staff. Corruption, harassment of traders and lethargy are general maladies. Many operational modernisation projects have not been extended for a long time even after successful experimentation at one or two places. The Kelkar Committee was emphatic about the requirement of a change in mindset away from controls rigidly administered, towards a more liberal policy environment in line with international standards. Matching change is needed in the mindset of private parties, traders, operators and business executives to adapt to a regime based on trust.

## II. Trade Facilitation—WTO Agenda

There is no standard definition of trade facilitation in public policy discourse (Sengupta, 2006). In absence of that it is impossible to say exactly what does trade facilitation entail for any country. The *UNCTAD Compendium of Trade Facilitation Recommendations* includes 237 recommendations. Only 19 of these recommendations have been subject to WTO discipline in some form or other. In WTO Trade Facilitation Symposium, March 1998 the trade facilitation items in WTO included GATT 1994 Articles V, VII, VIII, IX, X, Agreements on Customs Valuation, Import Licensing Procedures, Pre-shipment Inspection, Rules of Origin, Technical Barriers to Trade, Sanitary and Phytosanitary Measures, GATS and TRIPS. Only on three Articles of GATT 1994: Article V (Freedom of

Transit), Article VIII (Fees and Formalities relating to import and export), and Article X (Publication and Administration of Trade Regulations) no Agreement is in existence. Thus, trade facilitation is not a new issue into the WTO agenda although the term has not been used. At this moment the term has a very limited scope in WTO parlance, as pertaining to GATT Articles V, VIII and X. There were differences in opinion whether *status quo* should be maintained with respect to the three GATT Articles or not. Some members favoured more binding rules and commitments with strong dispute settlement mechanism. Some other members felt that GATT Articles V, VIII and X should be left as at present, and trade facilitation works should be undertaken autonomously, being guided by numerous international conventions and other organizations. The Doha declaration was that "In the period until the Fifth Session, the Council for Trade in Goods shall review and as appropriate, clarify and improve relevant aspects of Articles V, VIII and X of the GATT 1994"

The Uruguay Round had replaced the less effective forum approach of GATT by stringent rule based agreements. But it came under heavy criticism for compelling the developing and least developed countries to spend large sums from their meagre development budgets in order to meet their WTO obligations. Questions were raised whether the money has been well spent, whether better opportunities of investments have been overlooked (Finger, 2000). Developed countries and development agencies provided some technical assistance. But these were not binding commitments for them. In effect, the developing countries and LDCs had to make commitments first and then seek technical assistance, sometimes as forced priorities to meet commitments. Ever since the founding of the WTO, proposal for any new task has been plagued by this fundamental problem. At Cancún, the fear of being forced to take unjust additional commitments was at the root of the unrelenting opposition, particularly by the Group of 90, that represented the poor African, Asian and Latin American countries. Long before Cancún it was clear[2] that reaching agreements would be easier if the different Singapore issues were not pushed as a single bundle. Some of the developing countries had suggested before the Ministerial meet that the Singapore issues need not be treated as a 'single undertaking'. Some of the major developing countries have indicated that they may consider one or the other of the four Singapore issues. But most of the small and poor countries are stubborn in their resistance to any new issue. There was no consensus.

The aftermath of the Cancún Conference in September 2003 made all concerned to do serious rethinking. A new beginning was made in the General Council meeting in July 2004 when a Decision on Doha Work Programme was adopted by consensus. For arriving at a consensus the General Council made amendments in its approach. Three of the four Singapore issues were dropped. The Members decided *inter alia*, to commence negotiations on Trade Facilitation on the basis of a ten-point list of modalities (Annex D). The work programme adopted in 2002, immediately after the Doha Conference, consisted of three items—(i) clarification and improvement of Articles V, VIII and X of the GATT 1994, (ii) identification of trade facilitation needs and priorities of developing and least-developed countries, and (iii) technical assistance and capacity-building. The modalities agreed in 2004 included in addition to these items some significant modifications meant to take care of the concerns of developing countries, LDC and other groups with specific problems. These are:

- ❖ Special and differential treatment for developing and least-developed countries; the treatment should extend beyond the past practice of merely granting transition periods for implementing commitments.
- ❖ Least-developed country members to undertake commitments only to the extent that is consistent with their limited needs and capacities.
- ❖ Identification of trade facilitation needs and priorities would be done along with cost implications of proposed measures.
- ❖ Vital importance of technical assistance and support for capacity-building was recognized. It was also mentioned that in cases where required support and assistance for such infrastructure is not forthcoming, and where a developing or least-developed Member continues to lack the necessary capacity, implementation will not be required.

For Trade Facilitation issue, 'capacity-building' was made the key term relegating 'commitments' to the second place. The Annex D inverts the primacy between commitments and technical assistance by adding such clauses in modalities like: "the extent and the timing of entering into commitments shall be related to the implementation capacities of developing and least-developed Members. It is further agreed that those Members would not be obliged to undertake investments in infrastructure projects beyond their means", or "Least-developed country Members will only be required to undertake commitments to the extent consistent with their individual development, financial and trade needs or their administrative and institutional capabilities."

The modalities also included working with relevant international organizations and taking account of their work and a final commitment about the actions to be taken for immediate commencement of the agreed negotiation. At the Hong Kong Ministerial Conference the Ministers reaffirmed the mandate and modalities for negotiations on Trade Facilitation contained in Annex D and agreed to continue negotiations on the basis of the proposals already received and any new proposals to be presented.

If all the points in the agreed modalities are duly incorporated in the concluding Agreement on Trade Facilitation, multilateralism will usher into a new era. There is also a fear that ultimately, the negotiations will conclude on a conventional text with only lip service given to the concerns of the developing countries and the LDCs.

## III. India—Meeting WTO Regime

Until an Agreement is actually made, we would not know what are the tasks and how much additional effort is actually needed. At this moment only a tentative exercise can be done. The best that we can do is to pick up the latest WTO indicative document for our purpose. ANNEX E to Hong Kong Ministerial Declaration includes the Report by the Negotiating Group on Trade Facilitation to the TNC lists the 'Proposed measures to improve and clarify GATT Articles V, VIII and X'. The following is an extract from the list and a comparative presentation of India's position.

| Sl No. | Annex E List | Indian Situation |
|---|---|---|
| 1. | Publication and Availability of Information – PUBLICATION OF TRADE AND PENALTY REGULATIONS, INTERNET PUBLICATION, ESTABLISHMENT OF ENQUIRY POINTS/ INFORMATION CENTR | All the rules and notifications are available real time on the DGFT website and a large part of license applications are being filed and processed on-line. The CBEC website has gone online in August 2000. However both these websites carry only a fraction of the necessary information. Given the present facilities, the comprehensive notification on customs procedure, ruling, or guideline of general application that is needed for international trade is not difficult to meet; but a systematic effort is lacking.<br>There are numerous laws, regulations, procedures and practices. A WTO regime may consider the coverage in Indian system sufficient. Alternatively, it may impose greater demand, whose merit may not be in question, but will make considerable demand on India. |
| 2. | Interval between Publication and Entry into Force | Customs and Central Excise procedures are being changed rather frequently. New procedures come into effect from the date they are brought to the notice of field offices. Each instruction contains a direction to the field offices to issue suitable public notices/trade notices to inform the trade. Not only does this catch the trade by surprise but it may also happen that a procedure has been in force but is not complied with for the reason that the trade may not have been aware of it. Invariably, such situation also leads to compliance issuance and disputes. This again is an area where a WTO regime may make a difference.<br>This is not just a goodwill issue. There are problems that would require capacity building. For example, the departmental systems personnel are unable to modify their software, if required (Sengupta and Bhagabati, 2003). |
| 3. | Prior Consultation and Commenting on New and Amended Rules | Informal prior consultation goes on before budget and some other policy announcements. Customs and Central Excise procedures are framed in consultation with the field officers and there is no apparent involvement of the trade and industry. This is one area where political will is lacking. The Kelkar Committee recommended constituting a Standing Committee on Procedures or some such institutional mechanism. |
| 4. | Provision of Advance Rulings | Advance Rulings exist in the Customs Act, and also in the Finance Bill, 1999. Procedures and organisational set up for advance rulings may be developed in due course. |
| 5. | Appeal Procedures | Well established, with several tiers—Commissioner (Appeals), Customs, Excise and Service Tax Appellate Tribunal (CESTAT, earlier CEGAT) and an alternative system of Settlement Commission set up in 1998 to deal with tax and trade related disputes and offences. The EXIM Policy (1999-2000) proposed the appointment of an Ombudsman at Mumbai. However, there is a serious constraint in manpower. |

(*Contd.*)

| Sl No. | Annex E List | Indian Situation |
|---|---|---|
| 6. | Establishment of a Code of Conduct | Does not exist |
| 7. | Computerized System to Reduce/Eliminate Discretion | Yes |
| 8. | Specific Parameters for Fees/Charges, Publication/Notification of Fees/Charges, Prohibition of Collection of Unpublished Fees and Charges, Periodic Review of Fees/Charges | WTO Customs Valuation Agreement is followed. Fees and Charges are in order. |
| 9. | Reduction/Minimization of the Number and Diversity of Fees/Charges | Not much. |
| 10. | Non-discrimination | Not many dissenting view. |
| 11. | Reduction/Limitation of Formalities and Documentation Requirements | Were too many. Over the years the number of documents required and the number of copies needed has been somewhat reduced. But Single Administrative Document is not initiated. |
| 12. | Use of International Standards | Limited use |
| 13. | Uniform Customs Code | The country uses a single system. |
| 14. | Acceptance of Commercially Available Information and of Copies | Much need to be done. But efforts are on. |
| 15. | Automation | Yes |

*(Contd.)*

| Sl No. | Annex E List | Indian Situation |
|---|---|---|
| 16. | Single Window/One-time Submission | A "single-window" concept is practical and feasible only in an electronic environment. Acceptance of a system of Single Window for submission of documents/data and EDI connectivity with all customs locations involve enormous cost. |
| 17. | Elimination of Pre-Shipment Inspection | PSI system was never used by India. |
| 18. | Phasing out Mandatory Use of Customs Brokers | Use of Customs Brokers is not mandatory. |
| 19. | Prohibition of Consular Transaction Requirement | Never used |
| 20. | Border Agency Cooperation | The present format of Shipping Bill, evolved in 1991, is a notable success in simplification of Customs procedures. It is already a common document used by various departments, such as Customs, Reserve Bank of India (RBI) and Port Trust. For issuance of permission for trans-shipment from gateway port, a single window system has been introduced, where applications for trans-shipment are processed expeditiously with computer usage. The drawback payment system has been re-engineered to provide for direct disbursement of the amount into the exporters' bank accounts after the goods have been exported. A Committee looked into the feasibility of evolving a single transport document, and suggested that the Multi-modal Transport document may be used for this purpose. On the import side, the Sunder Committee (GoI, 1999) recommended evolving a SAD in the lines of the EC. But implementing this suggestion requires the acceptance of these documents by several agencies, including banks and insurance. No initiative has been taken as yet. |
| 21. | Pre-arrival Clearance | No |
| 22. | Expedited Frocedures for Express Shipments | Limited arrangement, but exists. |
| 23. | Risk Management/Analysis, Authorized Traders | India has already reduced the percentage check on consignment to about 2%. A codified risk management module has been tested recently for import consignments. |

(Contd.)

| Sl No. | Annex E List | Indian Situation |
|---|---|---|
| | | Use of authorised trader system is questionable. Kelkar Committee felt that this might discriminate against small traders. Though allowed, Customs officials rarely accept self-sealing of export containers and Fast Track Scheme for Customs clearance. They feel that there are numerous incentive schemes provide immense scope of frauds leading to loss of revenue. The developed countries can allow these because of complementary mechanism like Post-Clearance Audit. |
| 24. | Post-Clearance Audit | Some five years back a self-assessment scheme was introduced. A system appraisal procedure has been introduced by Customs, but very few have come forward to avail this opportunity. Post-clearance Audit is being launched through a few pilot projects. The feedback from the pilot projects would be taken as the basis for designing the whole process.<br>Considerable ground will have to be covered and a great deal of details spelt out for implementing the Post-clearance Audit (Sengupta, 2006). |
| 25. | Separating Release from Clearance Procedures | This is possible with Post-Clearance Audit, which takes a long time to introduce. The Risk management system recently introduced is the first step. |
| 26. | Establishment and Publication of Average Release and Clearance Times | Being done though irregular |
| 27. | Objective Criteria for Tariff Classification | Major problem area. Almost one-third of consignments are wrongly classified. |
| 28. | Matters Related to Goods Transit | Quite a lot need to be done. |

## IV. Do Benefits Outweigh the Cost?

ANNEX E to Hong Kong Ministerial Declaration also includes a list of 'Cross-Cutting Submissions' which are essentially, the tasks of the WTO. These are like:

- ❖ Needs and Priorities Identification
- ❖ Technical Assistance and Capacity Building
- ❖ Identification of Trade Facilitation Needs and Priorities of Members
- ❖ Cost Assessment
- ❖ Inter-Agency Cooperation
- ❖ Inventory of Trade Facilitation Measures
- ❖ Assessment of the Current Situation
- ❖ Timing and Sequencing of Measures.

*What has been done in these matters?*

In May 2002, the Members had requested the WTO Secretariat to prepare a compendium of the existing material on Members' trade facilitation needs and priorities. The paper (WTO, 2002) would cover all relevant inputs since the beginning of WTO work on trade facilitation following the Singapore Ministerial. The Secretariat personnel observed, "most of the examined material does not address trade facilitation needs and priorities of Members *per se*, but rather focuses on particular experiences with trade facilitation measures and programmes, or proposes approaches to future WTO work on this subject." The situation has not changed since then.

Many developing countries, including India, have been pursuing trade facilitation autonomously. There may be different ways of meeting the same goal. If one is adopted the countries which were pursuing the other course will have to change their ways. The developing countries fear that the ways of the developed countries like EU will be forced on them compelling them to abandon their reforms and initiating new ways. In one of the meetings a developing country Member asked whether EC will have to do anything as additional reform or all the reforms will have to be done by the developing countries.

Trade transaction costs include directly incurred costs, such as expenses relating to supplying information and documents to the related authority, and indirectly incurred costs, such as those arising from procedural delays. Empirical studies[3] suggest that directly incurred trade transaction costs related to border procedures each amount to 1-15 per cent of traded goods' value. Indirectly incurred Trade transaction account for a similar percentage. These estimates include transaction costs of both imports and exports. Trade facilitation can reduce this cost though not eliminate it altogether. The potential for the realisation of benefits from trade facilitation varies across countries, sectors, and types of traders. In countries where best practices are already applied, further efficiency gains will be difficult to achieve. But if border clearance costs are substantially above those encountered under best practices, room for improvement through suitable measures of trade facilitation is considerable. On a rough estimate, the potential savings from trade facilitation is of the order of 2-3 per cent of world GDP. Estimates for India were made by EXIM Bank of India (2003); Sengupta and Bhagabati (2003), and most recently by Chaturvedi (2006).

Another serious fallacy in the benefit-centred arguments for pushing trade facilitation through WTO is that investment decisions are made on the basis of comparative advantages not merely on the basis of net benefits. Trade facilitation may be beneficial. But is it the best opportunity for deploying scarce resources? Trade facilitation is beneficial. As G-90 alliance proclaimed, the Singapore Issues were not priority issues for them. Simplification of import and export procedures, reduction of data and documentation requirements, publication of information, consultation, non-discriminatory treatment and excellent scope of review and appeal would not serve any purpose without the requisite infrastructural capacity to clear the trade consignments. India faces severe capacity constraints in infrastructure. It is open to question whether trade facilitation works mandated by WTO would indeed, be the right priority for investment over investments in certain infrastructural opportunities. That trade facilitation is beneficial does not sanctify a WTO agenda on this issue. Instead, there are legitimate apprehension that powerful developed country lobbies having scant concern about the priorities of developing countries and LDCs, would prevail in framing of any WTO rules.

An appropriate approach for benefit analysis will be to compare marginal benefits of multilateral rules over autonomous reforms. This has to be compared with the cost of (a) introducing additional reforms over national policies in trade facilitation and also (b) to modify the architecture of some national initiatives to adjust to the WTO requirements. At the same time, a multilateral rule may prevent Indian trade facilitating activities deviating away from international systems, which is often the case in stand-alone developments. For example, in several areas of harmonisation of data, documents and classification, the measures taken in India are not always in harmony with international systems. Quite often the creativity of technical staff developing the systems find their ways overriding the need of universal standards required in transactions. Another area where a set of binding rules may help is completion of reforms. Lackadaisical approaches to reforms are quite common. Many operational modernisation projects have not been extended for a long time even after successful experimentation at one or two places. Prohibitive infrastructure cost is not the only reason why Single Administrative Document is not developed at a quicker pace. Essentially, these are what the proponents of trade facilitation have argued are the reasons for desirability of binding obligations.

## END NOTES

1. Though small, India's share at the time of independence was 2.5 per cent of global trade. Since then, international trade has increased in leaps and bounds.
2. For example, "While some of these matters (relating to Investment and to Competition Policy) remain highly controversial among WTO members, I believe it can be said that members are all broadly supportive of the general aims of the trade facilitation agenda. There is therefore a reasonably good chance that in Cancun we can move forward to agree upon a negotiating mandate, provided of course that the game of linkages (one sector being made conditional on progress or agreement in another) does not raise external obstacles to the pursuit of what are clearly common objectives." —Deputy Director-General Roderick Abbott, in a speech at the launching of the World Trade Point Federation website in Geneva, on 19 February 2003. http://www.wto.org/english/news_e/news03_e/world_trade_point_19feb03_e.htm
3. For example, Dee *et al.* 1996; WTO, 1997; SWEPRO, 1985; 2002; Messerlin and Zarrouk, 1999; Wilson *et al.*, 2005; OECD, n.d.; 2002; Hellqvist, 2003a; 2003b; Lucenti, 2003; Walkenhorst and Yasui, 2003.

## REFERENCES

Chaturvedi, S. (2006). 'Trade Facilitation Priorities in India and Commitments at WTO: An Overview of Current Trends', RIS Discussion Paper 109.

Dee, P., C. Geisler and G. Watts (1996). '*The Impact of APEC's Free Trade Commitment*', Staff Information Paper (Industry Commission of Australia).

EXIM Bank of India, 2003. 'Transaction Costs of Indian Exports: A Review', *Working Paper* 4. EXIM Bank of India.

Finger, J. M. (2000). 'The WTO's Special Burden on Less Developed Countries', *Cato Journal,* 19 (3): 425-437. Available at: http://www.cato.org/pubs/journal/cj19n3/cj19n3-9.pdf

Government of India (Ministry of Commerce, Government of India), (1999). '*Report of The Expert Committee on an Integrated Approach to the Movement of Goods in International Trade*'.

Hellqvist, M. (2003a). 'Trade Facilitation: Impact and Potential Gains', Swedish National Board of Trade.

———— (2003b). 'Trade Facilitation from a Developing Country Perspective', Swedish National Board of Trade.

Kelkar, V. (2002). *Final Report on Indirect Taxes,* New Delhi.

Lucenti, K. (2003). 'Is there a case for more multilateral rules on Trade Facilitation?', in Simon J. Evenett and the Swiss State Secretariat of Economic Affairs (eds.), *The Singapore Issues and The World Trading System: The Road to Cancun and Beyon*d, chapter IV, pp. 261-302. www.seco-admin.ch/imperia/md/content/aussenwirtschaft/wto/pub_seco_the _Singapore_issues.pdf

Messerlin, P. A. and J. Zarrouk (1999). 'Trade Facilitation: Technical Regulations and Customs Procedures', WTO-World Bank *Conference on Developing Countries' in a Millennium Round*, 20-21 September 1999, WTO Secretariat, Geneva.

OECD, (n.d). 'Costs and Benefits of Trade Facilitation', by Anthony Kleitz, Trade Directorate. www.unece.org/trade/forums/forum02/presentations/session_ii/akleitz.pdf

———— (2002). 'Business Benefits of Trade Facilitation', Matsudaira, T. supervised by Anthony Kleitz, Working Party of the Trade Committee. (TD/TC/WP/2001/21/FINAL). http://www.oecd.org/trade

Sengupta, N. (2006). '*The Economics of Trade Facilitation*', New Delhi: Oxford University Press.

———— and M. Bhagabati. (2003). 'A Study of Trade Facilitation Measures from WTO Perspective', Interim Report for the Department of Commerce, Government of India.

Staples, B. R. (1998). '*Trade Facilitation (Draft)*', prepared for the WTO 2000 Conference, Geneva, www1.worldbank.org/wbiep/trade/papers_2000/BPfacil.pdf

SWEPRO (Sweden Trade Procedures Council). (1985). 'Data Interchange in International Trade'

——— (2002). 'Trade Facilitation – Impact and Potential Gains'.

UN/CEFACT, (2001). 'Compendium of Trade Facilitation Recommendations', United Nations, (Internet).

Walkenhorst, P and T. Yasui (2003). '*Benefits of Trade Facilitation: A Quantitative Assessment*', prepared for presentation at the APEC Capacity-Building Workshop on 'Quantitative Methods for Assessing NTMs and Trade Facilitation', Bangkok/Thailand, 8-10 October 2003, www.usitc.gov/ntm/Walkenhorst_paper.pdf

Wilson, J.S., C.L. Mann and T. Otsuki (2005). 'Assessing the Potential Benefit of Trade Facilitation: A Global Perspective' in Dee Philippa, and Michael Ferrantino (eds.), *Quantitative Methods for Assessing the Effects of Non-tariff Measures and Trade Facilitation*, Singapore, APEC Secretariat. pp121-160.

WTO (1997). 'Trade Facilitation – Background Note by the Secretariat', G/C/W/80, 23 May 1997.

——— (2002). 'Trade Facilitation Needs and Priorities of Members—Compilation of existing material by the Secretariat', G/C/W/393, 11 July 2002.

*Chapter* **11**

# Trade Facilitation and Transaction Costs as an Agenda for Global Trade Negotiations

JAYANTA ROY*

## I. Introduction

Trade Facilitation has been a neglected issue in global trade liberalisation process, although its importance cannot be overstated. It is beginning to be recognized as an important component of national trade reform agenda. There is also a discussion afoot to put it in the WTO agenda.

Trade facilitation is the other name for reduction in transactions costs. According to a recent study carried out by the OECD the cost of poor border procedures could vary between 2 per cent to 15 per cent of the total transaction value of global trade. This highlights the wasteful costs involved considering that the average post-Uruguay tariffs on industrial goods amounts to a mere 3.8 per cent.

According to a study undertaken by the UNCTAD, direct and indirect transaction costs i.e. banking and insurance, customs, business information, transport and logistics etc. add up to 10 per cent of the total value of world trade (USD 400 billion) (UNCTAD, 1994).

In another special report by Wilson (*World Bank Development Outreach Magazine*, 2003), improving the performance of below average countries (i.e. countries with trade facilitation parameters below global average) in terms of port efficiency will increase global trade by USD 117 billion. An improvement in customs procedures in

* Principal Advisor, Confederation of Indian Industry, New Delhi.

such countries up to the global average levels will lead to gains in trade of around USD 22 billion.

The findings are clear. Reduction of transaction costs in trade through trade facilitation can bring enormous gains in trade, and as such are necessary and important for the development of global trade. All countries accept this fact, and the gains from Trade Facilitation in itself are not under dispute. In addition, the reduction of other types of barriers has brought border-crossing costs to business, such as waiting time and customs procedures into new focus. The need for trade facilitation is underlined further by the plethora of the procedures that have to be gone through at the border when importing or exporting. Such procedures have increased in recent years, especially in USA and other countries after 9/11 incident, adding to the cost of trading both for governments and business and yet at the same time the volume of international trade has expanded relative to the size of many national economies, making it more difficult for administrations to cope on the basis of unchanged resources.

Thus, Trade Facilitation assumes even greater importance now in the arena of international trade given recent trends in the structure of goods (and services) traded and the sophistication of such products.

Modern supply chain management techniques and the rapid spread of information technologies and e-commerce have progressively increased the use of just-in-time techniques by manufacturing industry and encouraged the growth of integrated global supply, production and distribution systems. In this environment, where manufacturers rely on the uninterrupted reception of the necessary components to meet production contingencies, business cannot afford to have imported or exported goods tied up for long periods because of unnecessary or over-complicated trade procedures and requirements.

Goods and Services traded across borders have become increasingly sophisticated, at the same time the rules and regulations that govern tariffs and non-tariff measures have become increasingly complicated over time. Preferential trade agreements have added to this complexity a proliferation of rules of origin. Threats to national security have also increased in recent times. All these factors add up to make the process of goods and services crossing borders far more difficult than they used to be half a century ago. Threats to national health and consumer welfare have also become greater and tend to have global repercussions (a good recent example is the SARS in East and South East Asia).

Given this background, it is important to meet this basic challenge, i.e. to make trade as easy and quick as possible to harmonize global supply chains and production process while ensuring that Governments are able to efficiently administer customs and safeguard national health and security.

## II. Trade Facilitation Indicators and Related Areas that Need Reform Focus

The ambit of Trade Facilitation is very broad and touches upon several areas. While some of these falls directly under initiatives that need to be taken by the Government, others involve a partnership between private stakeholders and Government initiatives. The main indicators of trade facilitation and the areas of reform required in them are briefly presented below.

***Port Logistics***

- Cargo Dwell time (see Table 11.2 in section 4).
- Warehousing facilities (including refrigerated warehouses for perishables).
- Rail and road links from hinterland to ports.

***Customs Procedures***

- Electronic Data Interface (EDI).
- Signature less, Internet based process for filing customs related documents.
- Trust based systems.
- Post-clearance audit.
- Pre-Shipment Inspection Agreements (PSI).
- Risk analysis and assessment.

***Standards Harmonisation***

- Reform of domestic Standards setting and monitoring authorities.
- Moving towards regional and global convergence on standards.
- Mutual Recognitions Agreements on Standards.

***Business Mobility***

- ❖ Movement of Professionals and transparent visa systems.
- ❖ Adequate Financial systems including Banking, Insurance and Clearance mechanism.

***Trade Information and E-business Facilities***

- ❖ Proper channels and access to market information, legal systems and standards and regulations.
- ❖ Availability of information electronically through the internet.
- ❖ E-business infrastructure to enable business to business contacts.

***Administrative Transparency and Professionalism***

- ❖ Simple and transparent procedures for export and import.
- ❖ Non-discriminatory approach to enforcement based on risk assessment techniques.
- ❖ Public Private cooperation and information sharing to improve enforcement and compliance.

## III. Trade Facilitation in the Multilateral Context

The principle behind the multilateral framework of WTO lies in the formation of a rules based trading framework for all countries. The WTO has achieved remarkable success in this direction in reference to trade liberalisation and removal of barriers in terms of tariffs, and to some extent Non-Tariff Barriers. The time has come for the WTO to explore areas beyond tariffs and NTB's that are impeding trade. Trade Facilitation is definitely one area that all countries will have to cooperate in for their mutual benefit, and multilateral framework of the WTO provides an excellent forum to explore this issue. But it should be recognized clearly at the outset, that removal of impediments to trade facilitation would take time in most developing countries, given their lack of essential capacity to undertake reforms. Multilateral and bilateral institutions must earmark provisions of substantial resources towards capacity-building process in developing countries.

Trade facilitation came rushing to the foreground of WTO issues as the international business community increasingly expressed concern for greater transparency, efficiency, and procedural uniformity of cross-border transportation of goods. Trade Facilitation came into the WTO agenda after studies done by APEC and World Bank came up with two major conclusions:[1]

- Clearing the red tape at country borders would generate approximately twice as much gain to GDP than tariff liberalisation would.
- Trade facilitation measures would particularly benefit developing countries, where the inefficiencies and inconsistencies in administering border measures, especially non-tariff border measures are sometimes more costly to industries than are tariff barriers.

In response, WTO members added trade facilitation to the agenda at the Singapore Ministerial Meeting in 1996. The Singapore Ministerial Declaration calls upon the Council for Trade in Goods (CTG) to conduct exploratory research into cross-border barriers, and analyze the effects of those barriers on traders and consumers.

Aspects of Trade Facilitation are not new as issues in WTO/ GATT. Even though Trade Facilitation was first included at the 1996 WTO Ministerial Conference, there are several GATT provisions that are related to trade facilitation. In addition to Article VII (Valuation for Customs Purposes) and Article X (Marks of Origin) a number of specific agreements have been negotiated during the Uruguay Round that are directly relevant to trade facilitation viz.,

- *Customs Valuation Agreement*: It sets out rules and guidelines for customs valuation.
- *Agreement on Rules of Origin*: It contains principles for origin determination in a neutral transparent, non-trade restricting manner. However actual origin rules are yet to be finalized for which intense negotiations are going on for the last seven years.
- *Agreement on Pre-shipment Inspection (PSI)*: It provides for pre-shipment inspection to avoid delays and to resolve disputes.
- *Agreement on Import Licensing Procedures*: It lays down rules for issuance of import licenses in respect of goods requiring licence.

- *Agreement on Technical Barriers to Trade (TBT)*: It provides that product standards should be based on scientific information and evidence and should not be so applied as to cause unnecessary obstacles to trade.
- *Agreement on the Application of Sanitary and Phytosanitary (SPS) Measures*: It provides that sanitary and phytosanitary regulations are not so formulated and applied as to create unnecessary obstacles to trade.

### *Issues on Trade Facilitation for Developing Countries*

While there is across-the-board agreement on the necessity for trade facilitation, developing countries are not enthusiastic to negotiate a multilateral agreement of trade facilitation commitments. Developing country concerns over Trade Facilitation can be summarized into the following points.

- They argue that they do not have the resources necessary to update their customs procedures to more modern technological standards.
- They are also reluctant to take on additional legal obligations that may subject them to NTB's and increase their exposure to disputes.
- If members insist on creating standards through a WTO agreement, developing countries feel that this agreement should only be a list of voluntary guidelines, or an agreement focused on capacity-building, rather than a legally binding, rules-based agreement.
- Some developing countries suggest that trade facilitation remain a national, bilateral, or regional concern. This has been the Indian stand at Cancun.

## IV. Trade Facilitation in India: Current Status and Strategic Issues

India has several problem areas in Trade Facilitation and there are substantive transaction costs involved in trading with India. While some impressive gains have been made over the last decade in terms of eradicating transaction costs, a lot of work still needs to be done to bring India up to the global standards in this area. The major work will involve simplification of export/import procedures and streamlining customs procedures and improving port logistics. Another major area of work will involve bilateral and multilateral initiatives that work towards agreements on Mutual Recognition (MRA) of Standards and Pre-Shipment Inspection (PSI).

### *Export and Import Procedures*

In spite of major trade liberalisation introduced since June 1991, the administrative procedures associated with trade are probably the most complex and irrational procedure-bound in the world. Table 11.1 shows that in order to export, one needs to obtain 258 signatures, make 118 copies of the same information, keypunching of which takes 22 hours. It of course, involves dealing with a multitude of GoI agencies separately. This evokes hardly a protest from established exporters who have a knack of going around the system and having prompt clearance by paying bribes. But for the new global players, this is posing a major irritant. Moreover, the Government should promptly remove a major source of complex administrative procedures and corrupt practice.

**Table 11.1:** Documents Required for Export Clearance

| | *Documents* | *No. of Copies* | *No. of Signatures Required* | *Time Required for Typing* |
|---|---|---|---|---|
| 1. | Proforma Inv. | 4 | 4 | 1 hour |
| 2. | Buyers Order | 8 | 16 | 1 hour |
| 3. | Letter of Credit | 1 | 4 | 1 hour |
| | *Total* | *13* | *24* | *3 hours* |
| | *Shipper's Documents* | | | |
| 4. | Shipping Instructions | 2 | 2 | 1/2 hour |
| 5. | Commercial Invoice | 11 | 27 | 2 hours |
| 6. | Packing List | 10 | 26 | 2 hours |
| 7. | GRI (Exch. Cont.) | 2 | 4 | 1/2 hour |
| 8. | Freight Certificate | 2 | 2 | 5 minutes |
| 9. | Origin Cert. Form 'A' | 2 | 2 | 1/2 hour |
| 10. | AR4/AR4A | 2 | 4 | 1/2 hour |
| 11. | G. Receipt | 3 | 6 | 15 minutes |
| 12. | AR4 or AR4A | 4 or 5 | 16 or 20 | 1/2 hour |

(*Contd.*)

**Table 11.1** (*Contd.*)

| *Documents* | *No. of Copies* | *No. of Signatures Required* | *Time Required for Typing* |
|---|---|---|---|
| 13. T. Tax (BAHETI) | 2 | 3 | 10 minutes |
| 14. Inspection Certificate | 2 | 2 | 15 minutes |
| 15. Insurance | 3 | 3 | 2 hours |
| *Total* | *46* | *101* | *9 hrs. 15 min.* |
| *Clearing Agent* | | | |
| 16. Shipping Bill | 10 | 72 | 1 hour |
| 17. Carting Order | 4 | 5 | 15 minutes |
| 18. Forwarding Note | 2 | 7 | 10 minutes |
| 19. Spl. Custom Inv. (Visa) | 2 | 4 | 15 minutes |
| 20. G.S.P. | 4 | 4 | 1 hour |
| 21. Meas. Certificate | 4 | 4 | 1 hour |
| 22. Fumigation Certificate | 3 | 3 | 15 minutes |
| 23. Container Load Plan (CLP) | 3 | 3 | 1/2 hour |
| *Total* | *31* | *105* | *3 hrs. 40 min.* |
| *Carrier* | | | |
| 24. Railway Receipt | 2 | 2 | 10 minutes |
| 25. N. Forms | 2 | 2 | 10 minutes |
| 26. Mate's Receipt | 3 | 3 | 10 minutes |
| 27. Bill of Lading | 18 | 18 | 1 hour |
| 28. Freight/Cargo Manifest | 2 | 2 | 4 hours |
| *Total* | *27* | *27* | *5 hrs. 30 min.* |
| *Bank* | | | |
| 29. Application to Bank for Negotiation | 1 | 1 | 1/2 hour |
| *Total* | *118* | *258* | *22 hours* |

*Source*: Roy, J. 2002.

## *Cargo Dwell Time and Port/Airport Logistics*

The current performance of India's Ports and Airports are far below global norms, and remain an impediment to India's greater integration with the world economy.

**Table 11.2:** Typical Cargo Dwell Time

| *Transaction* | *Location* | *Norm* |
|---|---|---|
| *Air Freight* | *Delhi Airport* | |
| Export | 2.5 days | Less than 12 hours |
| Import | 15 days | Less than 12 hours |
| *Containerized Sea Freight* | *Mumbai* | |
| Ship Waiting Time | 3-5 days | Less than 6 hours |
| Export Dwell Time | 3-5 days | Less than 18 hours |
| Import Dwell Time | 7-14 days | Less than 24 hours |

*Source*: Roy, J. 2002.

Table 11.2 above clearly shows that premier Indian entry points i.e. Delhi and Mumbai perform far below par of international norms, and thus reforms are urgently needed.

Reforms are also urgently needed in India's customs and regulatory practices that remain inefficient relative to International norms despite improvements in the recent past.

India has problems in other fronts also, most notably in Trade Information and enquiry point. As of now there is no officially designated inquiry point for traders dealing with the Indian market.

## Reforms and Initiatives

A major step towards trade facilitation in order to reduce transaction costs in India was taken with the recommendations of the Task Force on Indirect Taxes (December, 2002). Some of the most important recommendations that were accepted by the Government of India, were as follows:

- Customs clearance procedures should be based upon trust and be uniformly applied to all importers and exporters of all goods.
- The verification of declaration through pre-clearances examination, where necessary, should be based on intelligence and risk assessment techniques.
- Use of Post-Clearance Audit.
- Online filing of electronic declarations.
- Establishment of warehouses by shipping/airlines/couriers/ freight forwarders etc. within the port/airport area to reduce dwell time.

- High-level Inter-Ministerial Committee may be set up under the Chairmanship, CBEC to resolve inter-agency issues.
- A permanent Trade Facilitation Committee should be constituted at each Port/Airport/ICD/CFS comprising senior representatives of all agencies including Customs House Agents (CHA's) under the chairmanship of the Commissioner of Customs.

While noticeable progress has been made towards the reduction of transaction costs, it is recognized that fuller attention is required to expedite implementation of the recommendations, and this is necessary to make India a world-class global player. With this aim in mind, the Government of India has recently constituted a Working Group on Trade Facilitation with a view to further reduce transaction costs and harmonize procedures and trade practices in accordance to International norms. This Working Group, under the Chairmanship of Dr. Jayanta Roy, and comprising of the senior officials of Central Board of Excise and Customs (CBEC), will look into and suggest measures in the context of the following areas:

- Reduce extensive documentation requirements,
- Ensure total use of information technology,
- Bring about transparency and accountability,
- Introduce audit based controls,
- Introduce cooperation among all the Government agencies involved in the clearance of cargo,
- Introduce self-assessment,
- Reduce examination of goods to a minimum,
- Introduction of risk assessment techniques, and
- Reduction of the dwell time for clearance of cargo.

It is felt that there is a need to regularly monitor the convergence towards global standards in all areas of Trade Facilitation with special focus on cargo dwell time and enforcement standards. For this, it is necessary to fully operationalize EDI in all major customs points.

## V. Trade Facilitation at WTO: Re-appraisal of Pros and Cons

India's traditional stand on Trade Facilitation at WTO has been that it should be a voluntary (as opposed to compulsory) yardstick, and not an Agreement subject to compulsory standards thus party to dispute settlement mechanisms. India's stand stems from the legitimate concern that some members might use Trade Facilitation as a tool for retaliatory market protection. While such a concern is logical, time has come to also take a fresh look at the advantages of a Trade Facilitation in a multilateral context.

The key advantages of achieving a WTO undertaking in the area of trade facilitation would be renewed political impetus to make border controls more efficient and strengthened international coherence in tackling the issue. Some specific advantages of this are discussed below:

- The need to enhance efficiency in order to face an increasingly complex international trading environment has been an important driving force behind customs reforms undertaken at national level around the world in recent years. However, it has frequently not gone far enough to do away with deeply entrenched outdated institutional settings and cumbersome procedures. To be successful, a trade facilitation agenda needs wide political support and the sustained commitment of those involved in the formulation and implementation of trade policy, both within the administration and among the economic actors. Decisively launching the reform process and keeping it on the right track is crucial for achieving well-designed trade facilitation reforms that pay off quickly and end up being self-sustaining. Overcoming resistance to change from vested interests requires a considerable political effort that is not easy to muster without a high level of motivation. Trade facilitation rules in the framework of the WTO could offer this missing impetus at the multilateral level, providing an external discipline to ensure continuing domestic political commitment and shield from temptations to backtrack.
- Coherence is also essential. Trade facilitation efforts, national or international, need to be consistent between different policy areas. Partial approaches that lack coherence appear a sure recipe for failure. Speeding up Customs clearance, for example, will not help move goods faster if there is no road system to carry them. It is also a question of better co-ordination between the narrow area of trade facilitation and the areas of customs valuation, rules of origin, import licensing or sanitary

controls. A coherent multilateral setting would also provide a solid background for designing well targeted technical assistance and capacity-building projects, overcoming regional divides, ensuring that the projects' different components are mutually supportive and better targeting aspects of co-operation between border agencies of concerned countries.

## VI. Conclusion

Issues related to trade facilitation are an essential component of unilateral trade liberalization; hence it has featured prominently in most World Bank adjustment loans and IMF standby programmes.[2] It is also evidence of the seriousness with which multilateral and Governmental institutions emphasize the role of the diverse aspects of trade facilitation. Unfortunately, Governments often tend to look at the idea of trade facilitation piecemeal and not in a holistic fashion. A holistic approach will cover the areas of logistics, customs and procedural reform, and trade information in conjunction with development of transport infrastructure and other purely logistical issues such as refrigerated warehouses for perishables. Information Technology (IT) is revolutionizing the work on Trade Facilitation, and India has a comparative advantage over many other countries in IT. Some notable IT related initiatives in Trade Facilitation involve, tracking of global cargoes through automated identification devices, EDI and E-Commerce replacing old paper based systems, use of smart cards and satellite tracking systems for containers etc. While market based solutions (or a Public-Private partnership) are required in areas that involve purely logistical issues, the Government is the sole agency of reform in customs, procedures and port oriented problems (the concept of private ports being alien to most developing countries). Thus, a holistic approach towards Trade Facilitation, exploring all avenues including multilateral approaches, is the need of the hour.

*The author is grateful to pritam Banerjee (c 11) for invaluable assistance in prepares this.*

## END NOTES

1. Wilson and Woo, (2000). New Directions for APEC's Trade Facilitation Agenda, APEC and Maskus, Wilson and Otsuki (2000), Quantifying the

Impact of Technical Barriers to Trade, World Bank Policy Research Working Paper No. 2512

2. For a detailed discussion on World Bank's role in Trade Facilitation activities, refer Dr. Jayanta Roy's work on this area i.e. Trade Facilitation: The World Bank Experience. Paper presented at the Trade Facilitation Symposium, WTO. Geneva, March 9-10, 1998.

## REFERENCES

OECD Policy Brief (2003). 'Business Benefits of Trade Facilitation'.

Roy, J. (1998). 'Trade Facilitation: The World Bank Experience', paper presented at the Trade Facilitation Symposium, WTO. Geneva.

——— (2002). 'Towards International Norms for Indirect Taxes and Trade Facilitation in India', paper prepared for the Task Force on Indirect Taxes, Government of India.

Staples, B. R., (2002). 'Trade Facilitation: Improving Invisible Infrastructure', in B. Hoekman, A. Mattoo and P. English (eds.), *Development, Trade and the WTO*, World Bank Publication.

UNCTAD, (1994). 'Report on Trade Barriers'.

Wilson, J. S. (2003). 'Trade Facilitation, WTO Rules and Capacity-Building; What's at Stake?', Special Report, *Development Outreach Magazine*, The World Bank Institute. July Edition. Available at: http://www1.worldbank.org/devoutreach/july03

*Chapter* **12**

# Efficacy of a Multilateral Agreement on Transparency in Government Procurement: A Developing Country's Perspective

THILOTHAM R KOLANU*

## Introduction

Procurement of goods and services by Governments and their enterprises as well as their sub-agencies are considered to be significant opportunities for international trade. For instance, it is estimated that procurement by public authorities alone accounts for about 11 percent of the EU's GDP (OECD, 1999). As has been the practice across the world the Governments' procurement tends to favour local (domestic) suppliers. There has been considerable debate and discussion on public procurement of goods and services in the international trade arena because of its vastness and the future growth prospects. Transparency in public procurement has been hotly debated and contested in various international fora. While transparency is no longer an issue for negotiations at WTO since July 2005 but it continues to remain an important public policy concern at the domestic level in India from good governance perspective.

This paper attempts to understand the various dimensions surrounding issue of transparency in government procurement as it evolved at WTO from the perspective of various countries especially

* Consultant, Environment and Renewable Energy, Administrative Staff College of India, Hyderabad.

developing countries. It also tries to evaluate the efficacy of a multilateral agreement on transparency in government procurement from the point of view of developing countries with specific reference to India. The first section of the study dwells on the meaning and the various facets of government procurement as enumerated by scholars. The second section of the study provides an overview of evolution of government procurement as a subject-matter of international trade and its implications for developed and developing countries. Both groups of countries namely, which are supporting and objecting to introduction of transparency in government procurement at multilateral level, have made substantive submissions on different dimensions to the issue. An attempt is made in this paper to critically analyse the positions of major countries. While India is one of the critics of introduction of transparency in government procurement at the international forum but in the last decade there have been positive changes in its public procurement-procedures, which are attempting to enhance transparency levels. In this regard, section three discusses the procurement procedures at the Central Government level and the Indian Railways (the largest public enterprise) to evaluate it against the requirements of transparency provisions as discussed in the Working Group on Transparency in Government Procurement at WTO. Section four presents concluding remarks and recommendations.

Before dwelling on the politico-legal and economic implications of having a multilateral regime of transparency and non-discrimination in government procurement it would be pertinent to understand what one means by government procurement and whether or not and if so how lack of transparency and discrimination leads to international trade distortions as it is a primary focus of attention of World Trade Organization (WTO).

## SECTION I

*What is Government Procurement?* There is no agreed definition of government procurement. The term is used generally to cover purchases of goods and services made by Government entities using the funds allocated to them from either budgetary resources or from those that they receive from international donor agencies as aid (Rege, 2001). All the procurement of goods and services of Government entities other than defence are perceived to come under the purview of government procurement. Government entities here would not-only mean the national government but also the other entities like public sector undertakings and sub-national government entities (e.g., state and local self governments). One definition of *Government procurement* refers to it as *all the goods and services bought by the Government for consumption and investment but not for resale. It generally covers two main types of expenditure: consumption expenditure and expenditure on capital formation, i.e. investment expenditure. These two types of expenditure are usually classified by government function*. Public procurement to put in simple words means procurement by a procuring entity using public funds (World Bank, 1995). Unlike private procurement, public procurement "is a business process within a political system and has therefore significant consideration of integrity, accountability, national interest and effectiveness" (Wittig, 2001).

Some of the mechanisms used by Governments for discrimination of foreign suppliers of goods and services in favour of domestic sourcing include:

- Outright exclusion,
- Preferential price margin,
- Domestic content requirement, and
- Non-transparent tendering and bidding procedures.

A positive public purchasing policy applicable to all public authorities falls into the category of an economic instrument. The preferential treatment given to the domestic industries or entities while procuring goods and services would partially contribute either in encouraging domestic players or in a broader context in achieving social or economic policy objectives. As detailed in the literature the four major functions of public procurement in domestic economic policy include:

1. Increase public spending in domestic market,
2. Protect national industry against foreign competition,
3. Improve competitiveness of certain industrial categories and sectors, and
4. Remedy regional disparities by attaining redistributory objectives.

According to Martin, other (social) functions of public procurement include encouraging job creation, giving preferential treatment to the marginalized sections of the population, and encouraging good environmental and labour practices (Martin, 1996).

The aim of government procurement practices in most of the countries are geared to ensure effective competition by increasing transparency of procurement procedures, to minimize the scope for manipulation by officials in procuring agencies (departments) and to enhance efficiency levels (savings and better resource allocations).

Most of the economic literature on government procurement states that in a perfectly competitive market discrimination against international players on the domestic market does not have any efficiency rationale. Baldwin (1984) along with others has argued that discriminatory procurement policy affects neither domestic supply of goods and services nor does it impinge on trade flows except that it could lead to greater private demand for imports in case of limited domestic supplies.

However there is also a contention that discrimination may increase national welfare provided that the domestic firms have a cost disadvantage in producing the goods to be procured and that there are only a limited number of foreign firms that bid for the contract. Other researchers further elaborated this argument stating that even if the cost structures of domestic and foreign firms are identical and when one accounts for the social costs and benefits, discriminatory procurement policy may be optimal (Hoekman, 1998). Supporting the contention that discriminatory government procurement procedures can contribute towards lowering the imports if the Government demand takes the form of an ad valorem premium above import prices and is subject to cash limits (Santoni, 2001).

Other researchers like Lowinger (1976) have supported the view that huge welfare gains would be derived from non-preferential procurement policies. Economists have shown that outright exclusion of foreign firms in bidding for Government purchase of goods and services increases the costs of procurement. Increasing efficiency by introducing greater competition in government procurement, an empirical study shows, could result in saving for the Government up to 20 per cent or more without compromising on the quality of purchases (Domberger, Hall and Lee, 1995). In one of the studies that undertook simulations of auctions it was found that cost discrimination against foreign firms would raise procurement costs significantly yet these would be lower than imposition of outright ban on foreign bidding. Hence it is shown that preferential price policies bring in only marginal welfare as the benefits from shifting profits to domestic firms are ultimately offset by increasing procurement costs (Deltas and Evenett, 1997).

Through an empirical analyses of US procurement practices, Francois *et al.* (1997) have shown that the potential impact of preferential practices on the overall market access was relatively limited except in certain specific sectors like construction, maintenance and repair services etc. In spite of having many suppliers, positive discrimination in favour of domestic suppliers is considered beneficial provided the products procured are intangible or if monitoring of contractors and enforcing compliance are costly (Evenett and Hoekman, 2003).

There is information asymmetry in favour of suppliers and given the requirements of contract compliance monitoring it is stated that Government entities can economize on the costs of monitoring by choosing suppliers that are located within their jurisdictions. A recent analysis of effect of government procurement on market access and the multilateral trade regime has shown that potential international disciplines on procurement policies both in relation to transparency and to non-discrimination, need not translate into simultaneous improvements in market access and national welfare (Evenett and Hoekman, 2003). All attempts to estimate the impact of discriminatory procurement policies without taking into account their effects on bidding behaviour of domestic and foreign firms tend to produce biased results (Mattoo, 1996). Thus the long-term effects of discriminatory government procurement cannot be assessed unless it is correlated with domestic competition and investment policies.

## SECTION II

*Evolution of Government Procurement as a Multilateral Trade Concern:* For long government procurement has been excluded from the international trade deliberations (as reflected in Article III: 8 (a) and Article XVII: 2 of GATT and Article III: 2 of GATS). The first initiative in this respect was the successful completion of a plurilateral Agreement on Government Procurement in 1976, which came into effect in 1978. While the Uruguay Round of negotiations on GATT were carried out, simultaneously the Agreement on Government

Procurement (GPA) was also deliberated which resulted in its signing at Marrakesh in 1994. This GPA came into effect on January 1, 1996 with 22 parties to the agreement endorsing it. GPA is a plurilateral agreement, meaning that it imposes obligations only on those countries, which become its members. GPA, 1996 extended its scope both in terms of the disciplines as well as entities coverage. With respect to discipline, apart from goods procured beyond thresholds it extended its scope to services and construction work as well, and with respect to entities covered it included sub-central governments, public and regulated private companies along with Central Government. The exact coverage is determined by national schedules of purchasing entities and of services attached to the Agreement. Currently there are around 28[1] WTO member countries who have participated in the GPA and several countries have observer status in the WTO Committee on Government Procurement. There are around 23 nations as observers—a category that imposes certain basic obligations concerning transparency in government procurement (IISD, 2003).

Most of the participating countries in GPA are OECD countries and these countries demonstrated eagerness to bring government purchases under the multilateral framework. For understanding the rationale for this eagerness it is suggested that in the post-cold war era most of the developed world witnessed what is termed as a 'retreat of state' by way of privatization of public enterprises and reduced budgetary allocations etc. Faced with reduced budgetary allocations governments in these countries encouraged competition so as to reduce non-welfare expenditure. Secondly, firms that were being privatized had enhanced options of sourcing goods and services as well as limited prospects of bailout by government. These factors prodded the firms to make their procurements more efficient. Thirdly there is a realization of the potentially large market of public procurement across the world, which does not come under the multilateral framework. According to an OECD estimate the government procurement market is estimated to be over $ 2,000 billion in 1998 that is equivalent to 7 per cent of the World GDP and 30 per cent of the world merchandise trade (OECD, 2001). Studies have shown that though currently as percentage of their GDP developed countries' government procurement market is higher i.e., 5-8 per cent in comparison to the developing countries but in the coming decade it is projected that government procurement in the developing countries like China, India, Brazil etc. is poised to grow significantly high. It is argued that perceiving the potential benefits for their domestic firms developed countries like US, Japan, EU, Australia etc. along with Korea are pushing on the one hand for increasing the membership of GPA and on the other hand for a multilateral framework on transparency in government procurement.

The GPA of 1996 has clearly established rights and obligations of the member nations concerning their national procurement policies, regulations and practices whereby they are obliged to apply the principle of national treatment and extend most favoured nation (MFN) rule to suppliers of products and services among the signatories of GPA. All the goods are subject to GPA discipline except for those, which are exempted for a nation either while negotiating or while accessing the agreement. When it comes to services similar to GATS they are mentioned in the positive list. For each member nation GPA enlists a positive list of all sub-central entities and public enterprises to be covered. GPA has specified threshold values that are applicable to government procurement bids. In case of Central Government procurement the threshold is Special Drawing Rights (SDR) 130,000. Similarly for the purchases of sub-central government entities, the threshold ranges around SDR 200,000. With respect to public enterprises and services the threshold is SDR 400,000. In case of construction activities it is SDR 5 million.

International (both multilateral and bilateral) donor agencies like the World Bank and others have their own procurement guidelines, which are implemented and strictly monitored on project basis. Apart from this, for assessing the capacities of implementing agencies of developing countries in procuring goods and services in accordance to its procedures World Bank undertakes the Country Procurement Assessment Reports (CPARs) and the Country Financial Accountability Assessments (CFAAs). This forms a part of the Bank's fiduciary mandate to improve procurement and disbursement mechanisms both system-wide and for Bank projects in the fund receiving countries (World Bank, 2000). But the Bank's traditional focus of attention almost exclusively at the project level and only on financial accounting and auditing systems has in many instances been shown to be insufficient. In spite of the elaborate procurement guidelines one comes across a rising incidence of fraud and corruption and it shows the brittleness of "ring fencing" at the project level (Singal and Chakrapani, 2000). Another major concern is the existence of multiple donors in developing countries with different procurement and disbursement procedures that add additional administrative burdens and inhibit the development of coherent domestic procurement systems in developing countries (World Bank, 2000).

*Transparency in Government Procurement as a Singapore Issue*: Inclusion of Government Procurement as a new part of the four new Singapore Issues in 1996 Ministerial Conference at Singapore has resulted in new interest on this issue at the international forums. The Working Group formed on the subject of transparency in government procurement (WGTGP) is assigned to conduct a study on transparency in government procurement practices by taking into account national policies. Based on the study, WGTGP is assigned the responsibility of developing elements for inclusion in an appropriate multilateral agreement on transparency in government procurement. The WGTGP has been conducting its deliberations to build consensus among WTO member nations on the issue. These discussions have resulted in identification of the elements that could be considered as transparency provisions and therefore included in the proposed Agreement on Transparency. With respect to transparency in government procurement, Doha Ministerial Declaration 2001 in its para 26 states:

> "Recognizing the case for a multilateral agreement on transparency in government procurement and the need for enhanced technical assistance and capacity-building in this area, we agree that negotiations will take place after Fifth Session of the Ministerial Conference on the basis of the decision taken, by explicit consensus, at that session on the modalities of negotiations. These negotiations will build on the progress made in the Working Group on Transparency in Government Procurement by that time and take into account participants' development priorities, especially those of least-developed country participants. Negotiations shall be limited to the transparency aspects and therefore will not restrict the scope for countries to give preferences to domestic supplies and suppliers. We commit ourselves to ensuring adequate technical assistance and support for capacity-building both during the negotiations and after their conclusion".

There was a clear development with respect to transparency in government procurement as a result of the Doha Declaration. The Declaration has stated that there needs to be an explicit consensus for inclusion of transparency in government procurement along with the other Singapore Issues in the Cancun Ministerial Conference.

The stated objective of introducing transparency in government procurement under the multilateral framework (i.e., WTO) is to contribute to the liberalisation and expansion of world trade. Eliminating discrimination against and between foreign products, services and suppliers by enhancing transparency of laws and practices and ensuring fair, prompt and effective enforcement of international provisions on government procurement would contribute towards achieving the above objective.

The Working Group not only studied the transparency related provisions in the existing international instruments and in national procedures and practices but also continued discussions related to technical assistance and capacity-building. Transparency in government procurement according to the Working Group means ensuring information about a government's procurement regime and individual procurement opportunities to be made available to all interested parties, including potential (domestic and foreign) suppliers and service providers. It acknowledges the right to access such information whereby all the government procurement related policies and practices become transparent (WT/WGTGP/M/18, 2003).

Critical elements of transparency in World Bank procurement procedures are:

1. Notification and advertising (allowing sufficient time for participation),
2. Open competitive bidding preferred, use of other methods restricted,
3. Use of standard bidding and contract documents,
4. Pre-disclosure of relevant information (including bid evaluation method),
5. Public bid opening (and opening immediately following the deadline for bid submission),
6. Evaluation of bids in monetary terms (rather than merit point system),

7. Qualification of bidders on basis of pass/fail requirements,
8. Award to the lowest evaluated responsive bidder meeting the stated qualification criteria, without negotiations,
9. Accessibility of applicable laws and regulations,
10. Appeal mechanisms,
11. Debriefing, and
12. Publication of awards.

There are twelve sub-items on which transparency requirements have been deliberated in the Working Group and these issues were considered to be of paramount value during the negotiating phase [JOB (99) 6782 of November 1999]. These twelve issues include:

1. Definition and scope of government procurement,
2. Procurement methods,
3. Publication of information on national legislation and procedures,
4. Information on procurement opportunities, tendering and qualification procedures,
5. Time periods,
6. Transparency of bid documents, qualifications and decisions on contract awards,
7. Transparency on qualification of suppliers,
8. Domestic review procedures and institutional provisions,
9. Dispute settlement,
10. Language, maintenance of records of proceedings,
11. Information to be provided to other governments (notification), and
12. Technical cooperation and special and differential treatment for developing countries.

Though a larger degree of consensus existed in the WGTGP in comparison to other Working Groups on Singapore Issues such as those concerned with investment and competition policy but on a large number of issues such as definition and scope of government procurement, domestic review procedures as well as linkage to the WTO's DSU there have been contentions among member nations. Few notable developed countries (e.g., US, EU, Japan, Australia etc.) suggested that the Working Group should agree that the phase of study and work analysis has been completed and that it should seek authorization from the General Council for commencement of negotiations for developing an Agreement on Transparency in Government Procurement (Rege, 2001).

*Rationale for a Multilateral Framework in Government Procurement:* The rationale for international deliberations on transparency and non-discrimination negotiations with respect to government procurements stems from the consideration that they play a critical role in maintaining downward pressure on costs of goods and services purchases, giving taxpayers value for money, improving the quality of government services and permitting better allocation of resources. According to the Report of WGTGP to the General Council (2003), which also summarized the benefits of having a multilateral agreement on transparency in government procurement, the following are highlighted:

1. Enhances efficiency and increased innovation as the rule based transparent public procurement fosters increased competition whereby stimulating innovation among suppliers of goods and services,
2. Better value-for-money as transparent tendering leads to effective competition, reduces the level of bids, and this in turn reduces public expenditure,
3. Encourages domestic and foreign investment and partnerships between local and foreign suppliers, which is beneficial especially to developing countries,
4. Reduces corruption as a side-effect,
5. Contributes towards good governance—an essential requirement for economic development, and
6. Introduces legal certainty to existing procurement procedures.

This apart, public procurement of goods and services face the challenge of political favouritism that can be avoided by making the procurement procedures transparent (OECD, 1999). But the critical obstruction to progress on the subject of transparency in government procurement is the lack of clarity regarding the concept of transparency (Arrowsmith, 2003). It is argued that there is a case for a multilateral agreement on transparency in public procurement that is much stronger than the economic case for banning discrimination (Evenett and Hoekman, 2000) as it is held that the price to be paid for a transparency agreement would be relatively low compared to the potential benefits deriving from the optimisation of public expenditure (WT/WGTGP/W/41). However there are certain limitations of introducing transparency such as:

- ❖ It might enable collusion of bidders leading to conflict between the desire to promote competition and the desire to prevent corruption and favouritism (OECD, 1999).
- ❖ Increasing the transaction costs of procurement. The proposition that more competition is better than less rests on the assumption that there are no transaction costs of running the bidding competition or of participating in it (or that any such costs are small). However these transaction costs not only exist but also are large enough to matter for the way the procurement is organized (McMillan, 1998).
- ❖ Transparency of outcome enhances the ability of cartels to detect and punish cheating. Hence in certain public procurements private negotiations with potential suppliers are less likely to lead to collusion than public tender processes (OECD, 1999).
- ❖ Transparency alone may not be sufficient to curb corruption or political favouritism as the agent of the procurer in charge of the procurement can be influenced:
    - ■ to design the procurement process in favour of a particular firm or group of firms,
    - ■ to interpret the prerequisites with corrupt intentions during the process, and
    - ■ to manipulate the evaluation process for achieving desired outcome.

Accepting that there is no dispute regarding the merits of introduction of transparency in government procurement, developing countries like Brazil have observed that there is a need to demonstrate and understand how an agreement on transparency in government procurement would enhance relations among Members and how one Member applying enhanced transparency in government procurement affected and benefited its trading partners. Though the largest government procurement opportunities currently are available in the developed countries but the emerging economies offer major potential.

### *Why developing countries were reluctant to bring Government Procurement on to the multilateral framework?*

While accepting the fact that transparency in government procurement might entail benefits to developing countries (Deardorff and Stern, 2003) one needs to understand it from the perspective of developing countries for better appreciation of their position at WTO. Each country evaluates the gains that would accrue to it (both in terms of export gains and the efficiency gains in the domestic market) as against the costs (both in terms of administrative burden and the economic costs of changing the rules and procedures). There are substantial governance gains for the developing countries if they can bring transparency in their public procurement procedures as the procurement process in most of these countries is still shrouded by secrecy, inefficiency, corruption and undercutting. In all these cases, huge amounts of resources are wasted although several of them are reforming their procurement procedures (Odhiambo and Kamau, 2003). The gains that developing countries can derive by reforming government procurement procedures are not so much due to their capacity to gain international contracts but more due to the improved resource utilisation through more transparent and competitive government procurement practices. From an international trade point of view as most government purchases relate to services rather than merchandise trade, the concerns that arise are essentially related to liberalisation and national treatment of foreign service providers (Michalopoulos, 1999). Unfortunately these domestic efficiency and governance gains are not enough motivations for the developing countries to embark upon a multilateral framework on public procurement.

The asymmetry in access to information that the developing countries suffer with respect to procurement of goods and services and the lack of experience in bidding for such goods and services is a major disincentive for the developing countries to look at government procurement as a window of opportunity. Instead they perceive it as window of threat. While accepting the theoretical and actual benefits associated with transparency in government procurement, developing countries have been arguing that it is not a sufficient basis upon which to create multilateral rules (WTO, 2003, WT/WGTGP/7). They are arguing that it is necessary to demonstrate and understand how an agreement on transparency in government procurement would enhance relations among WTO members and how one Member applying enhanced transparency would affect and benefit its trading partners in the WTO. Developing countries like India, Pakistan, Malaysia and Egypt oppose the very concept of a multilateral agreement that is legally binding. Most of the developing countries are wary of the obligations that a treaty of this nature might impose on them. There is an apprehension among officials of developing and least developed countries regarding the threshold levels to which this multilateral agreement on Transparency in Government Procurement would apply.

**Box 12.1:** E-Procurement in Developing Countries

One area that has witnessed remarkable changes in recent years is government procurement. Government procurement in developing countries (e.g., Chile and Mexico) is witnessing remarkable changes as some of them are using E-procurement avenues for increasing transparency, reducing transaction costs and curb red tape and corruption in the government purchasing practices. In Chile (*www.compraschile.cl),* all companies that wish to be considered for a public contract register themselves according to their business activity (for example, construction, IT consulting, office furniture, etc.). When a public agency needs to purchase goods or services, it files a request in the new electronic system. An e-mail message soliciting bids is then sent automatically to all companies registered in the relevant business area. And once a decision is made, all information concerning the companies, their bids, and the results of the decision-making process are posted electronically. It shows that E-government solutions like this can generate cost savings for government and reduce opportunities for corruption, leading to increased public confidence in government (World Bank, 2000).

Going by the deliberations of WGTGP some of the developing countries fear that this agreement would not stop at transparency itself but would be expanded beyond once the negotiations on this subject starts (Evenett, 2003). There is a fear that these developing countries may no longer be in a position to use government procurement as a pool instrument for promoting domestic industry and lose the current discretion that they enjoy in pursuing value for money. A federal country like India is apprehensive of the compliance and enforcement requirements of an agreement of this nature as most of the government procurement activities (i.e., large number of limited value purchases) are carried out at sub-national levels like Panchayats, urban local bodies, municipalities etc. These are some of the valid reasons for the developing countries to be apprehensive about entering into serious negotiations with respect to a multilateral agreement on government procurement.

But today there is a wide array of technological avenues like use of Information Technology for improving government procurement procedures at limited costs. E-Procurement as experienced in some of the developing countries (*see* Box 12.1) provide good insights into the possibilities of improving transparency and procedural efficiency. It shows that not only procurement becomes more transparent but it also becomes efficient whereby it can lead to saving of administrative and transaction costs along with improved accountability (Moïsé and Grosso, 2003).

**India's Position on Transparency in Government Procurement**

While the Indian Government is willing to negotiate an agreement on transparency in government procurement it is opposed to extending this to a market access agreement. Similarly India does not perceive any benefits of inclusion of state governments and public sector enterprises to a market-access agreement. It perceives enormous transaction and other economic costs, which outweighs the potential benefits that would accrue to it. But there are economists who have argued that there is little to justify both within and outside India our objection to the introduction of the transparency in government procurement in the multilateral framework, unless we accept that complete national sovereignty is a higher social good over improved domestic policy and procedure and increased access to foreign markets (Mattoo and Subramanian, 1999)

## SECTION III
## GOVERNMENT PROCUREMENT PROCEDURES IN INDIA

*Evolution of Government Procurement in India:* In 1860 the British Government in London established the Indian Stores Department for purchase of imported stores. With the establishment of Indian Munitions Board in 1917 centralized purchasing in India was made effective for controlling purchases and enhancing indigenous base for Government purchase. By 1922 it was converted into the India Stores Department. During the pre-independence period the Indian Government procurement department has undergone numerous changes. The Directorate General of Supplies and Disposal (DGS&D) was established as the Central Purchase Organisation after Indian Independence i.e., in 1951 essentially for the procurement of goods and services required by various Central Government Departments/Ministries. Thus it became the exclusive executive arm of the Supply Division concerning conclusion of Rate Contracts for common user items, procurement of stores, inspection of stores, shipment and clearance. DGS&D is an attached office under the Supply Division and is the nodal body/agency for purchase and inspection of stores for the Ministries/Departments and offices of the Central Government. The Supply Division (erstwhile Department of Supply) in the Ministry of Commerce and Industry, Department of Commerce is basically concerned with formulation of policies and procedures relating to purchases by Government of India.

While there is no separate law or policy on public procurement in India but there are rules and orders in the General Financial Rules (GFR) and Delegation of Financial Powers Rules (DFPR) that govern purchase of goods and services by Union Government. These apart, there are legislations such as Indian Contract Act, 1872 and Sale of Goods Act, 1932 that have provisions for guiding government procurement. Apart from this the General Financial Rules (GFR) issued by Ministry of Finance, Government of India act as guidelines for government procurement. The Manual of Office Procedure for Supplies, Inspection and Disposals (MOPSID) popularly known as 'DGS&D Manual' continues to be the guiding document for undertaking all procurements either through DGS&D or by government departments directly. Based on these guidelines the procurement process as outlined by DGS&D is geared towards:

- ❖ Encouraging development of indigenous production as far as possible,
- ❖ Extending price preference up to specified limit (as specified by Government of India from time-to-time) to Small Scale Industries and Public Sector Undertakings, and
- ❖ Ensuring quality of products/services and timely supplies (DGS&D Manual).

According to the DGS&D Manual the objective of public procurement of goods and services are:

- Meeting the specified quantity and quality.
- Acquiring on a competitive basis at the lowest price.
- Ensuring delivery in a timely and planned manner.

Reflecting the changing economic policies of the Government DGS&D also underwent changes in its focus and attention. Decentralization of procurement of functions has been the major thrust of these changes, which are more evident after the liberalization policy in 1991. In the post 1991 phase, in spite of decentralization of the public procurement process the 'DGS&D Manual' continues to be the guiding document for undertaking all procurements by government departments. Apart from DGS&D, agencies such as Ministry of Railways, Ministry of Defence, CPWD, etc. have evolved their respective purchasing manuals giving specificity to their purchasing procedures. DGS&D Manual contains the entire gamut of procurement of goods and services which lays down guidelines/ instructions on all the important terms and conditions, inspection, bid evaluation, placement of contract, post-contract management, rate contracts, delegation of powers, dispute resolution etc. (Government of India, 2003).

According to the scheme of decentralisation, procurement against the ad-hoc indents was transferred from DGS&D to the indenting Ministries/Departments. However DGS&D continues to handle procurement on the rate/running contract. Only in cases of exceptions ad-hoc purchases are to be handled by DGS&D. These exceptions include:

1. Indented item is sophisticated in nature,
2. Lack of adequate expertise in purchasing department, and
3. For any other specific reason that is stated and approved by Secretary/Head of the Ministry/Organization.

The preferences extended to different sectors of industry as per the procurement procedures laid down by DGS&D get operationalized in the form of:

- Product Reservation,

- Purchase Preference, and
- Price Preference (DGS&D Manual).

*Product Reservation:* Some of the major product reservations applicable to government procurement in India are as follows:

1. Purchase of Khadi (hand-spun and hand-woven textiles) items are reserved exclusively from Khadi and Village Industries Commission (KVIC).
2. Purchase of all handloom textile items required by Central Government Departments are reserved for exclusive purchase from KVIC and/or notified Handloom Units through the Association of Corporations and Apex Societies of Handloom (ACASH).
3. About 358 items are reserved for exclusive purchase from Small Scale Industries (SSI). The Standing Review Committee at DGS&D periodically reviews this list of items. For these items in the process of procurement other things being equal, the purchase would be in favour of KVIC/ACASH/SSI in that order.

*Price Preference:* A price preference up to 15 per cent over the lowest offer from the large-scale private sector should be extended to SSI. But in cases where Cottage and Small Scale Industries have established themselves as suppliers of certain specified items and have competitive advantage over the Large Scale Industries then no price preference needs to be extended. Similarly if SSIs have previously supplied goods without availing the benefit of price preference or with lower price preference then there is scope for examining extension of price preference by the procurement officer.

*Purchase Preference for Public Sector Undertakings (PSUs):* In situations where both public and private sector units are competing for purchase preference in favour of PSUs, provided the quoted prices of PSUs are within 10 per cent of the lowest acceptable price offer of private sector, purchase preference may be granted at the lowest acceptable price to PSUs[2].

Until the 1990s DGS&D played a paramount role in procurement of goods and services by all the Union Government departments and Ministries. But gradually this function has been decentralized to the respective Ministries, which have evolved their own procurement procedures but follow the basic tenets of DGS&D Manual. The General Financial Rules specify threshold limits of procurement by different levels of authority as well as threshold limits for open tender, price preferences to small scale and cottage industries, purchase of imported plant and machinery and goods, methods of obtaining earnest money or security deposit from the bidders etc. (Muthuswamy and Brinda, 2000)

As per the scope defined in the deliberations at WGTGP the following entities come under the purview of government procurement in India:

- All the Departments and Ministries of Government of India except Ministry of Defence.
- All the Departments of the State Governments.
- Municipal Corporations, Municipalities etc. in Urban Areas.
- District, Mandal or Block and Village level (i.e., Zillas, Mandals or Taluks and Panchayats).
- Public Sector Enterprises under the Central Government like NTPC, ONGC, NMDC, NFC, SBI, IFFCO etc.
- Public Sector Enterprises at the State level like RTCs, Milk Cooperatives, State Cooperative Banks etc.

Given the federal nature of Indian Polity there is no uniform procurement policy that governs procurement activities of all the above entities. But for each of these entities there are fairly well documented procedures for purchasing of goods and services. The World Bank procurement guidelines are used in procuring goods and services within the government entities that receive its funding but the same entities follow different procurement procedures when it comes to purchases with its sanctioned budgetary resources.

An estimate carried out recently by Shrivastava indicates a range between 3.5 to 5.9 per cent of GDP as the share of government procurement in India. These estimates take into account the estimated value of purchases by state governments as well as public enterprises along with the procurements carried out by Government of India. For the year 2000-01 in value terms it is estimated to be in the range of Rs. 784.5 billion to Rs. 1283 billion [Central Government Rs.141.94 billion to Rs. 265.27 billion; PSEs Rs. 545.25 billion to Rs. 828.77 billion; and State Governments Rs. 184 billion to Rs. 349.5 billion] (Shrivastava, 2003)

Assessing Indian financial accountability, analysts from the World Bank (Sahgal and Chakrapani, 2002) have stated that incidence of fraud, waste and abuse of public funds is reportedly widespread. The systems of financial management and accountability in the States are essentially a replica of those at the Union Government level and are often influenced by the procedures and practices of the Union Government.

In order to curb corrupt practices in all the Central Government Departments and its Public Enterprises as well as local authorities the Government of India has constituted Central Vigilance Commission in 1999 through an ordinance and it has been further strengthened through an Act of Parliament entitled The Central Vigilance Commission Act, 2003.

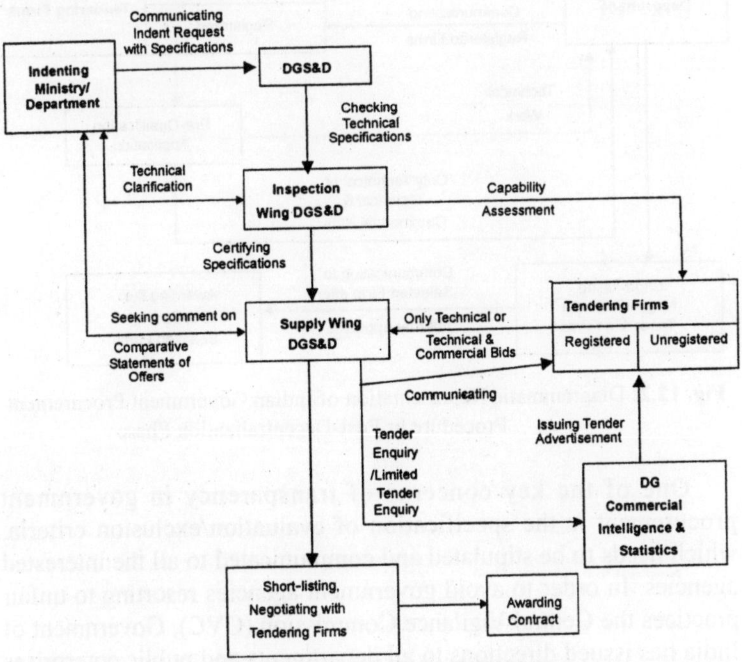


**Fig. 12.1:** Diagrammatic Representation of Indian Government Procurement Procedure in Pre-Decentralization Phase

Some of the important powers and functions of the CVC are:

- Investigation of offences alleged to have been committed under the Prevention of Corruption Act, 1988.

- ❖ Giving directions to the Delhi Special Police Establishment for the purpose of discharging the responsibility entrusted to it.
- ❖ Inquiry or investigation on a reference made by the Central Government wherein it is alleged that a public servant being an employee of the Central Government or its agencies has committed an offence under the Prevention of Corruption Act, 1988 or under the Code of Criminal Procedure, 1973.
- ❖ Advising Government and its agencies on matters referred to it etc.

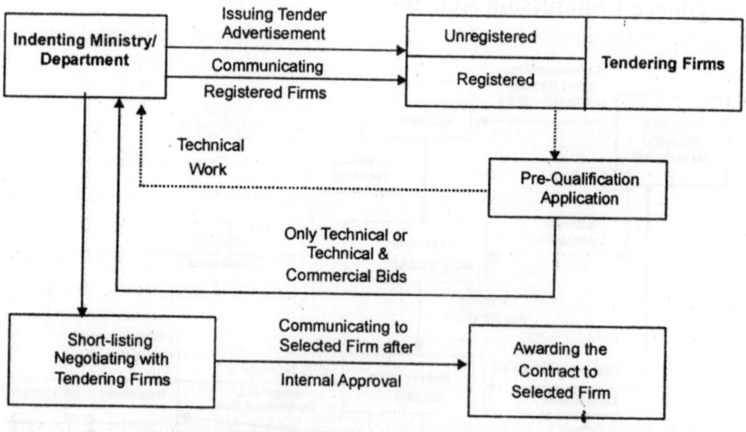


**Fig. 12.2:** Diagrammatic Representation of Indian Government Procurement Procedure in Post-Decentralization Phase

One of the key concerns of transparency in government procurement is the specification of evaluation/exclusion criteria, which needs to be stipulated and communicated to all the interested agencies. In order to avoid government agencies resorting to unfair practices the Central Vigilance Commission (CVC), Government of India has issued directions to all departments and public enterprises in its order No. 33/7/03 stating that "whatever pre-qualification, evaluation/exclusion criteria, etc. which the organization wants to adopt should be made explicit at the time of inviting tenders so that basic concept of transparency and interests of equity and fairness are satisfied" (CVC, 2003).

The general procurement procedure followed especially by the departments and agencies of Government of India while sourcing goods and services is enunciated as broad steps in the following:

- *Step I—Inviting Tenders:* A number of different possibilities exist in this respect: An open bid is globally advertised and foreign and Indian firms responding to these tenders are given equal consideration. In some cases, limited tenders are issued to selected suppliers that are already known and registered with the issuing organization or Ministry. In order for this list of suppliers to be selected, limited tenders are often preceded by an invitation for firms to register with the issuing organization, allowing quality and reliability to be judged. A brief overview of the tendering process in India is given in Box 12.2.
- *Step II—Evaluation Procedure:* Based on the nature of goods or services procurement evaluation procedure can be either single bid system or two-bid system. In the single bid system the bidders are required to submit their technical and commercial offers simultaneously for evaluation. But in the two- bid system bidders are requested to submit both technical and commercial bids separately and the evaluation is carried out in stages. In the single bid system only the eligible suppliers' commercial bids are opened and the lowest financial bid of the suppliers is selected for awarding the contract. But in the two stage bid system technical bids are required to be submitted by the suppliers in the first stage. Evaluations are made on the basis of bids limited to the technical specifications, from which a shortlist of eligible suppliers is prepared. These short-listed suppliers are asked to submit commercial bids from which the lowest financial bid would be selected for awarding the contract. As per the CVC procedures the procuring agency or department can negotiate only with the lowest financial bid suppliers.
- *Step III—Evaluation Criteria (Special and differential treatment for domestic firms):* In granting procurement contracts, a price preference of 15 per cent is given to "indigenous equipment" suppliers, for example, in telecommunications. In the shipping sector, price preferences of up to 30 per cent apply to Indian bidders on procurement contracts.

- *Step IV—Awarding of Contract:* The contract is usually granted within three months of submission.

To increase transparency in its bidding procedures, the Indian Government completed the development of standard bidding documents based on the World Bank's procurement guidelines, 1995/96, in July 1997. India has adopted the World Bank's standard bidding document for the procurement of goods, works, supply and installation, and pharmaceuticals and vaccines, and has finalized national competitive bidding documents for use in World Bank funded projects in India. The India-specific standard bidding documents are being prepared and are expected also to be used in contract/procurement manuals for Government Ministries and Departments.

**Box 12.2:** Tendering Procedures in India

*Essential Features of Tender*: According to the Supreme Court a valid tender must:

1. be unconditional.
2. be made at the proper place.
3. conform to the terms of obligation.
4. be made in the proper time.
5. be made in the proper form.
6. be made by a person who is able and willing to perform the obligation.
7. provide a reasonable opportunity for inspection.
8. be made to the proper person.
9. be of full amount.
10. if the offer of performance relates to a delivery, the promisee must be afforded a reasonable opportunity of ascertaining that what is offered is what the promisor is bound to deliver. In case of joint promises, an offer of performance to any one of them is a valid offer.

*Forms of Tendering*: There are several ways in which bids and tenders may be invited. Some of the more commonly used methods for government procurement in India are:

(a) *Competitive Tendering Process*: This process involves awarding the contract to the bidder who offers the most competitive terms. This obviously ensures the award of contract to one who offers the lowest price other things being equal.

The scope for bias and favouritism is, therefore, greatly limited or even eliminated if the process is properly carried out. Disadvantages of this process include:

1. the possibility of inferior quality goods or services being provided,
2. increased possibility of breach of contractual obligations,
3. use of lesser skills in implementation,

All or some of the above may occur due to the narrow profit margins involved, and may exclude quality bidders. Competitive tendering can be carried out two ways:

(i) Open public tendering involves inviting tenders by publication or other advertisement. As per government procurement procedures this is carried out in following two forms:

1. *Advertised Tender Enquiry*: when the estimated value of demand is Rs. 2 lakh and above.
2. *Global Tender Enquiry*: when wider competition on global scale is considered necessary.

(ii) Selective tendering process is where an invitation to tender is issued to a select number of tenderers/contractors, usually those who are on the Purchasing Department's approved list. This process is also called Limited Tender Inquiry. This method according to DGS&D manual should be adopted in all cases in which the estimated value is less than Rs. 200,000. It may also be followed for more than above stated value provided:

1. There are sufficient reasons to indicate that it is not in the public interest to call for tenders by advertisement,
2. There is urgency of demand which could not be anticipated, and
3. When the sources of supply are definitely known and possibility of fresh sources are remote.

(b) *Negotiated or Non-Competitive Tendering Process*: This process is also known as non-competitive tendering and helps both parties to arrive at a mutually acceptable price. This is called Single Tender Enquiry and it is usually employed when it is known that only a particular firm is the manufacturer of the goods in demand or as per Government Policy, purchases are to be made only from selected firms. Non-competitive tendering is also used especially in Defence and Aviation sectors. In this process after submission of the quotation, tentative price is determined after considering all factors, which forms the basis of negotiations with the supplying agency. The negotiations take place, a final price is arrived at and thereafter the contract executed.

(c) *The Process of Auction*: Government has used this method extensively for awarding licences/rights. Rules have been framed under certain State statutes prescribing the procedure for conducting auction sales and the confirmation of bids by the competent authorities. Such law gives the right to the bidders to insist that their transactions with the government should be in accordance with these provisions. The provisions of these rules can be legally enforced. In auctions for government contracts, a binding contract comes into existence not at the time of the fall of hammer, but when it is signed by the officer having the authority to make such contracts. This is a departure from the rule applicable to contracts entered into by individuals through the process of auction.

The current policy places emphasis on positive discrimination towards public sector enterprises as well as the small-scale sector in government procurement of goods and services so as to encourage them and ensure their viability. This translates in the form of specification of products that ought to be procured from the small-scale sector, including 75 items that may be procured from the handicraft and handloom sector. A price preference of up to 15 per cent applies to procurement from the sector on a tender-to-tender basis depending on whether the small-scale unit has successfully secured contracts by competing on a non-preferential basis with large-scale units.

Since 1993, there has been a gradual elimination in preferences for procurement from the public sector. Price preferences for the sector were eliminated in January 1992 and the number of items exclusively reserved for procurement from the public sector was reduced from eight to six, namely, coal, arms and ammunition, mineral oils, atomic energy, minerals related to atomic energy, and railway transport. Mining of iron ore, manganese ore, chrome ore, gypsum, sulphur, gold and diamonds, copper, lead, zinc, tin, molybdenum and wolfram were removed from the list of industries reserved for the public sector in 1991.

In understanding and evaluating the procurement procedures and their effectiveness the author has sourced (for most of the analysis in the following section) from an analytical study carried out by CVC (CVC, 2002).

In its efforts towards streamlining the public procurement procedures Government of India has constituted a Task Force for Revision of Norms for Procurement of Goods and Services by the Government so as to bring greater transparency, competition, fairness and elimination of discretion in procurement of goods and services by Government. This task-force after deliberations has submitted its recommendations for the consideration of the Government. Some of the major recommendations of the task force are enlisted in the following (Government of India, 2003):

- Increasing comprehensiveness of the contents of the bid document and making them user friendly.
- Transparency in bid notifications by giving wide publicity.
- Eligibility criteria for bidders needs to be clearly specified.
- Qualification criteria for bidders such as experience, technical and financial capability etc. needs to be clearly indicated in bid document.
- Technical specifications of required goods needs to be clearly specified.
- Time period needs to be specified and adhered to for different types of tenders.
- Bid evaluation criteria needs to be precisely defined including the weightages for different aspects of bid.
- Regarding negotiation with bidders it recommends to abide by Central Vigilance Commission direction that if negotiation is unavoidable it is permitted only with lowest responsive bidder.
- The names of the successful bidders should be notified in departmental bulletins/website/notice boards etc.
- Unsuccessful bidders should have the right to ascertain the grounds for rejection of their bids.
- Mechanism for settlement of disputes needs to be mentioned in the contract.

With respect to increasing efficiency, economy and accountability in public procurement, the major recommendations of the Task Force are as following:

- *Procurement Law*: GFR needs updating, modifications and restructuring in a comprehensive manner as it does not cover all the essential areas of purchase management
- *Threshold Limits:*
  - For small purchases of up to Rs. 1,000, purchases up to Rs. 5,000 may be made without inviting tenders/ quotations. For purchases between Rs. 1,000 – 10,000 Heads of Departments were authorized to purchase goods and services without calling tenders or pre-select DGS&D rate contract items. But quotations must be invited for different suppliers. This limit is recommended to be raised to between Rs. 5,000 – 30,000
  - Currently in the case of all orders up to Rs. 2,00,000 Limited Tender System is being adopted. This outer limit is recommended to be raised to Rs. 5,00,000.
  - The Rs. 2,00,000 lower limit in almost all cases for any good or service for Open Tender System is recommended to be raised to above Rs. 5,00,000.
- *Bidding Documents:* There is need for evolving a common basic structure of the bidding document for procurement of all goods with a limited scope of minor variations that do not violate the basic structure and the essential parameters of public procurements.
- *Standardization of Bidding Documents:* It is recommended that Standardized Bidding Documents for different value of purchases needs to be evolved. But these documents should not be more than two including one for a higher value purchase (above Rs. 5,00,000) and other for a lower value purchase (between Rs. 30,000 to Rs. 5,00,000).

According to the assessment of the World Bank, after introduction of liberalisation process in India the changes in the public procurement procedures brought them to the level consistent with the requirements of the plurilateral Agreement on Government Procurement of the WTO (Debroy and Pursell, 1997).

***Procurement Procedures in Indian Railways***

The Railways broadly has three systems of tenders such as:

- Open tender system,
- Limited tender system, and
- Single tender system.

In the open tender system, the tender notice is given due publicity through prescribed channels/media and suppliers eligible to bid for the work are informed. Under the limited tender system, tender notices are issued only to select-firms/entities which are short-listed in advance on the basis of their credentials, expertise and specialization vis-à-vis the requirements of the work in question. In other words, such agencies are those who are to be on the 'approved list' maintained by the Department. The single tender system, on the other hand, is taken recourse to only in emergencies and exceptional cases—where the other tender-routes cannot be followed an account of exigencies of the given situation.

**Table 12.1:** Stages, Players and their Functions in the Tendering Process

| *Stage* | *Authority/Official in Charge* |
|---|---|
| Opening of Tender | One representative (supervisory level) each of Executive & Finance Departments. |
| Technical Evaluation | An Officer of the Executive Department. |
| Making of Comparative Statement & Briefing Note | An Officer of the Executive Department. |
| Vetting of Briefing Note | An Officer of the Finance Department. |
| Convening of Tender Committee (TC) | Convener—The executive in charge of coordinating the award of tender. |
| Finalizing the TC recommendations | The Convener, Finance member and the third TC member which is from a department different than the executive. |
| Drafting TC recommendations & forwarding them to Accepting Authority | Convener. |
| Decision on TC recommendations | Accepting Authority can accept, modify or reject TC recommendations. |
| Issue of Letter of Acceptance of Offer to the selected firm | An officer of the executive department. |
| Signing of Contract. | An officer of the executive department. |

*Source*: Sainini, 2002.

The procedures governing the open tender and limited tender system are fairly well defined and documented. Despite this it is possible to manipulate the system to favour a supplier over the deserving one and as a result either quality of the good or service procured suffers or cost escalates to the disadvantage of the Department. If the evaluation committee, in case of Railways, the Tender Committee is 'managed' appropriately then there is enough scope and leverage within the system for manipulating it to the advantage of the predetermined supplier. Often the approving authority [i.e., Tender Accepting Authority (TAA)] endorses the decision due to the highly technical nature of the subject matter under-evaluation or when the TC was unanimous in giving its recommendations. Experiences of such evaluation committees elsewhere have shown that the convener/chairman of the committee plays a critical role either positively or negatively in steering the committee and its proceedings towards the recommendations.

The above mentioned study by CVC of the cases (total 341) referred to and handled in the year 2000 showed that manipulation of awards/tenders (34%) and irregularities in procurement (17%) account for more than half of the total cases handled. This shows the scope and extent of opportunities that currently exists in manipulating the public procurement procedures and activities to the detriment of the interests of the organization (in this case Railways). Some of the common irregularities observed in this study are as follows:

- Enhancing the rate of contracts.
- Compromising on the quality of works executed.
- Finalizing an undeserving supplier.
- Releasing enhanced payments for unfinished or under-finished work.
- Failure to carry out quality-checks.
- Misappropriation of materials by contractors and/or officials, in conspiracy with each other.
- Manipulations at the tender-processing stage with a view to favour a particular contractor and/or to eliminate a more deserving/eligible one.

Some of the recommendations for improving procurement procedures at Indian Railways by practitioners (Sainani, 2002) include:

- Posting all tendering rules, regulations and procedures on websites of the Railways
- All units of Railways that deal with tenders should make all information (primarily time taken in each stage of each tender, the party to and rate at which it is finally allotted etc.) public on their websites, particularly on tenders costing over say one million rupees. In the first stage of implementation this information could be posted at least every fortnight listing the details of all tenders finalized up to the previous week. In the second stage, the information could be made available online.
- All parties whose offers are not accepted should be informed electronically about the reasons for the same, within one day of the decision on tender. The reasons could be higher price (which is and should be the reason in most of the cases), technical unsuitability, lack of required experience, financial credentials, non-compliance to special conditions of contract etc.
- The parties whose offers are not accepted should be given the right to appeal to the highest authority of the unit in which the tender is being finalized. There could be a time limit of say three days for filing an appeal and seven days for disposing off the appeal. The letter of decision to award the contract should be issued only after all pending appeals have been finalized. This condition of withholding the decision to award the contract should be applicable only at the first level of awarding the contract. This means that if on the basis of appeal the earlier decision to award the contract is changed, the right to appeal would not be available at the revised decision. This is suggested to check the possibility of a series of appeals and consequent delays. The recommendations of the TC meeting and decision of Tender Accepting Authority (TAA) can be made public and posted on the website at the second stage of implementation.

An over review of procurement procedures in Central Government, and Indian Railways procurement procedures presented above reveal that the transparency requirements are almost similar. The differences in procurement procedures relate more to the type of procurement rather than level or type of procuring agency. With respect to degree of transparency in procurement is a function of value of procurement. Often the higher the value the greater is the demand for transparency in government procurement in India. While threshold levels for transparency requirements are similar in most of central government organizations and public enterprises but they differ from state to state. It is similar to the conclusion drawn in the study of procurement procedures of other countries (Moïsé and Grosso, 2003).

**Table 12.2:** Evaluation of Transparency in Government Procurement Procedures in India

| *Sl. No.* | *Required Transparency Element in Procurement Procedure** | *DGS&D Procedures* | *Indian Railways Procedures* |
|---|---|---|---|
| 1. | Notification and advertising (allowing sufficient time for participation) | ☆☆☆ | ☆☆☆ |
| 2. | Open competitive bidding preferred, use of other methods restricted | ☆☆ | ☆☆ |
| 3. | Use of standard bidding and contract documents | ☆ | ☆ |
| 4. | Pre-disclosure of relevant information (including bid evaluation method) | ☆☆ | ☆☆ |
| 5. | Public bid opening (and opening immediately following the deadline for bid submission) | ☆☆☆ | ☆☆☆ |
| 6. | Evaluation of bids in monetary terms (rather than merit point system) | ☆☆☆ | ☆☆☆ |
| 7. | Qualification of bidders on basis of pass/fail requirements | ☆☆☆ | ☆☆☆ |
| 8. | Award to the lowest evaluated responsive bidder meeting the stated qualification criteria, without negotiations | ☆☆ | ☆☆ |
| 9. | Accessibility of applicable laws and regulations | ☆☆ | ☆☆ |
| 10. | Appeal mechanisms | ☆☆ | ☆☆ |
| 11. | Debriefing | ☆ | ☆ |
| 12. | Publication of awards. | ☆☆ | ☆☆ |

* On the basis of World Bank Procurement Requirements.

☆ = Low on requirements; ☆☆= Partly meeting requirements;

☆☆☆= Fully meeting requirements of transparency.

*Source*: Author's Evaluation of Procurement Procedures

An assessment of the procurement procedures in India (*see* Table 12.2) based on the secondary sources of information against the transparency requirements as enunciated in the World Bank procurement procedures show that of the 12 critical elements of transparency requirements on 4 elements the current procedures meet the requirements fully, on 5 elements the requirements are met partially and on 3 elements the procedures are not meeting the requirements. This reveals that there is a need to introduce certain critical elements of transparency in government procurement procedures in India so as to enhance efficiency of utilizing public resources, to reduce the transaction costs for suppliers of goods and services, and to address corruption concerns in public procurement. This entails certain costs to the economy but the experience elsewhere has shown that benefits would outweigh the costs. This does not mean that there is a justification for a multilateral agreement on transparency in government procurement because there is no system evaluation of the pros and cons of such an agreement on the international trade of developing countries in general and India in particular.

## Conclusions

There are considerable international trade opportunities in government procurement markets across the world. Given the development function that government procurement procedures in different countries serve there has been resistance for inclusion of government procurement under multilateral trade regime by both developed and developing countries for long time. In the last decade some of the developed countries especially the OECD countries have moved forward in bringing government procurement under an international regime by strengthening the plurilateral agreement on government procurement. Given the apprehensions that a large number of developing countries have the membership of the plurilateral agreement is not growing at the pace desired by most of the developed countries like US, Japan, EU etc, they have sought to bring this subject of government procurement under the multilateral framework as a Singapore Issue in WTO in 1996. But here the focus was just confined to transparency in government procurement. The deliberations in the Working Group formed on this subject shows that there is a considerable degree of agreement as none of the WTO member countries have disputed the efficacy of transparency in public procurement.

Looking at the procurement procedures in Government of India, the DGS&D procedures as well as procurement procedures of Indian Railways show that there are certain gaps with respect to the requirements of transparency in government procurement as per the existing procedures. There is evidence to show that policy-makers are enlivened to these needs and are attempting to move forward towards introducing transparency elements in the procurement procedures.

It is the contention of the developing countries like India, Egypt, Malaysia, Pakistan etc. that transparency in government procurement devoid of non-discriminatory provisions in the multilateral framework portends no significant gains for international trade. This is because transparent access to foreign procurement markets does little to stimulate competition if overt discrimination against foreign bids is considerable (Evenett, 2003). Transparency in government procurement is more a means to an end rather than an end itself. However neither the Ministerial Declaration nor the deliberations of WGTGP have clearly specified which international trade related objectives transparency in government procurement intends to fulfil. This lack of clarity is creating trepidations among developing as well as least developed countries as they either perceive bringing government procurement into the WTO framework as unduly intrusive and/or it indicates some hidden agenda of the developed countries (Arrowsmith, 2003). Hence it becomes more of a domestic governance concern than an international trade concern.

## END NOTES

1. Parties to the GPA comprise Austria, Belgium, Canada, Denmark, European Communities, Finland, France, Germany, Greece, Hong Kong China, Iceland, Ireland, Israel, Italy, Japan, Korea, Liechtenstein, Luxembourg, Netherlands, Netherlands with respect to Aruba, Norway, Portugal, Singapore, Spain, Sweden, Switzerland, United Kingdom, and the United States.
2. For greater details on preferences and most current list of reserved items latest DGS&D Manual needs to be referred.

## REFERENCES

Arrowsmith, S. (2003). 'Transparency in Government Procurement: The Objectives of Regulation and the Boundaries of the World Trade

Organization', *Journal of World Trade*, 37(2): pp. 283-303, Kluwer Law International.

Baldwin, R.E. (1984). 'Rent Seeking and Trade Policy: An Industry Approach', *Weltwirtschaftliches Archiv*, 4(120): 646-77.

Calster, G. V. (2002). 'Green Procurement and the WTO: Shades of Grey', *RECIEL*, 11 (3), Blackwell Publishers Ltd.

Centre for International Trade, Economics & Environment (CUTS), Transparency in Government Procurement, State of Play—Issue Paper 9, Jaipur, India, 2003.

Central Vigilance Commission, Office Order No. 33/7/03, CVC, Government of India, New Delhi, July, 2003.

Choi, I. (1999). 'Long and Winding Road to The Government Procurement Agreement: Korea's Accession Experience', Prepared for Presentation at the World Bank—PEEC Trade Policy Forum seminar on East Asia and Options for the WTO 2000 Negotiations, Manila, July 19-20.

Deardorff A. V. and R. M. Stern (2003). 'Enhancing the Benefits for Developing Countries in the Doha Development Agenda Negotiations', Research Seminar in International Economics, Discussion Paper No. 498. Downloaded from http://www.fordschool.umich.edu/rsie/workingpapers/wp.html

Debroy, B. and G. Pursell (1997). 'Government Procurement Policies in India' in Bernard M. Hoekman and Petros C. Mavroidis, (eds.), *Law and Policy in Public Purchasing: The WTO Agreement on Government Procurement*, pp. 189-202. Ann Arbor: University of Michigan Press.

Deltas. G. and S. J. Evenett (1997). 'Quantitative Estimates of the Effects of Preference Policies', in B. M. Hoekman and P. C. Mavroidis (eds.) *In Law and Policy in Public Purchasing. The WTO Agreement on Government Procurement,* pp. 73-92, Ann Arbor: University of Michigan Press.

DGS&D. Manual of Office Procedure for Supplies, Inspection and Disposals, Directorate General Supply and Disposal, Ministry of Commerce, Government of India, New Delhi, downloaded on April 4, 2004 from http://dgsnd.nic.in/October, 1999.

———— Annual Report, (2002-03), Directorate General Supply and Disposal, Ministry of Commerce, Government of India, New Delhi, 2003.

Domberger, S., Hall C. and E.A.L. Lee, (1995). 'The Determinants of Price and Quality in Competitively Tendered Contracts', *Economic Journal* 105:1454-70.

Evenett, S. (2002). 'Multilateral Disciplines and Government Procurement' in *Behind to Borders: Trading Issues*, pp. 417-27. Washington D.C.: The World Bank.

———— (2003). 'Is there a case for new multilateral rules on Transparency in Government Procurement', in SECO and S. J. Evenett (eds.), *The Singapore Issues and the World Trade System: The Road to Cancun and Beyond*, World Trade Institute Berne.

——— and B. M. Hoekman, (2000). 'Government Procurement of Services and Multilateral Disciplines' in Pierre Sauvé & Robert M. Stern (eds.) *GATS 2000: New Directions in Services Trade Liberalization*, Boston: Brookings Institution.

——— (2003). 'Government Procurement: Market Access, Transparency and Multilateral Trade Rules', November, Washington D C: The World Bank.

Francois, J., D. Nelson, D. Palmeter (1997). 'Government procurement in the U.S.: A post-Uruguay Round Analysis', in B. Hoekman and P. Mavroidis (eds.), *Law and Policy in Public Purchasing*, pp. 105-124, Ann Arbor: University of Michigan Press.

Gordon H., S. Rimmer and S. Arrowsmith (1998). 'The Economic Impact of the European Union Regime on Public Procurement: Lessons for the WTO', *The World Economy*.

Government of India (2003). 'Report of the Task Force on Revision of Norms for Procurement of Goods & Services by Government', Ministry of Finance, Government of India, New Delhi, November.

Hoda, A. and B. Suchi (2004). 'Transparency in Government Procurement', WTO Research Series No. 6, Indian Council for Research in International Economic Relations (ICRIER), New Delhi, November.

Hoekman, B.M. (1998). 'Using International Institutions to Improve Public Procurement', *World Bank Research Observer* 13: pp 249-69.

——— (2002). 'Developing Countries and the Political Economy of the Trading System', Working Paper No. 2002/126, United Nations University, Tokyo, December.

——— and P.C. Mavroidis, (1995). 'The World Trade Organization's Agreement on Government Procurement Expanding Disciplines, Declining Membership?', The World Bank Policy Research Working Paper No. 1429.

Hunja Robert, R. (2003).'The UNCITRAL Model of Law on Procurement of Goods, Construction, and Services and Its Impact on Procurement Reforms', in *Public Procurements: Global Revolution*, pp. 97-109.

IISD (2003). Government Procurement in the World Trade Organization, International Institute for Sustainable Development (IISD), IISD Trade & Development Brief No. 4, Spring 2003.

Jasson, S.S. (1985). 'The GATT Agreement on Government Procurement: Canada and Australia', Australian Economic Papers, June, pp. 76-94.

Lowinger, T.C. (1976). 'Discrimination in Government Procurement of Foreign Goods in the US and Western Europe', *Southern Economic Journal* 42: pp. 451-460.

Martin, J.M.F. (1996). 'The EC Public Procurement Rules: A Critical Analysis', London: Oxford University.

Mattoo, A. (1996). 'The Government Procurement Agreement: Implication of Economic Theory', *The World Economy* 19(6): pp. 695-720.

——— and A. Subramanian, (1999). 'India and the Multilateral Trading System after Seattle: Towards a Proactive Role', presented at the World

Bank-NCAER Workshop on South Asia and the WTO, New Delhi, December 20-21.

McMillan, J. (1998). 'Competition in Government Procurement', July downloaded from http://www.irps.ucsd.edu/irps/faculty/Taiwan_procurement.html

Michalopoulos, C. (1999). 'Developing Countries Goals and Strategies for New Millennium Round', World Bank Policy Research Working Paper No. 2147, The World Bank Development Research Group Trade, July.

Ministry of Personnel, Public Grievances and Pensions (MPPGP) (1999). 'Impact of Decentralization of Ad-hoc Purchases of Directorate General, Supplies and Disposals—A Study Report', MPPGP, Government of India, New Delhi, February.

Moïsé E. and M. G. Grosso (2003). 'Transparency in Government Procurement: Benefits of Efficient Governance and Orientations for Achieving it', Organization for Economic Co-operation and Development (OECD) TD/TC/WP(2002)31/FINAL.

Muthuswamy and Brinda (2000). General Financial Rules, Chennai: Swamy Publishers (P) Ltd.

Odhiambo W. and P. Kamau, (2003). 'Public Procurement: Lessons from Kenya, Tanzania and Uganda', Organization for Economic Cooperation & Development (OECD), 208, March. Downloaded from www.oecd.org/dev/Technics.

OECD, (1999).'Competition Policy and Procurement Markets, Directorate for Financial, Fiscal and Enterprise Affairs', Committee on Competition Law and Policy, Organization for Economic Cooperation & Development (OECD) DAFFE/CLP/(99) 3/Final. Downloaded from http://www.oecd.org/daf/clp

———— (2001). 'The Size of the Government Procurement Markets', *Journal of Budgeting* 1(4): 1-66. Available at: http://www.oecd.org/dataoecd/12/36/33657593.pdf.

Rege, V. (2001). 'Transparency in Government Procurement: Issues of Concern and Interest to Developing Countries', *Journal of World Trade*, 35 (4): pp. 489-515.

Sahgal, V. and D. Chakrapani (2000). 'Clean Government and Public Financial Accountability', OECD Working Paper Series, No. 17 (Summer). Washington D.C: The World Bank.

———— (2002). 'India: Evaluating Bank Assistance for Public Finance Accountability in the 1990s', OECD Working Paper, Washington D.C.: The World Bank.

Sainani, A. (2002). 'Enhancing Accountability in Tendering System on Indian Railways: A Policy Recommendation', downloaded on December 12, 2003 at http://www.irastimes.org/enhancing_accountability_in _ tendering _system.html.

Santoni. M. (2001). 'Discriminatory procurement policy with cash limits can lower imports: An Example', Working Paper 03. Dipartimento di Economia Politica e Aziendale Università degli Studi di Milano.

Shrivastava, V. (2003). 'India's Accession to the Government Procurement Agreement: Identifying Costs and Benefits' in A. Mattoo and R. M. Stern, (eds.) *India and the WTO*, Washington DC: The World Bank, August.

Swami A. 'Transparency in Tendering System: Need for a Holistic Approach' downloaded on December 12, 2003 from http://www.irastimes.org/transparency_in_tendering_system.html

Trionfetti, F. (1997). 'Government Procurement, International Specialization, and Income Inequality', Athens: Ohio University.

———— (2000). 'Discriminatory Public Procurement and International Trade', *World Economy*, 23(1): pp. 57-76.

Wittig, W.A. (2002). 'Building Value through Public Procurement: A Focus on Africa', March 30. Published by International Trade Centre/UNCTAD/WTO, pp. 1-20.

World Bank, (1995). 'Guidelines: Procurement under IBRD Loans and IDA Credits', Washington D.C.: The World Bank.

———— (2000). 'Reforming Public Institutions and Strengthening Governance: A World Bank Strategy', Washington D.C: The World Bank, November.

———— (2003). 'India Country Procurement Assessment Report', Report No. 27859, Procurement Services South Asian Region, December 10.

World Trade Organization (WTO). 2002. WT/WGTGP/7 Available at: http://docsonline.wto.org/DDFDocuments/t/WT/WGTGP/7.doc.

## Chapter 13

# WTO and Issues in Agricultural Trade

K.P.C. RAO*

World trade in industrial products has grown rapidly after the Second World War. While the world economy grew only at around 3 per cent per year, trade in industrial products expanded at a rate of nearly 10 per cent per year in the last five decades. At the conclusion of the Second World War, the average tariff on industrial products was around 40 per cent. But over the last six decades, the average tariff on industrial products has fallen to 3.8 per cent. Several rounds of the GATT and WTO have achieved this reduction and contributed to growth in trade. There are two extreme and opposite perceptions about world trade. Some consider it as an instrument in the hands of rich countries to exploit the poor countries (Mehra *et al.*, 2004). The other extreme view believes that it contributes to maximization of welfare of all the citizens in the world by exploiting the principle of comparative advantage. India largely subscribed to the first view and followed import substitution policies since the time of independence. As a result, it lost its share both in terms of total trade as well as in terms of agricultural trade between 1947 and 1991 (Rao, 1994). However, after the advent of new economic policies, there is a considerable shift of emphasis from import substitution to export orientation (Goyal and Noor Mohd, 2001). But even after embracing new economic policies since 1991, it has not improved its share in world trade in any significant way.

Whether one likes it or not, trade with other countries is a

* Principal Scientist (VLS), International Crops Research Institute for the Semi-arid Tropics (ICRISAT), Patancheru, Andhra Pradesh.

compelling necessity (Balassa *et al.*, 1971). Experience has shown that it contributes to development of the poorer countries even when the trade terms are marginally loaded against them (Bacchetta and Jansen, 2003). Countries like South Korea, Taiwan, Hong Kong, Singapore etc., which have taken a positive view of international trade, have prospered and increased their shares in world trade, while India, which has taken a negative view of international trade, lost its share and became marginalized.

While the people of India have taken the economic reforms in their stride, the overarching attitude to international trade and globalization is still negative. Strong campaigns against the GATT, WTO and Globalization have contributed to this negative stance of the Indian psyche.

When the World Trade Agreement, 1994 was signed, a number of organizations in the country opposed it without understanding the implications of such an action and demanded that the government should walk out of GATT. But, the government took a pragmatic view, remained in the GATT and became a founder member of the WTO. But it did not make enough efforts to explain the logic of membership of GATT to the people of the country. However, it has been trying to improve the terms of the agreement by raising the implementation issues during the Ministerial Meets of WTO, which took place in Singapore (1996), Geneva (1998), Seattle (1999), Doha (2001), Cancun (2003) and Hong Kong (2005). The developing countries have become more articulate and united over the years in the negotiations at these Ministerial Meets. Yet, the fact remains that the developed countries still account for a lion's share in the world trade and are still calling the shots.

**Agricultural Trade**

The Uruguay Round of talks has initiated the process of trade liberalization in agricultural commodities. Trade in agricultural commodities was never discussed in the earlier seven rounds of GATT negotiations. Countries were constantly afraid of a Third World War breaking out between the NATO group and WARSAW pact group of countries. Thus no country wanted to depend on other markets for the supply of food and other important agricultural commodities in such an uncertain environment (Ingco and Nash, 2004). The implications of depending on others and facing problems of supply in the event of a war were unpalatable to them. Hence, every country tried to achieve self-sufficiency in foodgrains irrespective of the comparative advantage and cost of production. Countries like European Union, Japan, South Korea etc., have heavily subsidized production (Tokarick, 2005). Some (18) countries, which believed that they have a comparative advantage in the production of agricultural commodities, met at Cairns in Australia and demanded liberalization of trade for agricultural commodities as was done in case of the industrial commodities (Vousden, 1990). Countries that were subsidizing agricultural production heavily opposed the inclusion of trade in agricultural commodities as an agenda item for the eighth Round of GATT negotiations. They contended that agricultural sector in multi-functional and should not be treated as a mere supplier of commodities (Anderson, 2000). Agriculture has many other roles such as retaining scenic beauty, maintenance of ecological balance, provision of employment opportunities etc. (Freeman and Roberts, 1999). Because of these conflicting arguments, trade in agricultural commodities found a place in the agenda in a limited way. The 1994 agreement led to the opening-up of trade in case of agricultural commodities in a small way.

In this paper, we try to explain the provisions and implications relating to the three major issues in the Agreement on Agriculture viz., Market Access, Aggregate Measure of Support and Export Subsidies. Since the Sanitary and Phyto-sanitory measures (SPS) and Technical Barriers to Trade (TBT) influence trade in agricultural commodities, both of them are elaborated in the next section. Similarly, Intellectual Property Rights (IPR) that have a bearing on agriculture like Geographical indications, Patents and Plant Variety Protection Certificates, are also discussed briefly in the subsequent part of the paper. The paper also reviews India's experience with the Agreement, highlighting the divergence between what was expected and what has resulted. Finally, the paper surveys the broad proposals that emanated from the Hong Kong Meet, 2005 and the outlook for the next Agreement, if and when it happens.

### *Three Major Pillars of the Agreement on Agriculture (AOA)*

The Agreement on Agriculture signed in 1994 dealt with three major issues, viz., Market Access, Aggregate Measure of Support (AMS) and Export Subsidies (GATT Secretariat, 1994). We shall discuss them in detail to flag the issues arising out of the Agreement.

### *1. Market Access*

Member countries were advised to convert all non-tariff barriers into tariffs and to provide some minimum access to their markets. But the spirit of trade liberalization was considerably weakened by the process of voluntary tariffication, which resulted in what has come to be known as 'dirty tariffication', and minimization of gains from trade. The member countries were asked to reduce tariffs (including those in lieu of tariffication) by 36 per cent in case of the developed countries over a period of six years and by 24 per cent in case of the developing countries over a period of 10 years. Least developed countries were exempted from market access commitments. Member countries were also asked to compute current access by comparing imports with average levels of domestic consumption in the three-year (1986-89) base period. Thus if current access is zero or less than the minimum market access, minimum access has to be provided while if current access is higher than the minimum access, it has to be maintained. Minimum access is defined as 3 per cent of the average domestic consumption to start with in case of the developed countries, to reach a level of 5 per cent over a period of six years. In case of the developing countries, minimum access has to start at 2 per cent of the average domestic consumption and should reach 3.3 per cent at the end of ten years. The maximum tariff that can be charged from the importers till the minimum access level is reached is only 32 per cent.

Member countries can be exempted from the minimum market access commitments in case of products that are inimical to the national security of the country. Similarly, countries experiencing balance of payments (BOP) problems can be temporarily permitted to have quantitative restrictions (QR) with the condition that when they come out of this problem, quantitative restrictions are to be eliminated in a phased manner. There is also a provision that member countries may impose additional tariffs if there is a sudden surge in the quantity of imports or if there is a sudden drop in the prices of domestic products due to imports.

The least developed countries are totally exempted from the market access commitments. The United Nations Organisation (UNO) recognizes 53 countries in the world as least developed countries of whom 35 are already members of the WTO. These poor countries are exempted from granting minimum market access to the products of other countries.

## *2. Aggregate Measure of Support (AMS)*

This is the major bone of contention among the member countries. Over the years, domestic subsidies in agriculture assumed alarming proportions, particularly in the European Union, Japan, South Korea and United States (De Gorter *et al.,* 2004). The Cairns group of countries have been demanding a drastic reduction in the domestic subsidies. But the 1994 agreement addressed this issue only marginally. This agreement exempted several general services like research, extension, training, inspection, quality control etc., from the definition of the domestic support. There is also no upper limit on the expenditures incurred on these general services. Calamity relief, pest and disease control and insurance participation by the governments were also included in these 'Green Box' items. The United States even got the income support measures included in the 'Green Box' in the 1994 agreement. Thus the US government announces minimum guaranteed prices for some commodities but does not interfere when the prices fall below the guaranteed prices. But the farmers can seek compensation from the government treasury for the loss of revenue by selling their output below the guaranteed prices. Although this form of income support appears to be not interfering with the price mechanism in the short run, it keeps the production capacity of the farmers intact (Hennessey, 1998). This measure invites the farmers to over produce and, in the long-run, *effectively* distorts the markets. The US government is able to conceal a considerable part of its domestic support under the 'Green Box' due to this provision.

The European Union indulges more in 'Blue Box' support, which is aimed at harmonizing supply with demand (Diakosawas, 2002). The European Union very often resorts to this form of support to their farmers. If it is found that the demand for a particular commodity has fallen relative to the supply, they advise the farmers to set aside, a particular proportion of their land as fallow and the government compensates the farmers for the loss of revenue. The only saving grace in case of 'Blue Box' support is that there is an upper limit to the support extended under this provision. The acreages and the livestock numbers during the base years (1986-88) are the limits with reference to which the set aside programmes are administered. The 1994 agreement specified five per cent of the value of output as the upper limit on the 'Blue Box' support.

Some special exemptions are given to the developing countries in the 1994 agreement (Keck and Low, 2004). The major provision among these special exemptions relate to capital subsidies on surface irrigation projects. In the developing countries, investments on surface irrigation projects are treated as part of development expenditure and the capital costs are never recovered from the beneficiaries. This amounts to providing capital subsidies and the GATT Agreement, 1994 has taken note of it and agreed to exempt capital subsidies to surface irrigation projects in developing countries. The second provision relates to the support provided by governments to the resource poor farmers in the developing countries. Any support or subsidy provided to resource poor farmers is entitled to be exempt from the computation of Aggregate Measure of Support (AMS). The Government of India has notified to WTO that any farmer owning less than 4 hectares of land is a resource poor farmer. In AMS computations, the Government of India is now confining itself to the support given to farmers owning more than 4 hectares of land only. The third exemption is in case of incentives provided to the farmers for switching over from illegal crops (like Opium) to legal crops. Cultivation of illegal crops is confined to only a few pockets in the developing countries. The 1994 Agreement took note of this and encouraged the governments to motivate farmers to shift from illegal to legal crops. The support provided by developing countries to facilitate voluntary abandonment of illegal crops by the farmers is exempted from the computation of AMS.

*Computation of AMS*

After allowing for exemptions under ‘Green Box’, ‘Blue Box’ and special exemptions granted to the developing countries, whatever support is provided by the union, regional and local governments to the agricultural sector has to be computed and notified to WTO as the Aggregate Measure of Support (AMS). AMS has to be computed for 21 basic agricultural products figuring in Annexure-1 of the 1994 agreement and also for the entire agricultural sector. In case of each of the basic agricultural products, both the market support and non-market support have to be computed and added up. Market support is computed by subtracting the average annual domestic price from the external reference price of the commodity and by multiplying it with the quantity of output. The external reference price is the *c.i.f* price in case of normally imported commodities and the *f.o.b* price in case of normally exported commodities. The external reference price in dollar terms prevailing in the base years are to be considered at the current exchange rate. The non-market support refers to selective subsidies provided for the cultivation of the crop. If the total product specific support is more than five per cent of the value of the product (in case of developed countries) and more than 10 per cent of the value of output (in case of developing countries), the support is liable to be reduced by the concerned country. The excess support has to be reduced by 20 per cent over a period of six years in case of the developed countries and by 13.33 per cent over a period of ten years in case of developing countries. Just as in case of the basic agricultural products, the value of input subsidies extended by the governments to the agricultural sector has to be computed as sector specific support. The subsidies provided for fertilizer, irrigation and power and the interest subsidy given on agricultural loans are to be added up to arrive at the sector specific support. The exemption limits and the liability to reduce the excess support are the same as in case of product specific support. When there is excess support either in case of products or agricultural sector, the member country has to notify the reduction commitments over the implementation period to the WTO well in advance. The sector specific or the product specific support, which is liable for reduction, is referred to as the 'Amber Box' support.

### *3. Export Subsidies*

Many developed countries subsidized their agricultural sector quite heavily and accumulated stocks of many agricultural commodities (Gardener, 1996). Thereafter they started subsidizing export of agricultural commodities to clear the stocks. The developing countries in general and Cairns group of countries in particular, have demanded the abolition or substantial reduction in export subsidies during the Uruguay Round negotiations (Hoekman and Olarreaga, 2004). The GATT Agreement, 1994 asked its member countries to reduce export subsidies by 36 per cent over a period of six years in case of developed countries and by 24 per cent over a period of ten years in case of the developing countries. Besides reducing export subsidies by 36 per cent or 24 per cent as the case may be, the member countries also had to reduce the subsidized export quantities by 21 per cent in case of the developed countries and by 14 per cent in case of the developing countries. It also restrained the member countries that were not providing any export subsidies in the base year from introducing them afresh during the period of implementation. However, developing countries were permitted to reimburse internal and external freight charges and marketing costs, which together can add up to about 30 per cent of the export price. Thus, the 1994 Agreement provided for only a limited reduction in the export subsidies.

### Sanitary and Phyto-Sanitary (SPS) Measures and Technical Barriers to Trade (TBT)

Although these measures do not form a part of the Agreement on Agriculture (AOA), they influence agricultural trade substantially. There is a wide heterogeneity among the members of the World Trade Organization with respect to per capita incomes and safety perceptions. While the poorest of the developing countries have a per capita annual income of $ 100, the richest among the developed countries have annual per capita incomes exceeding $ 40,000. It is natural for the rich to follow high safety standards while the poor are unaware of the deleterious effects of lower safety standards. Even when the rich are willing to pay a premium price for higher safety, it is very difficult for the farmers and processors in the developing countries to meet those standards. There are international bodies like CAC (Codex Alimentarus Commission), HACCP (Hazard Analysis and Critical Control Point) mechanism etc., which set the standards for different products. In their assessment any standards lower than the prescribed ones could lead to adverse health effects. But some of the rich countries want even higher standards than those prescribed by the international bodies. In several poor countries, the standards are far lower than the ones prescribed by the international bodies. Sanitary and phyto-sanitary standards deal with microorganisms, toxins, pesticide residues, heavy metals etc., which if present beyond some threshold level in the foodstuffs, could cause ill health to human beings, animals and plants that feed on them. The 1994 Agreement upholds the right of member countries to set the safety standards at their will provided they are enforced on a non-discriminatory basis and not for protecting their markets from competition. But at the same time, it recommends that the member countries may follow the standards set by the international bodies. The countries, which set higher standards, should apply the same ones to their own domestic production and to the imports from different countries without discrimination. Many developing countries perceive that the developed countries are setting un-reasonable standards only to protect their markets from competition. Very often, SPS standards are referred as the 'Second Tariffs'.

Technical Barriers to Trade (TBT) refer to the quality standards of the product such as size, colour, nutritive value and health risk to the handlers. The preferences of consumers in different countries can vary with respect to the colour and size of the onions (for example). Toys should be safe for the children to play with and medical equipment should not cause any problems to the patients or technicians. Just as in case of SPS, member countries have the right to specify the quality of the product, which their consumers want, provided it is done on a non-discriminatory basis. In today's world, the consumer is the king and trading opportunities are available only to those who are willing to meet them. In case of both SPS and TBT, the member countries should notify the standards they would like to follow sufficiently well in advance so that the suppliers will have enough time to prepare themselves for meeting the standards. A mutual understanding is required on the part of both the suppliers and the consumers. Suppliers should try to meet the genuine concerns of quality while the consumers should try to keep the demands of quality well within the reasonable reach of the suppliers.

### Trade Related Intellectual Property Rights (TRIPS)

This agreement covers ten different types of intellectual property rights of which three are relevant for agricultural commodities, namely, geographical indications, patents and plant variety protection certificates.

### Geographical Indications

These refer to some special characteristics of a product, which are attained when it is grown in a particular geographical area. The products grown in that area are to be given a special trade-mark protection indicating the place of origin of the product e.g. Basmati rice. Some of the varieties of rice acquire the characters of long slender grain with aroma, which further elongates upon cooking when they are grown in north-western parts (Punjab, Haryana and parts of

Uttaranchal) of India. The same varieties if grown in other areas, say, Eastern Uttar Pradesh or Rajasthan would not attain the same qualities. Other examples of geographical indications are Darjeeling Tea, Ratnagiri Alphanso Mangoes and Muzaffarpur Litchis. The principle involved in the geographical indications is to avoid the misleading of the consumers about the true origin of the product. The 1994 Agreement gave a higher protection to wines (Champagne) and spirits (Scotch Whisky). The developing countries are voicing demands to get the same level of protection for their geographical indications at par with those given to wines and spirits.

**Patents**

These are the strongest forms of intellectual property rights and are obtained when the inventors establish their claims of novelty, usefulness and inventive step, which are not obvious to an ordinary practitioner of the art. Patents provide an exclusive right to the inventor to market the product for some years. Such a right and the chances of making a profit from it attract investments into the R&D activity and encourage inventive efforts. The 1994 Agreement exempts new plant and animal forms from patenting but makes it obligatory to grant patents to microbiological processes. The new plant varieties are to be given protection either through patents or through a *sui generis* method of protection. Countries have to provide protection to both process and product inventions. But in case of countries where product patents are not in vogue for some of the products, a grace period of 10 years is provided for the introduction of the product patents. However, the member countries have to provide exclusive marketing rights for a period of 5 years if that company has obtained a product patent for the same product in another member country. The period of patent protection is for 20 years and importation should be treated as working of the patent. In the United States of America, all asexually reproduced plants are given patent protection while sexually reproduced plants are protected by Plant Variety Protection (PVP) Certificates.

**Plant Variety Protection Certificates**

These are issued to the inventors if they establish Distinctiveness, Uniformity and Stability (DUS) of characters in case of new plant varieties. The requirements for PVP certificates are far less stringent than those for the patents. The governments can continue to give rights to farmers to grow even the protected varieties and use the saved seed for the next crop and to breeders to make use of the protected materials for their R&D activities under the *sui generis* clause of the agreement. Even farmers and farmers' groups can get the PVP certificates if they can prove the DUS characters of the variety which they have evolved over time. The Plant Variety Protection and Farmers Rights Bill passed in the Parliament incorporates many of these safeguards to limit the gains of companies earning PVP certificates.

**India's Experience with the Agreement**

When the Government of India signed the 1994 Agreement there was an optimism that the implementation of the GATT 1994 Agreement will lead to a reduction of domestic production and export subsidies and to an increase in the world prices of agricultural commodities, thereby helping the agricultural exports and the farmers in the country. Similarly, the policy-makers thought that there would be no need to open up the domestic market because of the balance of payments problem experienced by the country at the time of signing the Agreement. They also argued that the interests of the farmers can be safeguarded by following the *sui generis* method of plant variety protection. But, the production subsidies provided by the developed countries have actually increased over the years as they increased the 'Green Box' support to a greater extent compared to the reductions under the 'Amber Box'. This has led, among other things, to a reduction in the prices of agricultural commodities in the global markets. The Government of India succumbed to the pressure of consumer and trade interests and reduced the applied tariffs on edible oils and sugar for some years. Due to this, the fall in global prices was transmitted into the domestic markets, which adversely affected the viability of selected producer groups. But, very soon, the applied tariffs were raised sufficiently to protect the interest of the farmers. These tariffs are high enough to prevent any major import of commodities other than edible oils. Thus the adverse fallout of the decline in international agricultural prices was arrested by raising the applied tariffs for several agricultural products.

The product specific support in India has been largely negative because of high external reference prices that prevailed in the base years and subsequent depreciation of the Indian rupee. At the current exchange rates, the external reference prices (in the base years) are far higher than the average domestic prices. Due to this, there was never an occasion when product specific support has to be reduced. But if the current external reference prices are considered, it is likely that they may exceed domestic prices at least in case of some basic agricultural products. The sector specific support is also hovering around two to three per cent after the Government of India started excluding the support provided to resource poor farmers. There is ample scope to raise the sector specific support by three to four times provided the Government can find resources to do so.

Similarly, the Government of India managed to maintain Quantitative Restrictions (QR) till March 31, 2001. With the increase in foreign exchange reserves after signing the Agreement, IMF declared by 1996 that India is out of the balance of payments problem. Subsequently, there was considerable pressure from US, UK and other developed countries to remove the Quantitative Restrictions. After a long negotiation process, India eliminated QR's from April 1, 2001. But since India had already raised the applied tariffs, there was no adverse effect of removing the QR's. However, although, the impact of liberalization of agricultural trade has been quite limited on the agricultural sector, there is always a perceived import surge that can result from any future liberalization. There is also a tendency to blame WTO even for the problems arising out of domestic policies. A pragmatic approach is needed to isolate the impact of domestic agricultural policies and those caused by the implementation of WTO provisions.

India has always been a net exporter of agricultural commodities although its overall trade balance was always negative (Experts Committee Report, 2002). Around 2000, the value of agricultural exports was about two and a half times that of the value of agricultural imports (Table 13.1). But in the recent years, the rate of growth of agricultural imports has been slightly higher than that of agricultural exports. Although in the latest trade statistics, the value of agricultural exports is far higher than that of the agricultural imports, the gap between the value of agricultural exports and the value of agricultural imports is narrowing down over the years. The share of India in the world agricultural exports has slightly increased from 1.4 per cent in 1994 to 1.7 per cent in 2003.

After the implementation of the Agreement, the share of the developing countries in agricultural exports has marginally increased from 42 to 44 per cent (World Trade Report, 2005a). However, even this cannot be judged as the outcome of the implementation of the World Trade Agreement since, as the developing countries recorded relatively higher growth rates, it is natural to have a marginally increased share in agricultural exports. Moreover, this increased share of developing countries is on account of good performance of China, Brazil and other Latin American Countries. If these countries are excluded, there is hardly any improvement in the combined share of other developing countries.

**Table 13.1:** India's Total and Agricultural Exports and Imports before and after WTA (in Million US $)

| *Indicator* | *Triennium (1992-1995) Average* | *Triennium (1998-2001) Average* | *Per cent Change* |
|---|---|---|---|
| Total exports | 22368 | 38124 | 70.44 |
| Agricultural exports | 3928 | 5887 | 49.87 |
| Percent share of agricultural exports to total exports | 17.63 | 15.66 | –11.17 |
| Total imports | 24614 | 47299 | 92.16 |
| Agricultural imports | 1468 | 2363 | 60.95 |
| Percent share of agricultural imports to total imports | 5.99 | 5.07 | –15.36 |
| Percent share of agricultural imports to agricultural exports | 38.12 | 40.3 | 5.72 |

*Source*: Computed from basic data drawn from DGCIS Reports, Government of India

There are several instances of rejection of export consignments due to stringent sanitary and phyto-sanitary standards set by some of the developed countries. But this is an inherent hazard in international trade. Unless we are able to negotiate with trade partners for lower standards, it will be mandatory for the exporters to take all necessary steps to meet the safety requirements of the companies and the countries. But the popular perception is that the developed countries are using the SPS standards as a mechanism to prevent imports into their countries. While opposing such tendencies, we should also respect their concern for safety and meet the obligations.

In case of Intellectual Property Rights (IPRs) also, India had to face litigations in several cases. The liquor manufacturers in India were restrained from advertising their products as close substitutes to Scotch Whisky because of the strong protection to which the spirits and wines were entitled. Basmati exporters faced the threat of losing the special trademark protection to Basmati Rice, when the Ricetech Company in US claimed patent protection for the varieties evolved by them. They (the Ricetech Company)) made 20 claims for patent protection, which covered the whole range of properties unique to Basmati rice. The Basmati Rice Exporters Association and Indian Council of Agricultural Research (ICAR) opposed those claims in the US courts. When challenged, the Ricetech Company withdrew 15 claims for protection and the Basmati exporters were relieved that the generic name 'Basmati' will no longer be used by that company. But the Ricetech Company obtained patents for three varieties and two of their claims are still pending in the courts. The Ricetech Company claimed that their varieties are not geographical indications as in case of Basmati and that they can perform similarly at several locations under varied climates. The ICAR is probing into the patents used in the breeding programme of the three Texmati varieties for which patents were obtained. Similarly, when two non-resident Indians obtained patent claims on turmeric for healing surgical wounds, the National Chemical Laboratories (NCL), Pune opposed them and got the patents revoked by establishing that it is well documented that turmeric can heal wounds when the umbilical chord is cut at the time of child birth. But the Canadian company, which identified and isolated the chemical compound from the Neem oil which has the property of fighting tooth decay could retain the patent on the exclusive use of that compound, even when, NCL opposed it. These IPR related cases emphasized the need for thorough documentation in case of native herbs, land races and processes, which are in use, but for which no IPR's were obtained.

### Outlook for Hong Kong Meet

In 2001, the Ministerial Meet held at Doha resolved to take up a work programme, which was named as the 'Development Round'. The terrorist attacks of September 11, 2001 influenced the thinking of developed countries and in a bid to build coalitions, attention was paid to the concerns of the developing countries. But the concrete proposals put forth by the developing countries to liberalize agricultural trade and incorporate development concerns faced stiff resistance from the developed countries in the Cancun Ministerial Meet and in the subsequent negotiations. The Hong Kong Ministerial Meet held from December 13-18, 2005 agreed upon some broad proposals for liberalization of agricultural trade while postponing the decisions on ranges of tariffs and the exact cuts that will be applied in the next agreement to a later date (WTO Report, 2005a). The elements of the Hong Kong Agreement concerning different aspects of agricultural trade are detailed below.

**Market Access**

Although the market access provisions in the 1994 Agreement appear to be reasonable and rational, the purpose of having this provision was defeated due to tariffication of non-tariff measures and the modest cuts suggested in the tariffs. The effective access of developing countries to the markets of developed countries remained constrained due to the tariff peaks (tariff levels on products of interest to the developing countries) and tariff escalation (increase in the level of tariffs with the advancement in the stage of processing). These provisions limited market access for the developing countries and forced them to remain as the primary producers (WTO, 2002).

There is also a divergence of views on whether the Uruguay formula or the Swiss formula should be used in deciding the tariff cuts. The Swiss formula suggests deeper cuts as the level of tariffs go up and the Uruguay formula suggests average cuts on all products irrespective of the range of tariffs to which a commodity belongs.

There is also a fundamental divergence over the basic approach to sensitive products. Many developing countries want to keep the sensitive products out of tariff cuts. Some countries want to designate one per cent of their tariff lines as sensitive products while some other countries want to keep up to 15 per cent of tariff lines as sensitive products. A consensus is needed in the WTO as to what percent of tariff lines should be allowed as sensitive products in case of the developing countries.

The Hong Kong meet specified the following range of cuts in the tariffs (Tables 13.2 and 13.3).

**Table 13.2:** Developed Countries: Four Bands of Tariff Rates. Cut Over 5 Years

| *Band* | *Thresholds* | *Range of cuts (%)* |
|---|---|---|
| Band 1 | 0%-20/30% | 20-65 |
| Band 2 | 20/30%-40/60% | 30-75 |
| Band 3 | 40/60%-60/90% | 35-85 |
| Band 4 | >60/90% | 42-90 |

**Table 13.3:** Developing Countries: Four Bands of Tariff Rates Cut Over 10 Years

| *Band* | *Thresholds* | *Range of cuts (%)* |
|---|---|---|
| Band 1 | 0%-20/50% | 15-25 |
| Band 2 | 20/50%-40/100% | 20-30 |
| Band 3 | 40/100%-60/150% | 25-35 |
| Band 4 | >60/150% | 30-40 |

## Aggregate Measurement of Support (AMS)

Although the 1994 Agreement made a beginning for liberalizing agricultural trade by reducing the production subsidies, the rate of reduction was so low that it hardly made any impact on the production subsidies (Sykes, 2003).

The proposals regarding the reduction of AMS agreed at the Hong Kong Meet are summarized below:

- ❖ The current right of developed countries to exclude a minimal ("de minimis") level of support from reduction commitments would be halved from 5 per cent of agricultural production to 2.5 per cent over a five year period. There will be no such cut in case of the developing countries, which do not have AMS. In case of those developing countries, which have AMS, the cut would be less than 2/3rd of the cut for the developed countries.
- ❖ In case of 'Blue Box' support, the current ceiling of 5 per cent of the value of the agricultural output will be reduced to 2.5 per cent over the period of agreement.
- ❖ The 'Amber Box' support will be reduced by different countries based on the formulae given in the table below. Both the ranges of thresholds as well as the cuts in the AMS are supposed to be determined in the course of the negotiations (Table 13.4).

- Even the contents of the 'Green Box' support may be reformed to accommodate the concerns of the developing countries.

**Table 13.4:** Proposed Thresholds and Cuts in AMS

| *Band* | *Thresholds (US $ billions)* | *Range of Cuts (%)* |
|---|---|---|
| Band 1 (EU) | > 60 | 70%-80% |
| Band 2 (US & Japan) | 10-60 | 53%-75% |
| Band 3 (Other developed) | 0-10 | 31%-70% |

## Export Subsidies

The Cairns group of countries along with China and India among others proposed an immediate elimination of the export subsidies during the negotiations under the Doha Work Programme. While the developing countries negotiated for a rapid reduction, the developed countries wanted a slower phase out of the export subsidies.

The developed countries have agreed to bring down the export subsidies on agricultural products to zero by the end of 2013. In case of cotton, the export subsidies by the developed countries will be brought down to zero before the end of 2006 itself. The exact rates of reduction between the commencement of the Agreement and the end of 2013 will be determined in the course of negotiations. But export subsidies hardly account for a mere 2 per cent of the total subsidies. Hence, any liberalization of trade requires an equally drastic reduction in the production subsidies as in case of export subsidies. There is also the contentious issue of subsidized export credits provided by some countries. This measure also has an equivalent effect of supplying commodities at a cheaper price in the international market. Several member countries argue that the subsidized export credits should be disciplined in the same way as the export subsidies. The Hong Kong Declaration, which committed for the total abolition of export subsidies by the end of 2013, also hinted at disciplining other equivalent measures that are likely to have the same effect as export subsidies. It is yet to be seen whether the subsidized export credits will also be treated at par with the export subsidies.

### The Next Agreement

In view of the continuing differences among the member countries, it is anybody's guess whether or not there will be a new agreement. There was a total breakdown in talks in June 2006 and the possibility of a re-approachment appears remote at the moment. The developing countries along with China and Cairns group of countries are pressing for greater liberalization in agricultural trade. While there is a broad consensus about it, the exact reduction in the level of support is still being debated. The United States says that it is willing to reduce the support levels by 60 per cent provided the European Union and Japan reduce their levels of support by 75 per cent. It also wants that there should be an upper cap for Blue Box support at 2.5 per cent of the value of the agricultural output. Other countries want that US should eliminate implicit subsidies provided through export credit guarantee scheme and also agree to remove the income support clause from the Green Box (Vercammen,1998). The developed countries as a block want greater access to the markets of the developing countries in case of non-agricultural products. The European Union is not willing to concede a sharp reduction in the production and export subsidies. With such sharp differences, an agreement looks improbable unless there is a sudden reversal of positions by the developed countries. India has walked out of the talks and the Commerce Ministry has declared its inability to yield in some aspects of agriculture unless more is gained in other aspects of agriculture.

Dr. Pascal Lamy, the Director General of WTO, has argued that the developing countries will stand to gain from the New Agreement. He also issued a veiled threat that the developed countries can easily increase the support by about $ 57 billion within the provisions of the earlier agreement. The developing countries contend that since the expected gains from the earlier agreement did not materialize, they find it difficult to believe in the expected gains predicted for the next agreement. At present, there are conflicting expectations of different countries about the next agreement. In the face of uncompromising positions of different groups of countries, pessimists are already predicting the end of multilateralism in world agricultural trade. On the other hand, the regional trade blocks and preferential trade agreements are growing, thus limiting the scope of multilateral trade agreements. Perhaps, only a miracle can produce an agreement and save the World Trade Organization from extinction.

## REFERENCES


Anderson, K. (2000). 'Agriculture's "multifunctionality" and the WTO', *The Australian Journal of Agricultural and Resource Economics*, 44(3): 475-494.

Asia-Pacific Economic Co-operation (APEC), (2000). *'Study into the Nature and Extent of Subsidies in the Fisheries Sector of APEC Members Economics'*, Singapore. APEC#00-FS-01.1, www.apecsec.org.sg accessed on 15/07/06.

Bacchetta, M. and M. Jansen, (2003). 'Adjusting to Trade Liberalization: The Role of Policy, Institutions and WTO Disciplines', *Special Studies* 7, Geneva, WTO.

Balassa, B *et al.* (1971). 'The structure of protection in developing countries', Baltimore: John Hopkins U. Press for the World Bank and the Inter-American Development Bank.

De Gorter, H., M. D. Ingco, and L. Ignacio, (2004). 'Domestic Support Economics and Policy Instruments', in M. D. Ingco and J. D. Nash (eds.) *Agricultural and the WTO: Creating a Trading System for Development*, Washington, D.C. World Bank.

Diakosawas, D. (2002). 'How to Measure the Level of Agricultural Support : Comparison of the Methodologies Applied by OECD and WTO' in China in the Global Economy: Agricultural Policies in China after WTO Accession, Paris: OECD, pp. 217-45.

Freeman, F. and I. Roberts, (1999). 'Multifunctionality: A Pretext for Protection?', *Australian Bureau of Agricultural and Resource Economics Current Issues*, 99(3): 1-6.

Gardner, B. (1996). 'The Political Economy of U.S. Export Subsidies for Wheat' in Anne O. Krueger (ed.) *The Political Economy of American Trade Policy*, pp. 291-331. Chicago: University of Chicago Press.

GATT Secretariat, (1994). 'The Results of the Uruguay Round of Multilateral Negotiations', The Legal Texts, Geneva: GATT Secretariat.

Goyal, A. and Noor Mohd (eds.) (2001). *WTO in the New Millennium* (Fifth Edition), New Delhi: Academy of Business Studies.

Hennessy, D. (1998). 'The Production Effects of Agricultural Income Support Policies under Uncertainty', *American Journal of Agricultural Economics*, 80 (August): 46-57.

Hoekman, B. and M. Olarreaga, (2004). 'Agricultural Tariffs or Subsidies: Which are more important for Developing Countries?', *World Bank Economic Review*, 18(2): 175-204.

Ingco, M.D. and J.D. Nash, (2004). 'Food Security and Agricultural Trade Policy Reform', in Ingco M.D. and J.D. Nash (eds.) *Agriculture and the WTO: Creating a Trading System for Development*, World Bank and Oxford University Press.

Keck, A. and P. Low (2004). 'Special and Differential Treatment in the WTO: Why, When and How?', WTO Working Paper ERSD-2004-03, Geneva: WTO.

Mehra, M.K., M. Sinha, and S. Sahu (2004). 'Trade related Subsidies – Bridging the North-South Divide', An Indian Perspective, Winnipeg: International Institute for Sustainable Development.

Nogues, J. (1989). 'Latin America's Experience with Export Subsidies', World Bank Policy Research Working Paper 182, Washington, D.C: World Bank.

Rao K.P.C. (1994). 'India's Liberalization Policies and Dilemma on Dunkel Draft' in Rahim B. Talukdar (ed), *Management of Change in South Asia*, Dhaka: University Press Limited. pp. 93-106.

Report of 'The WTO Experts Committee' (2002). Department of Agriculture, Government of Andhra Pradesh.

Sykes, A.O. (2003). 'The Economics of WTO Rules on Subsidies and Countervailing Measures', John M. Olin Law and Economics Working Paper No.186, The Law School, University of Chicago.

Tokarick, S. (2005). 'Who Bears the Cost of Agricultural Support in OECD Countries?' *The World Economy*, 28(4): 573-593.

Vercammen, J. (1998). 'Export Credit as a Mechanism for Price Discrimination', *Canadian Journal of Economics*, 31:279-294.

Vousden, N. (1990). *The Economics of Trade Protection*, Cambridge: Cambridge University Press.

WTO, (2002). 'Members' Usage of Domestic Support Categories, Export Subsidies and Export Credits – Background Paper by the Secretariat', TN/AG/S/1, RESTRICTED, Geneva: WTO.

——— (2005a). *World Trade Report 2005*, Geneva: WTO.

——— (2005b). 'Doha Work Programme: Ministerial Declaration—Adopted on 18 December 2005'. WT/MIN (05)/DEC, Geneva: WTO.

# Index